Southern England: An Archaeological Guide

Archaeological Guides

General Editor: GLYN DANIEL

Sicily Margaret Guido

Southern Greece Robert and Kathleen Cook

Denmark Elisabeth Munksgaard

Malta D. H. Trump

Persia Sylvia A. Matheson

Southern Italy Margaret Guido

Central Italy R. F. Paget

Southern England:
An Archaeological Guide

the prehistoric and Roman remains

JAMES DYER

FABER AND FABER LIMITED
LONDON

First published in 1973
by Faber and Faber Limited
3 Queen Square, London W.C.1.
Printed in Great Britain
by Alden & Mowbray Limited
at the Alden Press, Oxford
All rights reserved

ISBN 0 571 10317 0
(Hard bound edition)

ISBN 0 571 10334 0
(Paper covers)

DA90
D95

FOR MY PARENTS
who have lived with this book for so long

Contents

Illustrations

Acknowledgements for Photographs
Aerofilms Ltd. 7, 16, 19, 21, 33, 35, 46, 72; Paul Ashbee 43;
G. W. G. Allen, Ashmolean Museum 39, 40; Michael Avery 50;
Department of the Environment 47; Alfred Dolbé 2, 3; Fishbourne
Roman Palace 60; John Hobley, Coventry Museum 63; David Leigh
34; John Lingwood 11; Barry Marsden 37; Peter Reynolds 76; J. K. St.
Joseph, Crown Copyright Reserved, Cambridge University Collection
5, 6, 9, 12, 17, 18, 25, 26, 27, 30, 38, 42, 49, 54, 55, 56, 58, 59, 61,
62, 67, 68, 74, 75; Verulamium Museum 41. Remaining photographs
taken by the author

Foreword

This book is for those who love the English countryside and believe passionately that the only way to understand it is to explore it in all weathers and at all seasons of the year. It is a book for field archaeologists, for those who want to seek out ancient sites and to know something of their history. Today we have more leisure than ever before and it is natural that many of us will spend this in the country. We can give more purpose to our travels if we use them to explore the wealth of archaeological sites with which the landscape is endowed. To this end I have collected together a personal selection of some of the finest sites in southern England that I consider worth visiting. There were thousands more that I had no room to include, but with practice the reader will soon develop an 'archaeological eye' for the countryside and find those for himself.

For the impatient reader, a car will enable him to see many sites in a limited time, though fortunately some of the best are still remote from the main roads. The railways, which could once have taken us to a lot of the sites, are for the most part, alas, no more. But the proper way to visit the monuments of our downs and moors is on foot, with a waterproof coat, stout shoes, an Ordnance Survey map, a packet of sandwiches and a flask of tea. There is nothing to beat a trek along the Berkshire Ridge Way or across Dartmoor to get the real flavour of field archaeology, and as an aid to this end the writer offers this book.

At the outset I should like to record my thanks to three people who, more than any others, have made my study of the field monuments of southern England so pleasurable: firstly, Richard Atkinson who in 1949 led a party which included six enthusiastic fifteen-year-olds on their first visit to some of the major earthworks of Wessex, and instilled in at least one of them a desire to know more. The work of Leslie Grinsell has always been a source of inspiration and I have valued his friendship and guidance throughout my field work. My debt to him is obvious from the frequency with which I have referred to him in my bibliographical notes. Finally Tony Hales has been my constant companion, friend and advisor when visiting so many of the sites described in this book. To all of them I offer my sincere thanks.

I have also received help and advice from Paul Ashbee, G. P. Burstow, Patricia Christie, Anthony Clarke, David T. D. Clarke, H. D. H. Elkington, Peter Gelling, Jillian Greenaway, Brian Hobley, Ronald Jessup, David E. Johnston, F. W. Kuhlicke, Peter Reynolds, Trevor Rowley, R. A. Rutland, Nicholas Thomas, D. R. Wilson and Andrew Woodcock. Finally I should like to thank Dr. Glyn Daniel for suggesting that I should write this book, Miss Elizabeth Gordon for her help over the manuscript, and Mr. Alan Pringle of Faber and Faber Ltd. for being so patient and understanding with a manuscript that 'just growed and growed'.   JAMES DYER

Using this Guide Throughout the Guide sites are described alphabetically by counties and numbered within counties. The index maps are on pages xxxvi to xlv. The numbers of the 1-inch Ordnance Survey maps and National Grid references are included in each entry of the text so that sites may be pinpointed. Directions for finding monuments are also given, but the inclusion of a site in this Guide does not necessarily mean that the public have right of access, and permission from landowners should first be obtained. At the end of each entry I have given bibliographical references, where they are of value, that will lead readers to more information about the places described. Where none is given I have usually relied entirely on my own field observations.

Radio-Carbon Dates Most radio-carbon dates quoted in this guide have been corrected by tree-ring calibration based on the best information at present available.

Ownership and Trespass All archaeological sites belong to someone. Many of them are owned by the state through the National Trust and the Department of the Environment, but thousands are privately owned. Landowners are the guardians of our ancient monuments; sometimes they do their job well, sometimes they do it badly. Frequently they welcome interested visitors provided that they observe the countryside code, but occasionally they can be very hostile and there is little that a genuine enthusiast can do about it. The Military are perhaps the worst offenders here, and many miles of important archaeological land in Wiltshire and Dorset is constantly damaged and barred to access. Whilst archaeologists may feel very sore about this, there is again little that can be done. The law of trespass is very clear:

'Trespass is the act of entering or remaining upon land of another without his permission. If the permission originally given is later withdrawn, a trespass will be committed. A landowner can take a person trespassing to Court without proving loss or damage to his land. Any actual damage he can show will entitle him to increased compensation.'

So before visiting a site make sure that you have obtained permission. Most of the latest editions of the Ordnance Survey maps show public footpaths and rights-of-way.

State-owned Sites Sites controlled by the Department of the Environment fall into two groups: those which may be visited at any time without charge, and those where a custodian is employed and an admission charge made. These usually open at standard hours, which with a few local exceptions are:

	Weekdays	*Sundays*
March–April	09.30–17.30 hours	14.00–17.30 hours
May–September	09.30–19.00 hours	14.00–19.00 hours
October	09.30–17.30 hours	14.00–17.30 hours
November–February	09.30–16.00 hours	14.00–16.00 hours

All monuments are closed on Christmas Day and Boxing Day.

Most prehistoric sites owned by the National Trust may be visited at any time, although a few Roman sites have admission charges and set hours of opening. A few privately owned sites also have an admission charge and fixed hours. Where possible details of these have been included in the Guide.

Museums There are hundreds of museums in southern England, many of them displaying archaeological material. Each is administered by its own officers, opens at its own times, and sometimes charges an admission fee. At the end of each county section in the gazetteer a list of museums has been given, although no attempt has been made to give details of hours of opening which change from year to year. This information can be found in the annual publication *Museums and Galleries in Great Britain and Ireland* published by ABC Travel Guides Ltd. Nor is the inclusion of a museum in the list a guarantee of the quality of its contents. Some may display only a few sherds of pottery or flints, whilst others may have a number of rooms devoted to archaeology.

For the visitor on a short visit to England, the Prehistoric and Roman galleries of the British Museum in London make an excellent starting point. The Museum is open on weekdays from 10.00 to 17.00 hours, and on Sundays from 14.30 to 18.00 hours. An admission charge (to the eternal shame of the British nation) may be made. One other museum stands out above all others for the wealth of its archaeological collection, and should on no account be missed: that is the Museum of the Wiltshire Archaeological and Natural History Society at Devizes in Wiltshire. (It is closed on Sundays and Mondays.)

Excavation On no account should the visitor attempt to dig on the sites described in this book. Excavation is a difficult science requiring great skill and understanding and it must be left to those qualified to undertake it. Many English sites are protected by scheduling laws and the public are liable to prosecution should they damage them in any way. These rules apply equally to landowners. Readers wishing to take part in excavations should apply to the Council for British Archaeology, 8 St. Andrew's Place, London, N.W.1, who publish monthly lists throughout the summer of excavations where assistance is required. (80p. per annum including postage.)

In recent years treasure hunters using metal detectors have caused considerable damage by looting archaeological monuments. Such activity is to be deplored. Any readers seeing sites being pilfered in this way should report it immediately to the landowner, and in writing to the Council for British Archaeology, as they should any other damage to a site which they feel is unreasonable.

Southern England in prehistoric and Roman times

Anyone who has travelled through the desolate windswept country-side of northern Norway with its frequent lakes and rocky outcrops, its grey lichen-covered stunted pines and kilometres of cotton-grass, with here and there infrequent herds of wandering reindeer and their hunters, will have glimpsed the sort of countryside that was England during the earliest ages of man. That it was inhospitable is beyond doubt, and this is borne out by the lack of material remains from that remote period that archaeologists call the Palaeolithic or Old Stone Age (500,000 to 10,000 B.C.). Although our museums can show us hundreds of flint and stone hand-axes made by man at this time, when their numbers are considered against the immense span of years over which they were made it will be realized that only sporadically did man wander to that part of the European continent that was England, during the long cold periods of the great Ice Ages, or the hot, semi-tropical times in between. And when he did come, his stays were probably short-lived: a few months' camping beside a river and then off after the game on which his life depended. Sometimes the winters were spent sheltering in the mouths of caves, where his discarded animal bones and broken tools have survived for us to find. In southern England these caves are few, but good examples exist, particularly in the Mendips.

With the final withdrawal of the ice from Britain, forests of pine and later oak spread across the land. Mesolithic or Middle Stone Age man (10,000 to 4000 B.C.) sought a livelihood hunting in the forests and fishing in the rivers, lakes and marshes that abounded in the aftermath of the ice. It was on the river gravels and sand hills that man was most at home, and the minute microlithic flint implements that he made are most frequently found there. His life was itinerant and seldom did he construct a home that has left a tangible trace in the soil. One such structure, at Abinger in Surrey, can still be seen, as can the overhanging rocks beneath which he sheltered in Kent and Sussex. About 8000 B.C. the land bridge that connected England to France was finally breached by the sea and Britain became an island. From that time onward human development had to be of an entirely insular kind, unless new influences were brought into the country by way of trade or migration from the European mainland.

The arrival of small groups of farmers and stockbreeders in the British Isles may be taken as the starting point for the Neolithic or New Stone Age (4000 to 2000 B.C.). These people ventured rapidly into many parts of the country, often settling not far from the sea or along the chalk ridges that formed their routeways into the hinterland. They left little trace of their presence; perhaps some of them were itinerant, returning only to one spot to bury their dead, whilst others, living in wooden huts, cleared land for their seed-corn and developed small fields around them. They introduced the first baggy pottery,

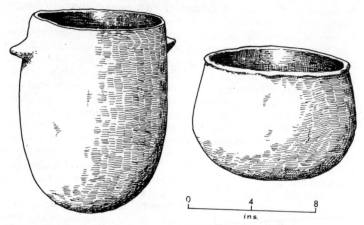

Fig. 1   Early Neolithic pottery

undecorated and with simple rims, known to archaeologists as Hembury and Windmill Hill wares (Fig. 1). In order to build they needed tools of flint and to this end the first flint mining began on the South Downs of Sussex. With polished flint axes they could trim timber for their homes and the wooden mortuary structures in which their dead lay before burial in earthen long barrows.

During the Middle Neolithic period (3500 to 2500 B.C.) earthern long barrows became commonplace in southern and eastern England, whilst stone chambered tombs developed in the west country. Any number of bodies, sometimes previously stored in a nearby mortuary enclosure, were buried under the higher end of the earthen long barrows. The corpses were often stored for long periods until their flesh disintegrated and the bones became disarticulated. They were then placed in a wooden or turf enclosure or hut, which was completely covered with earth quarried from ditches along either side of the barrow. Once constructed, the earthen barrow could not be easily re-entered since the burial chamber quickly rotted and collapsed. In Dorset the earthen long barrows sometimes took on excessive length and are known as bank barrows.

In the stone regions of south-western England and the Cotswolds the place of the wooden burial hut was often taken by stone-built burial chambers consisting of a long central gallery entered from a forecourt at the higher end of the barrow. Sometimes branching off from it there might be as many as six side-chambers or transepts. A large blocking stone sealed the tomb's entrance. These gallery graves were family or tribal vaults in which successive generations of burials could be placed over many hundreds of years (see West Kennet, Wiltshire). There were regional variations, and as time went on, modifications. Sometimes the blocking stone apparently sealing the tomb entrance would be a false portal, the true tomb being elsewhere in the mound, often in the form of three or four individual chambers entered from the sides of the barrow. In Cornwall and the Isles of Scilly there are a number of small circular cairns with single rectangular burial chambers entered directly from their sides, known as entrance graves. These are related both to the gallery graves and a class of circular barrows containing stone burial chambers, known as passage graves, found in Wales and Ireland, but which did not occur in the area covered by this book.

On some of the hilltops of the south the first causewayed camps were constructed: curious enclosures with banks and intermittent ditches that seem to have served as meeting places for tribal and ritual functions of both a secular and religious nature. Knap Hill and Windmill Hill, both in Wiltshire, are excellent examples of these. Farming settlements must also have existed. One imagines that these involved wooden buildings, perhaps raised on stilts above the ground, that have left little trace for archaeologists to find. The pottery that was produced during the Middle Neolithic became thicker, perhaps for added strength, and was decorated in a variety of simple impressed patterns. This developed pottery is known according to its regional variations as Abingdon, Ebbsfleet, Whitehawk and Mildenhall wares; names that are taken from the type-sites where it was found.

The need for flint increased and new mines were opened in Wiltshire, the Chilterns and at Grime's Graves in Norfolk (Plate 47).

Plate 1   Neolithic stone axes

Towards the end of the Middle Neolithic the first of the ritual henge monuments appeared, perhaps having some function similar to that of the causewayed camps which they may have replaced. One of the earliest recorded is the small site at Arminghall in Norfolk, with its horseshoe setting of great posts. To this time, also, belongs the earliest mound of Silbury Hill, erected perhaps as a cenotaph, or as an observation platform for some religious or dedicatory ceremony.

Further regional divergencies appear in the Late Neolithic period (2500 to 2100 B.C.) and the heavy, decorated pottery of the Peterborough school spread through southern England, at first in the Mortlake style, and later, after influence from beaker pottery, in the Fengate style (Fig. 2). At the same time the henge builders spread

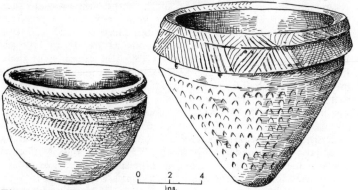

Fig. 2   Late Neolithic pottery

throughout the south constructing larger and more sophisticated monuments, often with timber or stone circles within them, and leaving specialized grooved-ware behind them. During this time such famous monuments as Avebury, Stonehenge and Durrington Walls were first built.

It was into this scene that a group of simple peasant agriculturalists arrived in eastern England from the Rhine delta between 2500 and 2300 B.C., who buried their dead in single graves under round barrows, together with pottery of bell-beaker type and sometimes trinkets of gold. Ethnographically the newcomers can be distinguished from the natives by the rounder shape of their heads, which contrasted noticeably with the longer skulls of the indigenous population. Comparatively few of their settlement sites have been uncovered and where houses have been found they are small and circular or oval in plan. A second and varied group of Beaker people arrived around 2200 and 2100 B.C. from the middle Rhinelands, who settled initially in the Thames valley and northern England. Their beakers were

Plate 2   Beaker pottery

taller, more slender and better made and decorated than the earlier bell-beakers (Plate 2). They brought with them a knowledge of metallurgy, which they developed in Britain, eventually resulting in their exploitation of Irish copper and gold. Their material culture included the bow with barbed and tanged arrow-heads, wristguards, tanged daggers and battle-axes.

The divergent home backgrounds of particular groups of Beaker folk led to a number of regional variations in British beaker types. Increasing insularity followed, and at the end of the Neolithic three separate beaker traditions were established, in East Anglia, northern Britain and southern England. Of these, that in the south grew and flourished, only to be suddenly submerged about 1700 B.C. by the appearance of a new aristocracy, perhaps from the middle Rhine, with highly developed metallurgical techniques that enabled them to exploit and control the native population and emerge as a particularly dominant group of Wessex chieftains.

Bronze manufacture, combining copper and tin ores, required organized prospecting leading to industrial growth which in turn brought trade and prosperity to those engaged in exploiting it. A wealth of new equipment resulted not only in bronze daggers and axes, but in luxury goods of gold, shale, amber and faience. It was the aristocratic Wessex chieftains who were responsible for the new-found wealth which introduces the Early Bronze Age in southern England (2100 to 1700 B.C.). Their superiority is marked by cemeteries of round barrows of divergent types scattered over the downs and moors.

Plate 3   *Bronze Age pottery: a collared urn on the left, incense cup centre*

Under them cremation burials with a varied assortment of grave goods were common.

Round barrows had first appeared in the Late Neolithic period, frequently containing the crouched burials of the Beaker folk. Although some Wessex chieftains preferred inhumation burial, others introduced the idea of cremation. Either the ashes of the dead placed in collared urns (Plate 3), or flexed corpses, were buried at the centre of the barrows, accompanied by a variety of daily and luxury goods, amongst them necklaces and pendants of amber, battle-axes and bronze pins of German types, bronze daggers with hilts sometimes decorated with gold inlays, as well as a selection of gold jewellery and trinkets and the curious incense cups, all of British manufacture. The round barrows exhibited a variety of architectural types, dominated by the great bell-barrows, consisting of a central mound surrounded by a flat platform or berm, and enclosed by a ditch and outer bank. These barrows seem to have been used exclusively for male burials (Fig. 3). Women were buried in disc-barrows, in which the central mound was reduced to a minimum but still surrounded by a wide berm, ditch and outer bank. Women were also buried under saucer-barrows in which a low central mound spread to the edge of the enclosing ditch. The most curious of the Early Bronze Age barrows is the so-called pond-barrow, in which a sunken central area, sometimes

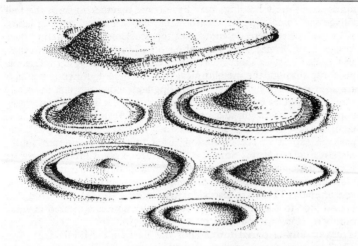

Fig. 3   British barrow types: long, bowl, bell, disc, saucer and pond

containing cremations, is surrounded by a bank of earth. Henge monuments still played an important part in the religious life of the people, and settings of stones were often placed at their centres, or free-standing stone circles were set up, particularly on the moors of the south-west.

Whilst an aristocracy was developing in Wessex and spreading into East Anglia, the native peasantry continued in a developed neolithic tradition to depend on agriculture for their livelihood. By about 1700 B.C. the Middle Bronze Age, marked by new metalwork designs including rapiers and palstaves, and a change in religious customs requiring that cremation burials no longer be accompanied by grave goods, had come into being. Although there is no clear-cut transition discernible in everyday life, for the technologists the Late Bronze Age (1200 to 700 B.C.) is marked by the introduction of a lead-bronze alloy which enabled improved casting and finer products. New objects to appear included leaf-shaped swords and spearheads, and socketed axes. Farming settlement, composed of groups of circular huts with adjoining fields and ranches, flourished throughout the period, and from about 900 B.C. we may even see the beginning of the first defended hilltop forts.

The Early Iron Age (700 to 400 B.C.) has no really obvious beginning, for it followed steadily on from the Late Bronze Age. The first rare objects of iron were produced and jealously owned, until their production proliferated and they became commonplace. Much of the population lived as we have seen in farming communities in which a

number of family holdings may have come together to form the first
village settlements, perhaps with communal fields and grazing lands.
Here and there were defended hill top stockades, some dating back
to the Late Bronze Age, suggesting occasional localized skirmishes,
and built in styles that must reflect contacts with western Europe,
probably through the metallurgical trade. These continental contacts
are seen most strongly in southern England about 400 B.C. in locally
produced angular bowls, and the appearance of La Tène-type daggers,
both clearly based on designs current in France. Whether these
Gaulish ideas indicate nothing more than trade contact, or if we should
perhaps expect to see indications of a folk movement into south-
eastern England at this time, it is premature to say. Certainly there are
signs of large-scale building and strengthening of hillforts in the south-
east suggesting the presence of hostile newcomers searching for land
and animals. There are also signs that during this Middle Iron Age
period (400 to 100 B.C.) the first rectangular houses appeared in small
numbers alongside circular ones on domestic sites. There are few
traces of formal burial throughout the Early and Middle Iron Age.
This suggests that it was no longer necessary to bury the cremated
dead, the scattering of their ashes becoming normal practice. Alternatively, perhaps the corpses were exposed in public shrines and then
allowed to disintegrate by natural agencies.

One developing feature of the Middle and Late Iron Age was the
growth of the curvilinear art style used to decorate both pottery and
metal work, whose origins can also be seen in the La Tène cultures of
central Europe. From its wealth and regional variety it is clear that
the metalsmiths enjoyed a special place in Iron Age society which
allowed them time to experiment and develop their skills without
being tied to the land.

From the end of the Bronze Age attempts had been made to fortify
hilltops by ringing them with a line of rampart and ditch (univallate
fort). With the Middle Iron Age some defences became more complicated as the lines of defence were multiplied (multivallate). Ramparts might follow the natural contour of a hilltop, thus creating
contour forts. On lower ground, where no suitable hills existed,
plateau forts were built, often with particularly strong defences.
Sometimes a steep-sided hill-spur was defended by throwing up a
line of defence across its neck, thus creating promontory forts. On
the coast rocky headlands were cut off in a similar manner to produce
cliff-castles, whilst a specialized hill-slope fort on the hillside was used
for cattle ranching and sheep penning. Only a few forts had more than
two entrances, since these were always a point of weakness (Fig. 4).
These had wooden gates arranged in a variety of ways to increase their
strength. Often they had a bridge to carry a sentry-walk over the gate
passage. The ramparts were normally strengthened with large vertical

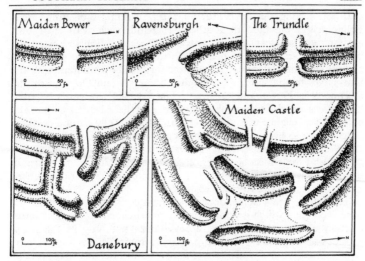

Fig. 4   Hillfort entrances of simple (above) and complex types (lower)

posts at the front and back, tied together with horizonal cross-timbers and faced with thousands of fencing posts or a dry-stone wall. The greatest danger for the wooden forts came from attack by fire. Ditches were deep and V-shaped and natural slopes were often steepened or scarped to make them more difficult to climb. A number of forts were left unfinished, and study of these enables us to understand how they were constructed (see Ladle Hill, Hampshire).

Around 100 B.C. there was the first of at least two migrations to England of Belgae from the area of modern Belgium, most clearly recognized in their practice of cremating the dead and burying their ashes in pear-shaped pedestal-urns. This first appears in the Aylesford and Swarling area of Kent and marks the beginning of the Late Iron Age. Since no settlements of this earliest migration are known we might ask if the first Belgae came as invaders or as traders and missionaries, perhaps led by their scholars and priests, the Druids. A second group arriving in about 50 B.C. seem to have been much more warlike, with intentions of making permanent settlements. In response to their arrival the native hillforts frequently strengthened their defences at this time, some of them increasing in size to become tribal capitals controlling large areas, whilst the Belgae established a number of open settlements defended by outlying dykes, which were sometimes called *oppida* by the Romans. Sometimes the Belgae took over native hillforts and refortified them with wide ditches and loose rubble glacis ramparts.

It was during the 1st century B.C. that a number of strong non-Belgic tribes emerged in southern England, each with their own customs and allegiances. In central and eastern England were the Trinovantes and Iceni, to their north the Coritani, west between the Severn and the Cotswolds lay the territory of the Dobunni, with the Durotriges to the south in Wiltshire, Somerset and Dorset, and the Dumnonii in Devon and Cornwall. The first Belgic arrivals imposed themselves on the Cantii of Kent and established control over the native Catuvellauni of southern Hertfordshire. The second wave of Belgae were to become the Atrebates and Regni of Berkshire, Hampshire and west Sussex. It is the rivalry between these two Belgic groups and the efforts of their non-Belgic neighbours not to be drawn into their feuds, that occupies much of the political history of southern England prior to the Roman conquest.

The Belgae had a tremendous effect upon the material culture of the Late Iron Age, which is dominated by wheelmade pottery. The introduction of the wheel created a revolution, not only in the mass-production of pottery. In the home the rotary quern for grinding corn speeded up the production of flour and resulted in a finer product. The wheel as an aid to transport had been introduced to Britain perhaps during the 3rd century B.C., but now it came into its own for light and fast war-chariots, as well as transporting goods of all kinds. The Belgae were amongst the first tribes to introduce gold, silver and bronze coins, often inscribed with the names of their leaders, the first names in British history. At their death these leaders were cremated and their remains placed in princely burial vaults, richly furnished and filled with gifts of food and wine in Roman amphorae, cauldrons and spits for cooking, bowls and jugs for serving, and jewellery, clothing and musical instruments for the funeral feast.

Julius Caesar's brief visits to Britain in 55 and 54 B.C. left little effect on the native population of southern England, and only the Catuvellauni and their allies, under their leader Cassivellaunus, came into serious but short conflict with him. But with the Claudian invasion of A.D. 43 things were very different. A bridge-head having been established at Richborough on the Kentish coast, the Roman commander Aulus Plautius began his march forward to attack the Catuvellaunian capital at Colchester. Whilst tribes like the Catuvellauni and the Dobunni put up some resistance to Rome, others like the Atrebates of Hampshire signed treaties of friendship and were allowed to retain their own native kings. Where resistance was met in the hillforts of the west it was soon put down by brute force, and the legions burned and cut their way to the line of the Fosse Way, which by A.D. 47 marked the limit of their initial conquest. In the next few years they progressed into the Welsh Marches, so that by A.D. 60 the whole of southern England, with the exception of the south-west beyond Exeter, was under Roman control. In that year Boudicca, Queen of the Iceni, led a revolt against the occupying forces that resulted in the destruction of their new towns of Colchester, Verulamium and London. Once the rebellion had been put down and reprisals made, southern England settled down to enjoy the consequent benefits of colonization. Fine towns grew up that became centres of commerce and fashion, and were linked together by a network of efficient roads that allowed for speedy communication between them. The luxury of public baths, theatres and civic buildings must at first have seemed as bewilderingly out of place to the natives, as did those of the first British colonists in India.

The native Briton could be engaged in any of a multiplicity of industries that the Romans introduced, as potters, carpenters, builders, brickmakers, butchers, tanners and a host of other trades. If he lived in the country, then food production as farm labourer or market gardener provided him with a worthwhile livelihood. For those with initiative well-paid employment meant increasing wealth and the means to climb the social ladder. With money wooden huts could be replaced by half-timbered houses with stone foundations and plastered walls. From such buildings grew the villas or country houses of Romanized Britons and Roman officials. Similarly, in the towns, progress from market-stall to lock-up shop could be relatively swift for those with ability.

Temples were built for the official state religion and the worship of local gods. In A.D. 312 Christianity became the religion of the Roman Empire, although it has left surprisingly few material traces from that period in England. Burial, for the most part, by inhumation or cremation, was in flat cemeteries outside Roman settlements. Occasionally important citizens were cremated and their ashes interred in conical round barrows, some of which rose to a considerable height (see Bartlow Hills, Essex).

Intermittently from the end of the 3rd century A.D. the coasts of southern England suffered from bands of raiding Saxon and Irish pirates, and a number of Saxon Shore-forts were built from the Isle of Wight to the Wash in an effort to check them. These were only partially successful; but it was a series of troop withdrawals towards the end of the 4th century that robbed the country of its protectors and made way for deeper and more serious inroads by the Saxons and Picts. With the final withdrawal of Roman troops by A.D. 400 Britain was left to defend herself, which she did at first with the aid of Saxon mercenaries, who in turn rebelled against their masters, so that by A.D. 442 'Britain passed under the authority of the Saxons' as a Gallic chronicler says. Slowly the remains of Roman civilization in Britain crumbled or became the quarries of their successors, and were eventually forgotten by time and man.

Glossary

Acheulean. Hand-axe making industry of the later stages of the Lower Palaeolithic period.

Agger. The raised foundation of a Roman road.

Aldbourne cup. Small pottery vessel of Bronze Age date decorated with incised lines and dots, of type found in barrow at Aldbourne (Wiltshire) and presumed to have been used in funerary ritual.

Atrebates. Belgic tribe of Berkshire, Hampshire and west Sussex, with their native capitals at *Calleva Atrebatum* (Silchester) and near Chichester.

Awl. Small handled tool of copper or bronze used for boring, often found in female graves. Might have been used in tattooing.

Barrows. Mounds of earth, circular or elongated in plan, covering burials.

Beaker. Finely made pottery vessels, perhaps used for drinking, which appear in many different designs, but are basically of two shapes. The earliest have the S-shaped bell-beaker profile revealing their continental ancestry (2500 to 2300 B.C.), and the later examples reflect insular developments, with bulbous bodies and long necks (2200 to 2100 B.C.) (See Plate 2).

Beaker folk. Late Neolithic people who introduced beaker pottery (see page xviii).

Belgae. Warrior people of mixed Celtic and Germanic origin who came to Britain from the area of modern Belgium about 100 B.C. and settled initially in Kent, later spreading to southern Hertfordshire and Essex. About 50 B.C. a second group, the Atrebates and Regni, moved into Berkshire, Hampshire and west Sussex.

Berm. Flat area separating a mound or bank from a quarry ditch. Normally found in hillforts and bell- and disc-barrows.

Bronze Age. The period when bronze was the main metal used for the manufacture of tools and weapons (although flint continued to be used). From 2100 B.C. to about 700 B.C. in southern Britain.

Burh. A stronghold often of Saxon foundation that frequently developed into a borough in later times.

Burghal Hidage. An early 10th-century A.D. line of ancient fortresses established for the defence of Wessex against the Danes.

Capstone. Large stone forming the roof to burial chamber.

Caesar, Julius. Roman general who undertook reconnaissance expeditions to Britain in 55 and 54 B.C. but did not bring sufficient troops to conquer the islands.

Cairn. Mound composed of stones, rather than soil, usually covering a burial.

Catuvellauni. A native tribe of the Chilterns in the Late Iron Age, whose chieftain, Cassivellaunus, led their resistance to Caesar. The tribe had been overrun by the Belgae who adopted its name, perhaps because of its proud native ancestry.

Causewayed camp. An enclosure composed of one or more roughly concentric rings of quarry ditches, whose excavated material was piled up to form internal banks. The ditches were broken by frequent causeways of undug chalk (see Windmill Hill, Wiltshire).

Cella. Name given to the central room in a Romano-Celtic temple.

Celt. Name sometimes used for the blade of an axe or adze of stone or bronze. Pronounced with soft 'c'.

Celtic fields. Small rectangular fields, often on sloping ground, with slight banks or lynchets marking their sides and lower edges. Seldom more than 0·2 ha in extent they were in use from the Late Bronze Age in spite of their misleading name. Normally associated with small farmsteads and sometimes divided by hollow-ways, they represent the farming pattern prevalent in Britain in the last millennium B.C.

Celts. A cultural and linguistic group of iron-using people, also known as the Gauls and Galatians, who lived in central Europe north of the Alps before 800 B.C. and spread widely in western Europe and the eastern Mediterranean. Their influence is reflected particularly in their art styles. Direct evidence of Celtic migrations to Britain are seen in the Arras culture of Yorkshire and the Aylesford culture of Kent.

Chambered long barrows. (See page xvi).

Cist. A burial pit, sometimes lined with stones and covered with a capstone. A cist too small to be called a burial chamber may also be built of stone on the land-surface beneath a barrow.

Cliff-castle. A hillfort on a coastal spur (see page xxii).

Collared urns. Pottery vessels with high collars originally used for food storage, but later adapted to contain cremation burials. Common throughout the Bronze Age, they survived in derivative shapes into the ensuing Iron Age. (See Plate 3, page xx.)

Coloniae. Towns deliberately built by the Romans to house soldiers retired from the army, who would provide a second line of defence and help to spread the Roman way of life amongst the native population. Colchester and Gloucester were both *coloniae*.

Contour fort. A hillfort designed to follow the contour of a hilltop.

Corbelling. A means of roofing a stone chamber, in which successive layers of stone rise above and overhang each other until they meet, or leave a gap which can be bridged by a single capstone.

Counterscarp bank. A small bank on the outer, downhill edge of a fort ditch, often the product of successive cleanings-out of the ditch.

Courtyard house. Found in Cornwall, these large oval-shaped houses have a series of rooms leading off a central courtyard. The rooms may have had corbelled or lean-to roofs, whilst the yards were open to the sky. They were often grouped into small villages. Chysauster is the best example.

Cromlech. A general name used in south-western England and Wales to describe megalithic tombs, in particular those that have lost their covering mounds.

Crouched burial. A burial whose knees are drawn up to the chin in a crouched sleeping position.

Cup-and-ring marks. Small circular egg-shaped hollows cut into the rock, and sometimes surrounded by one or more carved rings. Found on standing stones and walls of burial chambers, mostly in northern England.

Currency bars. Sword-shaped bars of iron, 70 cm to 90 cm long, with squeezed-up 'handles' at one end, and used in Britain for currency until the introduction of coinage by the Belgae.

Cursus. William Stukeley's name for a long avenue bounded by banks and ditches, of unknown purpose, but associated with long barrows, and dated to the neolithic period (see Stonehenge Cursus, Wiltshire). (Stukeley (1687–1765) was an antiquary and field archae-ologist who wrote valuable books on Stonehenge and Avebury, but in his later years became obsessed with unfounded information on the Druids.)

Deverel–Rimbury culture. A culture found in southern England towards the end of the Middle Bronze Age, from about 1300 B.C., typified by circular wooden houses and Celtic fields, storage pits and weaving combs, coarse globular and bucket-shaped urns, and an economy clearly based on stock-rearing and agriculture.

Disc-barrow. This barrow of the Early Bronze Age was normally built to cover female burials, and consists of a small central mound on a wide, flat circular platform or berm, contained by a surrounding ditch and outer bank. There can sometimes be more than one mound within the enclosure. (See Fig. 3.)

Dobunni. A non-Belgic tribe of the Late Iron Age who occupied the area between the Severn estuary and the Cotswolds. They may have had a capital at Bagendon, Gloucestershire.

Dolmen. The stone remains of a burial chamber that has lost its covering cairn. It is often of indeterminate form.

Druids. A Celtic priesthood found in Gaul and Britain during the 1st centuries B.C. and A.D. They led local resistance to the Romans and were finally exterminated in Anglesey in A.D. 60 by Paulinus.

Durotriges. A non-Belgic Late Iron Age tribe located in Dorset and Somerset. Their capital may have been at Maiden Castle.

Earthen long barrows. See page xvi.

Entrance graves. See page xvii.

Faience. A form of glass made from a fusion of sand and clay, often coloured with copper salts. In Britain normally used for beads of Early Bronze Age date.

False portal. The dummy entrance, sometimes within a forecourt, at the higher end of a long barrow. The burial chambers are normally hidden in the sides of the mound. Belas Knap, Gloucestershire, is the classic example.

Fogou. Normally an underground passage, lined and roofed with stone, associated with Iron Age settlements in Cornwall. It often has side-chambers and branch passages, and may have been used for food storage or as a hideout (see Carn Euny, Cornwall).

Forecourt. A paved area, often semicircular, in front of the entrance to a chambered long barrow. It was there that the main funerary rites probably took place.

Glacis. A scree (or dump) of loose chalk or stone rubble.

Grape-cup. A small ritual vessel of incense-cup type, whose sides are covered with small, grape-like knobs of clay, and dated to the Early Bronze Age.

Grave goods. Personal objects such as jewellery, weapons or pottery buried with the dead. Reached their zenith in the Early Bronze Age graves of Wessex.

Halberd. A Bronze Age weapon in which a bronze dagger-like blade was fixed at right-angles to a wooden shaft. Perforated models of these made of gold and amber were hung on necklaces as halberd pendants.

Hand-axe. An oval or pear-shaped tool of flint that seems to have been used for many purposes. The majority of British examples belong to the Acheulean phase of the late Lower Palaeolithic period, from about 350,000 B.C.

Henge Monument. A circular or oval banked enclosure with an internal ditch, that was probably used for religious purposes. One, two or sometimes four entrances cut through the earthworks. Most henges are on low or sloping ground beside water and sometimes, as at Marden (Wiltshire) water forms a side of the monument. Constructed in the Late Neolithic, henges continued in use into the Bronze Age, when they sometimes had stone settings placed within them (see Stonehenge, Wiltshire).

Hillforts. See page xxii.

Hollow-way. A sunken road or track that through constant use has been worn down to below the surrounding land surface. Sometimes such tracks may have been deliberately cut so that they should not be in the open field of view.

Hut platform. A hollow or flat scoop, often in the hillside, on which a hut once stood. Very marked examples can be seen at Hod Hill, Dorset.

Iceni. Non-Belgic tribe who occupied Norfolk and Suffolk during the Late Iron Age. In A.D. 60 under their Queen Boudicca, they revolted against Roman rule.

Incense cup. Small pottery vessel of uncertain purpose, usually accompanying cremation burials. It might have held the sacred embers of a funeral pyre.

Inhumation. A burial which has not been cremated.

Iron Age. The period when iron was the main metal used for the manufacture of tools and weapons, although some bronze and flint continued to be used. In southern England it lasted until the arrival of the Romans, although it did not immediately stop at that time, but continued with varying degrees of Roman influence. The culture that resulted is referred to as Romano-British.

La Tène culture. The second Iron Age culture of central and western Europe, which came into existence by the mid 5th century B.C. and lasted on the Continent until the 1st century B.C. when it became dominated by Roman or Germanic control. In Britain its influence was first felt about 400 B.C. and it lasted into the mid 1st century A.D.

Lintel Stone. Horizontal stone across the top of an arch or doorway.

Long barrow. See page xvi.

Lynchet. A bank of soil found on the scarp face of the downs associated with Celtic fields, caused by the downward creep of soil during contour ploughing operations. Strip-lynchets probably represent the fields created by the ploughing of the Saxons, and occur in long terraces.

Megalithic. Structure made of large blocks of stone, usually a burial chamber or stone circle. From the Greek words meaning 'great' and 'stone'.

Menhir. A single standing stone, usually erected for ritual purposes.

Mesolithic. The Middle Stone Age (10,000 to 4000 B.C.) during which man lived by hunting and fishing in the forests and lakes that appeared after the final withdrawal of the Ice Age glaciers. He used minute flint implements known as microliths during this time.

Microliths. See Mesolithic.

Mithras. A Roman god of Persian origin, who was particularly popular in military circles. He was a god of truth and light, who constantly fought against the powers of evil.

Mortuary enclosure. A hut-like enclosure of wood or turf in which corpses were stored until a barrow could be erected. Sometimes the barrow was built over the mortuary enclosure (see earthen long barrows, page xvi).

Mosaic. Pavement composed of small cubes of stone and formed into geometrical or pictorial designs. Introduced by the Romans for decorating the floors of their town houses and country villas. Most common in England in the 4th century A.D.; a few are known from the earlier centuries of Roman occupation.

Multivallate. A hillfort with three or more roughly parallel ramparts and ditches, one within the other.

Neolithic. See page xv ff.

Oppidum. A term used by Caesar to distinguish the chief settle-ments of the British tribes. These might be hillforts or open villages defended by lines of dykes. Some archaeologists define an *oppidum* as any pre-Roman settlement where coins were minted.

Palaeolithic. The Old Stone Age (500,000 to 10,000 B.C.). The time of earliest man and the manufacture of simple tools of stone, lasting through the Ice Ages until the final melting of the glaciers around 10,000 B.C. It was in the final part of this period, called the Upper Palaeolithic, beginning about 40,000 B.C. that man sometimes occupied the mouths of caves, and also painted on their walls (though not in Britain). It was a time when he lived by hunting and fishing during extreme climatic conditions.

Palstave. Bronze axe-head with side flanges and stop-ridge, of Middle Bronze Age date.

Parallelithon. Word coined by Dr. C. E. Prior (1872) to describe parallel rows of stones forming avenues.

Peristalith. A kerb of stones surrounding and often retaining a barrow or cairn.

Pillow mound. Small oblong mounds of uncertain age or purpose, possibly constructed in medieval times as artificial rabbit warrens.

Platform-barrow. A form of Bronze Age round barrow with flat top.

Pond-barrow. An embanked circular area used for burial and mortuary purposes (see Fig. 3).

Porthole entrance. A circular hole cut into blocks of stone, to form the entrance to neolithic gallery graves, mainly in the Cotswolds (see Avening, Gloucestershire).

Pound. Walled enclosure found on the moors of south-west England, usually containing a farm or small village of Middle or Late Bronze Age date.

Promontory fort. See page xxii.

Pygmy cup. Alternative name for incense cup (see Plate 3).

Quoit. Cornish name for a cromlech; usually the vestiges of a stone burial chamber that has lost its covering mound (see Lanyon Quoit, Cornwall).

Regni. A Late Iron Age tribe centred on Hampshire and west Sussex.

Revetment. A wall of stone, timber or turf used to stop the sides of a rampart or burial mound from slipping or collapsing.

Ritual pit. Defined by Leslie Grinsell as 'any pit found by archaeologists, the purpose of which is not evident to them'. Sometimes dug to receive libations, food offerings and gifts for religious purposes.

Romano-British. The native British population, living in Britain during the Roman occupation, and showing clear signs of Roman influence, particularly in their homes, dress, coinage, pottery and metalwork.

Round barrows. See page xix.

Robbers' trench (also looters' pit). The hole made in a barrow by a treasure hunter or early antiquary in fairly recent times.

Sarsen stones. Naturally occurring sandstone blocks found on the Downs of north Wiltshire and the south Dorset downs, and used in the construction of megalithic monuments such as Avebury, Stonehenge and Wayland's Smithy. The name is derived from saracen—a foreigner.

Saucer-barrow. A low circular mound surrounded by a ditch, normally covering a female cremation burial. Constructed in the Early Bronze Age. (See Fig. 3.)

Saxon Shore. See page xxv.

Scarping. Artificial steepening of a hillside to increase its defensive potential. Associated with some hillforts.

Sherds. Broken fragments of pottery.

Standing stones. Stones standing on end, and deliberately set up by man, perhaps for some religious, astronomical or architectural purpose.

Storage pits. Holes varying in width and depth, but often about 1 m in diameter and 2 m deep, frequently found on Late Bronze Age and Iron Age settlement sites, used for storing food, especially grain; for water supply when lined with clay, and as latrines.

Tesserae. Small blocks of stone, brick or glass used to make decorated mosaic pavements, and introduced into England by the Romans.

Timber lacing. Method of obtaining maximum strength for a hill-fort rampart by securing horizontal cross-timbers through the body of the rampart connecting vertical posts at the front and rear. The best-known method is the Hollingbury type, named after the hillfort near Brighton (Sussex) where it was first recognized. The method can also be used with stone revetting.

Trilithons. Two upright stones, with a third lying horizontally across the tops, as at Stonehenge, Wiltshire.

Trinovantes. Late Iron Age tribe living in the eastern Chilterns and Essex. A non-Belgic group who were constantly at war with the Catuvellauni, their western neighbours, and who were later absorbed by the Belgae.

Tump. A barrow or burial mound; often applied to the small mounds at the centre of disc-barrows.

Univallate. Hillfort with a single line of rampart and ditch for defence.

Villa. The living quarters of Roman country estates, which were often farming establishments but were sometimes connected with indus-tries, such as pottery making or iron working. Some villas were quite luxurious with hypocaust (under-floor) heating, wall paintings and mosaics (see Chedworth, Gloucestershire).

Metric Conversion Tables

The bold figures in the central columns can be read as either the metric or the British measure. For example 1 inch = 2·54 centimetres; or 1 centimetre = 0·39 inches.

Cm		Inches	Metres		Feet	Metres		Yards
2·54	1	0·39	0·30	1	3·28	0·91	1	1·09
5·08	2	0·79	0·61	2	6·56	1·83	2	2·19
7·62	3	1·18	0·91	3	9·84	2·74	3	3·28
10·16	4	1·57	1·22	4	13·12	3·66	4	4·37
12·70	5	1·97	1·52	5	16·40	4·57	5	5·47
15·24	6	2·36	1·83	6	19·69	5·49	6	6·56
17·78	7	2·76	2·13	7	22·97	6·40	7	7·66
20·32	8	3·15	2·44	8	26·25	7·32	8	8·75
22·86	9	3·54	2·74	9	29·53	8·23	9	9·84
25·40	10	3·94	3·05	10	32·81	9·14	10	10·94
27·94	11	4·33	15·24	50	164·04	91·44	100	109·36
30·48	12	4·72	30·48	100	328·08	457·20	500	547·00

Km		Miles	Hectares		Acres
0·40	¼	0·16	0·405	1	2·471
0·80	½	0·31	0·809	2	4·942
1·21	¾	0·47	1·214	3	7·413
1·61	1	0·62	1·619	4	9·884
3·22	2	1·24	2·023	5	12·355
4·83	3	1·86	4·047	10	24·711
6·44	4	2·49	8·094	20	49·421
8·05	5	3·11	12·141	30	74·132
16·09	10	6·21	16·187	40	98·842
32·19	20	12·43	20·234	50	123·553
80·47	50	31·07	30·351	75	185·329
160·93	100	62·14	40·468	100	247·105

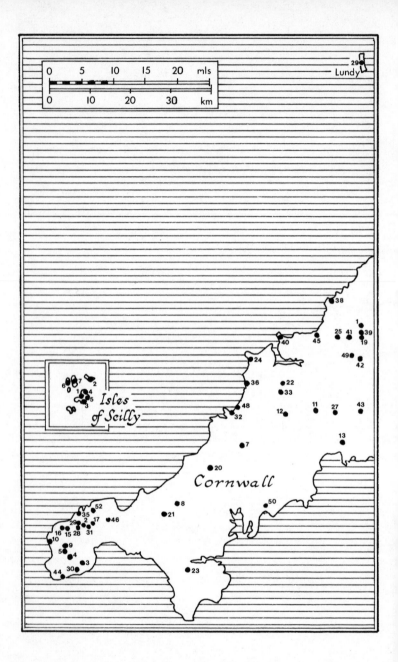

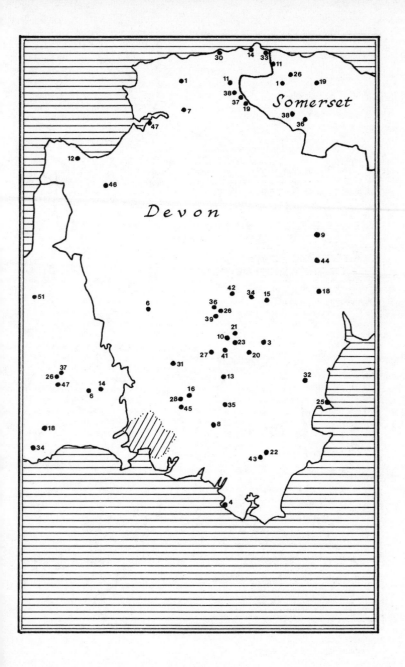

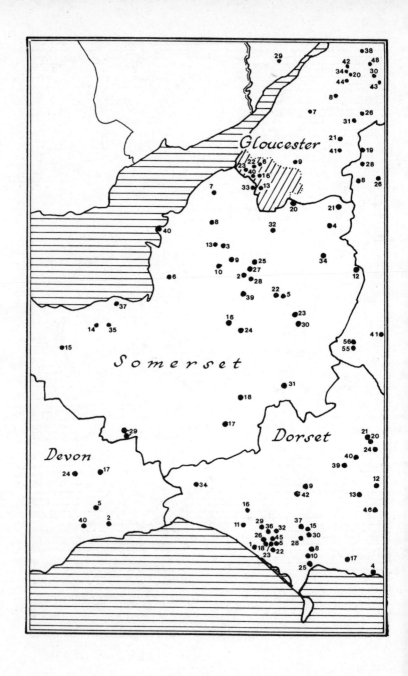

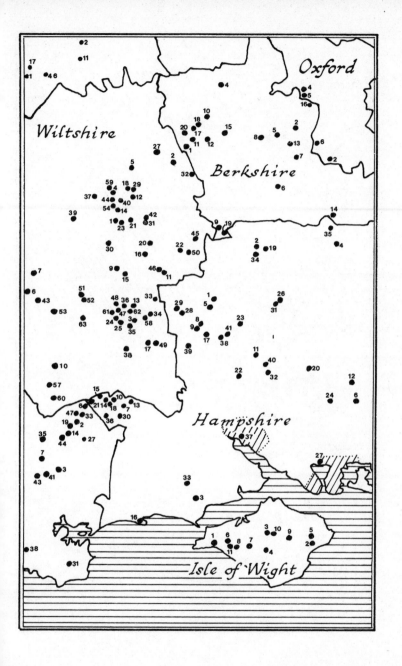

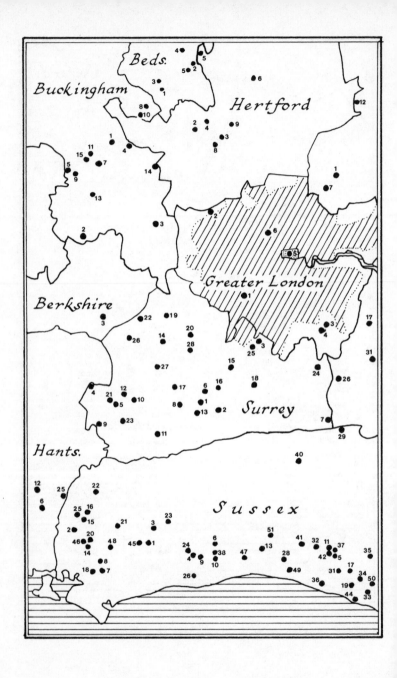

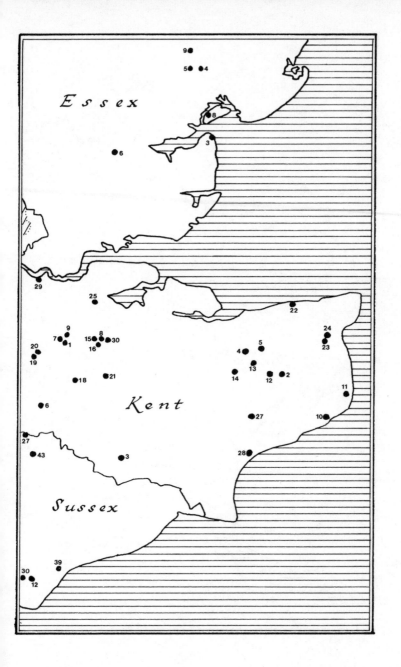

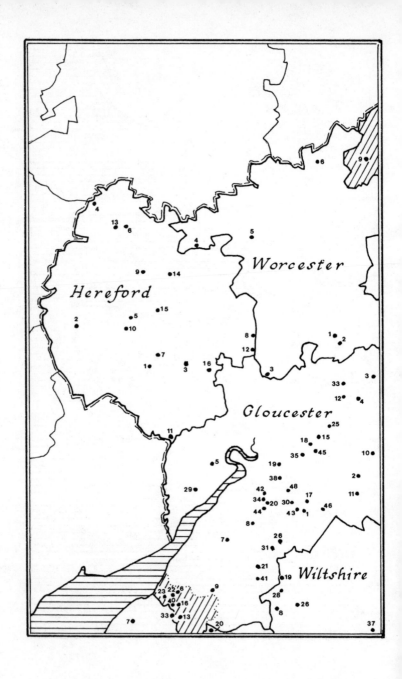

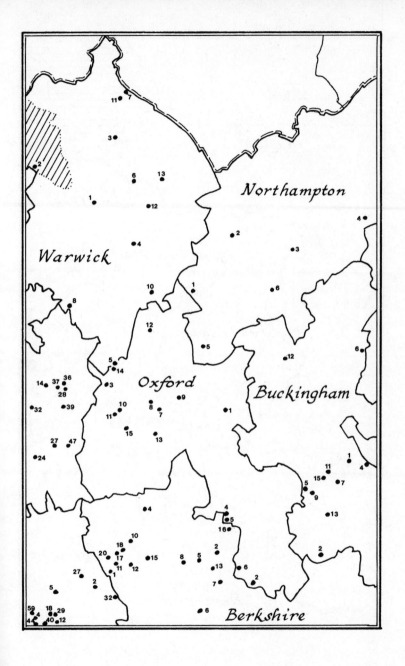

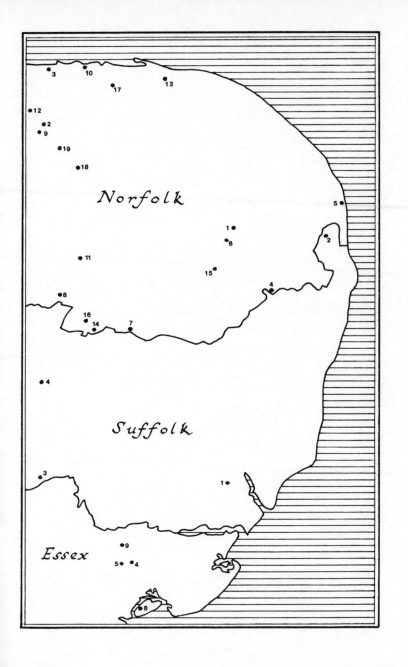

Plate 4   The Five Knolls barrow cemetery, Bedfordshire

I   FIVE KNOLLS BARROW CEMETERY (Plate 4)

Dunstable

Neolithic–Bronze Age
147 (TL:007210)

On the northern extremity of Dunstable Downs.

Although more than a hundred round barrows have been identified in the Chilterns, only two barrow cemeteries of any size remain. These are the Five Hills at Therfield, Herts. (page 183) and the Five Knolls at Dunstable.

In spite of the name there are seven burial mounds on the northern spur of the downs. From the north-west they consist of a bowl-barrow, a triple bell-barrow (that is, three barrows enclosed by a single ditch) and another bowl-barrow. To the east of this line are two pond-barrows.

The north-western bowl-barrow was opened in 1928 and contained a crouched female burial, with a curiously thin skull, suggesting the wearing of a wig or head-dress, and a polished flint blade of Late Neolithic type. In the Bronze Age cremations were added to the barrow, one in an inverted urn, another wrapped in cloth. During the late Roman period some thirty bodies with hands tied behind their backs were buried in the south side of the barrow; perhaps the victims of a Saxon raid. By Norman times the barrow probably had a gallows on its summit for more than sixty skeletons of people executed at various times lay over the barrow and the Saxon cemetery.

The bell-barrows within the continuous ditch have all been dug into at various times, but there is no accurate record of their contents, nor do we know if the most southerly bowl-barrow has been opened. Two of the barrows were opened during one day in August 1850 without result. Those watching included a 'large assembly of persons of the middle and working classes, who exhibited much interest in the progress of the works, and whose conduct was extremely orderly'.

Although noticed by Stukeley, the pond-barrows were first recognized as such by L. V. Grinsell. Their hollow, pond-like shapes are unexcavated, but may contain cremations. Such barrows are often slightly later than bell-barrows.

South-west of the cemetery is a long, narrow mound. It has been suggested that it covers a neolithic mortuary enclosure.

J. Dyer: *Bedfordshire Magazine* **8** (1963) 15

2   GALLEY HILL   Neolithic–Roman
     Streatley   147 (TL:092270)
Footpath from the A6 opposite St. Margaret's Home.

There is nothing very spectacular about this hilltop today, but the two almost flattened round barrows on its top are of some interest. The most northerly was originally kidney-shaped. Although the burial from the central grave had been robbed, a shallow pit at one side contained the remains of two young men whose bodies were partially disarticulated and mixed together. Pieces of Windmill Hill pottery with them suggest a date around 3500 B.C. During the Roman period the surface of the barrow was the site of a mass burial of men, women and a child, probably victims of a skirmish between Saxons and Romanized Britons. In the Middle Ages the barrow was used yet again, this time as the site of a gibbet on which at least half a dozen people were hanged, including, perhaps, one suspected of witchcraft. At the foot of the gallows a horse's skull had been buried with a dice on the end of its nose and it has been suggested that the horse's skull represented the witch's 'familiar'.

The southern barrow was much disturbed, and the central grave had again been robbed, but pottery of early Iron Age date was found bearing grain impressions.

At the foot of Galley Hill is the site of an Iron Age boundary dyke called *Dray's Ditches*. It ran from Great Bramingham (TL:075266) to Warden Hill (TL:090265) and consisted of three parallel V-shaped ditches 1·8 m deep and 4·6 m wide running for about 1·6 km with massive wooden stockades between them. The purpose of the dyke seems to have been to form a barrier across the Icknield Way, and thus control the flow of traffic, checking surprise attacks and cattle rustling. The dyke can be dated to the beginning of the Iron Age, perhaps around 700 B.C. It now marks the northern edge of a housing estate, and little can be seen, except at TL:084265.

J. Dyer: *Ant. J.* **116** (1961) 1 for Dray's Ditches (material on barrows unpublished)

Plate 5   Maiden Bower plateau fort, Bedfordshire

3 MAIDEN BOWER (Plate 5)   Neolithic, Iron Age
   Houghton Regis   147 (SP:997224)

Approached from Sewell by a footpath beside a chalk quarry.

This small Iron Age plateau camp is circular in shape. It encloses 4·4 ha and is defended by a single rampart, still 2 m high in places, and a silted-up V-shaped ditch about 3·7 m deep. Excavations in 1913 suggested that the only entrance on the south-east was funnel-shaped, perhaps with a rampart walk or bridge over it.

There are indications that a neolithic causewayed camp lies asymmetrically beneath the Iron Age camp. A number of disconnected ditch sections containing broken human and animal bones were found during chalk quarrying in the last century, and both neolithic and Iron Age ditch sections are still visible in the quarry face. Neolithic pottery and an antler comb have been obtained from the site.

J. Dyer: *Bedfordshire Magazine* 7 (1961) 320

4   BEDFORDSHIRE

4 SHARPENHOE CLAPPER HILLFORT   Iron Age
   Streatley   147 (TL:066302)

National Trust property. Access from the Streatley to Sharpenhoe road.
Small lay-by for parking at the top of the hill.

This small promontory fort commands superb views of central Bedfordshire. A wide, flat ditch and damaged (possibly unfinished)
rampart cut off the tree-covered fort spur from the main hill mass to
the south. The steep hill-slopes on three sides must have provided
sufficient protection to require no obvious fortification. It is undated
by excavation.

J. Dyer: *Bedfordshire Magazine* **8** (1963) 112

5 WAULUD'S BANK   Neolithic
   Luton   147 (TL:062247)

In a public park around the source of the river Lea.

A denuded bank and external ditch surround the curved side of a D-
shaped enclosure of some 7 ha at the source of the river Lea. The bank
was made up of dumped chalk and gravel dug from the ditch, and
revetted on the outer edge by a stack of turves. The ditch is broad and
flat-bottomed, 9·1 m wide and 2·1 m deep. Neolithic grooved-ware
pottery and flint arrow-heads have been excavated from the earthwork,
and it seems likely that it belongs to the class of ritual sites similar to
Durrington Walls and Marden in Wiltshire. The position of the earthwork around a natural amphitheatre at the source of a river suggests
that religious ceremonies in which water played a part were important
to the builders of Waulud's Bank. Part of the site was re-used in the
Iron Age, and the ditch on the northern side of the site was enlarged
in the Roman period when a large amount of refuse of 2nd-century
date was dumped into it.

A. Selkirk: *Current Archaeology* **3** (1972–3) 173

Museums containing archaeological material
Bedford Museum, The Embankment, Bedford
Luton Museum and Art Gallery, Wardown Park, Luton

BERKSHIRE

1 ALFRED'S CASTLE   Iron Age
   Ashbury   157 (SU:277822)

By bridleway round south side of Ashdown Park from B4000, and foot-
path north to Ashbury. Site lies on north-west edge of park.

Described as irregularly hexagonal in shape, this camp of 0·8 ha lies on gently sloping ground, and is defended by a single rampart and ditch, with an extra external ditch on the south-east where there is an original entrance. This 'outwork' may be part of a barbican entrance. There may also be an entrance at the north-west, but this remains to be tested. Although the site is unexcavated there are surface indications to show that the rampart was stone-faced with sarsen boulders. Aerial photographs have shown that an elongated enclosure of about 3 ha stretches north from the earthwork, though no sign of this is visible on the ground. A considerable range of pottery of Iron Age, Romano-British and perhaps Saxon date, has been found on the surface at various times.

M. A. Cotton and P. Wood: *Berks. A.J.* **58** (1960) 43

2 BLEWBURTON HILL   Iron Age
  Blewbury   158 (SU:547862)

Approached off bridle road between Blewbury and Aston Upthorpe.

Blewburton is an outlying chalk hill commanding the angle between the Berkshire Downs and the Goring Gap. Round its oval summit runs a single rampart and ditch, enclosing about 4 ha, and broken by an entrance at the western end. The fort has been excavated by A. E. P. and F. J. Collins between 1947 and 1953, and again in 1967. In its earliest form the hilltop seems to have been occupied by a small farming settlement of about 2 ha, protected by a single palisade, and dated to about 550 B.C. or earlier. About 400 B.C. a rampart with horizontal timber lacing was constructed with a narrow level berm and V-shaped ditch outside it. The gate on the west was 4·9 m wide and might have had a bridge-walk over it. After a period of decay the fort was refortified by recutting the ditch and dumping the material obtained over the earlier rampart, and erecting a breastwork on top at the same time: probably about 100 B.C. The entrance passage was widened and faced with dry-stone walling. Traces of a second outer ditch may belong to this period. The burials of four complete horses and fragments of others were uncovered in the entrance passage and seem to belong to the Iron Age. Somewhere towards the middle of the 1st century A.D. the western entrance seems to have been abandoned, perhaps burnt, and its walls collapsed. Whether this was the result of Belgic expansion westwards or the arrival of the Romans soon after A.D. 43 is at present uncertain.

A Saxon cemetery has been excavated inside the fort, and there are a fine series of lynchet terraces on the hillside.

D. W. Harding: *The Iron Age in the Upper Thames Basin* (1972) 45

3 CAESAR'S CAMP   Iron Age
   Easthampstead   169 (SU:863657)

Public recreation area on the south side of Ninemile Ride.

This is a contour fort of about 8 ha. It follows the 400 feet contour line closely, and in plan resembles an oak leaf. The camp is defended by a single high rampart and ditch, with traces of a counterscarp bank here and there. There seem to be two original entrances, at the north and south, whilst gaps on the other sides are likely to be recent. The fort, which is covered with trees, is unexcavated, but probably began life in the early Iron Age.

M. A. Cotton: *Berks. A.J.* **60** (1962) 43

4 CHERBURY CAMP   Iron Age
   Kingston Bagpuize   158 (SU:374963)

Footpath south from the A420 passing Lovell's Court Farm.

When first constructed this low-lying earthwork was surrounded on three sides by a stream and marshes. Only on the north-east was it possible to reach the camp on dry land, and it is here that the only original entrance is to be found. Cherbury is the only multivallate fort in Berkshire. Three banks and ditches, with traces of a slight counterscarp bank, encircle an area of 3·6 ha. Excavations by J. S. P. Bradford in 1939 showed that the ditches were broad and fairly shallow whilst the innermost bank was composed of dumped sandy material faced with fine dry-stone walling on the inner and outer edges. There was no sign of walling to support the outermost bank. The entrance, midway along the eastern side, was lined with dry-stone walls, and closed by gates slung on two large posts. The road had been metalled, but had worn away with continuous use, and was pitted with wheel ruts about 1·5 m apart. Pottery, now in the Ashmolean Museum at Oxford, suggests that the fort was in use during the 1st century B.C.

J. S. P. Bradford: *Oxoniensia* **5** (1940) 13

5 CHURN FARM BARROW CEMETERY   Bronze Age
   Blewbury   158 (SU:515837)

On the south side of Churn Hill, east of Churn Farm. Metalled road south-west from the A417 at Blewbury.

The Berkshire Ridge Way runs across this part of the downs with various minor antiquities lying on either side of it. Numerous round barrows in the area have been destroyed by ploughing, but a few are still visible. Three east of Churn Farm (formerly four) measure between 24·4 m and 38 m in diameter, and are each about 0·9 m high. Two of them join one another. The third was opened by Dr. J.

Wilson in about 1840 and produced a cremation burial and 'pale pottery'. About 0.8 km south-east of the farm (SU:520833) are two bell-barrows with poorly defined berms, each about 2.4 m high and 23 m to 27 m in diameter. The larger barrow produced a riveted bronze dagger and cremation. On the north side of Churn Hill, beyond the wood, is Churn Knob (SU:522847), a fine, upstanding round barrow, whilst south-west of Churn Farm is Fox Barrow (SU:506831) cut by the later Grim's Ditch (see page 8).

L. V. Grinsell: *Berks. A.J.* **40** (1936) 42

6 GRIMSBURY CASTLE   Iron Age
  Hermitage   158 (SU:512723)

In Fence Wood, 0.8 km south of Hermitage. A minor road passes through the fort.

Situated on the watershed between the Kennet and the Pang at 500 feet (152 m) above sea level, this fort of 3.2 ha is triangular in shape, with a single rampart, ditch and counterscarp that follow the contour of the hilltop very closely. Excavation has shown that the inner bank and the high counterscarp were both of simple dump construction, whilst the ditch between is wide and U-shaped. There are three possible entrances of which one, slightly inturned on the west, has been proved by excavation. Both this, and a simple entrance gap at the northern apex, have hollow-ways leading up to them. A narrow causeway across the ditch at the south-east corner may indicate a postern entrance connecting with nearby springs. Pottery from the excavation dated the occupation to between the 3rd and 1st centuries B.C. There is an additional arc-shaped length of defence sweeping round 55 m west of the fort, consisting of a bank to the north and a bank and ditch further south.

P. Wood: *Trans. Newbury District Field Club* **11** (1963) 53

7 GRIM'S DITCH   Iron Age
  Aldworth   158 (SU:546785–570792)

There are two major groups of earthworks known as Grim's Ditch on the western end of the Berkshire Downs, and further sections to the east in the Chilterns. It is impossible to decide if they are all part of a related system, or all of the same age, though it is now generally accepted that they are of Iron Age date. The group in the Aldworth–Streatley area comprise three main stretches of earthwork, in each case consisting of a bank with a ditch on the north, and an average height of 1.8 m between the ditch bottom and bank crest. The main section near Aldworth stretches from Beche Farm for 1.6 km to the east, splitting in two where it crosses beneath the road from Hungerford Green. This line seems to continue to the east near Streatley, where an o·8 km length lies between the A417 near The Grotto and Hurdle Shaw (SU:593796). 2·4 km south is a tree-covered section on Hart Ridge, to be seen in Broom Wood and Bowler's Copse (SU:584775). It is noticeable that the Aldworth and Hart Ridge sections both cut across the same hill-spur and seem to isolate territory between them. Their size hardly makes them defensive, and perhaps we should consider them as demarcating grazing lands, as opposed to arable, on the top of the downs. They might then be seen as outworks of *Perborough Castle* hillfort to the west (SP:520780). This univallate hillfort is denuded and scarcely worth a visit. It can be approached from Cow Down to the north. Its main interest lies in that it seems to have been built over a Romano-British field system.

8 GRIM'S DITCH   Iron Age
   East and West Hendred and Blewbury   158 (SU:423845–542833)
This earthwork can be reached by various field tracks north of the Berkshire Ridge Way.

This earthwork can be traced intermittently for about 13 km for most of its course lying north of the Ridge Way. Whilst it may once have been more complete than today, it was probably never continuous for the whole distance, wherever steep slopes or woodland made construction difficult. The greatest surviving height of the earthwork from the crest of the bank to the bottom of the ditch is about 1·8 m. Its date is uncertain, though its antiquity is demonstrated by the number of parish boundaries that run along it. In all probability it delimits Iron Age farming territory, perhaps associated with the hillforts of Perborough or Grimsbury Castle, 9·7 and 12·9 km to the south. If this is true, then the length of ditch at East Garston (SU:363780 to 366796) might also be considered as part of the system.

9 INKPEN LONG BARROW (COMBE GIBBET)   Neolithic
   Inkpen   168 (SU:365623)
Beside a bridle-path on the ridge between Walbury Hill and Inkpen Hill.

This fine long barrow is magnificently sited on the crest of Inkpen Hill, where it is crowned by a recently restored gibbet. The barrow, which is apparently unexcavated, measures 61 m long, 22·9 m wide and is 1·8 m high at the eastern end. It has side ditches still 4·6 m wide and 0·9 m deep. It has been a cause of considerable concern in recent years due to motorists driving over it and thus causing damage.

10 KINGSTON LISLE ROMAN BARROW   Roman
Kingston Lisle   158 (SU:328882)

On the east side of a minor road, north-north-east from Kingston Lisle,
opposite a modern cemetery.

This barrow is conical in shape and stands about 1·8 m high. Its
position on low-lying land suggests a Roman rather than prehistoric
origin. This might be supported by the name of the adjacent hamlet,
Fawler, which according to the English Place-Name Society is derived
from the Old English *fagan flore*: spotted floor, meaning a tessellated
mosaic pavement. A villa might well be expected in the vicinity.

S. Piggott: *Antiquity* **1** (1927) 478

11 KNIGHTON BUSHES   Iron Age–Romano-British
Compton Beauchamp   158 (Centre at SU:300830)

Approached by minor road from Upper Lambourne passing Maddle Farm,
then by cart track.

On the downs north-east of Ashdown Park some 809 ha of Celtic fields
have survived, with at least three Romano-British settlements and a
cross-dyke amongst them. Evidence for the survival in the form of low
lynchets, supplemented by aerial photography, seems to show the fields
mainly on the west and south slopes of the hills. Ancient trackways
ran through the fields and linked the settlements, which are now poorly
preserved and very indistinct. The largest of these enclosures lies on
the east side of the ridge known as Compton Bottom (SU:286843). It
is on rough grassland and is surrounded by ploughed downland. It is
approximately polygonal in shape and encloses about 0·8 ha. Excavation in 1950 produced plentiful Romano-British occupation material
including pottery, a coin of Victorinus, a needle, brooch and ox-goads.
1·6 km to the south-east at Knighton Bushes is a sub-rectangular
enclosure of less than an acre, surrounded by a low bank, which is
broken on the north side (SU:298831). The interior has produced much
Romano-British pottery, a brooch and a number of Constantinian
coins.

The third enclosure lies in the hollow between Uffington Down and
Woolstone Down (SU:302853) and is separated from the Celtic fields
by a massive cross-ridge dyke. The enclosure is small, only 21·3 m by
15·2 m, and marked by a shallow ditch 1·2 m wide, with traces of an
inner and outer bank near the south-east corner. Romano-British
pottery has again been found on this site.

There is no direct evidence to link the fields and enclosures, though
it seems probable that the fields were still being worked when the
enclosures were occupied.

P. P. Rhodes: *Oxoniensia* **15** (1950) 1

Plate 6   *The Lambourn Seven Barrows, Berkshire*

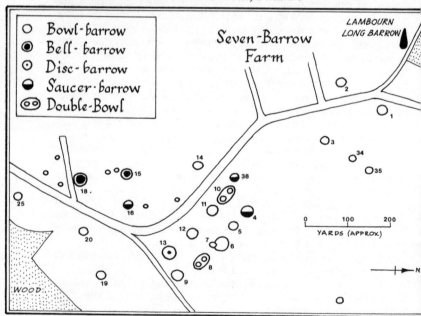

Fig. 5   *Lambourn barrows, Berkshire*

12 LAMBOURN SEVEN BARROWS (Plate 6)

Late Neolithic–Bronze Age

Lambourn 158 (SU:328828)

Mostly east of the minor road from Lambourn north to Kingston Lisle (see plan, Fig. 5).

About forty round barrows lie close to the boundaries of Lambourn and Sparsholt parishes, but only those in the famous 'Seven Barrows' group beside the road are accessible, and consequently described in detail. The numbering of L. V. Grinsell and Humphrey Case has been retained. The barrows are described commencing at the north-western end of the row furthest from the road:

No. 4. This was a large disc- or saucer-barrow 36·6 m in diameter, with a bank outside the ditch. It seems only to have produced a small piece of charcoal when it was dug into by Edwin Martin Atkins between 1850 and 1858.

5. There are no records of the opening of this bowl-barrow which is 1·8 m high and 21·3 m in diameter.

6 and 7. A large bowl-barrow 1·8 m high and 24·4 m in diameter overlaps a very small barrow on its southern side.

8. This consists of two mounds, each 1·8 m high, enclosed within a single ditch.

9. This bowl-barrow is 1·8 m high and 18·3 m in diameter. When it was examined by Martin Atkins it was found to contain a four-walled sarsen stone cist with a capstone, in which an early collared urn containing the cremated remains of a woman had been placed. A small mound of sarsens, flint and wood ash had been piled over the cist before the barrow mound had been constructed. A crouched secondary burial was also found in the surrounding chalk mound.

10. This is another double barrow with two mounds enclosed by a single ditch. The northern mound was opened by Atkins, and produced the bones of an ox and 'a dog apparently something of the lurcher kind'.

11. A bowl-barrow, 3·1 m high and 30·5 m in diameter, which has been clearly opened although no record is known.

12. This bowl-barrow is about 2·4 m high and 21·3 m in diameter. There is a tree-planting bank around it.

13. This is the only disc-barrow in the main group. It is 30·5 m in diameter and has a central mound 0·3 m high and 18·3 m in diameter. Nothing is known of its contents.

38. A small saucer-barrow 13·7 m in diameter, with a ditch 0·9 m deep, and a slight outer bank.

Mention can also be made of a fine bell-barrow (No. 18) not far from the road and crossed by a hedge line some 183 m south of the group described. The mound is 1·8 m high and 18·3 m in diameter, and is separated from its ditch by a berm 3·7 m wide. In the centre of the southern side a circular sarsen cist was found containing a cremation, a bronze awl, a shale ring and a jet amulet. The cist is thought to have been added to the barrow as a secondary burial.

Immediately east of the road, 229 m north of the main group, is another fine bowl-barrow (No. 1). It contained two cremations at its centre, accompanied by a small bronze knife, a biconical pygmy cup and a bronze awl. The surface of the barrow was covered with secondary cremation burials: fifty-four were protected by sarsen stones, and another fifty-nine by cinerary urns. Martin Atkins took twenty days to excavate the barrow in 1850, during which time he drew plans and sections to scale. After the excavation he restored the mound to its original shape. This was truly remarkable work considering the normal standards of excavation in his day.

The *Lambourn long barrow* (SU:323834) lies 0·4 km north-west at the south-east end of Wescot Wood. Badly denuded it can be reached along a cart track which passes over it. It is 82·3 m long and 21.3 m wide at its eastern end where it is still 1·2 m high. Martin Atkins dug into it and found a number of skeletons, but has left us no further details. More recent rescue work by John Wymer showed a core of sarsen stones, and a crouched burial in a rough sarsen cist, together with some sea shells, lying in the head of the mound; but clearly not forming the primary deposit.

H. J. Case: *Berks. A.J.* **55** (1956–7) 15

13 LOWBURY HILL   Roman
    Aston Upthorpe   158 (SU:540823)
3 km north-east of Compton along a bridle road.

Standing on the highest point of the eastern Berkshire Downs, this site commands splendid views. It consists of a rectangular banked enclosure with rounded corners, 54·9 m long by 43·3 m wide, covering the footings of a rough flint wall, with an entrance in the middle of the eastern side. In the south-west corner of the enclosure at the base of the wall was the skeleton of a middle-aged woman with a cleft skull. Donald Atkinson, the excavator, suggested that this might have been a dedicatory burial. He dated the walled enclosure to about A.D. 200 and suggested that it remained in use until about A.D. 400. There was plenty of pottery evidence to show that the site had been occupied for an even longer time, probably from the Early Iron Age, though whether at that time it had been enclosed was uncertain. The Roman occupation involved wooden buildings of uncertain form in two corners, each with tiled roofs. Opinions differ as to the purpose of the site, Sir Ian Richmond considering it to have been a farm, whilst others, including the Ordnance Survey, have interpreted it as a Romano-Celtic temple.

A barrow east of the earthwork contained a primary Saxon burial.

H. Peake: *Archaeology of Berkshire* (1931) 115

14 MORTIMER COMMON BARROW CEMETERY Bronze Age
   Stratfield Mortimer   158/168 (SU:643651)

On the west side of Mortimer Common, north of the road to Ufton Nervet and west of the road to Burghfield.

On the edge of Holden's Firs plantation are five barrows close to the road, with two bowl-barrows further north. On the south-east, nearest the road is half of a bowl-barrow, originally about 15·2 m in diameter and 0·6 m high. To the north-west is a low bowl-barrow 12·2 m in diameter and only 0·3 m high. North-west again is a fine bell-barrow 1·8 m high and 44·2 m in overall diameter. Some 18 m further west is a large but indistinct disc-barrow 54·3 m in diameter with a central mound 12·8 m in diameter and only 0·3 m high. It is surrounded by a ditch and bank, both 5·8 m wide. On the west this barrow overlaps a small but typical bell-barrow. There is no record of the contents of these barrows if they have ever been opened.

15 SEGSBURY CAMP (LETCOMBE CASTLE)   Iron Age
   Letcombe Regis   158 (SU:385845)

This large D-shaped hillfort of 10·5 ha lies 91 m north of the Ridge Way. It is defended by a single rampart and ditch, with a counter-scarp bank on the north-west side. The rampart was faced with blocks of sarsen stone. Thomas Hearne, writing in 1725 records 'within the Bank that lies on the Inside of this Camp . . . they dig vast red Stones, being a red Flint, some of which a Cart will hardly draw. They have dug up a great many Loads of them, and with many of them they build. They are placed in the Banks of the Dike or Trench in form of a Wall.' The original entrance on the east is flanked by out-turned rampart ends. The other breaks seem to be modern. Digging in the southern bank of the rampart in 1871 a Dr. Phené found a cist containing human bones, flint scrapers, perhaps the umbo of a shield and fragments of pottery. This sounds like a Saxon burial, but might possibly be an Iron Age dedicatory burial. Pottery found within the fort suggests that it was occupied in the 4th century B.C.

M. A. Cotton: *Berks. A. J.* **60** (1962) 43

16 SINODUN CAMP   Iron Age
   Little Wittenham   158 (SU: 570924)

Car-park and footpath beside the road from Brightwell to Little Witten-
ham.

Until recently the twin peaks of the Sinodun Hills have proudly
dominated this part of the Thames valley. The southern hill, crowned
by the wood known as Wittenham Clumps had been a landmark for
generations. Now they are rivalled by a vast power-station that does
nothing to improve one of the most beautiful corners of England. The
south-eastern hilltop bears the 4 ha fort known as Sinodun Camp or
Castle Hill. Soil from a deep ditch has been thrown downhill to build
an outer rampart. If there was ever an inner one, then the soil has
crept down the hill behind it and slowly buried it. The entrance, a
simple straight-through type, is on the west. Iron Age pottery has been
found within the earthwork which is unexcavated, and also outside the
entrance and under the modern car-park.

   The tree-clad *Brightwell Barrow* (SU: 576918), which has produced
Iron Age pottery, is clearly visible on the summit o·8 km east.

P. P. Rhodes: *Oxoniensia* **13** (1948) 18

17 UFFINGTON CASTLE   Iron Age
   Uffington   158 (SU: 299864)

One-way road signposted 'White Horse' from the B4507. There is a car-
park on the hilltop. The fort lies due east of this. (Department of the
Environment: access at any time.)

'A fine earthen work of verdant turf uninjured by the plough' was how
Sir Richard Colt Hoare described this fine hillfort in 1819. In more
recent years motor cycles caused trouble here in their efforts to scramble
over the ramparts. Wire fences have now been set up to check their
progress.

   A single rampart and ditch, broken by an entrance facing west
towards Wayland's Smithy, encloses about 3·2 ha. The rampart
curves outwards on either side of the entrance causeway and seems to
join up with a small counterscarp bank. Martin Atkins, digging through
the ramparts in about 1850 found that the chalk rubble had been piled
between two rows of posts. A number of sarsen stones have also been
observed protruding from the rampart, suggesting a facing of these
stones, but it is uncertain how they are related to the timber work.
A silver coin of the Iron Age tribe, the Dobunni, was found within the
camp, though it may be related to the nearby White Horse.

   Two oval mounds lie east of the hillfort and above the White
Horse. Excavated in 1857 one was found to contain forty-six Roman
skeletons, five of which had coins placed between their teeth to pay
Charon for ferrying them across the river Styx.

One of the finest stretches of the Berkshire Ridge Way runs along the southern side of the fort, and it is well worth the effort of walking the 2·4 km westwards to Wayland's Smithy.

M. A. Cotton: *Berks. A.J.* **60** (1962) 48

Plate 7   The Uffington White Horse, Berkshire

18 UFFINGTON WHITE HORSE (Plate 7)   Iron Age?
   Uffington   158 (SU:302866)

One-way road signposted 'White Horse' from the B4507. An 0·4 km walk north-east from the car-park leads to the Horse. (The Horse, Uffington Castle and Dragon Hill are in the care of the Department of the Environment and can be visited at any time.)

This curious, bird-headed horse is surely one of the strangest ancient monuments to have survived from prehistory. The existence of such a figure cut into the downland turf is due to the tremendous impact its presence must have had on generations of local inhabitants, who every few years (seven is often mentioned), scoured the chalk amidst celebrations and festivities which included horse and ass races, cudgel playing and wrestling and the rolling of cheeses down the steep valley known as the Manger. As the Horse was scoured a local ballad was chanted in Berkshire dialect:

The old White Horse wants setting to rights,
    And the Squire has promised good cheer,
So we'll give him a scrape, to keep him in shape,
    And he'll last for many a year.

He was made a long, long time ago,
    With a good deal of labour and pains,
By King Alfred the Great, when he spoiled their conceit
    And caddled those wosbirds the Danes.

The Blowing-stone in days gone by
    Was King Alfred's bugle horn,
And the thorning-tree, you may plainly see,
    Which is called King Alfred's thorn.

There'll be backsword play, and climbing the pole,
    And a race for a pig and a cheese,
But we think as he's a dummel soul
    Who don't care for such sports as these.

(caddled = harassed; wosbirds = a term of abuse; dummel = dull)

The Horse, which measures 111·3 m from the tip of its tail to its front ear, was probably first cut in the Late Iron Age, its design resembling that found on certain Belgic coins and metalwork of the period. It may have been an emblem of the Dobunni or Atrebates, tribes who might well have occupied the adjoining hillfort of Uffington Castle. Since the Horse is best viewed from 3 or 4 km away to the north, along the Longcot to Fernham road, for example (SU:277909), one cannot help wondering how its constructors first laid it out. In modern times megaphones or even radio might be used to position markers on the hillside from the valley below, yet the Uffington horse is scarcely visible from the nearby valley. Some sort of flag system was possibly used.

There are various legends connected with the Horse and surrounding district. It was considered lucky to wish when standing in the Horse's eye. Tradition says that St. George slew the dragon on the flat-topped Dragon Hill below the horse. The bare patch of chalk is where the dragon's blood spilled; no grass has grown there since. The odd shape of the hill is quite natural, but it is curious that drawings made of it 200 years ago also show the same bare patch of chalk. Perhaps the White Horse is St. George's charger, or even the dragon!

The *Blowing Stone* mentioned in the poem stands in a cottage garden at the foot of Blowing Stone Hill (SU:324871). It is a block of natural sarsen stone, with a hole in it about 46 cm long. Blown in a particular way it produces a loud, siren-like note, which can be heard for 3 or 4 km on a suitable day. For a few pence visitors may try to blow the stone. King Alfred is supposed to have blown through the stone to summon the Saxons to battle. Unfortunately this story seems to be less than 300 years old, and the stone has no archaeological significance.

The White Horse and the Blowing Stone both figure in Thomas Hughes's classic *Tom Brown's School Days*. Hughes lived at Uffington until he was eight.

L. V. Grinsell: *White Horse Hill* (1939)

19 WALBURY HILLFORT   Iron Age
   Combe   168 (SU:374617)
The minor road from Inkpen to Combe Hill passes beside the fort and the Berkshire Ridge Way runs through it.

The defences of Walbury enclose the trapezoidal top of the highest chalk hill in Britain at a height of 974 feet (297 m) above sea level. 33 ha lie within the single rampart and ditch of this contour fort which has slight traces of a counterscarp bank. At the north-west corner is an inturned entrance, and there is a smaller one at the south-east. Hollow-ways outside both are connected with minor earthworks, and two cross-banks at the north-west seem to check progress across the neck of land. The inner one of these may be connected with some kind of barbican outwork. Circular depressions inside the fort could represent hut circles, but confirmation of this must wait until it is excavated.

M. A. Cotton: *Berks. A.J.* **60** (1962) 42

20 WAYLAND'S SMITHY CHAMBERED BARROW (Fig. 6; Plate 8)
                                                             Neolithic
   Ashbury   158 (SU:281854)
In beech trees 1·2 km south of Ashbury, and 1·2 km north-east of the B4000 walking along the Berkshire Ridge Way: alternatively 2·4 km west of Uffington Castle car-park. (Department of the Environment. Open at any time.)

'At this place lived formerly an invisible Smith; and if a traveller's horse had lost a shoe upon the road, he had no more to do than to bring the horse to this place, with a piece of money, and leaving both there for some time, he might come again and find the money gone, but the horse new shod.' Thus wrote Francis Wise in 1738 and the tale has been retold many times.

Wayland's Smithy is a unique chambered barrow with a burial chamber at one end of a long trapezoidal mound, which in turn encloses an earlier chalk-built barrow containing a timber structure. That the barrow is of two distinct periods was shown by excavations in

Plate 8 Wayland's Smithy chambered tomb, Berkshire

1962–3 by Professor Richard Atkinson. The Period I barrow contained a wooden mortuary hut shaped like a ridge tent, but with a sarsen stone floor. Into this some fourteen bodies had been brought; some in an articulated condition, others with limbs separated as though they had been stored elsewhere until the flesh had disintegrated, and were then brought to the mortuary hut for final burial. When the hut was full, sarsen boulders were placed around it, and chalk from ditches on either side was piled over the top. The whole mound was kept in position by a kerbstone of boulders. None of this barrow is visible today.

The Period II barrow consists of the mound now visible, 54·9 m long, 14·6 m wide at the front, tapering to 6·1 m at the back. At the wide end of the cairn four of originally six great sarsen stones, each about 3 m high, flank the entrance to the burial chamber, which consists of a stone-lined passage 6·7 m long, with a single chamber or transept on either side. The roof of the passage, where it still exists, is about 1·8 m high, whilst that of the side-chambers reaches 1·4 m. Dry-stone walling was used to fill gaps between the stones. During excavations in 1919 the left-hand chamber (west) was found to contain about

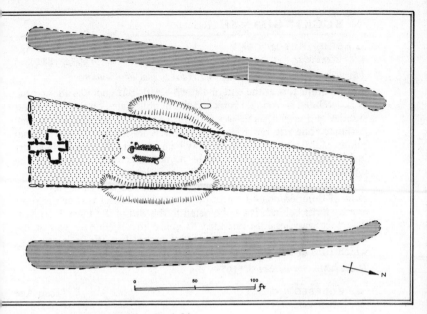

Fig. 6 Wayland's Smithy, Berkshire

eight skeletons including one of a child. What were thought to have been two Iron Age currency bars found at the same time have since been shown to be parts of 18th-century barn hinges! The new excavations showed that the material for the final barrow was excavated from ditches on either side of the mound, each 1·8 m deep and 4·6 m wide, and was held in place by a continuous kerb of sarsens. Revised radiocarbon dates suggest that the barrows were both constructed between 3700 and 3400 B.C.

Wayland's Smithy has been restored by the Department of the Environment. The two missing sarsen stones beside the entrance have been marked by irregular dry-stone work in the front façade. The present entry behind the façade from the east is also modern.

Museums containing archaeological material
Abingdon Borough Museum, County Hall, Abingdon
Newbury Borough Museum, Wharf Street, Newbury
Reading Museum and Art Gallery, Blagrave Street, Reading

The Ashmolean Museum, Beaumont Street, Oxford, also exhibits Berkshire material

1 BODDINGTON CAMP   Iron Age
Wendover   159 (SP:882080)

Through the housing estate off the A4011, east of Wendover.

This contour fort at the end of a steep-sided spur encloses about 7 ha. It is defended by a single bank and ditch, obliterated on the north-west side. A gap at the south-western end of the fort may be an original entrance, but the more likely position is at the north-west. Aerial photographs suggest that there may be a smaller, possibly earlier, fort inside the earthwork. This might be an inner quarry ditch for the existing rampart. Unfortunately this area is now planted with trees. When the rampart was examined in 1964 it was shown to have been built of dumped chalk held in position by a stack of turf at the front and by flints behind. It can be dated to the end of the Early Iron Age. The fort was possibly intended to guard the Wendover gap at the northern end of the Misbourne valley, as well as the Icknield Way which runs at its foot.

R.C.H.M. Bucks. South (1912) 184

2 BOLEBEC'S CASTLE   Iron Age
Medmenham   159 (SU:807847)

East of the minor road from Medmenham to Bockmer End.

This small wooden Iron Age contour fort is situated on a spur above the valley of the Thames to the north-east of Medmenham church. Although the fort is much damaged on the east, sufficient remains to show that the site enclosed 619 ha and was defended by a single rampart 4·6 m high and a ditch, now about 0·9 m deep, with traces of an outer bank on the west. There is what appears to be an original entrance on the north-west, whilst a bank protects a pathway on the south-west which leads down to a spring.

Less than 2 km east of Bolebec's Castle was a second Iron Age fort at *Danesfield* (SU:816846). Originally it covered about 8 ha, but today only parts of the double northern and eastern ramparts survive, in places more than 4·6 m high. Between the ramparts is a ditch 3·1 m deep and 21·3 m wide. There is little doubt of the fort's Iron Age origin in spite of a local tradition ascribing it to the Danes.

R.C.H.M. Bucks. South (1912) 256

3 BULSTRODE CAMP   Iron Age
Gerrards Cross   159 (SU:994880)

Reached from the A332 along Camp Road, 0·4 km south of A40 cross-roads. Public open space.

This Iron Age plateau camp stands on level ground at a height of 275 feet (84 m) above sea level. It is roughly oval in shape and its western side follows a steep escarpment. Enclosing 9 ha, and one of the largest Chiltern forts, it is surrounded by a double rampart and ditch, except on the west and north-west sides where the outer ditch has been destroyed. The entrance was probably on the north-east. The gap at the south-west is not original. Excavations in 1924 were inconclusive, and suggest that the ramparts were constructed of dumped sand and gravel without timbering.

C. Fox: *Records of Bucks.* **11** (1924) 283

4 CHOLESBURY CAMP   Iron Age
Cholesbury   159 (SP:930072)
Surrounding the village church. A footpath leads left from the church driveway on to the rampart.

One of the strongest plateau forts in the Chilterns surrounds the church of St. Lawrence. Oval in shape, and enclosing 6 ha, it has two ramparts still 1·8 m high, with a ditch between them which was 4 m deep when excavated. An extra rampart and ditch have been constructed on the southern side of the camp facing down the adjoining dry valleys. On the west the two ramparts are separated by a broad triangular area that terminates at a low cross-ditch. In prehistoric times the clay land to the north was forested, and may have required less protection. There are also indications of minor earthworks running north-east and north-west from the camp to join Grim's Ditch just over 1·6 km away. These may have enclosed an area for cattle and pig husbandry. The main entrance to the fort was probably where the path to the church cuts the rampart, although the gap on the north-east is also a possibility. Pottery excavated from the site was considered to be not necessarily earlier than the 2nd century B.C., and distinctively native in character.

K. Kimball: *J. Brit. Archaeol. Assn.* **39** (1933) 187

5 THE COP BARROW   Bronze Age
Bledlow   159 (SP:773011)
Reached from the B4009 midway between Chinnor and Bledlow. A steep climb from the Upper Icknield Way leads into woods where a track leads across Wain Hill, near to the barrow which stands in a clearing.

In 1937 a small round barrow on Wain Hill was excavated by J. F. Head. About 1·8 m high and 18·3 m in diameter the barrow had no surrounding ditch, but was built of material scraped from the surrounding hillside: a common feature in the Chilterns. The barrow may have contained a crouched female burial, but its centre had been much disturbed and only a jaw-bone remained. At all events the burial seems to have been covered with a layer of clay, perhaps as a water-

proof covering. Also in the grave was part of a polished axe-head of
Cornish greenstone and a tanged bronze dagger. Later in the Bronze
Age a cremation without an urn was added to the barrow, as well as a
bone bridle-piece. In the Saxon period cremation and inhumation
burials took place at the barrow.

About 0·8 km south-west beside the same footpath on the open hillside are two further barrows enclosed within a single ditch (SP: 767006).
It is reported that an iron spearhead and bronze sword-chape were
found in one of the barrows in 1885, and that the mounds, which are
much disturbed, were largely constructed of flints. They lie beside an
Iron Age occupation site, and it is possible that the barrows may be of
the same date.

J. F. Head: *Records of Bucks.* **13** (1938) 328

6 DANESBOROUGH HILLFORT   Iron Age
   Wavendon   146 (SP: 922348)

Numerous bridleways through Wavendon Wood pass close to Danes-
borough, but careful map-reading will be required.

This small hillfort lies in deep woodland close to the county boundary,
on the greensand ridge, above the Roman town of *Magiovinium* (Fenny
Stratford). Although the fort, which is roughly rectangular, only
encloses 3·4 ha, it is quite strongly defended by two ramparts separated
by a ditch. A simple straight-through entrance is on the south-western
side. The north-eastern end of the fort may be unfinished, but it is so
densely planted that it is impossible to be sure without excavations.
There are extensive outworks for almost 2 km south-east of the fort,
which may be connected with cattle ranching. Danesborough is well to
the north of the Icknield Way and it was probably concerned with
protecting the Ouzel valley along which traffic passed from the
Chilterns to the Great Ouse valley. A second fort in the same valley,
Craddock's Camp, north of Leighton Buzzard, has been totally
destroyed.

R.C.H.M. Bucks. North (1913) 311

7 GRIM'S DITCH   Iron Age
   Chilterns   159 (various references: see below)

This linear earthwork runs for 40 km through the central Chilterns.
Nowadays it is generally accepted as of Iron Age date, although it is
still uncertain at precisely what time during that long period it was
constructed. It runs in a series of scallops along the top of the Chiltern
escarpment, curving south into the river valleys, and suddenly breaking
off where it would have to descend to lower ground to cross wooded
and marshy valleys. The ditch of the earthwork faces south, often on
the uphill side, and it is clear that the dyke was not defensive, but

intended only to mark a boundary. Perhaps it was built by a people who came late to the Chilterns and had to live on the heavier clay lands to the south, where they may have practised cattle and pig husbandry. The best section of the Grim's Ditch can be seen at Great Hampden between SP:835022 and Hampden Church. Notice the entrance gap at the angle of the dyke at SP:838029. Smaller sections are visible north-west of Chambersgreen in the wood (SP:901073); north of Kiln Farm (SP:926092); on Pitstone Hill (SP:948142); and on the edge of Whipsnade Zoo (Bedfordshire: SP:998186).

J. Dyer: *Antiquity* **37** (1963) 46

8 IVINGHOE BEACON   Iron Age
    Ivinghoe   159 (SP:960168)

Approach from the road linking the B489 with Ashridge. Car-park and picnic area. National Trust property.

An early contour fort, enclosing 2·2 ha, rings the summit of Beacon Hill, about 0·8 km north of the Icknield Way. A level platform, marking the course of the filled-in ditch, is almost all that is visible of the fortification today. Excavation has proved that a very simple, slightly inturned entrance existed at the eastern end of the fort, marked by a double row of posts forming an entrance passage only 2·4 m wide. On the south-east the fort had a double bank and ditch, but the steeper west side and north face do not seem to have required extra protection. The rampart had been composed of stout wooden fences at front and back, the space between them filled with chalk. Although this barrier seems to have averaged 2 m wide, there were places where it was as narrow as 0·9 m. Outside it was a ditch 3·1 m wide and 2·4 m deep. There were slight traces of huts within the fort, and pieces of a bronze sword and a bronze razor were found. Together with the pottery these finds suggest a very early Iron Age date, probably in the 7th century B.C.

At the highest point inside the fort is a round barrow, and there are two others outside the eastern entrance. Between the fort and the car-park to the south are further barrows on the small hill summits west of the path. There are no records of the opening of any of these barrows.

M. A. Cotton and S. S. Frere: *Records of Bucks.* **18** (1968) 1

9 LODGE HILL   Bronze Age
    Saunderton   159 (SP:789004)

Farm track from the Bledlow to Bledlow Ridge road runs up towards Lodge Hill. Barrows can be viewed from west end.

At the north-western end of this low chalk spur are two large ploughed bell-barrows. With the exception of the unusual examples at Dunstable, these are the finest of their kind in the Chilterns, and still stand 0·9 m

high and 22·9 m in diameter. They are particularly clear in growing
corn, when the buried ditches show up as darker growth in the crop.
Because Lodge Hill rises immediately to the south, it is possible to look
down on to these crop marks. The barrows were opened in the past
with negative results, although human bone fragments, pieces of
beaker pottery and flint saws have been scattered in the plough soil.

On the southern slopes of the hill are a number of depressions which
probably represent hut circles and storage pits. These cover an area of
about 0·8 ha and end abruptly at a curving bank and ditch on the west.
From surface finds this site was almost certainly occupied in the Early
Iron Age and again in Romano-British times. Yet another Iron Age
occupation site was situated close to where the bridleway leading to
Lodge Hill leaves the Bledlow to Bledlow Ridge road (at SP:786006).

J. F. Head: *Early Man in South Buckinghamshire* (1956) 51

10 PITSTONE HILL FLINT MINES, ETC.   Neolithic
   Pitstone   159 (SP:950142)

*Access from the minor road linking B488 to Ashridge. There is a car-park
at SP:955148.*

This hill, above a large cement works, has many archaeological sites
upon it. These include flint mines, boundary dykes and field systems.
The flint mines are situated at the western angle of the hill (SP:949142)
and consist of two deep hollows 3·7 m and 3·1 m deep respectively, and
a third 1·8 m deep. Although the mines have not been excavated there
is good reason to believe that they are of neolithic date. The paucity of
flint in the Chiltern chalk probably explains why there are not more
pits.

Along the west and north-west escarpment of Pitstone run further
sections of the Grim's Ditch (No. 7), perhaps best seen beside the flint
mines, or at SP:952148 where it is cut by a deep hollow-way. Much
of the eastern and southern slopes of Pitstone Hill are covered with
early field boundaries of Celtic and strip-lynchet types. The romanized
section of the Icknield Way also runs across the hill.

J. Dyer and A. Hales: *Records of Bucks.* **17** (1961) 49

11 PULPIT HILL   Iron Age
   Great Kimble   159 (SP:832050)

*A minor road south of Great Kimble church runs uphill to the fort. It is
metalled for part of the way.*

This small but strong hillfort is situated in woodland on a spur of the
Chilterns which would have commanded extensive views in all directions, and is roughly circular in plan. Its eastern side is defended by
a double rampart and ditch, with traces of a 4·6 m wide berm behind

the outer rampart. This effectively cuts off the fort from the main hill mass to the east. Only single defences exist on the north-western and south-western sides where the natural slope is steeper. The main entrance is on the east and is of the simple straight-through type. A second break on the west might have allowed access to a look-out post. There are many low boundary banks in adjoining Pulpit Wood, which may have been connected with Iron Age agriculture.

R.C.H.M. Bucks. South (1912) 164

12 THORNBOROUGH ROMAN BARROWS   Roman
    Thornborough   146 (SP:732333)

North of the B4034, 230 m east of Thornborough Bridge.

Two large Roman burial mounds lie north of the road 3·2 km east of Buckingham. That on the west is about 4·6 m high and 36·6 m in diameter, whilst its eastern companion is 4 m high and 27·4 m across. Both barrows were opened by the Duke of Buckingham in 1839 and 1840. One, he discovered, had been opened previously and robbed. The other was richly furnished. A small wooden vault had been constructed over the corpse, which had been cremated on a limestone floor. Around the burial were placed pots, glass and bronze vessels, a gold ornament and a ring, two wine jars, iron weapons and a lamp with a chained lid. Joan Liversidge has dated the burial to the late 2nd century A.D.

Roman roads from Towcester, Irchester and Magiovinium met close to the barrows, near a head stream of the Great Ouse. On the opposite side of the stream and 110 m south of the road, a Romano-Celtic temple was excavated in 1964. Nothing of it is visible today.

J. Liversidge: *Records of Bucks.* **16** (1954) 29

13 WEST WYCOMBE HILLFORT (Plate 9)   Iron Age
    West Wycombe   159 (SP:827949)

North-west of the village of West Wycombe, whose church stands inside the fort.

This small contour fort on Church Hill encloses just under 1·2 ha within a rampart, ditch and counterscarp bank. The rampart still rises 3·4 ha high on the north-east, but on the south-east the construction of the 18th-century Dashwood mausoleum has totally destroyed it. The church and churchyard, also within the fort, have considerably damaged the interior. The original entrance probably coincided with the modern north-western gate into the churchyard. The fort lies on the southern tip of a long, narrow ridge which terminates to the north at Lodge Hill, Saunderton (see No. 9).

The caves below Church Hill are of medieval and later date.

R.C.H.M. Bucks. South (1912) 318

Plate 9   Church Hill fort, West Wycombe, Buckinghamshire

14   WHELPLEY HILL   Iron Age
  Ashley Green   159 (SP:996039)

A footpath passes on the south side of the camp from the Bovingdon to Whelpleyhill road.

This small camp is now almost ploughed out. It covers 1·8 ha and is bounded by a single bank and ditch. A gap in the rampart on the south-east may indicate an original entrance. The camp, which in prehistoric times would have been surrounded by forests, is on the same ridge as the Cholesbury fort (No. 4) and may have been strategically linked to it. Both forts overlook the valley of the Bulbourne to the north and east.

R.C.H.M. Bucks. South (1912) 16

15   WHITELEAF BARROWS   Neolithic
  Monks Risborough   159 (SP:822040)

From the Monks Risborough to Great Hampden road a footpath leads up to the barrows from a little beyond the base of the Whiteleaf Cross.

The Whiteleaf barrow stands on a false crest of the Chiltern escarpment, above the medieval chalk-cut hill figure, the Whiteleaf Cross.

The barrow was kidney-shaped in plan with a 'forecourt' on the eastern side. It is surrounded by a circular ditch about 24 m in diameter, which was shown to be 0·9 m deep.

The barrow was excavated between 1935 and 1939 by Sir Lindsay Scott. It contained a wooden burial chamber measuring 2·4 m by 1·7 m. Only the left foot of the skeleton of a middle-aged man lay in the chamber; the rest of the burial was scattered outside on the forecourt to the east. Many pieces of pottery of neolithic types were found in the soil immediately covering the burial chamber. The pieces represented fifty-one pots that had obviously been lying on the ground when the soil was scraped up to make the covering mound, but the fresh nature of their broken edges clearly indicated that they had been deliberately smashed just before the barrow building ceremony.

At the northern end of the Whiteleaf ridge is a small scraped-up barrow (SP:821043) about 10·7 m in diameter and 1·2 m high, whilst midway between it and the Whiteleaf barrow is what might be a pond-barrow, with a cross-shaped depression in it. It could, however, have also been a windmill base.

V. G. Childe and I. Smith: *P.P.S.* **20** (1954) 212

Museum containing archaeological material

Buckinghamshire County Museum, Church Street, Aylesbury

CAMBRIDGESHIRE

1 BELSAR'S HILL   Iron Age
   Willingham   135 (TL:423703)

On minor road east of Willingham. Footpath runs through camp to Aldreth.

A denuded oval fort some 268 m by 229 m consisting of a single rampart and ditch, lying on the western edge of Hempsals Fen. The rampart has been much reduced by ploughing and is best preserved north-west of the trackway. There is an entrance on the west and possibly traces of another on the east. The marshes must have provided excellent protection for this camp. The footpath passing through it leads to the Isle of Ely 14·5 km north-east. It follows a causeway beside which Bronze Age material has been found.

C. Fox: *Archaeology of the Cambridge Region* (1923) 137

2 CAMBRIDGESHIRE DYKES   Saxon
Pampisford, Great Abington, Newmarket, Great Wilbraham

135 and 148

In view of the absence of upstanding prehistoric and Roman monuments in Cambridgeshire, it is perhaps legitimate to mention briefly
five linear dykes of probable early Saxon date, three of which can
hardly be missed by any traveller in that area. Built to protect the
region to the north-east from south-westerly attack, they lie at right
angles to the Icknield Way and terminate either in woodland, marsh or
at rivers. Whilst at least one (Heydon Ditch) may have Iron Age
origins, most of them were probably thrown up soon after the battle of
Mons Badonicus early in the 6th century A.D. when the Saxons were
driven into East Anglia and attempted to protect themselves from the
British to the west. Visible dykes are:

Brent Ditch in Pampisford and Great Abington parishes. 2·4 km
long, it can be seen in the trees on either side of the lay-by at TL: 515474
(Map 148).

Devil's Ditch, Newmarket. 11 km long, running beside the race
course (TL: 580648 and TL: 620614) (Map 135).

Fleam Dyke, Great Wilbraham. 5·6 km long, best seen at TL: 548540
(Map 135 and 148).

Heydon Ditch (TL: 422419) is scarcely worth visiting, and the *Black
Ditches* (TL: 774684) are in Suffolk.

C. Fox: *Archaeology of the Cambridge Region* (1923) 123

3 CAR DYKE   Roman
Cottenham and Waterbeach   135 (TL: 461713 to TL: 496643)

The Car Dyke is one of a series of canals cut by the Romans, early in
their occupation of Britain, as part of their scheme to bring grain from
East Anglia to Lincoln and ultimately York. Running from the river
Cam at Waterbeach the Car Dyke ran north-west for 8 km to join the
Old West River 3·2 km south of Haddenham. In Roman times the
Old West River did not join the Cam; the section between the A10 and
the Cam is man-made. From the Old West River via the Ouse and
Conquest Lode or Cnut's Causeway, access was gained to the Nene.
The Lincolnshire Car Dyke then carried the boats on to Lincoln.

Excavations in 1947 dated the canal's construction to between A.D. 50
and 60, and showed that it remained in use until the end of the 2nd
century at least. Its dimensions, about 13·7 m wide, 2·1 m deep, with
a flat bottom 8·5 m wide, are comparable with modern-day canals.
A number of Romano-British settlements have been detected beside
the dyke, but there is little to be seen today. That at TL: 465702, for
example, consisting only of low banks and shallow depressions. In
places the Car Dyke has been reduced to little more than a field ditch;

a good section of it runs beside the Cambridge to Ely Road (A10) as it passes Waterbeach airfield at TL:485664.

G. Clark: *Ant. J.* **29** (1949) 145

4 MOULTON HILLS BARROWS   Romano-British
   Bourn   134 (TL:326571)

On the north side of the village on high banks above the road at Crow End and Caxton Road junction.

Known locally as Arm's Hills, these three barrows stand at the Caxton Road junction, two east of the road and one north-west. Of the two barrows together the northern is 20·7 m in diameter and 2·4 m high, with a marked ditch 5·5 m wide. Its neighbour is 25 m in diameter, 2·4 m high and surrounded by a ditch 6·7 m wide. The western sides of both barrows have been destroyed by road widening. Both barrows were dug into at the beginning of this century.

The northern barrow covered a cremation and pottery fragments, together with a coin of Aurelius (A.D. 161–80). The southern was more complicated, and was found to cover an earlier ditched barrow that held a cremation, together with scraps of metal and pottery of Romano-British character. The excavator considered that the outer barrow covering had been added in post-Roman times, but could provide no conclusive evidence. There were traces of Roman occupation on the land surface beneath both barrows.

The third mound on the opposite side of the road has also been damaged by road works. It was originally 1·5 m high, 18·3 m in diameter and with a ditch 4·6 m wide. It is believed to be unexcavated.

F. G. Walker: *P. Cambs. Ant. Soc.* **15** (1911) 166

5 WANDLEBURY HILLFORT   Iron Age
   Stapleford   148 (TL:493534)

6 km south of Cambridge on the north side of the A604, on the hill above the Gog Magog golf course.

Cambridgeshire is so lacking in conspicuous prehistoric monuments that Wandlebury must make up for all the rest. Lying in wooded ground administered by the Cambridge Preservation Society, it must once have been upstanding and impressive. Unfortunately landscaping for Lord Godolphin early in the 18th century required the removal of the ramparts and partial filling of the ditches. Even so the circular outer ditch, 304·8 m in diameter and in places 2·4 m deep, still survives.

Excavations in 1955–6 showed that the surviving ditch belongs to the earliest period of the fort, and together with a rampart 4·3 m wide, faced inside and out with timber, was constructed in about the 4th century B.C. The outer ditch, which was 4·6 m deep, had steep sides, and a flat bottom 2·4 m wide. After a lengthy period when the fort fell into disrepair and the ditch began to silt up, it was redefended. The ditch was widened to 10·7 m and given a steep outer side and sloping inner face. Material taken from it was piled into a counterscarp bank, whilst the rampart was reconstructed with further timbering. A new inner V-shaped ditch and rampart were also constructed at this time, which must have been early in the 1st century A.D.

The interior of Wandlebury was intensively occupied. Square and rectangular foundations may represent huts, and associated pits were probably for grain storage. Numerous small post holes and fragments of human skeletons found lying in the domestic rubbish of the fort suggest that bodies were exposed on wooden stands at death and left there until they disintegrated. This method of disposal of the dead seems likely to have been widely practised during the Iron Age, and accounts for a general lack of human burial material for the period.

The reoccupation of Wandlebury may be the work of the Iceni of Norfolk, setting up an outpost against Belgic expansion, or of a Chiltern tribe defending the Icknield Way and lands to the west from Icenian exploitation.

B. R. Hartley: *P. Cambs. Ant. Soc.* **50** (1957) 1

Museums containing archaeological material

University Museum of Archaeology and Ethnology, Downing Street, Cambridge

Wisbech and Fenland Museum, Museum Square, Wisbech

CORNWALL

1 ADVENT TRIPLE BARROW   Bronze Age
   Advent   186 (SX: 137834)

On left beside road, just beyond spinney. Passing place immediately beside barrow.

Triple bell-barrows are unusual in southern England and would seem to be more at home in Wiltshire. Here are three flat-topped mounds, each about 1·2 m high, enclosed within a single oval ditch whose greatest diameter is 61 m. Nothing is known of the contents of the barrow.

2 BODRIFTY VILLAGE   Late Bronze Age/Iron Age
                                                189 (SW: 445354)

From Newmill on the Penzance to Zennor road, turn west to 'Ding Dong', taking second turning on right and proceeding north-west to spot-height '603' on O.S. map. Site is on uncultivated heathland to east.

A low stone pound wall encloses an area of 1·2 ha. An entrance in its south-west corner leads to a village of about twelve houses each varying in size. Each house had inner and outer stone-facing walls filled with rubble, standing 1·2 m high, and timber frames inside to support a thatched roof. Most huts had a central hearth stone, and light penetrated from the doors that were usually on the south-west side facing the sun. They also had paved thresholds and some had drainage channels under the floor as at Chysauster, but unlike that site each hut at Bodrifty was separately built, without an adjoining courtyard. There were small fields, which can still be seen as low banks on the hillside above the village. From the end of the Bronze Age an open settlement existed with huts scattered amongst the fields. Later in the 2nd century B.C. people of Iron Age B culture rebuilt some of the huts and enclosed them with a wall. These are the remains visible today.

D. Dudley: *Arch. J.* **113** (1956) 1

3 BOLEIGH FOGOU   Iron Age
   Boleigh   189 (SW:437252)
North from the B3315 at SW:437250 to Rosemerrin House. Permission required to visit site in the garden.

Underground chambers or *fogous* as they are called in Cornwall are often found in, or close to, villages of courtyard houses, or sometimes on their own inside small, defensive earthworks. They can be fairly accurately dated to the end of the Middle Iron Age, and continue in use into the Roman period.

The Boleigh fogou has an entrance on the south leading into a stone-roofed passage 1·5 m wide and 12·2 m long. An L-shaped creep passage at the side has an airshaft hole in the roof. Fogous were probably used as cellars for food storage. It is unlikely that the older idea that they were hiding places for use in times of attack is true, since they were so easily found and would have proved veritable death-traps (but see Halligye fogou, page 41).

A. Fox: *South-west England* (1964) 151

4 BOSCAWEN-UN STONE CIRCLE   Bronze Age
   St. Buryan   189 (SW:412274)
Footpath south from the A30 near SW:411278 passing close to a clump of trees.

Here nineteen roughly rectangular blocks of stone are evenly spaced to form a circle 22·9 m in diameter. At the centre is a single leaning pillar stone, and there are four other stones on the circumference at the north-east. There are two barrows and two standing stones (SW:416276) close by, which together with the circle must relate to some ancient religious practices once observed at these sites.

5   BRANE, OR CHAPEL EUNY BARROW (Plate 10)   Bronze Age
      Brane   189 (SW:402282)

Approached by extremely narrow side road off A30 through Lower Drift to Brane hamlet. Follow signs to 'Carn Euny Ancient Monument' as far as Brane Farm where permission and directions may be obtained. (National Trust.)

The finest Cornish example of the small group of entrance graves confined to the Isles of Scilly and west Penwith, consisting of short stone-walled burial passages open at one end and covered by mounds of earth and stones. These are almost certainly the last vestiges of the great passage grave burial chambers found in western and northern Britain. At Brane the passage is 2·3 m long and 1·2 m wide, and is roofed with two large capstones. A kerb of large stones surrounds the barrow which is 2·1 m high and 6·1 m in diameter.

G. E. Daniel: *Prehistoric Chamber Tombs of England and Wales* (1950) 239

Plate 10   Brane or Chapel Euny Entrance Grave, Cornwall

6 CADSON BURY HILLFORT   Iron Age
   St. Ive   186 (SX:343674)

Approached by footpath from road running south of Newbridge to Crift.
(National Trust.)

A single rampart and ditch surround this steep isolated hill, on the
extreme eastern edge of Bodmin Moor. Below it, on the east, flows the
river Lynher. The hillfort is unexcavated and its original entrance is
uncertain.

7 CARLAND CROSS-ROADS BARROWS   Bronze Age
   Mitchell   185 (SW:845539)

Lay-by beside the A30 just west of Carland cross-roads with the A3076.

A fine bell-barrow lies immediately north of the A30. It is about
24·4 m in diameter and has an upstanding berm 3·1 m wide. The
mound, which has a deep robbers' pit in it, stands 1·8 m high. South
of the A30, but west of the Truro road are three other round barrows,
one of them ploughed. In all, there were some thirty barrows spread
across the fields to the south-west from the cross-roads, but the majority
have been destroyed by ploughing in recent years.

8 CARN BREA   Neolithic and Iron Age
   Redruth   189 (SW:685407)

Rough road to the summit from Carnkie at SW:686400.

The hillfort is situated at the eastern end of the hill between the
monument (surely the ugliest in Britain?) and the castle. A double
line of rampart enclosing 14·6 ha loops round from the monument
south-east towards the castle. The outer defence runs under the
cottage beside the road. The inner is lined with great slabs of stone,
and there was a simple entrance, perhaps with guard chambers, near
the monument. On the northern side of the hill the castle and monument are linked by a single masonry bank and external ditch with a
break about midway along it. There are hut circles within the fort
considered to be of Iron Age date, although recent excavations have
been almost devoid of material of that period. Large quantities of
neolithic (Hembury type) pottery, flints, pits and hearths have been
found on the south slope of the hill below the castle. It is probable that
these earliest inhabitants exploited the Cornish greenstone for axe
manufacture. The later occupants left behind a small hoard of Bronze
Age socketed axes of Breton type, as well as a hoard of Celtic coins
found in 1749.

R. Mercer: *Cornish Archaeology* **9** (1970) 53

Plate 11   Carn Euny fogou, Cornwall

9 CARN EUNY VILLAGE   Iron Age
   Sancreed   189 (SW:403288)

*Approached on extremely narrow side road through Lower Drift to Brane.
Car-park and 5-minute walk to site. Department of the Environment
signposts.*

The first timber-built huts dated from 200 to 150 B.C. and were circular, with beaten clay floors and stone covered drainage channels.
Pottery was on the whole plain, but included some decorated Glastonbury wares.

During the 1st century B.C. stone houses replaced wooden ones, and
a new type of pottery, 'cordoned ware', was introduced. Such pottery
probably originated in Brittany and is found on a number of Cornish
sites. The inhabitants were farmers and stockbreeders, but also involved in the tin industry. An unusual discovery in 1965 was a grain
storage pit: a common feature in south-eastern Britain, but almost
unknown in the south-west.

The most spectacular feature of Carn Euny is the fogou (Plate 11),
an underground passage about 20 m long with a low 'creep' passage at
the west end, and a circular corbelled chamber which seems to be
unique. It also had its own drains and paved floor. The purpose of these
strange monuments found exclusively in south-west Cornwall is the
subject of much speculation (see Boleigh, page 31) but the usual
explanations offered are that they were either cold 'larders', or hiding
places.

P. M. Christie: *Carn Euny* (1968) D. of E. pamphlet.

10 CARN GLUZE (BALLOWAL) BARROW   Bronze Age
    St. Just   189 (SW:355312)

*By lane south-west from St. Just at SW:364314 for 0·8 km. Barrow is
signposted beyond mine chimney. Department of the Environment.*

One of the most fascinating and complex Cornish sites was excavated
by W. C. Lukis and William Borlase in 1874. In the centre of the
barrow a T-shaped pit was dug 2·1 m deep into the bedrock. It contained no burials and was probably used for some ceremonial purpose.
Four small stone cists stood on the floor around the top of the pit and
contained small pots of Middle Bronze Age type, probably holding
food offerings. These cists can no longer be seen. Over the pit and
cists a great dome was built, oval in plan, and still surviving to a height
of 3·7 m. It consisted of an inner and outer corbelled stone shell filled
with tumbled stones to create a wall 1·5 m thick. It had no entrance,
and once built completely sealed off the ritual features inside, including
a further burial cist, containing pottery and lamb bones, built into the
wall at a height of 1·5 m. Outside the domed wall Borlase found two
more burial cists, one of which is still visible, slightly below ground
level. Eventually a massive oval stone wall, 20·4 m by 22·6 m in plan,
6·1 m wide and 1·5 m high, was built round the whole structure. In the
south-west side of this is a low, rectangular burial chamber, or
entrance grave, of neolithic type, which contained many cremated
human bones and Bronze Age pottery. It is surely significant that this
was the only part of the complete tomb which came into contact with
the outside world. Perhaps it was here that the local people deposited
their gifts and sacrifices to whatever spirits lurked within. Although the
pottery from the site suggests a Bronze Age date, the traditions seem
to be neolithic in outlook. Is it possible that here at the land's end,
there existed a religious shrine whose sanctity lasted for perhaps 1,000
years?

A. Fox: *South-west England* (1964) 52

11 CASTILLY HENGE MONUMENT   Neolithic
    Luxulyan   185 (SX:032627)

Beside minor road between the A30 and A391. Can be seen from the A30.

This small oval henge monument, measuring 48·8 m on its long axis
by 30·5 m east to west, is situated in a classic position on a northward
facing slope, with streams to east and west at the foot of the hill. Its
bank, still 1·8 m high, and internal ditch 5·5 m wide and 2·1 m deep,
are both covered with scrub and bushes, making examination difficult.
The entrance at the lower northern end is original, whilst that at the
south-west is modern. The interior is arable. Excavation has shown
that Castilly was later remodelled for use as a medieval theatre and for
defence during the Civil War. It lies close to the junction of two pre-

historic trackways; and five round barrows close by, as well as others showing on aerial photographs, indicate that prehistoric travellers may well have looked upon it as a suitable spot for worship on their journeys.

C. Thomas: *Cornish Archaeology* **3** (1964) 3

12   CASTLE-AN-DINAS   Iron Age
     St. Columb Major   185 (SX:946623)
Approached by bridle road signposted to 'Castle Down' west of Providence (SX:946617). Cars parked at bungalow (10p).

Three massive stone ramparts ring this hill enclosing 2·4 ha. The inner and outer ramparts have deep ditches outside them, the middle one was added later in an attempt to strengthen the inner enclosure, but was never completed. The unfinished work is particularly evident on the north where the ditch is not continuous. Traces of a fourth outer rampart can also be seen particularly in the south. There are a number of breaks in the defences, but only that on the south-west seems to have been an original entrance. Hut circles can be traced in the interior and a pond on the north side is fed from a local water supply. The nearby wolfram mine may be responsible for some of the disturbance inside the fort. During the summer months the earthworks are obscured by bracken. The Cornish word *dinas* means a stone-walled fort.

B. Wailes: *Cornish Archaeology* **2** (1963) 51

13   CASTLE DORE HILLFORT   Iron Age and Dark Age
     St. Sampson   186 (SW:103548)
Gate in hedge just east of B3269 between Lostwithiel and Fowey.

This well-preserved little fort consists of a circular inner rampart 97·5 m in diameter with an entrance gap on the east. A V-shaped ditch 2·4 m deep separates it from the ploughed outer rampart and 3·7 m deep ditch, which are egg-shaped in plan. They circle the inner rampart, but at the eastern end bulge out to form an enclosure in front of the inner entrance, and are themselves broken by an entrance at that point. Excavation has shown that the ramparts were made about 200 B.C. of stone and earth piled between turf retaining walls, and then completely covered with turf and soil. Later, about 50 B.C., the inner rampart was given a vertical stone outer face and raised in height. The inner entrance, which when first built was simply a gap in the rampart, was also remodelled at this time. An inturned wooden entrance tunnel was built, 9·1 m long, with a bridge for a rampart walk over the top. Traces of circular huts were found inside the fort, with conical thatched roofs supported between low stone walls and central poles. Excavation in the outer enclosure showed that a ditch-lined road had linked the inner and outer gates; the enclosed areas on either side presumably having been used for cattle pounding and farm buildings. A larger enclosure, marked by a slight bank, lies outside the entrances. It was probably a cattle paddock. The wealth of the community living in Castle Dore, which included imported glass beads and bracelets, was probably derived partly from agriculture, but largely by exploiting nearby tin and iron ores.

Abandoned early in the last quarter of the 1st century A.D., the fort seems to have been reoccupied in the 5th century for a number of generations. During that time two rectangular timber halls and a square kitchen building were set up. They may have been the home of King Mark of Cornwall who figures in the Tristan and Isolde legend. At the cross-roads 3·2 km south of Castle Dore is a 2·1 m high standing stone inscribed

'DRUSTANUS HIC IACIT
CUNOMORI FILIUS'

(Tristram lies here, the son of Cynvawr). It is the grave stone of a chieftain of the mid 6th century, and was moved to its present site from further north.

C. A. R. Radford: *J. R. Inst. Cornwall* (new series) **1** (1951) 1

14 CASTLEWITCH HENGE MONUMENT   Neolithic
   Callington   186 (SX:371685)

Turn off A388 to Castlewitch hamlet, and take left turn from there to Westcott. Site lies to left on hillslope.

This small henge monument is situated at the head of a valley in which rises one of the feed streams of the river Lynher. First recognized as such by Sir Cyril and Lady Fox in 1951, it is oval in shape with a single surrounding bank and internal ditch, and an entrance gap on the south. It has been somewhat damaged by ploughing. 0·4 km north on the crest of Balstone Down near the A388 is a small outcrop of Cornish greenstone rock, which provided the raw material for a number of stone axes identified as from Cornwall.

A. Fox: *Ant. J.* **32** (1952) 67

15 CHUN CASTLE   Iron Age
   Morvah   189 (SW:405339)

Signposted south-west from Bosullow Common. Parking at Trehyllys Farm. Short walk up hill.

Two strong walls surround this small hilltop fort. They are faced with blocks of granite quarried from external ditches. Originally these walls stood at least 3·7 m high and 6·1 thick; today they reach 2·7 m high in places. The outer wall is 85·3 m feet in diameter, and is broken by an entrance on the south-west. This is not immediately opposite the inner entrance gap, but is staggered some 15·2 m away from it, thus forcing those entering the fort to turn their flank towards the defenders on the inner wall. The massive gate-posts have been preserved. Beside the inner wall are a few circular Iron Age huts, but most of these are overlaid by 6th-century A.D. rectangular huts dating to a re-use of the fort during the Dark Ages. Hearths in some of the huts have been used for iron and tin smelting. There is a well on the north-west side of the interior. Like many of the other Iron Age settlements in this area, Chun must have been connected with the Cornish tin trade.

E. T. Leeds: *Archaeologia* **76** (1926) 205

16 CHUN QUOIT   Neolithic
       Morvah   189 (SW:402339)
Directions as for Chun Castle. It lies a short distance west of that site.

Four great slabs of stone form the sides of this well-preserved burial chamber which measures 1·8 m long and 1·7 m wide, with an enormous sloping rectangular capstone 2·4 m square. It stands at the centre of a low mound about 10·7 m in diameter. Scattered stones on its south side suggest that there may once have been an entrance passage.

17 CHYSAUSTER VILLAGE (Fig. 7; Plate 12)
                                              Iron Age and Romano-British
       Madron   189 (SW:472350)
Signposted from B3311 at Badgers Cross (SW:486332). Car-park beside road. Rough climb with stiles. Department of the Environment. Admission 5p. Open standard hours.

The village of Chysauster lies on the slopes below the ruined ring-fort of Castle-an-Dinas (Twednack, not St. Columb Major). Here a localized architectural development, the courtyard house, can best be seen. In south-west Cornwall at least two dozen villages were built, late in the Iron Age, with their houses and outbuildings constructed as a single unit around a central courtyard. Of these courtyard villages Chysauster, because it is maintained by the Department of the Environment, is the best example to see, although to some extent it suffers from being over mown and cared for, and in places rebuilt.

Nine houses line a narrow street 3·7 m wide, each with its attendant garden plot. Two or three other houses lie away from the street, No. 9 for example at the end of an alleyway between Nos. 3 and 5. Another on the south side of the village has a small ruined example of a fogou (underground chamber) attached to it. Five of the houses have been excavated completely. Each is roughly oval in shape and about

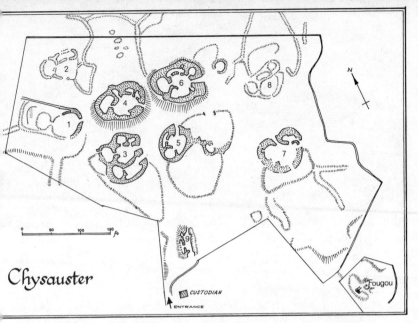

Fig. 7   Chysauster, Cornwall

27·4 m long. The thick walls still stand 2·7 or 3 m high in some cases. An entrance passage (6·7 m long in No. 6) leads into the courtyard which was open to the sky. At the far side is a small circular hut chamber, which had its own thatched roof supported on wooden posts, and paved floor. Some of these huts had open hearths and granite basins for grinding meal near their centres. On one side of the courtyard are long, narrow workrooms and sometimes additional living rooms with corbelled stone roofs, whilst opposite stabling space (perhaps roofed over) was available for animals. Amongst interesting features worth noting are covered drains with sumps (huts 4, 5, 6 and 7), a semi-detached house (No. 3), and the rather damaged hut 9 with its axis north-east to south-west.

Each house has its own terraced garden plot with a low stone wall round it, and beyond, up the hill-slope were small terraced fields. A track leads downhill from the settlement to a stream beside which tin working was carried out. Chysauster is only 6 km from St. Michael's Mount, from where the ore was shipped to France and beyond. Both track and workings may be as old as the village itself. The site was occupied from about 100 B.C. until well into the 3rd century A.D., although there is little evidence that the Romans had much influence on affairs there.

H. O. Hencken: *Archaeologia* **83** (1933) 237

Plate 12   Chysauster Iron Age village, Cornwall

18 DULOE STONE CIRCLE   Bronze Age
        Duloe   186 (SX: 235583)
In the centre of the village, east of the B3254.

A small stone circle only 11·3 m in diameter, but spectacular on
account of its eight large stones, one 2·7 m high. Unlike the other
circles and megaliths of the county the Duloe stones are composed of
quartz.

19 FERNACRE STONE CIRCLE   Bronze Age
        St. Breward   186 (SX: 144799)
0·8 km due south of Rough Tor. (See No. 39 for directions.)

On the south-western slope of the hill is a circle of granite stones of all
shapes and sizes, closely set together. 45·7 m in diameter, the circle
may have retained an earthwork forming some kind of ceremonial
enclosure. Of seventy visible stones, thirty-nine are still standing in the
circle and two others lie near the centre.

H. St. George Gray: *Archaeologia* **61** (1906) 33

20 FOUR BARROWS   Bronze Age
        Kenwyn   190 (SW: 762482)
*Beside the A30 between Carland and Redruth, 0·8 km north-west of
junction with A3075. Park in lay-by beside them.*

Lying across the Cornish Ridgeway along which the A30 now runs,
these four barrows are amongst the most prominent in Cornwall. The
example north of the road is 3·1 m high and has a deep looters' pit in its
top. The other three are of similar height. One was opened during
William III's reign. Known as Burrow Belles, it contained a large
stone burial cist.

21 GIANT'S QUOIT BURIAL CHAMBER   Neolithic
   Caerwynnen   189 (SW:650373)

3 km south of Camborne on north side of minor road from Troon to Praze,
a short distance up the hill from Caerwynnen. Through iron gate into
Pendarves Park, left by building, and can be seen across low hedge bank.

This monument has various names including the Giant's Frying Pan,
and consisted of a 10-ton capstone on three uprights. It collapsed in
1834 when it was restored, only to fall again in 1967. It now lies
dormant, but is worth a visit, if only for its great size. There are traces
of an oval mound which must once have covered it.

22 GIANT'S QUOIT   Neolithic
   Pawton   185 (SW:966696)

South of A39 at Whitecross for 1·6 km, taking very narrow road to
Haycrock Farm buildings. 55 m beyond minor power line crossing lane,
burial chamber visible over wall hedge to west. Accessible when crop off
field.

On the northern edge of St. Breoc Down, this burial chamber has one
enormous capstone originally measuring 4·0 m by 2·1 m and 0·8 m
thick, and supported by three of seven uprights in a rectangular setting.
Two further stones would have supported part of the capstone that has
broken off, forming a façade. The whole tomb has been somewhat
damaged of late and the oval mound 21·3 m by 15·2 m has been
reduced by ploughing. The narrow road up to the barrow is somewhat
off-putting, but the effort is worthwhile.

23 HALLIGYE FOGOU   Iron Age
   Mawgan-in-Meneage   190 (SW:712238)

Minor road north and east from Garras on B3293, footpath uphill from
edge of wood. Torch required.

This fogou was built below the defences of a small fortified homestead.
Today only the fogou remains. It consists of a wide subterranean
passage 16·5 m long, walled and roofed with slabs of stone. At its
eastern end is a massive north-south passage crossing the first like the
cross of a T. The northern end of this originally opened out into the
homestead ditch, but it is now blocked. At the western end of the main
passage, near the entrance, is a shorter passageway leading south.
Close to this point a block of rock 0·6 m high lies across the floor of the
passage. It has been explained as a deliberate stumbling block, introduced to warn anyone hiding in the fogou of the approach of strangers.
In this case the structure may have been built for defence rather than
storage. It probably dates from about 100 B.C. to the 3rd century A.D.

24 HARLYN BAY CEMETERY   Iron Age
  Harlyn Bay   185 (SX:877753)

*In a private garden, south of the road through Harlyn, and west of the
bridge. Usual hours of opening 10.45 to 12.30, 14.30 to 18.00. Closed
Fridays and Saturdays. Admission 5p.*

An Iron Age cemetery and adjoining midden were found when the
house was built about 1900. It is believed that some 130 graves lay on
an old shore line which was subsequently covered by 4·6 m of drifting
sand. Five of these graves can now be seen, covered with glass roofs in
the garden of the house, beside a museum where other objects found
during the highly unscientific uncovering of the cemetery are displayed. The graves consisted of rectangular holes in the ground, lined
with upright slate slabs. In them the dead were buried in contracted
positions, accompanied by jewellery dating from the 4th to 3rd centuries B.C. Slate slabs were also placed over the bodies. The graves are
claimed to have been orientated north-south, but this is not confirmed
by contemporary accounts. Iron Age burials of this date are almost
unknown in Britain, thus making the site particularly important.

O. G. S. Crawford: *Ant. J.* 1 (1921) 283

25 HELSBURY CASTLE HILLFORT   Iron Age
  Michaelstow   186 (SX:083796)

*Due west of B3266 on minor road to Treveighan. Enter by farm gate on
east side.*

Although very worn by ploughing this is a fine circular hillfort with a
single rampart and ditch crowning the top of a high outlying hill, with
a mutilated annexe or enclosure on the east. Both fort and enclosure
entrances face eastwards, towards a sunken approach road which may
be contemporary, but could equally well relate to later features. A
square enclosure on the summit of the hill contains the foundations of
a chapel dedicated to St. Syth. Numerous architectural fragments are
scattered over that part of the site. Two axe moulds were found in
Helsbury quarry in 1934.

A. Fox in Frere: *Problems of the Iron Age in Southern Britain* (1959) 41

26 THE HURLERS STONE CIRCLES   Bronze Age
  Minions   186 (SX:258714)

*On south-west side of the village of Minions. Approached along track from
car-park.*

On the mine-scarred eastern flank of Bodmin Moor lie the three stone
circles known locally as the Hurlers. According to William Camden
(1551–1623) the local inhabitants considered 'that they had been men
sometime transformed into stones, for profaning the Lord's Day with

hurling the ball'. The circles lie in a line from north-east to south-west and are almost contiguous. The smallest circle on the south side is 32 m in diameter and still has nine visible stones. The central circle is the largest, 41·1 m in diameter with seventeen stones standing, and a further stone in the centre. The northern ring measures 33·5 m across and still contains thirteen stones. Excavations have shown that the area inside the northern circle has a granite paving. All the stones seem to have originally been shaped, and it was apparently important to see that their tops were all at the same level. This was achieved by setting them in pits of different depths and holding them in place with small granite blocks. A path of granite slabs ran between the central and northern circles. (The Rillaton barrow is close by.)

C. R. Radford: *P.P.S.* 4 (1938) 319

27 LANIVET QUOIT   Neolithic
     Lanhydrock   186 (SX:072628)

Beside narrow local road bounded by high walls, visible through arable field gate, west of minor power-cable line.

This chamber tomb has a great granite capstone 3·1 m wide and 4·9 m long, which has fallen off its uprights, two of which lie nearby. There are traces of a surrounding, much ploughed, mound.

28 LANYON QUOIT   Neolithic
     Madron   189 (SW:430337)

Situated immediately north of the Madron to Morvah road, behind a high wall.

Traces of an overgrown long cairn can be seen lying north–south, and measuring 27·4 m by 12·2 m. At the south end are fallen stones which probably belong to a burial cist. At the north-east stands Lanyon Quoit, consisting of a great capstone 5·8 m long, supported by three upright stones, with a fourth lying under the northern end. The chamber collapsed in 1815 and a number of stones were damaged. It was re-erected in 1824 on a smaller scale and it is said that originally a man on horseback could ride under it. Lanyon is often pronounced 'Lan-ine'—'ine' as in wine.

29 MEN-AN-TOL   Neolithic
     Madron   189 (SW:427349)

Signposted along path leading north-east from road across Bosullow Common, opposite junction with road to Chun Castle. Lies in field on right, after passing farm buildings on left. Walk of 1 km.

Men-an-tol means simply 'stone of the hole'. It consists of a thin slab of stone with a perfectly circular hole in the centre, set upright between two pillar stones. These latter are known to have been moved in historic times. All the stones must have originally formed part of a burial chamber now destroyed. Folklore, connected with the site, included the passing of children through the hole as a cure for rickets and adults as a cure for ague. It was also considered to have prophetic qualities.

30 MERRY MAIDENS STONE CIRCLE (Plate 13)   Bronze Age
     St. Buryan   189 (SW:433245)

There is a small lay-by 0·8 km east of the turning to St. Buryan in an angle of the B3315.

This is probably the only complete stone circle in Cornwall. Nineteen evenly spaced rectangular blocks of stone, each about 1·2 m high, surround an area 24·4 m in diameter. Only on the north-east is there a gap in the ring, forming what is probably an entrance. It is sometimes known as the Dawns Men (pronounced Dorns Main, and Cornish for 'stone dance'.) Two standing stones called *The Pipers* are nearly 0·4 km north-east, and lie on a line drawn from the centre of the Merry Maidens. They stand 4·6 m and 4·1 m high, and can be seen from the B3315 (though not from the circle). The Pipers were turned to stone when they played music for the Merry Maidens to dance on the sabbath! To the west beside the B3315 is the recently excavated

Plate 13   The Merry Maidens stone circle, Cornwall

megalithic tomb called *Tregiffian* (SW:430244). It has cup-marked stones, and produced an urn and cremated bones.

31 MULFRA QUOIT   Neolithic
    Madron   189 (SW:452353)

A footpath leads off the Penzance to Porthmeor road at SW:454356.
A walk of 0·4 km uphill.

Three wall stones of this small rectangular burial chamber still stand upright. Against them leans the fallen capstone, almost 3 m across. The tomb seems to have stood in a round barrow, 12 m in diameter, of which traces remain.

G. E. Daniel: *Prehistoric Chamber Tombs of England and Wales* (1950) 238

32 NEWQUAY 'BARROWFIELDS'   Bronze Age
                                                     185 (SW:820623)

Of a group of seventeen or eighteen barrows only three now remain, the rest were destroyed in 1821. These are in a very forlorn state and are mixed up with a miniature golf course on the sea front. They stand about 1 m high.

33 NINE MAIDENS   Bronze Age
    St. Columb Major   185 (SX:937676)

A footpath by a field gate beside the A39 at SX:934676 leads straight to
the stones by a hedgerow.

A great many prehistoric maidens must have been turned to stone in Cornwall. This group forms the only stone row known in the county. It consists of nine stones spaced out along a line 106·7 m in length from north-east to south-west. Six of the stones stand apparently complete, the rest are broken, but can still be traced. 0·8 km north on the same alignment is a single stone, the *Magi Stone*, with a round barrow slightly to the south of it.

34 PELYNT ROUND BARROWS   Bronze Age
                                                     186 (SW:200544)

Take minor road west at Pelynt church, and turn right after 0·8 km

This much ploughed group of round barrows in Five Burroughs field was dug into on a number of occasions between 1830 and 1850. Some ten barrows can still be seen, none more than 1·2 m high. The group is important because of a short sword or dagger of Mycenaean type dated to the 14th or 13th century B.C. found in one of the graves and possibly indicating far-reaching trade connections. Most of the barrows covered cremation burials, the corpses appearing to have been burnt

on the spot. Some of the ashes were placed in urns of Cornish Bronze
Age type, and were sometimes covered with piles of stones beneath the
barrow mound. One grave contained an ogival dagger with large
rivets, lying under a stone 'in one of the smaller barrows' together
with a battle-axe of local greenstone.

J. Couch: *Report Royal Inst. Cornwall* **27** (1845) 34

35 PORTHMEOR COURTYARD VILLAGE   Romano-British
      Zennor   189 (SW:434371)
Path from B3306. Permission to visit from Porthmeor Farm.

Seven round huts and two courtyard houses are enclosed by a pound
wall. Further down the hillside is a second enclosure containing a
courtyard house and a remarkable fogou, with a passage 5·8 m long
and 1·5 m wide above ground level. It leads into a curved corridor
7·3 m long. Both passages have lost their roofs. The settlement at
Porthmeor dates from the 1st to 5th centuries A.D.

36 REDCLIFFE CLIFF-CASTLE   Iron Age
      St. Eval   185 (SW:848696)
At Bedruthan Steps, approached off B3276, 0·8 km north of Trenance.
Cliff-top footpath leads from northern car-park.

This small cliff-castle can be clearly viewed from Bedruthan Steps
to the south. Three lines of rampart are separated by two well-
marked ditches, the latter cut deeply into the rock. At one point it is
nearly 4·6 m deep. A single entrance way cuts through the centre of all
the fortifications. The enclosed area has been sadly reduced by erosion.

37 RILLATON BARROW   Bronze Age
      Linkinhorne   186 (SX:260719)
From the Hurlers west of Minions, follow an approximate alignment due
north for 0·8 km. The barrow is on the highest point of the hill with the
Cheeswring quarry to the left.

This large cairn of stones and turf, 36·6 m in diameter and 2·4 m
high, has a deep hole in its centre, clearly indicating that a primary
burial has been disturbed. On the eastern side of the barrow is a stone
cist, 2·3 m long, 1·2 m wide and 0·9 m high, which when opened in
1818 contained an extended skeleton of a man. It is almost certainly
secondary to the cairn, and was added to the mound at a later date.
With the burial was a gold cup, 8·3 cm high, decorated with horizontal
corrugated ridges, and held by a fine ribbon-like handle. The gold
cup seems to be a copy in metal of a handled beaker. The grave also
contained a Wessex-type ogival dagger, faience beads and pottery.

Shortly after the gold cup was discovered, its whereabouts was forgotten and the cup assumed lost. Persistent detective work by Christopher Hawkes in 1936 eventually revealed that the cup, which was treasure trove, had been sent to Queen Victoria at Osborne, and from there it had found its way via Marlborough House to King George V's dressing room in Buckingham Palace. Together with the bronze dagger it is now in the British Museum.

G. Smirke: *Arch. J.* **24** (1867) 189

38 ROCKY VALLEY CARVINGS   Bronze Age ?
   Tintagel   185 (SX:073893)

Car-park beside B3263 at SX:072891, opposite footpath signposted 'Trevillett Mill Rocky Valley'. The carvings are beside ruined mill buildings 0·4 km from gate on road.

On the cliff-like wall of the valley are two small labyrinth-type carvings, each about 22·9 cm across and pecked into the hard rock. Although such designs are often attributable to the Bronze Age, they are also common in many other periods. The position of these carvings beside an isolated mill building is frankly suspicious and may well have been the doodles of an idle miller.

39 ROUGH TOR SETTLEMENT AND HILLFORT
                                                   Bronze and Iron Age
   St. Breward   186 (SX:141815)

Minor road signposted 'Rough Tor' east from Camelford at SX:110839 to car-park after 3 km. It is worth studying the layout of the sites with field-glasses before leaving the car-park which affords a good viewpoint. Part National Trust.

A number of roughly oval enclosures with hut circles around their perimeters lie at the south-west end of Rough Tor, midway between the stream and the hilltop. The enclosures, which were probably paddocks, are often linked to one another by stone 'walls' with lynchets and tracks amongst them. Stones have been cleared from fields in prehistoric times and piled in lines along their boundaries. Examples of these occur just beyond the National Trust signboard near the stream, and run diagonally uphill towards the south end of Rough Tor.

   Between the two rock outcrops (and utilizing them) on the summit of the Tor, a small hillfort was constructed. On the west two lines of stone walls can be traced, but on the more precipitous eastern side little remains of an artificial defence. Hut circles exist inside the fort making it difficult to date, though it probably belongs to the Bronze–Iron Age transition somewhere between 1000 and 700 B.C.

Plate 14   The Rumps cliff castle, Cornwall

40 THE RUMPS (Plate 14)   Iron Age
  Pentire Head, St. Minver   185 (SW:934810)

*From Pentireglaze to Pentire Farm (parking) and then walk of 0·8 km
to Rumps Point (signposted). National Trust property.*

This is one of the most beautifully situated of Cornwall's forty cliff-
castles. Three lines of rampart and ditch isolate two rocky headlands
with a more sheltered hollow between them. The outer defence is not
as strongly marked as are the other two, and has a modern wall upon it.
Its associated ditch is shallow. The middle defence is the strongest,
and is built of weathered slate faced with a continuous kerb of boulders.
Its ditch is 4·6 m deep. The inner ditch is more shallow and provided
quarry material for the inner rampart, which is partly built on a
natural ridge of slate. The modern entrances follow the positions of
the prehistoric gates, which were placed across stoutly defended
passageways lined with timbers and dry-stone walling. At least three
successive prehistoric roadways ran into the fort, where a number of
hut foundations were found in the lee of Rumps Point. Pottery and
animal bones were also found behind the ramparts suggesting some
length of occupation in those areas. Cordoned pots common in Cornwall late in the 1st century B.C. and 1st century A.D. were found on the
site; these are similar to examples found in north-west France at that
time. Together with wine amphorae from the Mediterranean, they
suggest that the builders of The Rumps had strong continental
connections.

R. T. Brooks: *Cornish Archaeology* **3** (1964) 26; **5** (1966) 4

41 STANNON STONE CIRCLE   Bronze Age
  St. Breward   186 (SX:126800)
*On south side of minor road 4·8 km north-east from St. Breward to
Stannon Farm.*

A circle of stones 42·7 m in diameter, of which forty-one out of at
least eighty are now standing. A single stone lies near the centre of the
circle. As at Fernacre, the stones are very close together and may have
formed some kind of enclosure rather than a true stone circle of the
more usual Cornish type.

H. St. George Gray: *Archaeologia* **61** (1906) 36

42 STRIPPLE STONES HENGE MONUMENT   Neolithic?
  Blisland   186 (SX:144752)
*Minor road from the A30 at SX:136737 and walk up path from SX:
129748 passing the Trippet Stones and buildings on the left.*

On the slope of Hawks Tor is an embanked enclosure with internal
ditch 68·3 m in diameter. Inside it is an irregular circle of fifteen

(formerly twenty-eight) granite blocks, only four of which are still standing. Almost in the centre of the stone circle, which is 44·5 m in diameter, is a single recumbent stone, and three others lie outside the circle but within the earthwork. Excavation by H. St. George Gray in 1905 showed that the surrounding ditch was very irregular, but averaged 2·7 m wide and 1·2 m deep. It was broken by an entrance facing south-west towards the Trippet Stones. The Stones themselves were in shallow holes, none more than 0·8 m deep. The site is clearly a henge monument by the position of its internal ditch. The presence of the stones suggests a continuity between the neolithic henge and Bronze Age stone circle. Modern excavation might reveal that the earthwork is older than the stone setting.

H. St. George Gray: *Archaeologia* **61** (1906) 1

43 TAPHOUSE BARROWS   Bronze Age
    Broadoak   186 (SX: 143633)

Minor road off A39 towards Lanhydrock. (Extremely sharp junction if approached from west.) Gate at SX:140632.

A row of four fine round barrows run along the hill scarp from east to west. There are two others east of the barn on the hilltop. Yet two more originally completed the cemetery, but they have been destroyed. Most of them show the scars of trenches across them, or the hollows of central shafts, but no record of their contents survives. Locally they are claimed to be the graves of soldiers killed in the Civil War.

44 TREEN DINAS   Iron Age
    St. Levan   189 (SW: 397222)

Approached by footpath from Treen signposted 'To Treen cliff and Logan Rock'.

Treen Dinas (Treryn Dinas on the map) is another of the spectacularly sited Cornish cliff-castles, possibly constructed by immigrants to south-western England from north-west France from the 1st century B.C. onwards. The occupation at Treen seems, however, to belong to a number of periods, even going back to the 3rd century B.C., but without excavation this cannot be confirmed. Approaching the headland from the north one first meets a massive curved rampart fronted by a ditch. After a gap, three further lines of ditch and rampart cut across the headland, the middle one being the strongest (compare the Rumps and Trevelgue, pages 49 and 53). At the tip of the headland a fifth great ditch and stone-faced bank cut across the peninsula. This line is broken by a central entrance. Just inside the gate are two hut hollows. The Logan Stone, a natural rocking stone, is perched on one of these crags above the fort.

45 TREGEARE ROUNDS   Iron Age
    St. Kew   185 (SX:033800)

*Between Port Isaac and St. Teath. Reached from B3314 by gate south
of road at SX:032800, before hill starts to descend.*

The massive 3·1 m high rampart of this fort, contained by a modern
stone wall, is completely covered with trees and bushes making inspection difficult. The entrance, on the south-east side, leads into a large
enclosure with a smaller circular bank and ditch inside it, measuring
some 152·5 m in diameter. The rampart-ends beside the gateway are
raised up, presumably to provide better visibility.

    This is one of a series of multiple-enclosure forts, sited on the sides
of hills, and common in Cornwall, Devon and South Wales. Their
purpose seems to have been mainly concerned with cattle herding.
To this end, an additional enclosure or barbican has been added to the
south-east side of Tregeare Rounds, with a sunken road leading towards
a small stream in the valley bottom. The northern end of this enclosure
has been destroyed, probably by ploughing. Traces of occupation,
including Iron Age B pottery, have been found between the concentric
ramparts, further suggesting that the central area of the fort was used
for cattle herding during the 2nd and 1st centuries B.C.

Aileen Fox: *Arch. J.* **109** (1952) 9

46 TRENCROM HILLFORT   Iron Age
    Ludgvan   189 (SW:517363)

*Minor roads circle this hill which is National Trust property, and can be
reached by footpaths from north or south.*

This small fort which is oval in shape, crowns a granite massif.
A single dry-stone wall, faced inside and out with great stone slabs,
incorporates natural outcrops to create spectacular walls of almost
cyclopean dimensions! There are entrances to the fort on the east and
west, and it has no surrounding ditch. Inside are more than a dozen
overgrown hut circles. Surface pottery found at the site dates it to the
2nd century B.C.

47 TRETHEVY QUOIT (Plate 15)   Neolithic
    St. Cleer   186 (SX:259688)

*At the angle of a narrow lane between Tremar and Darite, behind a row
of cottages.*

This is a truly spectacular burial chamber, huge to behold from the
front. It stands 4·6 m high on its southern side. Seven stones form a
rectangular burial chamber 2·1 m by 1·5 m, whilst an enormous eighth
stone provides a great sloping capstone 3·7 m long. The rectangular

Plate 15   Trethevy   Quoit, Cornwall

chamber is divided into two parts. The inner area is almost completely
sealed off, except for a small opening in the corner of the doorstone at
the eastern end. This is just big enough for a body (alive or dead)
to pass through. Originally it may have had some kind of blocking
stone to cover it. It can be compared with entrances to other megalithic
tombs, which were sometimes circular, like portholes (compare
Men-an-Tol, No. 29, which probably served such a function). There
is an antechamber in front of the entrance stone, created by two side
stones jutting forward to the east. Although there is little trace of a
surrounding mound today, W. C. Lukis, in the last century recorded
that it was oval in shape and measured 7 m by 6 m.

G. E. Daniel: *Prehistoric Chamber Tombs of England and Wales* (1950)
239

48 TREVELGUE HEAD CLIFF-CASTLE   Iron Age
   Newquay   185 (SX:827630)
*By footpath beside putting-green, west of the B3276, just north of St.
Columb Porth.*

One of the most easily accessible of the Iron Age cliff-castles, Trevelgue
is a splendid example defended by six lines of ramparts and ditches
and a sea gorge. From the putting-green one immediately reaches the
first outer rampart and ditch. A wide enclosure follows taking in the
full height and width of the promontory, before three closely set
ramparts and ditches cut across the headland. As is often the case in
these cliff-castles, the middle rampart of the three is the strongest,
being 2·4 m high, with a 3·7 m deep ditch outside. There were probably
entrances at the southern end of the first two ramparts, and in the
centre of the third, where today the path leads onto a footbridge. A
deep sea-cleft cuts off the final island from the promontory. It seems
likely that there was still a land-bridge in Iron Age times. Once across
the footbridge the visitor is immediately faced with a further rampart
through which the path cuts a good archaeological section. After a
short distance the final, innermost rampart is reached. Huts have been
excavated inside this area, including one with stone-built walls,
14 m in diameter, with a ring of post holes around its central hearth.
Although the site was excavated in 1939 the results have not yet been
published. Finds included pottery and glass, a bronze horse-harness
and evidence of a small bronze foundry on the south side of the island.
It seems to have been occupied from the Bronze Age until well into
the Roman period. There are two Bronze Age barrows within the fort,
one on the hilltop just inside the outer defence at SX:828631, and the
second on the highest point of the island, with a deep gash in its side.
Although both have been dug, one in 1872 by William Borlase, nothing
is known of their contents.

   0·8 km further north along the coast are two more large round barrows.
They can be reached from a footpath off the B3276 or by following
the cliff-top walk north from Trevelgue.
P.P.S. **5** (1939) 254 for brief note

49 TRIPPET STONES   Bronze Age
   Blisland   186 (SX:131750)
*Along unfenced road to St. Breward across Manor Common for 1·6 km
from A30, turning north-east along cart track for 0·4 km. Site lies beside
telegraph pole on left.*

This is a small but impressive circle of eight standing, and four fallen,
stones, 33 m in diameter. Most of the stones are roughly rectangular
blocks, about 1·5 m high. In the centre is a modern boundary stone.

H. St. George Gray: *Archaeologia* **61** (1906) 25

50 VERYAN BARROW   Bronze Age
  Veryan   190 (SX:913387)
*Beside a minor road from Carne to Pendower Beach at a sharp bend in the
road.*

This monumental barrow, lightly covered with scrub, is one of the
largest in southern England, being at least 4·6 m high and 112·8 m
in diameter. It is magnificently sited above Gerrans Bay.

51 WARBSTOW BURY HILLFORT   Iron Age
  Warbstow   174 (SX:202908)
*Minor road off A395 at Hallworthy to Warbstow and Canworthy Water.
Park by house called 'Hillside' halfway down hill at SX:203907. Public
footpath through field-gate opposite, to fort.*

One of the finest hillforts in Cornwall with enormous views in all
directions except the south-west. There are two concentric rings of
ramparts and ditches, with an additional arc on the higher south-
western side close to the inner rampart. The outer ditch, in the same
area, has also been widened, suggesting that this was the most vul-
nerable side. It belongs to the group of hill-slope forts with widely
spaced ramparts, characteristic of south-western Britain (see No. 45).

A. Fox in Frere: *Problems of the Iron Age in Southern Britain* (1959) 49

52 ZENNOR QUOIT   Neolithic
  Zennor   189 (SW:469380)
*Approached by footpath from B3306 at SX:467387, opposite house
called 'Eagles Nest'.*

Five upright stone slabs form a completely enclosed burial chamber.
On the east is an antechamber with two vertical façade slabs in front
of it, with a narrow entrance gap between them. Over the back of the
tomb rests the collapsed capstone, measuring 5·5 m across. In 1881
a local farmer blasted the paving in the antechamber in search of
treasure, but only found a perforated whetstone. Excavation by
R. J. Noall a few years later produced cremated bones, flints and a
small neolithic pot.

G. E. Daniel: *Prehistoric Chamber Tombs of England and Wales*
(1950) 237

Museums containing archaeological material

Public Library and Museum, Cross Street, Camborne
Penzance Natural History and Antiquarian Museum, Penlee Park,
  Penzance
County Museum and Art Gallery,* River Street, Truro
Wayside Museum, Old Millhouse, Zennor
                    *Main county collection

1 BERRY DOWN BARROWS   Bronze Age
Berrynarbor   163 (SS: 569436)

On either side of the B3343 road, 0·4 km west and south-west of Berry Down Cross.

On the northern edge of Exmoor, this group of about nine round barrows stands at more than 800 feet (244 m) above sea level. The barrows vary in height from less than 0·3 m to 1·8 m, and in diameter from 9·1 m to 32 m. Some of them were opened by George Doe in 1883, and in one of them he found a ribbon-handled urn of Cornish Trevisker type, inverted over a cremation burial. It is now displayed in Exeter Museum.

L. V. Grinsell: *Archaeology of Exmoor* (1970) 59

2 BLACKBURY CASTLE   Iron Age
Southleigh   176 (SX: 187924)

Immediately south of the road from Lovehayne Common to Southleigh. Parking area beside road. Department of the Environment. Access at any time.

This oval enclosure of 1·6 ha, with only one original entrance in the south side, commands a narrow east–west ridge. The single line of rampart still stands 3·1 m high, and has an outer V-shaped ditch 2·4 deep and 9·1 m wide. The ends of the entrance are slightly out-turned. Excavation has shown that there were wooden gates, and perhaps a sentry walk-bridge over the gateway passage, which was 2·6 m wide. In front of this entrance is a large triangular-shaped barbican defence, with an embanked and metalled entrance passage 54·9 m long, and two triangular enclosures on either side. The whole thing resembles an early stage in the entrance defence of Maiden Castle's east gate. The excavators considered it unfinished. The triangular enclosures may have been used for the night protection of animals who by day roamed the ridge on which the fort lies. Although a hut has been found in the fort, evidence suggests that it was not extensively occupied.

A. Young and K. Richardson: *P.D.A.E.S.* 5 (1954–5) 43

3 BLACK HILL CAIRNS AND STONE ROW   Bronze Age
Manaton   175/188 (SX: 767793)

North of road between Manaton and Haytor Vale.

The ground here is 305 m above the river Bovey which flows to the north-east. There is a large cairn of stones 30·5 m north of the road, almost certainly of Bronze Age date. Stretching north from it down the hillside is a row of sixteen stones, with a larger stone at right angles at the far end. The row was probably double at one time, but it has been much robbed. At the southern end is another damaged cairn, about 15·2 m in diameter.

4 BOLT TAIL PROMONTORY FORT   Iron Age
   Malborough   187 (SX:670397)

(*National Trust.*) *Overlooking Bigbury Bay, south-west of Inner Hope, and 6·4 km west of Salcombe.*

This magnificent headland is isolated by a promontory fort of 4·9 ha. Across the narrowest part of the promontory a rampart 274 m long and 4·6 m high in places has been thrown up. There are indications of a stone facing wall on the outer eastern side. There is an inturned entrance approached by a hollow-way and guarded by an arc-like outwork on the north. The hollow-way leads north-west to a second minor fort on lower ground, in which a small promontory facing north to Bigbury Bay is cut off by a line of rampart running north-west to south-east, and about 2·7 m high. There is an entrance near the cliff edge on the north-west. The camp seems to have been an annexe for the larger fort, well sited to guard a fresh-water supply and observe Hope Cove below.

V.C.H. Devon **1** (1906) 578

5 BROAD DOWN BARROW CEMETERY   Bronze Age
   Farway   176 (SY:147963 to 172937)

Beside the B3174 between the 'Hare and Hounds' and Broad Down.

Scattered along the ridge road between Gittisham Hill and Broad Down are more than fifty round barrows. Some of them, unfortunately, have been irrevocably damaged by ploughing in recent years. Varying in height from a few centimetres to as much as 3·7 m, and in diameter from 7·6 m to 42·7 m, the barrows are externally typical of those found all over southern England. Excavations have shown that they contain cremation burials placed either in a cist, or on a 'pavement', often covered with heaps of flints. They range in time through the Beaker period and Early Bronze Age. A line of seven barrows on Broad Down (Ball Hill) may represent the burial ground of a dynasty of local chieftains. Two of this group had stone circles set around them, and the central example produced a carved shale cup in 1868. A second shale cup was found at Roncombe Gate. Others have yielded a grooved bronze dagger, a segmented bone toggle and a pottery pygmy cup. North-west of Broad Down on Farway Hill are twenty more barrows, a number of them clustering round a circular enclosure, 61 m in diameter, and consisting of a low bank and outer ditch (SY:161955) which may be a sacred enclosure of henge-type or only a tree-clump boundary circle. It has no apparent entrance. A barrow to the south-east of the enclosure (SY:164949) is ditched, 2·1 m high and 24·4 m in diameter, and has a boundary stone on its summit. Gittisham Hill has more scattered barrows including one (SY:152961) 42·7 m in diameter and 3·7 m high.

A. Fox: *South-west England* (1964) 72

6 BURLEY WOOD HILLFORT   Iron Age
    Bridestowe   175 (SX:495876)
In woodland. Footpath from south-east at Watergate.

A roughly triangular north-facing spur is cut off at its southern apex by three cross-ridge dykes. The most southerly, broken by two entrance gaps, is also the most massive. The middle bank has a simple straight-through entrance gap. Enclosed on the spur by the dykes is an oval fortification with an annexe at its south side. This fort, about 1 ha in extent, is surrounded by a single rampart and ditch, with traces of a counterscarp bank. An inturned entrance at the south connects with the annexe, which is entered on the west. There is a small enclosure in the north-east corner of the annexe which may have been a cattle pen.

Outside the fort to the north-east is a small but very strong motte-and-bailey castle earthwork.

7 BURRIDGE CAMP   Iron Age and/or Saxon
    Rodborough   163 (SS:569352)
Off the A39 1·6 km north of Barnstaple along minor road towards Brightlycott. Through gate on north of road near top of hill.

A single rampart and ditch surround this small hillfort of about 1·2 ha. They are broken on the east by an entrance gap and are damaged on the south. There is a second line of rampart and ditch facing east, about 368 m along the ridge to the east. Some doubt has been expressed as to whether this is an Iron Age fort, or whether it might be one of the four Saxon *burhs* of Devon constructed in Alfred's reign. One is known to have been erected to keep guard over Barnstaple Bay. On the other hand an existing hillfort might have been adapted to serve as a *burh*.

L. V. Grinsell: *Archaeology of Exmoor* (1970) 83

8 BUTTERDON HILL STONE ROW AND BARROWS   Bronze Age
    Harford   187 (SX:655587)
Footpath by minor road north-east from Ivybridge (SX:646576) or from Harford Moor Gate (SX:643596). Uphill walk of 1·6 km from either point.

There are at least six stone burial cairns around the summit of this hill. One of them is 30·5 m in diameter and 3·7 m high. Another,

11·3 m in diameter, has a stone retaining circle around it, and leading north from it a row of stones 1·9 km long, which now ends in a single tall pillar stone. This row passes another large cairn with a robbers' hollow in its top, 0·8 km to the north. Formerly the stone row continued past Hobajons Cross to the summit of Pile Hill where there is a fallen pillar stone called the Longstone.

9 CADBURY CASTLE   Iron Age
   Cadbury   176 (SS:914053)
Approached from south by track opposite entrance to Cadbury House, then beside wood for 0·8 km.

Crowning a hilltop west of the Exe valley, this roughly oval fort encloses about 1·6 ha with a single rampart and traces of a filled-in ditch on most sides. The rampart on the south, south-east and south-west is very high indeed, about 6·1 m in places on the outside. On the north-west the ground falls away steeply. There is a simple straight-through entrance at the south-east, and a probably modern gap at the north-east. About 30·5 m inside the fort on the southern side there is a marked ridge, in places 6 m high, running parallel to the outer rampart from the east to west sides of the fort. This has the appearance of representing an earlier line of rampart, flattened and replaced by the existing line. There is a deep hollow in the centre of the fort which was excavated in 1847 and found to be 17·7 m deep. Its mouth was funnel-shaped, and the whole shaft tapered from 2·4 m diameter at the top to 0·9 m near the bottom. The shaft was lined with puddled clay. As well as pottery and animal bone, the shaft produced twenty metal bracelets and four of shale, beads, a finger ring and an iron blade. No water was reached in the shaft, and it was probably dug for religious and votive purposes.

A. Ross, in Coles and Simpson: *Studies in Ancient Europe* (1968) 262

10 CHALLACOMBE STONE ROWS   Bronze Age
   North Bovey   175 (SX:690809)
By moorland footpath east from Warren House Inn, or south-east from minor road at SX:695815, amongst old tin mines.

Running from south to north down a hill-slope this triple row of stones is 161 m long today. Originally it was longer, but stones at both its extremities have been destroyed, although the southern end is marked by a large triangular blocking stone. The rows are parallel for the greater part of their length, but they narrow and come towards one another at the southern end. There is a large stone in the central row near the northern end which lies across the row. It was probably turned in fairly recent times. Just outside the rows, to the west of this transverse stone are a number of other blocks, all of which may once have formed a circle. Unfortunately the restorer has been at work here, and it is uncertain which stones are in their original positions.

J. Brailsford: *Antiquity* **12** (1938) 463

11 CHAPMAN BARROWS   Bronze Age
   Challacombe   163 (ss:695435)

A lane on to Challacombe Common leads from Parracombe to Two Gates (SS:690434). The group lie on the moor to the east.

This group of about ten round barrows run in a line along the hill from east to west. They vary in size from 9 to 30 m in diameter and in height between 0·3 and 2·7 m. The south-eastern barrow was opened in 1905 by J. F. Chanter. Layers of turves and a stone cairn covered a cremation burial. A low wall of stones had originally held the mound in position.

About 0·4 km south-east of the Chapman barrows is the *Long Stone*, the tallest standing stone on Exmoor. It is a block of Morte slate about 2·7 m high and 15 cm thick. Some distance south-east again is a large ditched barrow 2·4 m high and 30·5 m across. This is the Longstone Barrow and judging from the depression on its summit it has clearly been robbed. After two or three other barrows the Wood Barrow is reached. It lies on the county boundary and was one of the early boundary marks of Exmoor Forest. Legend has it that it contained a great brass pan filled with treasure.

L. V. Grinsell: *Archaeology of Exmoor* (1970) 59

12 CLOVELLY DYKES (Plate 16)   Iron Age
   Clovelly   174 (ss:311235)

Immediately north of the A39(T) and west of the B3237 turning into Clovelly opposite a garage. Permission to visit from East Dyke Farm.

This large hill-slope fort is sited at the junction of three ridge ways. It began life as two approximately rectangular enclosures, one within the other, strongly defended with a rampart and ditch, and a simple entrance in both on the eastern side. The outer rampart was the stronger of the two. It lay some 61 m outside the slighter inner rampart. Some time later the fort was enlarged by the addition of three rectangular strip-like enclosures on the west, and a single semi-circular enclosure on the east (partly east of the B3237). The original entrances in the central enclosures remained in use and linked up with another in the eastern enclosure opposite Clovelly Cross garage. The entrances to the western enclosures were all on the northern seaward side of the fort, facing nearby springs. The rampart ends at these entrances are higher and broader than elsewhere and have a distinctly 'knobbed' appearance. Although the fort is strongly defended it is

Plate 16   Clovelly Dykes, Devon

believed that multiple enclosures like Clovelly Dykes were used by Iron Age farmers for segregating domestic animals, and perhaps for herding cattle prior to exporting them or their hides to the continent from a nearby estuary or harbour.

A. Fox: *Arch. J.* **109** (1952) 12

13 CORRINGDON BALL LONG BARROW   Neolithic
   South Brent   188 (SX:670614)

From South Brent to footpath at SX:684603, or from footpath north of Didworthy Hospital at SX:679624. Walk of 1·6 km.

This is the only chambered long barrow on Dartmoor. Although the burial chamber is ruined, large stones at the south-east end clearly indicate its position. The mound which lies north-west to south-east is about 40 m long, 19·8 m wide and 1·8 m high at the south-east end.

Across the valley 0·4 km to the west (SX:666613) are seven short stone rows, a cairn and the circle of retaining stones that once surrounded a now destroyed barrow. The longer, north-western stone row, about 152 m long, is aligned on the cairn: the rest of the stones in two triple-rows align on the retaining circle which is 11·3 m in diameter. One triple-row is 79·2 m long, the other 66·8 m. All the stones are small, few being more than 30 cm high, consequently they should be visited when the bracken is low.

R. H. Worth: *Dartmoor* (1953) 231

14 COUNTISBURY PROMONTORY FORT   Iron Age
   Lynton   163 (SS: 741493)

On Wind Hill south of the A39, 1·6 km east of Lynton above Lynmouth Bay.

A steep-sided hill-spur between the sea and the East Lyn river is defended by one of the most massive ramparts on Exmoor. The rampart rises about 9 m above the bottom of a ditch, which lies on its eastern side. The earthwork, which isolates a promontory almost 1·6 km long, is itself almost 0·4 km in length. The gap through which the road passes may be the original entrance, though this has not been proved. Leslie Grinsell has suggested that Countisbury may be an invasion beach-head similar to Bindon Hill in Dorset.

L. V. Grinsell: *Archaeology of Exmoor* (1970) 83

15 CRANBROOK CASTLE   Iron Age
   Moretonhampstead   175 (SX: 738890)

Minor road from A382 at Easton and public footpath from SX:742889.

The river Teign is deeply incised in its valley at this point. The Iron Age fort of Cranbrook Castle sits on the highest hill to the south, opposite Prestonbury Castle on the north bank, in such a position as to suggest forts strategically placed on the edge of warring territories. A third fort, Wooston Castle, lies 2·4 km downstream to the east.

   Cranbrook is roughly square in plan, and encloses 3·2 ha. It has a single rampart 2·7 m high, faced with stone, on its east, south and west sides, but on the north where the ground falls away steeply there is only a line of loose stones, perhaps indicating an unfinished rampart, or the line of a wooden stockade. To the west and south there is a ditch still 3·4 m deep separated from the rampart by a berm 9 to 12 m wide. South again is an outer bank and ditch, which is much less distinct to the east and west, the ditch having disappeared. There are two entrances, one on the south-west, and another on the south-east which is slightly inturned.

S. Baring-Gould: *Trans. Devon Assn.* **33** (1901) 129

16 DRIZZLECOMBE STONE ROWS AND CAIRNS   Bronze Age
   Sheepstor   187 (SX: 592670)

Minor road east from Sheepstor to SX:576673, then south to Ditsworthy Warren House, and footpath north-east on to Moor. Sites between path and river Plym.

Attractively grouped on ground sloping south to the river Plym are a comprehensive group of Dartmoor monuments. Of three round barrows in a line on the side of the hill, two have stone rows descending from them. From the centre barrow 9 m in diameter, a single row of

stones runs south-west for 149 m and terminates at a standing stone
2·4 m high. To the right a second widely spaced single row of stones
84 m long terminates at a menhir 4·3 high. South of this menhir is
a large bracken-covered barrow called the Giant's Basin, because of
the depression 1·8 m deep in its top. This barrow is 21·3 m in diameter
and 3·1 m high. West of the barrow is the most southerly of the stone
rows, 148·7 m long, lying north-east to south-west, with a barrow at
the upper end, and a standing stone 3·2 m high at the other. This row is
partly double. 137 m north-west of the three barrows is a burial cist in
a barrow, whilst 91·4 m north-east is a roughly circular pound just
over 61 m in diameter with a ruined wall about 1·5 m thick around it,
broken by an entrance gap on the west. There are two hut circles within the enclosure. Almost immediately outside to the north-east is
another burial cairn. A second pound lies about 46 m to the north,
enclosing three hut circles. There are numerous other hut circles and
standing stones in the vicinity.

R. H. Worth: *Dartmoor* (1953) 209

17 DUMPDON GREAT CAMP   Iron Age
   Luppitt   176 (ST:176040)
*Leave A30 near Langford Bridge (ST:174015) and drive to east side
of Dumpdon Hill (ST:178044)*

Beautifully sited above the river Otter this tree-capped hill is a landmark for many kilometres. Roughly kite-shaped in plan it has a double
rampart and ditch on the north side, and a single defence elsewhere,
with traces of an outer counterscarp bank. There is an entrance on
the north-east which has an inturned entrance passage 30·5 m long.
Outside there seem to be some protective terrace works which restrict
direct access to the entrance. Part of the 2 ha interior has been ploughed,
whilst trees grow on the southern end. The defences are themselves
covered with bracken.

18 EXETER CITY WALLS   Roman
                                                     176 (SX:923925)

In Roman times Exeter was known as *Isca Dumnoniorum*, 'the people
of this land', and was the major town of the Dumnonii, a confederation
of Iron Age people who occupied south-west England. The earliest
settlement dates from about A.D. 45 to 75. It consisted of a small
military fort (not visible) to the east of South Gate, and a native settlement of timber-framed buildings spread out along a road running
down to a crossing place over the river Exe. After A.D. 75 a regular
street plan was laid out, public buildings were erected and houses of
brick and concrete set up. About A.D. 160 a ditch and earthen rampart
were thrown round the town, whilst at the end of the 2nd century a

stone wall 3·1 m thick and 6·1 m high was added and the rampart heightened. An area of 37 ha was thus enclosed. The wall still survives combined with medieval work. The Roman sections can be picked out by the chamfered plinth along the bottom and the dark purplish stone, Exeter trap, quarried around the castle, from which it is built. Some of the best work can be seen in Northernhay Gardens, Post Office Street, Southernhay West, and from South Street down to the river Exe. Nothing structural remains of the Roman gates which were almost certainly on the sites later occupied by the medieval gateways, although the site of a tower of the South Gate is marked out on the west side of South Street near the Inner By-pass.

Material from excavations within the city is displayed in the Rougemont House Museum, Castle Street (*Monday to Saturday 10.00 to 17.30 hours*).

A. Fox: *Arch. J.* **114** (1957) 178

19 FIVE BARROWS   Bronze Age
    North Molton   163 (ss:732368 centre)
There is a parking place at Comerslade on the ridgeway (SS:733373). The barrows lie around the summit to the south.

Nine barrows lie in a rough line east to west, and vary in diameter from 12 to 33·5 m, and from 0·3 to 3·4 m in height. There are no records of any of them having been excavated. On the south-east side of the summit is a good bell-barrow with a well-marked surrounding ditch.

20 FOALES ARISHES SETTLEMENT SITE   Bronze and Iron Age
    Widecombe   175/187 (sx:737758)
On the hillside, about 366 m south-west of road at Hemsworthy Gate (SX:742761). The ground is inclined to be marshy in patches.

This small village was originally much more extensive, but has been badly reduced in the past hundred years, and was considerably altered during the creation of modern 'enclosures'.

Eight huts were excavated in 1896, but only six can easily be identified today. The diameters of these structures measure between 5·5 and 9 m, with walls 1·2 to 1·3 m thick and 1·5 m high. The latter were faced with stone blocks and had a rubble core. The roofs had been supported on upright posts within the huts. Cooking holes were also found in some of them. One hut, 9·1 m in diameter, has a small rectangular barn or storeroom built against it, outside its entrance.

Running down the hill-slope between Pil Tor and Top Tor are long rectangular medieval fields. They cover the earlier Bronze Age fields whose banks run along the slope of the hill, sometimes up to the huts themselves. Each runs roughly from north-east to south-west and is seldom longer than 122 m. It is believed that originally these fields covered about 10 ha. Material from the excavations date them to the Bronze Age–Iron Age transition, between 1000 and 600 B.C.

C. A. R. Radford: *P.P.S.* **18** (1952) 71

21 GRIMSPOUND (Plate 17)   Bronze Age
       Manaton   175 (SX:701809)

Off road from B3212 at Shapley Common that runs south between Challacombe Down and Hamel Down. Signposted clearly.

This well-known site occupies a valley between Hookney Tor and Hameldon Hill. A small stream, the Grims Lake, runs through the north side of the pound passing under its walls. It tends to dry up in the summer months, so was not a dependable water supply. The wall is a massive affair, 3·1 m wide and 1·2 to 1·5 m high, but it was largely reconstructed during the last century. It is built of large slabs of stone with a core of smaller stones. There is a single original entrance on the east with side walls and paving. It faces up the slope of Hameldon. All the other gaps in the wall are modern.

Enclosing 1·6 ha the pound contains sixteen huts, six or seven store huts and three or four cattle pens. The huts vary in diameter between 2·4 and 4·6 m, with walls 0·9 m thick. Upright stones form jambs for the doors, two of which have porches open to the east. Each dwelling has a hearth, and also once contained central posts to support the roof. The store huts are much less substantial, with walls only one stone thick. They all lie on the north-east side of the village and are covered with heather. None of them contained hearths. Cattle pens were built against the pound wall and can be seen close to the modern entrance gap on the west side.

Although the excavations failed to date the site, it almost certainly belongs to the end of the Bronze Age, about 1000 to 800 B.C., and its inhabitants must have been pastoralists, dependent on the stream and neighbouring hill-slopes for water and fodder.

A. Fox: *Arch. J.* **114** (1957) 158

22 HALWELL CAMP   Iron Age
       Halwell   187/188 (SX:784532)

On B3207 0·8 km east of Halwell village.

Split in two by the road to Dartmouth this small fort has an upstanding rampart and outer ditch in the section north of the road, but that to the south has been largely destroyed. Its original entrance is no longer apparent. The camp is about 110 m in diameter and appears to be unexcavated. It has been suggested that it was the site of the *burh* of Halwell, which was one of the four *burhs* of Devon in the 10th century A.D.

There are a group of round barrows on the summit of Bickleigh Brake hill to the north.

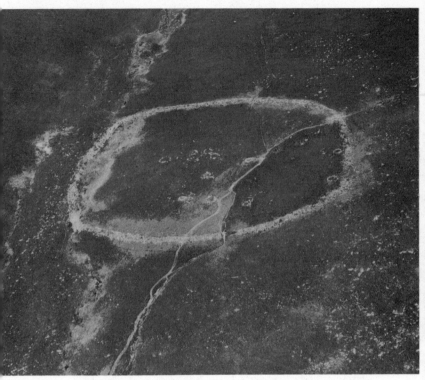

Plate 17   Grimspound, Devon

23   HAMELDOWN ROUND BARROWS   Bronze Age
Widecombe   175 (SX: 706795)

Approach from the B3212 by road from Shapley Common south to Grimspound, then follow footpath south on to Hameldown Tor and along ridgeway (2·4 km each way).

Strung out along this ridgeway are four named barrows. At the north is Broad Barrow with a mound 1·2 m high and 36·6 m in diameter; next comes Single Barrow, somewhat smaller in size; and then close together Two Barrows. When the northern of this pair was opened in 1872 in a far from scientific manner, a cremation was found south-east of the centre of the mound and covered by slabs of stone. With the cremated bones was a bronze dagger of Wessex type, whose pommel, made of amber, was decorated with a cross-shaped inlay of minute gold pins like those found at Bush Barrow and Winterbourne Stoke in Wiltshire. Unfortunately it was destroyed in 1943 when Plymouth Museum was bombed. The very incomplete excavation found a cairn of stones at the centre of the barrow, but failed to find a burial. The whole mound is about 1·2 m high and 12·2 m in diameter. The second barrow, to the south, is slightly smaller, but no record exists of its contents if it has been opened.

T. D. Kendrick: *Ant. J.* **17** (1937) 313

24 HEMBURY HILLFORT (Fig. 8; Plate 18)

Neolithic and Iron Age

Payhembury   176 (ST:113031)

Most easily approached through woods from north at ST:112035 or more conventionally off A373 at ST:112028.

Hembury is one of the most important sites in southern England. Visited in May when the bracken is low and the bluebells are in flower, it is also one of the most attractive.

The southern end of the spur was first occupied by a neolithic causewayed camp dated by corrected radio-carbon analysis to between 4200 and 3980 B.C. Eight sections of flat-bottomed ditches about 1·8 m deep and between 7·6 and 17 m long ran east to west across the promontory, with traces of a rampart on their southern side. At the west end a gate-structure of wooden posts was uncovered, as well as the footings of a small hut just inside the entrance. Further north, where the eastern Iron Age fort entrance is situated, another line of neolithic ditch was found with a line of eight post-holes for a palisade outside it. Domestic refuse including cooking pots, flints, bones and hearths were scattered over many parts of the hilltop.

In the Iron Age the hill was again occupied, this time by a large triangular hillfort which covered about 2·8 ha. On the north and west it was defended by three banks and ditches, but on the east by only two. These were broken by two entrances, one midway along the west side, and the other in the north-east corner. Both were inturned and had double gates in long entrance passages.

The excavation showed that the initial Iron Age defence had been by means of two closely spaced palisades and a small rampart. The great ditches and ramparts that we see today were constructed later; the inner rampart being 9 m above the ditch bottom. On the north the outer ditch was only half completed across the hill-spur. On the steep

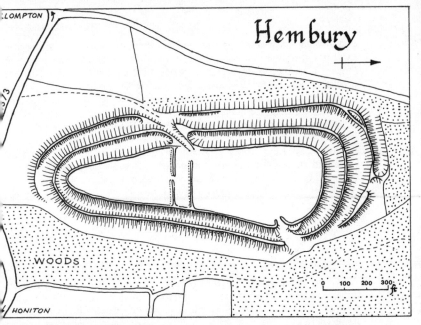

Fig. 8   Hembury hillfort, Devon

Plate 18   Hembury hillfort, Devon

east and west hill-slopes the ramparts had been made by scarping and by throwing the soil downhill into a rampart, creating a slope 17·7 m long. This stage of the fort's history, dating from the 2nd and 1st centuries B.C. seems to have been created by people using pottery characteristic of the middle Iron Age in south-western Britain: probably the Dumnonii.

Late in the Iron Age following a cultural change the fort was reduced in size by building two banks midway across the fort. The southern tip seems to have been used as a stock enclosure, whilst the northern part remained in use for human occupation although no huts have been found. The fort continued to be occupied until about A.D. 65–70, at which time the inhabitants moved to a new site, as yet undiscovered.

D. Liddell: *P.D.A.E.S.* **2** (1935) 135

25 KENT'S CAVERN   Palaeolithic
       Torquay   188 (SX:934641)
In Ilsham Road, signposted off Babbacombe Road. Free car-park.

Although occupied for much of the Palaeolithic period, little has been done to make this show-cave of interest to archaeologically minded visitors. Two main chambers and a series of galleries have produced material ranging in date from 100,000 to 8000 B.C., including a wide range of flint implements, antler and bone tools including three harpoons, one double barbed, a sewing needle and an ivory rod. Digging has been carried on spasmodically since about 1824, also producing evidence of prehistoric fauna including mammoth, woolly rhinoceros, cave-hyena, cave-bear and cave-lion. Visitors will probably gain more from the cave material displayed in the Museum of the Torquay Natural History Society, Babbacombe Road (*open weekdays 10.00 to 17.00 hours*), and the Natural History Museum in South Kensington, London, than from the site itself.

E. H. Rogers: *P.D.A.E.S.* **5** (1954–5) 68

26 KESTOR SETTLEMENT SITE   Iron Age
       Chagford   175 (SX:665867)
3 km west of Chagford. The minor road from Teigncombe to Batworthy passes through the site.

Excavation in 1951 and 1952 examined part of Kestor, a settlement with associated field systems of early Iron Age date. The main feature of the site is Round Pound, a walled enclosure 33·5 m in diameter, surrounding a circular hut 11·2 m across. This hut had stone wall-footings, a ring of posts for a somewhat irregular roof that may have been partially open to the sky, a drain, and an iron smelting furnace. A drove way connecting the open moor on the south-west with the

Batworthy brook on the north-east, joined the entrance to the pound on its west side. 91 m north-east a second hut was examined. It too had stone wall-footings and posts to support a conical roof. Up the hill-slope from Round Pound are a series of broadly contemporary fields, rectangular in shape, with, here and there, about twenty-five other unexcavated huts, varying in diameter from 3·7 to 11 m. Along the crest of the ridge is another drove way, also running north-east to south-west.

A. Fox: *Trans. Devon Assn.* **86** (1954) 21

27 LAKEHEAD HILL STONE CISTS   Bronze Age
    Lydford   187 (SX:644774)

From B3212 to Bellever (Youth Hostel) then footpath west uphill through woodland.

On the open hilltop are three stone cists, hut circles and pound, and a stone row. Of the three cairns the southernmost (SX:647774) is the most interesting, with an impressive rectangular cist composed of four wall slabs and a cover slab raised above ground level. Around it are six stones, all that remain of a circle 7·6 m in diameter. Leading for 13·4 m east of it is a row of eleven stones. The whole monument was restored in 1895 when the cist was made too large. North-west is another cairn circle (SX:643774) 6·4 m in diameter with a stone cist at its centre, whilst a third lies further north at SX:643777. At the northern end of the woodland clearing (SX:644782) is a pound containing hut circles.

28 LEGIS TOR POUNDS   Bronze Age
    Sheepstor   187 (SX:570654)

On north bank of the Plym reached from minor roads from Cadover Bridge to Brisworthy (SX:562654), then footpath beside river.

This pound of 1·8 ha consists of four enclosures. The first enclosure constructed was small, oval and close to the river on the south side. A second larger oval enclosure was added on its western side, and then a much larger third addition was made to both on the north-east. This latter contained a small internal enclosure cutting off the south-east corner. Within the whole pound are ten huts between 4·3 and 6·4 m in diameter; one, presumably the earliest on the site, is incorporated in the wall of the earliest pound. Most of the huts had entrances on the southern side, some had paved floors, stone hearths and adjoining cooking holes. Their walls were of stone, about 1·2 m high, and each would have had a roof of timber and thatch. The settlement is dated on pottery excavated from the site to between 1800 and 1500 B.C.

C. A. R. Radford: *P.P.S.* **18** (1952) 61

29 LUNDY HUT CIRCLES   Bronze/Iron Age
   Lundy Island   163 (ss:134476)

National Trust Property. Two-hour boat journey from Bideford or Ilfracombe.

A number of groups of hut circles and associated field systems are scattered over the island, especially in the centre and north. The earliest Late Bronze Age huts were found at the northern end of the island inside a rough stone wall which isolates the northernmost area like one of the pounds of Dartmoor. Iron Age huts 9 m in diameter have been found in the central part of the island called Middle Park (ss:136462), and with their associated fields on Beacon Hill near Old Light (ss:132444). There are a few barrows on the island, some of which must be Bronze Age in date, as well as a considerable number of later antiquities including Dark Age inscribed stones.

Current Archaeology **1** (1968) 196

30 MARTINHOE FORTLET   Roman
   Martinhoe   163 (ss:663493)

Through Martinhoe village to end of lane, then across two fields. Alternative coastal path between Woody Bay and Heddon's Mouth is most attractive but very steep.

In the middle years of the 1st century A.D. the Romans in north Devon were faced with the task of watching the hostile tribe known as the Silures who lived in South Wales, and who constantly gave them trouble. In order to do this two successive fortlets were established, the first at Old Burrow (No. 33) and the second at Martinhoe.

The Martinhoe fort dates from about A.D. 60 to A.D. 75. It consists of double ramparts and ditches making a strong enclosure with an entrance facing north towards the sea. 21 m outside this was an outer rampart and ditch, with an entrance facing south. If this outer gate was forced the attackers would have to make their way under fire half-way round the inside of the enclosure before reaching the inner gate.

Excavated by Lady Fox and Dr. Ravenhill in 1960–1, the fort was shown to have contained two wooden barrack blocks, providing sufficient accommodation for eighty men (a century), field ovens, and a furnace probably used by armourers. Traces of signal fires were found inside the outer enclosure, on the cliff edge. It was probably abandoned at about the time that the legionary fortress at Caerleon in South Wales was established, thus making the fortlet unnecessary.

A. Fox: *South-West England* (1964) 138

31 MERRIVALE STONE SETTINGS   Bronze Age
Walkhampton   175 (SX: 553746 centre)

Just south of the A384 on bend in road 0·8 km east of Merrivale village.

By far the easiest group of stone monuments to reach on Dartmoor, consisting of groups of hut circles on either side of the road, three stone rows, a stone circle and numerous cairns within easy distance of the road.

Two double rows of stones run parallel to each other from east to west. The northernmost is 181·8 m long and the southern 263·8 m long. Both are blocked by a triangular stone at the eastern end. Near the centre of the southern row is a round barrow with a circle of stones around it. South-west of this barrow is another with a single stone row leading south-west from it for 42·7 m. There are two other barrows nearby. A stone circle stands 91 m south of the last stone row, with a standing stone to the south beside a cairn. Nothing is recorded of the contents of the barrows and cairns.

J. Brailsford: *Antiquity* **12** (1938) 444

32 MILBER DOWN CAMP   Iron Age
Haccombe   188 (SX: 884699)

Road from Newton Abbot via Watcombe to Torquay cuts through the site. Public footpath at SX: 885698.

Four roughly concentric enclosures with ramparts and external ditches lie on the west-facing slope of Milber Down. None of the ramparts are of any great strength, and they are typical of that class of monument known as a hill-slope fort, and considered to have been used mainly for cattle herding. The outer enclosure is damaged on the north and east sides, and has a long sunken entrance passage on the west, turned inwards until it joins the third rampart. The other ramparts probably had entrances on the west also, but the road has destroyed them. The site, which has been excavated, was constructed in the 1st century B.C. and abandoned at about the time of the Roman conquest.

A. Fox *et al.*: *P.D.A.E.S.* **4** (1949–50) 27

33 OLD BURROW FORTLET   Roman
Countisbury   163 (SS: 788493)

Approached by path from Black Gate at SS: 788489, on the A39 between Lynmouth and Porlock.

Situated on mist-shrouded moorland 1100 feet (335 m) above sea level, this temporary Roman fortlet was occupied for about four years only, between A.D. 48 and 52. Excavations by Lady Fox and Dr. Ravenhill in 1963 showed that its outer enclosure, some 70 m across, was hastily

constructed. After which an inner double-ramparted enclosure 27·4 m
across was more carefully built inside. The outer enclosure had a gate
on the south side, whilst the inner gateway faced north towards the
sea. This inner entrance was paved and had a partially timbered gateway. Remains of a very large field oven were found within the fort.
The purpose of this isolated military post was to keep watch on the
Silures across the Bristol Channel and pass signals to the Roman fleet
(see Martinhoe, No. 30).

A. Fox and W. Ravenhill: *P.D.A.E.S.* **24** (1966) 1

34 PRESTONBURY CASTLE HILLFORT   Iron Age
    Drewsteighton   175 (SX:746900)
*South from the road between the hamlet of Preston and Drewston Woods
at SX:7469905, and north of Fingle Bridge.*

On the steep north bank of the Teign gorge, facing across the valley to
Cranbrook Castle hillfort, is a fine multiple enclosure fort. Its inner
enclosure of 1·2 ha is roughly oval and is surrounded by a rampart but
no ditch. There is an entrance on the east side. There is a second rampart on the north and east side of the inner enclosure, this time with an
external ditch. It protrudes well to the east forming an annexe. Much
further out from the main camp is a third line of defence forming an
outer rampart, again with its ends stretching to the steep gorge sides,
and with a strongly inturned entrance on the east, on the edge of the
ploughed field. This outer line forms a large enclosure, probably used
for cattle herding, and dating from the 2nd or 1st centuries B.C.

35 RIDERS RINGS SETTLEMENT   Bronze Age
    South Brent   187 (SX:678644)
*By minor roads north from South Brent to Shipley Bridge, then walk
beside Avon for about 1·6 km, keeping to west bank of river. Steep climb
on to moor.*

Riders Rings consist of two adjoining settlement enclosures or pounds
on a hillside sloping to the river Avon on the south-east. The southern
pound is circular and apparently earlier than the elongated enclosure
to the north. It encloses 1·2 ha and contains some sixteen huts most of
which lie beside the uphill north-western wall. The pound wall,
which stood about 2 m high, is composed of an inner and outer face of
large stones. Turves packed between them have disintegrated leaving
a core of small stones and rubble. The slightly later northern pound
encloses 1·4 ha and is about 213 m long. There are about a dozen certain huts mainly along the central axis of the enclosure. Against the
north-west wall a series of small rectangular enclosures seem to have

been stock pens. Similar structures elsewhere in the Rings may have been cultivation plots. An entrance connects both enclosures showing that they were both used together at some time in their history. There are seven other entrances facing in all directions, serving the needs of a herding community.

R. H. Worth: *Dartmoor* (1953) 147

36 SCORHILL STONE CIRCLE   Bronze Age
   Gidleigh   175 (SX:655874)
Through minor roads to Gidleigh and Berrydown, parking at SX:661877, and climb of 0·8 km.

This fine stone circle lies on the open moor close to a tributary stream of the river Teign. It measures 26·8 m in diameter, and contains twenty-three mainly pointed stones, as well as seven fallen ones. Originally it contained about forty more which have been removed from time to time. The largest stone stands 2·4 m high. Other stones were removed to line the banks of a leat about 61 m away.

R. H. Worth: *Dartmoor* (1953) 249

37 SETTA BARROW   Bronze Age
   High Bray   163 (SS:726381)
East of the ridgeway from Mole's Chamber to Kinsford Gate.

Situated on the crest of the moor and the county boundary, this round barrow is 29·2 m in diameter and 1·8 m high. Round it is a circle of stones originally intended to hold it in position. 320 m to the south is a smaller barrow, 24·4 m in diameter, that also has a retaining circle. This lies 2·7 m inside the modern edge of the barrow and clearly shows that it failed to do the job for which it was intended. There is yet another barrow to the north of Setta barrow with a retaining peristalith. South-west of Setta barrow is a row of three standing stones with a fourth almost at right-angles to the rest. Like the barrows, they are probably of Bronze Age date, and may be connected with them in some way.

38 SHOULSBURY CASTLE   Iron Age
   Challacombe   163 (SS:706391)
On moor, west of minor road between Five Cross Way and Mole's Chamber. Approached by field gate in hedgerow.

This is a rectangular hillfort enclosing about 1·6 ha with a single rampart 1·2 to 1·8 m high and a silted-up ditch. On the north, east and part of the west side is an incomplete line of outer rampart and ditch. The other sides are partially protected by the steep hillslope down to the river Bray. There is an entrance gap on the west side. In the north-east corner is a low mound about 9 m in diameter which has been variously described as a round barrow, watch-tower base and hut circle. The ground to the north and east of the camp is inclined to be marshy and should be approached with caution.

A. H. Allcroft: *Earthwork of England* (1908) 114

39 SHOVEL DOWN STONE ROWS   Bronze Age
    Gidleigh   175 (SX:660860)

From Chagford to Teincombe and Batworthy. Footpath to summit of Shovel Down.

Three stone rows, either double or parallelithon, lie on the north facing slope of Shovel Down. One row 167·6 m long runs south uphill from Batworthy corner to a low cairn which contains four roughly concentric settings of small stones. The stones of the row are 0·6 to 0·9 m high and are set in pairs about 1·2 m apart. The row is badly damaged at the northern end. At the point where it approaches the cairn two large menhirs have fallen across the alignment. Part of a cist slab can be seen at the centre of the cairn. A second row lies west of the first. It is 145 m long and consists of small stones in rows 1·2 to 1·5 m apart. At the southern uphill end is a single upright stone 0·6 m high. This row leads downhill in the direction of a stream, and seems to be aligned on the Scorhill circle nearly 1·6 km away. A third alignment south of the others is 114·3 m long and 1·5 m wide. It leads to a cairn just below the ridge to the south, in which the stones of a ruined cist can be seen. Over the ridge and to the south again is a single stone row, and then a double row slightly to the west which leads to the *Longstone*, a menhir 3·2 m high and 0·6 m by 0·9 m at the base. 167·6 m to the south is the only survivor of three standing stones known as the *Three Boys*; it is 1·4 m high.

A. Fox: *Arch. J.* **114** (1957) 155

40 SIDBURY CASTLE HILLFORT   Iron Age
    Sidbury   176 (SY:128913)

West of the A375 from Sidbury. Best approached from north at road junctions SY:125915.

This is a pear-shaped fort of about 4·4 ha with two strong ramparts separated by a single ditch. The main entrance is at the north-west where there is a strongly out-turned passageway, which is also curved. At the southern corner of the camp there are signs of an inner quarry ditch. The north and south ends of the camp are overgrown with bracken, and trees impinge on the fort.

41 SOUSSONS PLANTATION CAIRN CIRCLE   Bronze Age
  Manaton   175 (SX:676785)

On north of minor road linking Postbridge and Widecombe, just inside the plantation.

Two side stones of a central cist which measured 1·4 m by 0·6 m, are surrounded by a ring of twenty-two retaining stones, 8·5 m in diameter. They are almost all that remains of a once extensive burial cairn.

42 THE SPINSTERS' ROCK   Neolithic
  Drewsteignton   175 (SX:700908)

North-west of minor road linking A382 near Shilstone with Drews-teignton.

Traditionally set up by three spinsters before breakfast, this monument consists of three upright stones between 2 m and 2·7 m high, capped by a coverstone measuring 14·4 m by 3·1 m, and weighing about 16 metric tons (16 tons). There are no longer any traces of a covering mound which might have been long or circular, nor of any associated stone avenue to the west, nor stone circles, all of which were claimed to have existed at the beginning of the last century. The burial chamber collapsed in 1862 and has been restored, perhaps in not quite its original form.

J. Brailsford: *Antiquity* **12** (1938) 455

43 STANBOROUGH CAMP   Iron Age
  Halwell   187/188 (SX:773517)

East of the A381 and behind the Stanborough Lodge guest house.

This roughly circular camp encloses 1·4 ha. It is defended by a single rampart and ditch and commands wide views, especially to the south-east over Start Bay. Immediately west of the camp is a fine prehistoric ridgeway running from Dartmoor south-east towards the sea. To the north-east are a group of round barrows. The camp was the meeting place for the hundred court of Stanborough.

44 THREE BARROWS   Bronze Age
  Upton Pyne   176 (SX:913993)

West of the road north from Upton Pyne, south-east of Stevenstone Farm.

The Three Barrows are part of a much wider and more scattered group of barrows. Opened in 1869 the central mound of the Three Barrows contained a cremation burial, with a small grooved bronze dagger, bronze pin, a pygmy cup and a necklace with beads of lignite and fossil encrinite. North-east of Starved Oak cross-roads, south-east of the Three Barrows is a round barrow 39·6 m in diameter and 1·8 m high (SX:915991). A neighbouring barrow, opened in 1967, produced a cremation in a collared urn in a cist near its centre, and three other cremations in inverted urns on the ground surface. All were covered by a mound of sand into which five other cremations had been placed, before the mound had been topped with turves and red clay. The objects found are in Rougemont House Museum, Exeter. A corrected radio-carbon dating for the barrow suggests that it was built between 2000 and 1700 B.C.

H. M. Pollard and P. M. Russell: *Proc. Devon Arch. Soc.* **27** (1969) 49

45 TROWLESWORTHY WARREN   Bronze Age
    Shaugh Prior   187 (SX:574645)
Minor road from Shaugh Prior to Cadover Bridge to SX:567648. Hut groups lie north-west of this reference and 0.8 km south-east on slope of moor. National Trust property.

Three roughly circular pounds lie between the road and the river Plym to the north. Two contain huts of the early Bronze Age and that to the north-east is of Middle Bronze Age date. (Notice Legis Tor pounds north-east across the river Plym.) South-east on the moor are four other pounds each enclosing about 0.2 ha and containing five to ten huts. 0.4 km south-east is a stone retaining circle with a single stone row leading south from it, 130 m long. 91 m west of the circle is a second stone row running east–west 76 m long, its west end marked by a standing stone 1.2 m high.

46 WRANGWORTHY CROSS BARROWS   Bronze Age
    East Putford   174 (SS:384174 centre)
Between A388 and A39 on byroads. Most lie behind high hedges and are not easily seen.

Of this somewhat scattered barrow group the mound at SS:377177 is most easily seen. Rush Barrow, 183 m east along the road to Wrangworthy Cross is much ploughed. All the barrows vary between 12 m and 36 m in diameter and are about 1.8 m high. One of them contained a burial accompanied by a bronze dagger lying under a mortuary house. This had been built of thick timbers forming a gabled structure 0.9 m high and 1.5 m long, above which a cairn of stones had been placed. At the centre of another a row of posts had been set up with a sloping roof laid against them. This, too, covered a burial.

C. A. R. Radford and E. H. Rogers: *P.D.A.E.S.* **3** (1947) 156

47 YELLAND STONE ROWS   Bronze Age
    Fremington   163 (SS:491329)
Approach from the A39, leaving cars at Lower Yelland Farm. Walk along muddy path south of railway line, cross by first gate, and walk along

shingle bar. The site is very difficult to find and should be visited at low tide.

Discovered in 1932, there are two parallel stone rows 34·4 m long and 1·8 m apart, lying along a roughly east–west axis, and running out into the Taw estuary. The stones, each about 30 cm high, are placed at approximately 2 m intervals apart, and originally there would have been sixteen in each row. Today nine survive in the northern row and six in the southern. Excavation has found some of the missing stone holes. The rows probably date from the Bronze Age.

E. H. Rogers: *P.D.A.E.S.* **1** (1932) 201; **3** (1946) 109

Museums containing archaeological material

Ashburton Museum, 1 West Street, Ashburton
The North Devon Athenaeum, The Square, Barnstaple
Brixham Museum, Higher Street, Brixham
Rougemont House Museum,* Castle Street, Exeter
Honiton and Allhallows Public Museum, High Street, Honiton
Torquay Natural History Society Museum,* Babbacombe Road, Torquay
The Elizabethan House, 70 Fore Street, Totnes

* Main county collections

DORSET

1 ABBOTSBURY CASTLE HILLFORT   Iron Age
  Abbotsbury   178 (SY:555866)

2·4 km north-west of Abbotsbury. Approached off B3157 at SY:558862. Park in small quarry area.

Two ramparts separated by a single ditch surround this triangular hillfort which encloses some 1·8 ha. Only at the narrow south-east end has the defence been increased to four ramparts separated by enormous ditches. This seems to represent part of a later scheme to enlarge the fort. The only certain entrance is at the south-eastern end of the north-east rampart where a single rampart forms a protection. A gap in the north-western side may represent an original postern gate.

In the western corner of the fort is a small square enclosure whose ditch cuts through the hillfort ditch. Its commanding position, especially its views along the Chesil Beach towards Portland, makes it possibly a Roman signal station. In the centre of the camp are a number of hollows that may represent huts. There is also a round barrow 12·2 m in diameter and 1·5 m high.

R.C.H.M. Dorset I (1952) 31

2 ACKLING DYKE ROMAN ROAD   Roman
179 (SU:022178 to ST:967032)

This Roman road ran between Old Sarum and Badbury Rings. The *agger*, or metalled surface, of the road stands 1·8 m high, and is between 12·2 and 15·2 m wide. The side ditches, 26 m apart, which flanked it have for the most part been destroyed. It can best be seen on Oakley Down where it cuts two disc-barrows and the Dorset Cursus (SU:010152) and can be followed from there on foot for about 13 km to Badbury Rings.

3 BADBURY RINGS HILLFORT (Plate 19)   Iron Age
Shapwick   179 (ST:964030)

The B3082 passes along its south-western side.

This tree-clad hillfort is a conspicuous feature for many kilometres. 7·3 ha are enclosed by three lines of ramparts and ditches, of which the outermost ring is by far the weakest. There are two main entrances into the fort, at the east and the west. At the former the inner rampart is inturned. At the west a rectangular enclosure butts out from the middle rampart, with an entrance in the centre of its longest side. In addition there is an alternative south-western gate in the same enclosure, linking with a gate in the outer rampart which seems to have led to neighbouring fields. There is a distinct hollow about 30·5 m inside the western entrance which might indicate a hut or ritual shaft. At present the fort is unexcavated.

During the Roman period two roads were built, the Ackling Dyke running from Dorchester to Old Sarum and London, and the road from Bath to Hamworthy (Poole). These crossed each other about 183 m north-east of the fort. Although the actual crossing place is now ploughed, a fine stretch of the Ackling Dyke is preserved on the north side of Badbury Rings, actually touching the outer rampart at one point. Here the *agger* of the road is 12·2 m wide and about 1·5 m high, with clearly visible side ditches. On the north side of the Ackling Dyke close to the B3082 are three round barrows (ST:958029) which have been variously described as Bronze Age and Roman, but have not been scientifically excavated. Between them and the west entrance to the fort is a large, but much flattened disc-barrow.

O. G. S. Crawford and A. Keiller: *Wessex from the Air* (1928) 58

4 BINDON HILL   Iron Age
West Lulworth   178 (SY:825803)

Footpath from West Lulworth above the cove.

Identified as an invasion beach head of the early Iron Age, a small section of this earthwork was excavated by Sir Mortimer Wheeler in

1950. About 162 ha are enclosed by a bank and north-facing ditch which run for 2·4 km along Bindon Hill. A north–south cross-dyke cuts off about 5 ha at the western end of the hill. Only this small portion can be visited: the remainder is daily being smashed to pieces with army shells by people who ought to know better. Bindon Hill is one of the great tragedies of British archaeology.

R. E. M. Wheeler: *Ant. J.* **33** (1953) I

Plate 19   Badbury Rings hillfort, Dorset

5   BLACK DOWN, HARDY MONUMENT BARROWS   Bronze Age
   Portesham   178 (SY:613876)

There are some ten round barrows in the immediate vicinity of the Hardy Monument on Black Down. Although all have been dug into at some time, only one bell-barrow (SY:612874) has been recently excavated. It lies on the edge of gravel working and is much disturbed. It had a turf core that may have covered a primary burial, although this was not found. In the barrow mound four secondary Middle Bronze Age urns were found, three containing cremations.

Along the ridgeway east of the Monument lies the *Bronkham Hill barrow group* (SY:623873) in Winterbourne St. Martin parish. This is a great linear cemetery that stretches along the skyline for 1·6 km and contains about thirty barrows, including four bell-barrows and a double bowl-barrow. One of the bell-barrows is about 4·3 m high, and has a great robbers' trench gashing through it. Although most of the barrows have been dug into there are no records of discoveries. 3 km further west along the ridgeway at the point where it crosses the B3159 road is the huge disc-bell-barrow (SY:663866) with mound 2·4 m high and 24·4 m in diameter. Its outer bank is 76·2 m in diameter. It stands at the eastern end of a line of eleven barrows.

L. V. Grinsell: *Dorset Barrows* (1959) various

6 BOKERLEY DYKE   Roman
                                    167 and 179 (SU:022198 to 063168)
On either side of the A354 at SU:035198.

This impressive earthwork divided the downlands of Cranborne Chase from Salisbury Plain to the north-east. About 5·6 km long it cuts across a spur of chalk with its ends tucked into forest land. The rampart still stands about 2 m high and 10·7 m wide, with a ditch on the north-east about 10·7 m wide and, when excavated by Pitt-Rivers between 1888 and 1891, was V-shaped and 3·1 m deep. Its history is complicated but it seems to have first comprised the section south-east of the A354 road, and dated to early in the 4th century A.D. The Rear Dyke, west of the A354 and now invisible, was constructed about A.D. 367–8. Eventually the Fore Dyke, the visible section north-west of the A354, was built about A.D. 400. The Roman road, Ackling Dyke, underlies the A354 at this point, and the Rear and Fore Dykes were clearly concerned with controlling it.

A. Pitt-Rivers: *Excavations at Bokerley Dyke and Wansdyke* (1888–91)

7 BUZBURY RINGS   Iron Age
Tarrant Keynston   179 (ST:919060)
The B3082 road between Blandford and Wimborne cuts through the fort.

Buzbury belongs to a group of enclosures known as hill-slope forts and more usually found further south-west in Britain. It has an outer kidney-shaped enclosure bank of 4·9 ha with an eccentric inner enclosure of 1 ha, all lying on ground sloping down to the east, and overlooked from the north and west. There is a V-shaped ditch on the inside of the larger enclosure bank. These hill-slope forts seem to have been mainly concerned with stock-keeping. The central enclosure probably housed the occupants, whilst the outer area contained the animals. There are traces of other banks and ditches in this enclosure which may have served to divide different group activities. There was an entrance on the south-west. From the site direct access was gained to neighbouring fields, their divisions still marked by various ditches which radiate from the fort. In particular a ditch on the west seems to lead to the river Stour.

There is a small bowl-barrow 61 m north of Buzbury, and another larger example a further 183 m north. Nothing is known of either.

O. G. S. Crawford and A. Keiller: *Wessex from the Air* (1928) 64

8 CAME WOOD BARROWS   Neolithic and Bronze Age
     Whitcombe, Winterbourne Came, and Broadmayne
                                                      178 (SY:699855)

Between Ridgeway Hill on the A354 and Broadmayne.

There are twenty-six barrows in Came Wood and the fields to the east. Those in the wood are fairly well preserved and include two bell-barrows and a pond-barrow. The mounds in the fields beyond have been badly damaged by ploughing. The westernmost of these, Culliford Tree barrow, was examined in 1858 and contained four burials, one with a necklace of amber beads, two covered with gold. A bank-barrow lies on some waste ground (SY:702853), and is 183 m long with a flat overgrown top, which stands some 1·8 to 2·1 m above the bottom of its surrounding ditch. The round barrow at its western end overlies it, and is therefore later. Most of the barrows in the field to the west seem to be aligned on the bank-barrow.

L. V. Grinsell: *Dorset Barrows* (1959) 143

9 CERNE GIANT   Romano-British
     Cerne Abbas   178 (ST:667016)

Approached through Cerne churchyard at the north end of Abbey Street. Footpath to left through spinney and steep climb uphill. National Trust Property.

This enormously obscene hill-figure is unique in Britain. Standing 54·9 m high and 51 m wide, its outline has been formed by chalk-filled trenches each about 0·3 m wide and deep. The method of design has made it possible to show internally features such as the ribs, nipples and phallus: the latter the cause of so much embarrassed indignation over the past century, except to the local children who scramble all over the figure, quite unabashed. Although it has not been proven, there is good reason to consider that the figure was cut at the end of the 2nd century when the Emperor Commodus (A.D. 180–93) was endeavouring to revive the cult of Hercules.

Above the Giant is a small banked enclosure measuring 30·5 m by 27·4 m, with a raised disturbed centre. Known locally as 'The Trendle' or 'Frying Pan', the earthwork may represent an Iron Age burial mound: the tomb perhaps of the person represented by the 'Giant'. Until recently the 'Frying Pan' was the scene of May Day celebrations including Maypole dancing, a ceremony significantly concerned with fertility and phallic worship.

North-east along the hilltop just before the wire fence is reached, is a settlement site of probable Romano-British date. It includes an oval banked enclosure 41 m by 32 m across, with two entrances, which may have contained a hut. Midway between this part of the hill and the 'Frying Pan' lies a dyke, with bank to the south, perhaps demarcating grazing lands.

R.C.H.M. Dorset I (1952) 82

10 CHALBURY HILLFORT   Iron Age
    Bincombe   178 (SY:695838)

Beside minor road from Came Wood to Jordan Hill.

This univallate fort encloses about 3·4 ha, on an upstanding hill north of Weymouth Bay. The walls of stone and soil were retained by inner and outer facings of limestone, set on edge, and obtained from an internal quarry ditch. An entrance in the south-east corner is of simple construction. Numerous depressions within the fort represent hut circles and storage pits. Excavation revealed two phases of early Iron Age occupation, the first of which may be very early, perhaps 6th century B.C. One of the huts examined was 10 m in diameter and had substantial stone walls and an area of roughly paved floor. Apart from pottery and animal bones, finds included a small iron knife, personal ornaments, and spinning and corn grinding equipment. A scatter of human bones over the site has been interpreted as evidence for cannibalism, but may indicate a burial custom involving the exposing of corpses in small shrines within the fort, whose disintegrating bones later become scattered.

Margaret Whitley: *Ant. J.* **23** (1943) 98

11 CHILCOMBE HILL HILLFORT   Iron Age
    Chilcombe   177 (SY:530920)

Immediately south of the A35, approached from footpath uphill at SY:528922 (lay-by). Centre of the fort arable.

A single ditch with inner and outer rampart encloses an irregular rectangular earthwork of some 7·7 ha. The fort is much denuded and presents little evidence of strength. It seems to have had three original entrances, of which that on the north-west was probably the main one. Others are to be found on the eastern side and at the south-east. There is a round barrow inside the fort, close to the northern rampart.

R.C.H.M. Dorset I (1952) 97

12 COMBS DITCH   Iron Age and Roman
Winterborne Whitechurch   178 (ST:851021 to ST:890000)
Cut by the A354, 2·4 km north-east of Winterborne Whitechurch.

This linear dyke wound its way for 6·4 km across the chalk ridge
between the Winterborne brook and the river Stour. It is now visible
only for a distance of 4·4 km. It consists of a bank with a ditch on the
north-east side. The bank is between 0·3 and 1·5 m high and about 6 m
wide. The ditch averages 7 m wide, it is V-shaped and has been shown
to be about 1·8 m deep. Excavation showed that it was probably an
Iron Age field boundary in its original form, but was enlarged into a
defensive barrier during the Roman period.

R.C.H.M. Dorset III **2** (1970) 313

13 DEVEREL BARROW   Bronze Age
Milborne St. Andrew   178 (SY:820990)
*Footpath north from A354 just west of road cutting, 2·4 km east of
Milborne St. Andrew. Overgrown and enclosed by a wall.*

Though now only 0·9 m high, this famous barrow originally reached
a height of at least 3·7 m. It is clear that it had already been disturbed
when W. A. Miles cut a trench 1·8 m wide into its centre in 1824. He
found a semi-circle of sarsen stones covering a number of cists cut into
the chalk, containing seventeen cremations in globular or bucket urns,
whilst a number of other cremations lay on the barrow floor. Sir
Richard Colt Hoare, commenting on the discovery, considered that the
barrow had been a family vault opened on a number of occasions, and
that two large blocks of stone in the barrow had served as altars. The
barrow later gave its name to the Deverel–Rimbury culture of the
Middle Bronze Age.

W. A. Miles: *The Deverel Barrow* (1826)

14 DORSET CURSUS   Neolithic
Bokerley Down to Thickthorn Down
                                          179 (ST:970123 to ST:040191)

One of the largest prehistoric monuments in Britain, the Dorset Cursus
runs for 9·6 km from Bokerley Down to Thickthorn Down. It consists
of two parallel banks with external ditches lying about 91 m apart,
closed at each end by transverse banks and ditches. It is clear that the
Cursus was designed in two parts, one, possibly the earlier, from Thickthorn to Bottlebush Down (ST:018160), and the other from Bottlebush
to Bokerley. Much of the monument has been destroyed by ploughing
but it can be seen to the east and west from the B3081 road at Bottlebush, especially in the winter and spring. Incorporated into the Cursus
or closely associated with it are a number of long barrows. The Thick-

thorn barrows (No. 44, page 105) lie at the west end; from there the designers seem to have aligned it on a barrow on Gussage Down which lies between the two ditches. Another long barrow forms part of the north side of the Cursus in a wood south-east of Oakley Down, whilst close to the east end near Bokerley Dyke are two other long barrows, 53·3 m and 91·4 m long respectively, that may originally have formed a single barrow. There are entrance gaps in both the ploughed-out cursus ditches 0·8 km from the east end. That this monument was connected with the neolithic cult of the dead seems almost certain, but what its precise function was remains a mystery.

R. J. C. Atkinson: *Antiquity* **29** (1955) 4

15 DURNOVARIA   Roman
   Dorchester   178 (SY: 694900)

There is little to be seen of this once thriving Roman town. The line of the Roman and medieval city walls are marked today by the 18th-century city 'Walks', but only one area of Roman masonry survives, south of the Hardy statue at the West Gate.

Colliton Park building. In the north-west corner of the Roman town a small town house was excavated in 1937. Begun at the end of the 2nd century A.D., it was roughly L-shaped in plan, and had been added to at a later date. Built of flint and limestone, it contained seven main rooms, plus three bathrooms, a kitchen and possible servants' room. A verandah joined the baths and kitchen to the rest of the house. No doubt they had been built apart to eliminate fire risk. The best view of the house can be obtained from the staircase windows of the adjoining County Council offices.

The amphitheatre called Maumbury Rings is described separately (No. 30, page 96). Many Roman objects found in the town are displayed in the Dorset County Museum in Dorchester.

16 EGGARDON HILLFORT (Plate 20)   Iron Age
   Askerswell   177 (SY: 541948)

Minor trackway runs along the north-east flank of the fort from the road junctions to the east.

One of the most beautifully sited hillforts in Wessex. An area of 8 ha is surrounded by three massive ramparts with ditches between them. On the northern side there is a wide berm separating the outer ramparts. At the north-west where the ground flattens out an extra line of defence has been added 91 m from the main fort. There are entrances at this north-western end which cross the earthworks diagonally. The major entrance seems to be at the south-east where an inturned passage through the outer ramparts leads at a sharp angle into the hillfort. At some time after the fort was built a land-slip occurred on its southern

Plate 20   Eggardon Hill, Dorset

side, carrying with it much of the fortifications. The occupiers had to hastily throw up a new line of defence in the loose material lower down the hillside. The whole of the interior of the fort is pitted with dozens of depressions about 3·7 m in diameter. Five of these were excavated in 1900 and were shown to be pits 1·5 to 1·8 m deep, probably used for storage. They contained various pieces of flint, but no pottery.

In the angle made by the road and the north side of the track to the hillfort is what appears to be a large overgrown disc-barrow, or possibly a henge monument (SY:546946), 58 m in diameter, with a large central mound that has been considerably disturbed. There is a small round barrow on its south-western side which it seems to avoid. Breaks in the rampart and ditch on the north-west and south-east may constitute entrances if the site is a henge monument, in which case the central mound must be seen as a later round barrow.

R.C.H.M. Dorset I (1952) 13

17   FIVE MARYS BARROW CEMETERY   Bronze Age
    Chaldon Herring   178 (SY:790842)
Beside minor road linking A352 and East Chaldon
Along the top of a west–east ridge are a row of six round barrows, two of which are bell-barrows. All show signs of having been dug into in

the past. Two of them, perhaps the first and third from the west, were dug by the exiled Duchess of Berry before 1866, and produced crouched male and female burials with stag antlers at their shoulders.

R.C.H.M. Dorset II **3** (1970) 441

18 GREY MARE AND HER COLTS   Neolithic
    Long Bredy   177 (SY: 584871)

By trackway from SY:590867, keeping left of the hedge for the Grey Mare, and right for the Kingston Russell stone circle.

This chambered long barrow is in a poor state of preservation. It contains the remains of a burial chamber formed of three upright stones and a slipped capstone. There are traces of an original crescentic forecourt at the wider south-eastern end of the barrow and two or three peristalith stones. It was dug into in the early 19th century when human bones and pottery were recovered.

R.C.H.M. Dorset I (1952) 42

19 GUSSAGE HILL SETTLEMENT   Iron Age
                                                           179 (ST: 990140)

Footpath from the busy A354 at ST:987146.

Originally an extensive settlement site, it has now been largely destroyed by ploughing, and can best be seen as a soil or crop mark in winter or spring. The massive dyke system on the north is still well preserved, as is the Gussage Hill long barrow which is 50·3 m long, 21·3 m wide and 3·4 m high. The side ditches of the latter are filled up. At either end of the long barrow runs the Dorset Cursus (page 83) from south-west to north-east, but this is almost invisible here. The main features of the settlement which lay south-east of the water tank consisted of a circular enclosure, probably surrounding a farm, with adjoining roads and platforms for barns and huts, and accompanying fields, some divided from each other by small dykes, perhaps regulating droveways. There is a second smaller long barrow 137 m south-east of the first.

H. Sumner: *Ancient Earthworks of Cranborne Chase* (1913) 73

20 HAMBLEDON CAUSEWAYED CAMP   Neolithic
    Iwerne Courtney   178 (ST: 849122)

Immediately outside the south-eastern ramparts of the hillfort.

A site of 8·1 ha enclosing the domed summit to the south-east of the great Iron Age fort, and three cross-dykes on the spurs to the south and east. It has been badly damaged by flint digging and plough-ing. The enclosure is visible as little more than a scarp but excavation in 1951 confirmed its neolithic date. The cross-dyke to the south of the

enclosure still exhibits an interrupted ditch system and its bank is about
0·9 m high. A radio-carbon date for it has been recalibrated at about
3600 B.C. Between it and the enclosure is a small long barrow, 26 m
long, 12·2 m wide and 1·8 m high at the southern end. There are two
cross-dykes east of the enclosure, one within 30·5 m of it is almost
destroyed, the other 0·4 km east runs across the neck of the spur. Most
of the cross-dyke ditches are flat bottomed, between 0·9 and 2·1 m
deep and between 3·4 and 4·3 m wide. Neolithic pottery, axes, leaf-
shaped arrow-heads, cattle bones and two human skulls came from the
dykes.

R.C.H. Dorset III 1 (1970) 131

Plate 21   Hambledon Hill, Dorset

21 HAMBLEDON HILL HILLFORT (Plate 21)   Iron Age
     Child Okeford   178 (ST:845126)

*Approached by footpath from road between Child Okeford and Shroton
Lines, signposted at ST:847133, or numerous other paths.*

This magnificent hillfort constructed during the Iron Age, is clearly of
more than one period, but without excavation it is not certain which
parts of the earthwork belong to which phase. For the most part
double ramparts encircle the fort, and are duplicated with massive
outworks on the south-east at the neck of the spur. To a large extent
the ramparts are the result of scarping which has thus involved a mini-

mum of digging. There is a continuous quarry area inside the inner rampart. It seems likely that the original fort was of no great strength and occupied 3·2 ha at the northern end of the hill. Some time afterwards the size was increased to 6·1 ha, by extending as far south as the low cross-dykes 46 m north of the long barrow. These dykes seem to be the only surviving part of that camp. Later the defences were extended to take in the southern end of the hill, thus enclosing 12·5 ha. The complex nature of these massive defences suggests that they were probably not all contemporary, although a 'master hand' seems to have designed their final appearance. There are three entrances, at the north, south-west and south-east. The northern is now largely destroyed by quarrying, but seems to have been nothing more than a simple straight-through type. A long passage leads up to the south-western entrance which is slightly inturned. The south-eastern entrance is also slightly inturned; it is simple and faces north, but was approached by a long terrace along the edge of the escarpment to the east. Two hundred hollows inside the hillfort must, on analogy with neighbouring Hod Hill, be hut platforms. It should be remembered, however, that much flint digging occurred on Hambledon in the last century.

A long barrow lies within the hillfort at the highest point of Hambledon Hill; 73 m long and 16·8 m wide, it is 1·8 m high, and has been broken in two near the centre by digging in the past, although no record of its contents has survived. Its ditches are scarcely visible.

R.C.H.M. Dorset III **1** (1970) 82

22 HAMPTON STONE CIRCLE   Bronze Age
   Portesham   178 (SY: 596865)
Beside footpath between Portesham Hill and White Hill.

This small sarsen stone circle, excavated in 1965, is about 6 m in diameter, and was made up of nine stones, set in two arcs on the north and south sides. No excavation finds were made to date it accurately. An ancient track led up to the circle and stopped at its perimeter.

G. J. Wainwright: *Proc. Dorset N.H.A.S.* **88** (1966) 122

23 HELL STONE LONG BARROW   Neolithic
   Portesham   178 (SY: 606867)
By footpath 0·8 km north-east of Portesham.

This picturesque chambered long barrow is about 27 m long and 1·5 m high near the sarsen stone burial chamber which was wrongly restored by Martin Tupper in the last century. There are traces of a peristalith close to the chamber.

R.C.H.M. Dorset II **3** (1970) 432

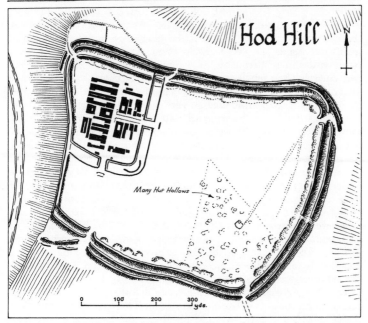

Fig. 9   Hod Hill hillfort, Dorset, with Roman fort in north-west corner

24 HOD HILL HILLFORT (Fig. 9)   Iron Age and Roman
    Stourpaine   178 (ST:857106)

Footpath uphill from the A350 near Steepleton House or by path from Stourpaine village.

When in the first years of the Roman conquest the future Emperor Vespasian captured twenty hillforts (*oppida*) there can be little doubt that one of the largest of those to fall was Hod Hill. Its ramparts enclose 22 ha in a circuit of 2·4 km. On the north, east and south stands a massive rampart 4·6 m high and backed by quarry scoops. Outside is a ditch 12·2 m wide and 6·1 m deep, and beyond that an outer rampart and ditch. Only on the steeper western slope is the fortification reduced to a single rampart and ditch representing an unfinished stage in the earthwork's history. Two ancient entrances break the defences. The largest at the northern end of the western rampart, known as the Steepleton Gate, does not appear to be very strong; it is slightly inturned and has a massive hornwork which prevents a frontal attack. The South-west Gate lies at the western end of the southern rampart. It seems to have been a simple 'water gate' down to the river Stour, 106·7 m below. Nevertheless it is protected by an extra line of rampart on its southern side. Excavation has shown that the existing earthworks represent the final stage in a sequence of at least three major periods of development. At first a box-like rampart faced with timber at front and back, and filled with chalk from a ditch, had encircled the whole hilltop. Later this rampart was enlarged in glacis form. Chalk from quarry pits behind the rampart was piled over the existing rampart to create an earthwork 10·7 m wide and 3·4 m high. This defence had a rampart wall 3·1 m wide at its top. At the same time as the rampart was enlarged a palisade was set up outside the old ditch. Soon, however, the ditch was redug and enlarged and the palisade covered by an outer bank of earth. In its final prehistoric phase the main rampart was topped by a flint-paved walk which increased the rampart height to 4·6 m and its width to 13·7 m. At this time a further outer ditch was commenced, but at the time of the Roman attack had only been completed round three-quarters of the fort. Inside the hillfort were hundreds of huts and allied structures. The hollows of some of these can still be seen in the unploughed south-eastern corner of the fortress. All except one of the huts excavated were circular, and one enclosed by a rectangular palisade may have been the home of some person of importance: perhaps a chieftain.

The Romans seem to have conquered the fort with *ballista* fire, concentrated on the area of the chieftain's hut. There is no evidence for a direct assault and we may conclude that capitulation and surrender were quickly agreed on. The occupants of the fort seem to have been driven off to some open settlement, perhaps in the river valley, and their huts were destroyed.

The Romans then took the unusual step of establishing a fort of their own on the north-west corner of Hod Hill inside the hillfort. Rectangular in shape, it measures 229·5 m by 178·9 m and encloses 4·5 ha. It is well sited to command extensive views in all directions. It had two main gates, the *Porta Praetoria* facing east towards the Steepleton Gate, and a *Porta Principalis Dextra* facing the native South-west Gate. In addition a water gate was cut through the native rampart at the north-west corner to enable drinking water to be obtained for men and beasts from the river below. Towers stood at each gate as well as at the south-eastern corner of the fort. Accommodation within the camp was cramped, suggesting that occupation was not intended to be permanent, but was sufficient to support a legionary detatchment of some 600 men and an auxiliary cavalry unit of about 250 men. It included the *Principia* or Headquarters Building, the houses of the Legionary Centurion and Cavalry Commander, Legionary and Cavalry Barracks, a hospital and various minor buildings. None of these are visible today, although the Roman fortifications, slighter than those of the Iron Age, are clearly visible. On the evidence of coins and pottery the Roman occupation of Hod Hill almost certainly belongs to the years A.D. 43–51: the first few years of the conquest. It was extensively excavated between 1951 and 1958, and most of the finds are in the British Museum.

Ian Richmond: *Hod Hill* **2** (1968)

25 JORDAN HILL TEMPLE   Roman
   Weymouth   178 (SY:698821)

Approached by a footpath from the A353 at SY:695821.

On the crest of the hill overlooking Weymouth Bay are the footings of a small Roman building, 76 m square, with walls 1·1 m thick. In all probability this was a Roman temple, for outside it to the north and north-east a cemetery of some eighty burials was uncovered by J. Medhurst, who first dug the site in 1843. In the south-eastern corner of the building was a rectangular shaft 3·7 m deep. At its base was a stone cist holding two urns, a sword and spearhead and various domestic objects. Above it were sixteen layers of ash and charcoal, each separated from the next by layers of roofing slabs, and each containing the bones of a single bird and a Roman coin. The birds were identified as ravens, crows, starlings and buzzards. Such a deposit clearly had some religious function. The temple was surrounded by an enclosure, but its size has not been determined. It seems to have been mainly used in the 4th and early 5th centuries A.D. After re-excavation in 1931–2 the temple was consolidated by the Inspectorate of Ancient Monuments, and is now cared for by the Department of the Environment. (It can be visited at any time.)

R.C.H.M. Dorset II **3** (1970) 616

26 KINGSTON RUSSELL STONE CIRCLE   Bronze Age
                                                         178 (SY:577878)

Signposted from the top of White Hill, 1·6 km north-east of Abbotsbury. Department of the Environment. Access at any time.

A long walk results in a not very impressive circle of eighteen stones. These gnarled blocks of limestone once stood on end, but now lie scattered around an oval measuring 24·4 by 27·7 m. They are best visited when the crop is off the field.

27 KNOWLTON CIRCLES (Fig. 10; Plate 22)   Neolithic
   Woodlands   179 (SU:025100)

Parking beside the central circle in Lumber Lane, off the B3078.

This group of monuments set roughly in a line and known as the Knowlton Circles are clearly very complex. They consist of a roughly

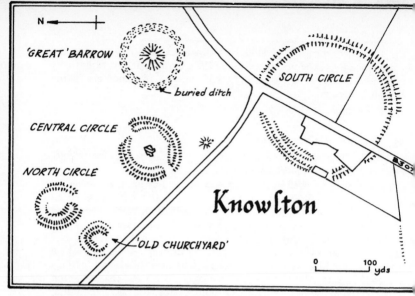

Fig. 10   Knowlton Circles, Dorset

D-shaped enclosure, mistakenly known as the Northern Circle, with a circular site between it and the Lane, 61 m in diameter, called the Old Churchyard. The Central Circle is the most clearly defined and contains the ruins of a 12th-century church with a 15th-century tower. East of this circle is the tree-clad Great Barrow 41·1 m in diameter and 6·1 m high. It is encircled by a ploughed-out quarry ditch, as well as a ditch and outer bank some 152·5 m in diameter about 18·3 m from the base of the mound. A further South Circle straddles the B3078 road and encircles Knowlton Farm. It is 243·8 m in diameter and has its bank outside the ditch. It is best preserved behind the farm.

With the exception of the Great Barrow, the only other monument clearly discernible is the Central Circle, which is maintained by the Department of the Environment in an impeccable condition. The circle is 106·7 m in diameter and consists of an irregular ditch 10·7 m wide, and an upstanding outer bank in places 3·7 m high. Two entrances, at the north-east and south-west, break through the earthworks. That on the north-west is most likely to be original. Like the other circles at Knowlton it is probably a henge monument; a religious centre, whose sanctity has been retained even into the Christian era by the construction of the church at its centre.

Near the road, south of the Central Circle, is a damaged and ploughed round barrow, and aerial photographs have shown many more in the vicinity, especially to the north-east of the Great Barrow.

N. H. Field: *Proc. Dorset N.H.A.S.* **84** (1962) 117

Plate 22   Knowlton Circle and church, Dorset

28   MAIDEN CASTLE HILLFORT (Plates 23, 24)

Neolithic and Iron Age

Winterborne Monkton   178 (SY:669884)

By Maiden Castle Way, south-west from Dorchester. Car-park, and publications hut open in the summer. In the care of the Department of the Environment, and accessible at all times.

'It may be likened', wrote Thomas Hardy, 'to an enormous many-limbed organism of an antidiluvian time, lying lifeless, and covered with a thin green cloth, which hides its substance, while revealing its contour.'

Due to the extensive excavations carried out between 1934 and 1938 by R. E. M. Wheeler this is the best known of the British hillforts. Its history is long and complicated, whilst its great bulk straddles two hilltops.

About 3000 B.C. a neolithic causewayed camp was constructed around the eastern end of the hill on which the later fort lies. It appears to have consisted of two concentric lines of causewayed ditches some 15·2 m apart, most of which were destroyed or buried by the Late Iron Age defences. Towards the close of the neolithic period a unique

Plate 23 *The southern ramparts of Maiden Castle, Dorset*

Plate 24 *The Romano-Celtic temple, Maiden Castle, Dorset*

long mound was constructed across the filled-up ditches of the cause-wayed camp. This mound is 545·6 m long and is flanked by ditches 18·3 m apart, and it runs for three-quarters of the length of the Iron Age fort. It should be added that due to deliberate destruction in antiquity and ploughing, it is difficult to trace today. At the eastern end of this mound were the burials of two six- or seven-year-old neolithic children, accompanied by a small cup. Close by were the dismembered remains of a young man that have recently been shown to be of Anglo-Saxon date (about A.D. 635).

The Iron Age occupation of the hill is more complex, but can be reduced to four apparent phases. At first about 350 B.C. people of early Iron Age culture ringed the eastern hill with a single rampart and ditch, following approximately the line of the causewayed camp and enclosing 6·5 ha. The rampart was faced with timbers at the front and back and was built of chalk quarried from an external ditch 15·2 m wide and 6·1 m deep. It was broken by entrances at the west, and a double entrance with two separate gate passages on the east. About a hundred years later a claw-like extension was built outside the eastern gates, creating barbicans which funnelled traffic into the two entrance passages. At about the same time the whole fort was enlarged to take in the western hill by extending the single rampart and ditch around an area of 19 ha, and providing a new western entrance, also with two passageways and barbican outworks. Period III at Maiden Castle is represented about 150 B.C. by people of Middle Iron Age B culture rebuilding the fortifications on twice their original scale. The rampart was enlarged and reinforced front and back with a stone wall, using material quarried from inside the fort. At the same time the ditch was enlarged to produce a scarp slope from the bottom of the ditch to the rampart crest of 24·4 m. Two additional ramparts and ditches were set out on the south side of the fort, with a further single line along the north. The defences at the entrances were strengthened at the same time. Some time between 100 and 75 B.C. further remodelling took place, in which the new defences of Period III were strengthened and the intricacies of the entrances developed. Further repairs took place at intervals until about A.D. 44 when the fort was attacked by the 2nd Legion under the command of Vespasian. The excavations revealed 54,000 sling-stones gathered from the Chesil Beach 13 km away, which, though quite effective when used against other Iron Age people, could not withstand the Roman artillery, who stormed the east gate, leaving a trail of carnage and destruction. Some of the British dead were later buried at the eastern gateway. The fort continued to be occupied, though not defended, for about another thirty years, until most of the inhabitants had probably been rehoused in the neighbourhood of *Durnovaria*, Roman Dorchester, less than 3 km away.

About A.D. 367 a small Romano-Celtic temple was built inside the northern part of the hillfort. A verandah 12·2 m square, surrounded an inner *cella* 6·1 m square. The interior walls had been plastered and painted, and the floors were tessellated, red on the verandah, and black and white within the sanctuary. Such temples were not un-common in the late 4th century when there appears to have been a pagan revival in the Roman Empire. North of the temple was a small two-roomed house. Both of these structures have been consolidated and are open to view. Objects found during the excavations are dis-played in the Dorset County Museum in Dorchester.

R. E. M. Wheeler: *Maiden Castle, Dorset* (1943)

29   MARTIN'S DOWN BANK BARROW   Neolithic
       Long Bredy   177 (SY:571911)
Footpath up hill at junction of A35 and road to Long Bredy.

This great bank barrow on arable land is best seen to advantage from a neighbouring hilltop. It is 196·6 m long and about 1·8 m high with ditches along either side. It is broken at one point by a gap. There is no record of its having been excavated. About 183 m south-east is a long barrow 35·4 m long and 1·5 m high. A cross-dyke south-west of the bank barrow marks the edge of arable land. Nine round barrows on the hill are in varying states of preservation.

Looking across the A35 from the northern end of Martin's Down one can see a rough standing stone 2 m high at SY:573915. West of the road junction to North Barn are two large bell-barrows, 22·9 m and 27·4 m in diameter, and about 1·8 m high. There is no record of their contents.

R.C.H.M. Dorset I (1952) 41

30   MAUMBURY RINGS   Neolithic and Roman
       Dorchester   178 (SY:690899)
On the south side of Dorchester beside the Weymouth Road (A354).

Excavations by H. St. George Gray between 1908 and 1913 showed that this site is of three periods. Initially it was a neolithic henge monu-ment consisting of an external bank and an irregular ring of pits within it, some more than 9 m deep, and between 2·1 and 4·3 m in diameter. The henge had an entrance at the north-east under the present day entrance. The Romans also used this gap when they redesigned the site as an amphitheatre, 100·6 m in external diameter. At that time they dug away 3·1 m of solid chalk to lower the floor of the arena, creating an oval area 58·5 m by 48·2 m. Seats were probably cut into the chalk banks, and revetted with timber. A gate 3·7 m wide closed the entrance at the north-east side. A rectangular room, perhaps a cage for wild animals, was uncovered on the south-west, opposite the entrance.

The site was again used in 1642 as part of the Parliamentary defence of Dorchester.

R.C.H.M. Dorset II **3** (1970) 589

31 NINE BARROWS   Neolithic and Bronze Age
   Corfe Castle   179 (SY:995816)
By footpath through trees from the B3351 at SY:987823 and climb up to the ridgeway.

A group of seventeen round barrows and a long barrow are strung out along the crest of the ridge. One of the round barrows contained a cremation, but it is not known which. The second barrow from the western end of the group is 14·6 m in diameter and 2·1 m high, and is unusual in having four causeways breaking the ditch. Another barrow in the centre of the group is 27·4 m in diameter and 3·1 m high, with a very wide ditch (6 m) surrounding it. The long barrow, which can be seen in silhouette from the south, is 34·1 m long, 0·9 m high, and 12·2 m wide. There are no records of its contents although it seems to have been opened.

R.C.H.M. Dorset II **3** (1970) 443 (Ailwood Down group)

32 NINE STONES STONE CIRCLE   Bronze Age
   Winterbourne Abbas   178 (SY:610904)
In fenced enclosure on sharp bend of A35 road, west of Winterbourne Abbas.

The peace of what must once have been a quiet sanctuary is now shattered by traffic charging round a bend on a busy main road. Nine irregularly spaced blocks of sarsen stone form a rough circle 8·4 m in diameter. The two largest blocks are 1·8 m and 2·1 m high respectively. The site is best visited in the autumn or spring months when leaves on the encircling trees do not make viewing difficult.

33 OAKLEY DOWN ROUND BARROWS (Fig. 11, Plate 25)
                                               Bronze Age
   Wimborne St. Giles   179 (SU:018173)
Best approached along the Ackling Dyke from the B3081 road at SU:016163.

Visited in early spring when the grass is short, this compact group o more than twenty round barrows provides one of the finest Bronze Age cemeteries in southern England. Almost all the barrows were opened by Sir Richard Colt Hoare at the beginning of the 19th century and the finds are in Devizes Museum. The accompanying plan is numbered according to Colt Hoare. Nos. 1 to 3 are bowl-barrows.

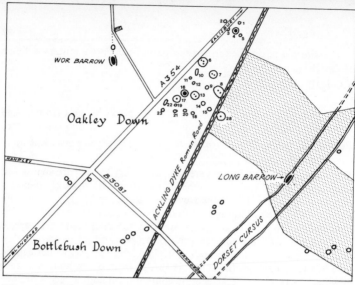

Fig. 11   Oakley Down barrow cemetery, Dorset

Barrow No. 4 is a good example of a bell-barrow, its mound 3·1 m high and 24·4 m in diameter is surrounded by a 3·7 m wide berm and 4·9 m wide ditch. In it lay a skeleton at a depth of 3·7 m, with two others 0·6 m above it. These were accompanied by a small handled vase with four feet, and a bronze dagger. Barrow No. 6 is a disc-barrow with three grave mounds. The central one covered a cremation accompanied by amber and faience beads, all placed in a large urn. The northern mound contained a disturbed cremation, and the southern one a cremation in a small circular pit. No. 7 is also a disc-barrow with two mounds that covered cremations and amber beads. Barrow No. 8 is a large oval disc-barrow, cut by the Roman road, the Ackling Dyke. This barrow also had two burial mounds, both of which covered cremation burials, bronze awls and beads: that furthest from the Roman road contained more than a hundred amber beads and the spacer-plates for a necklace, whilst that to the south held an Aldbourne cup. Bowl-barrow No. 9 was built for a crouched burial who clutched a four-riveted gilt-bronze dagger and four barbed and tanged flint arrow-heads similar to those made in Brittany. At his feet was a 'drinking cup' which Hoare did not bother to preserve. Nos. 10 and 22 are small oval barrows which produced an incense cup and amber beads. Bowl-barrow No. 11 held a cremation, but nothing is recorded from No. 12. One of the two mounds of disc-barrow 13 was excavated and produced a cremation and V-bored button of amber. Nos. 14 and 15 are both bowl-barrows, each about 1·5 m high. The first contained two cremations, one under an inverted urn. Colt

Plate 25 Oakley Down barrow cemetery, Dorset

Hoare found nothing in the bell-barrow 16. No. 17 is a disc-barrow, though the ditch is scarcely visible. It covered a cremation wrapped in cloth, placed beneath a large collared urn whose rim was perforated eleven times, presumably so that a cover could be tied over it. Traces of the fabric were found 'lying like cobwebs on the calcined bones'. The remaining barrows in the group are bowl-barrows, except for No. 28 which is a disc-barrow. Hoare's Nos. 24 to 27 are some distance from the rest of the group.

L. V. Grinsell: *Ancient Burial Mounds of England* (1952) 160

34 PILSDON PEN HILLFORT   Iron Age
    Pilsdon   177 (ST:413013)

From the B3164 road at Lob Gate (ST:414009) it is a short but steep walk uphill to the fort.

Another of the magnificently sited hillforts of Dorset, 900 feet above sea level. Double ramparts and ditches with counterscarp banks surrounded an area of about 3 ha. On the north-western side where the natural slope is absent, a wide space has been introduced between the lines of defence. There seem to have been two original entrances, at the north corner and half way down the south-western side. During recent years excavations have uncovered Iron Age hut sites including one which may have been used as a goldsmith's workshop since it produced a crucible with beads of gold still adhering to it. In the 1st century B.C. a rectilinear building was constructed in the centre of the fort. It seems probable that it was built around four sides of a square. The only completely excavated side was over 54 m long. Before the end of the Iron Age this building had gone, and the square was demarcated by four low banks. Amongst the recent discoveries has been the head of a Roman *ballista* bolt.

P. Gelling: *Proc. Dorset N.H.A.S.* 92 (1971) 126

35 PIMPERNE LONG BARROW   Neolithic
                                                178 (ST:917105)

Approached by bridleway opposite entrance to Blandford Camp on A354 road.

This impressive long barrow is 106·7 m long, 27·4 m wide and 2·4 m high at its south-eastern end. It has pronounced side ditches which are separated from the barrow mound by a berm. There is no record to show that it has been excavated.

36 POOR LOT BARROW CEMETERY   Bronze Age
    Kingston Russell   178 (SY:589907)

South of the A35 between Kingston Russell and Winterbourne Abbas. Good viewpoint from hillside to north.

There are at least forty-four barrows in this necropolis that lies at the junction of the three parishes of Winterbourne Abbas, Kingston Russell and Little Bredy. Closest to the A35 road is a linear cemetery of some twenty barrows of bowl type, together with a fine disc-barrow adjoining a very large ditched bowl-barrow that is 40·2 m in diameter and 3·7 m high. In the field to the south-east of the large bowl-barrow is another disc-barrow, and two bell-disc barrows of a local type intermediate between bell and disc.

Continuing 183 m further up the hill beside the fence a second line of barrows is reached, of which the largest, a bell-barrow, straddles the fence. It is 35·4 m across and 3·4 m high, and shows signs of disturbance. Adjoining it on the east is a small disc-barrow, beyond which lies a pond-barrow, a bell- and a further disc-barrow. Midway between this cemetery and the first lies another small bell-barrow 18·3 m in diameter and 1·5 m high. North of this are traces of two pond-barrows, the only sites in the group of which we have any excavation records. Both contained flint paving and small pits, but no trace of burials.

Nearly 0·8 km south-east of these cemeteries on the crest of the

ridge are two long barrows or bank barrows, of which the most
northerly is 95·1 m long, 13·7 m wide and 1·8 m high at its eastern end.
The southern example is 106 m long, 13·1 m wide and 1·5 m high at its
south-eastern end. It is cut by a modern trackway. Both barrows are
lower to the west, and have clear side ditches.

Before leaving the Poor Lot group note should be taken of the disc-
barrow and ditched triple-bowl-barrow in the field north-east of the
A35. The latter barrow lies at the corner of a flight of Celtic fields
(SY:592908). A twin bell-barrow with mounds 2·1 m high covered
with bushes and trees also lies north of the road (SY:591906).

L. V. Grinsell: *Dorset Barrows* (1959) various

37 POUNDBURY HILLFORT (Plate 26)   Iron Age and Roman
  Dorchester   178 (SY:683912)
*Reached by gates from the Poundbury Road, leading north-west from
Dorchester.*

Plate 26 Poundbury Camp, Dorset. Aqueduct above railway on right

This 5·7 ha hillfort lies 3 km north of Maiden Castle, and overlooks
the river Frome to the north and Dorchester to the east. It was originally
defended by two ramparts and ditches on all sides, but a number of

events seem to have destroyed quite a lot of the outer defences. Excavations in 1938 showed that the earliest rampart constructed in the Iron Age A period had been faced with vertical timbers above a V-shaped ditch 8·8 m deep and 4·3 m wide. Later in the middle of the 1st century B.C. a dumped glacis rampart had been piled over the earlier one, and a second bank and ditch constructed outside. At the same time quarry ditches inside the camp provided chalk blocks to revet the inner and outer faces of the inner bank. The only original entrance appears to be that in the centre of the eastern side, above the railway tunnel that cuts under the site. An extensive Roman cemetery existed to the north-east outside this gate and is at present (1971) under excavation.

On the north of Poundbury the outer rampart and ditch have been destroyed by the construction of a *Roman aqueduct* which carried water for some 19 km from the river Frome at Notton Mill (SY:609958) to *Durnovaria* (Dorchester). This aqueduct which ran along the southern side of the Frome valley, following each re-entrant valley, allowed the water to drop some 7·6 m between the source and the town. For most of its length the aqueduct formed an unlined ditch 1·5 m wide and 0·9 m deep with a bank on its outer edge. It has been estimated that it would have discharged 55,150,000 litres (12,958,000 gallons) of water each day. Today it can be seen as a terrace at a number of points along the Frome valley, but it is best preserved along the sides of the two combes west of Whiffield Farm at Fordington Bottom between SY:671917 and SY:674914, and from there it can be easily traced all the way to Poundbury where it forms a terrace along the north side of the camp. This can be particularly well seen from the north-west corner of Poundbury, or the A37 road to the north. From Poundbury the aqueduct ran along the 250 feet contour to discharge its water near the West Gate of Dorchester.

R.C.H.M. Dorset II **3** (1970) 487, 585

38 POVINGTON HEATH BARROW CEMETERY   Bronze Age
    Tyneham   178 (SY:876840)
Beside the B3070 between Lulworth and Wareham. This road is often closed without notice by the army.

These barrows, of which some twenty-four have been recorded on the Heath north of the Purbeck Hills, have been much damaged by the army, who continue to play at soldiers in this area, much to the annoyance of the general public. The Five Barrow group does in fact consist of six barrows running in a straight line from north to south along the summit of the ridge. The three barrows nearest the road are bowl-barrows, the second being 1·2 m high and 18·3 m in diameter. Then follow three bell-barrows, each about 1·8 m high, and more than

30·5 m in diameter. There are twin bowl-barrows enclosed by an oval ditch 3·1 m wide east of the B3070 at SY:8880841, on the summit of a slight hill.

R.C.H.M. Dorset II **3** (1970) 455

39 RAWLSBURY CAMP   Iron Age
       Stoke Wake and Hilton   178 (ST:767057)

A metalled road between Hazelbury Bryan and Bulbarrow Hill passes the site. Gate at ST:767059.

Situated on the western spur of Bulbarrow Hill, this pear-shaped hillfort of 1·6 ha commands breath-taking views across the Vale of Blackmoor. Two banks with a ditch in between form the essential part of the defences, though an outer ditch has been added on the west side. Although together at the west and south-east, the ramparts separate on the north and south to leave a space for enclosures up to 21·3 m wide between them. A number of trackways on the north side of the hill have damaged the earthwork. A wooden cross stands beside the entrance at the eastern end facing Bulbarrow. Here the rampart turns outwards to create a long elaborate entrance passageway, similar to that at Eggardon. The initial occupation of the fort probably dates from the mid 3rd century B.C., and there are slight depressions near its centre that may represent huts (on the southern side of the hedgerow). 152 m east of the fort and almost certainly related to it is a dyke 36·6 m long across the hill-spur.

R. A. H. Farrar: *Proc. Dorset N.H.A.S.* **76** (1954) 94

40 RINGMOOR SETTLEMENT   Iron Age
       Turnworth   178 (ST:809085)

Bridle road off the minor road between Okeford Fitzpaine and Winter-borne Stickland at ST:817084 leads to settlement at west end of wood.

A small oval enclosure 45·7 m by 33·5 m is surrounded by a bank and ditch with traces of an outer bank on the western side. There are signs of possible hut platforms on the western side. On the east, facing down the hill-slope, is an entrance with an outer flanking enclosure on the south. Ancient embanked trackways approach the enclosure and pass it on its north and west sides. The latter almost certainly linked with a second ploughed-out enclosure close by, now only visible from the air. There are extensive Celtic fields to the east and west.

A cross-dyke on Bell Hill, 0·8 km to the west (ST:797080) may have been connected with the settlement. It has been almost totally destroyed but can just be traced in the pasture south-east of the bridleway.

R.C.H.M. Dorset III **2** (1970) 291

41 SHAPWICK ROUND BARROW   Bronze Age
   Sturminster Marshall   179 (ST:934016)

Across fields from the A350 and close to power cables.

Opened in 1838, this round barrow contained a probable primary
cremation in a large pit covered by a flint cairn. Amongst the ashes
were 'ruby-coloured barrel-shaped glass beads'. The excavation took
eight days, and was the subject of the famous poetic dialogue *The
Barrow Diggers: a dialogue in imitation of the Grave Diggers in Hamlet*
by Charles Woolls:

> 'With Popish Tricks, and Relics rare,
> The Priests their Flocks do gull,
> In casting out the earth take care,
> Huzza! I've found a skull.'

L. V. Grinsell: *Dorset Barrows* (1959) 132

42 SMACAM DOWN SETTLEMENT   Iron Age
   Cerne Abbas   178 (SY:657994)

*By path west from the A352 at SY:663998. In bushes on crest of the hill
south of the path.*

This well-preserved little farming settlement is unusual in that the
adjoining field systems can be clearly seen to be related to it. The main
feature is a kite-shaped enclosure about 45·7 m by 36·6 m, with a
hut circle, about 10·7 m in diameter, inside. Outside the enclosure
to the west is a long barrow about 30·5 m long and 1·5 m high, whilst
54·9 m to the north-east of the enclosure is a low bowl-barrow 11 m in
diameter. The settlement is bounded on the west by a strongly marked
cross-ridge dyke with a ditch on the western side. All sides of the valley
to the south are stepped with Celtic fields and lynchets, facing east
towards the river Cerne.

R.C.H.M. Dorset I (1952) 83

43 SPETISBURY RINGS   Iron Age
   Spetisbury   178 (ST:915020)

Footpath south from Spetisbury under railway bridge.

This is a 2 ha fort protected by a single rampart and ditch on the
northern end of a spur overlooking the river Stour about 91 m away.
There is a simple entrance gap on the north-west, where the rampart
ends are turned slightly outwards. There are indications that the earthwork is unfinished, particularly on the north-east, near the railway.
It was this railway in 1857 that destroyed the north-eastern section of
the fort, and revealed a mass-grave of about 120 skeletons. They may

have been victims of a Roman advance perhaps connected with the construction or strengthening of the fort.

C. A. Gresham: *Arch. J.* **96** (1939) 114

44 THICKTHORN LONG BARROWS   Neolithic
   Gussage St. Michael   179 (ST:971123)

Beside the road. Gate at ST:972122.

These two long barrows lie under pasture close to the south-western end of the Dorset Cursus. The longer northern barrow is 45·7 m long, 20·4 m wide and 2·1 m high, and is surrounded by a U-shaped ditch. As far as is known it is unopened. The second barrow (to the south-east) is only 30·5 m long, 18·3 m wide, and also 2·1 m high with a horseshoe-shaped ditch. It was totally excavated in 1933 and proved surprising in that it contained no primary burial, although a turf structure in the centre may at some time may have held burials before the chalk mound was piled over the top. The ditch was broken at its south-eastern end by a causeway 18·3 m wide, on which were found three post holes, again possibly connected with part of the burial ritual. Pottery of Windmill Hill type indicated a date around 3500 B.C. for the barrow. This, together with two chalk phalli, found in the ditch, is now in the Dorset County Museum. Later, at least three secondary burials were added to the south-western side of the mound. In a shallow grave a young woman of about twenty and a child were buried in a crouched position, accompanied by a pottery beaker. Close by was the burial of a girl of seventeen or eighteen, also with a beaker.

C. D. Drew and S. Piggott: *P.P.S.* **2** (1936) 77

45 VALLEY OF STONES   Iron Age
   Littlebredy   178 (SY:597877)

Footpath between Littlebredy Farm and minor cross-roads to south-east, 1·2 km west of Hardy Monument.

Many of the sarsen stones used in the megalithic monuments of southern Dorset must have originated in this valley, left behind as the result of glacial action in the Ice Ages. On the sides of the valley are a fine series of Celtic fields ranging in area from 0·8 to 0·5 ha and bounded by lynchets, some as much as 3·7 m high.

R.C.H.M. Dorset II **3** (1970) 624

46 WOODBURY HILLFORT   Iron Age
   Bere Regis   178 (SY:856948)

Approached from minor road on east side of Bere Regis.

A single rampart and ditch with a counterscarp bank enclose the summit of this flat-topped hill. On the north where the hill is connected to the main spur, the counterscarp bank lies 61 m forward of the main rampart, but is badly damaged by ploughing. The entrance seems to have been at the point where the modern farm road enters the fort. The site commands extensive views, especially over Wareham Forest to the south-east.

R.C.H.M. Dorset II **3** (1970) 484

47 WOR BARROW LONG BARROW Neolithic
Handley 179 (SU:012173)

North-west of A354, on left of drive to Oakley Farm, which should be followed as far as first houses, then double-back beside hedgerow to barrow.

Following the total excavation of Wor Barrow by General Pitt-Rivers in 1893–4, the excavated earth was placed in piles on three sides of the site, where it remains today. The area covered by the barrow mound is now quite flat, and the ditches which Pitt-Rivers cleared out to their full depth of 4·0 m and width of 5·5 m, have partially silted up again. The excavation showed that there were two distinct phases in the barrow's building.

At first a rectangular wooden mortuary enclosure measuring 27·4 m by 10·7 m was set up, with a narrow entrance passage at its south-eastern end. Outside the enclosure a shallow ditch was dug in a series of connected pits, surrounding an area about 42·7 m by 27·4 m. Inside the mortuary enclosures two large posts were set up with three articulated male burials between them; then turves were placed over the bodies to form some kind of turf hut. Outside the hut, but within the enclosure, the bones of three other burials were piled, 'the limb-bones being laid out by the side of the skulls'.

Next a new ditch, the one to be seen today, was dug in four sections, destroying most of the earlier one. The chalk derived from this was piled up over the mortuary enclosure and turf hut, to form the long barrow mound which originally reached 45·7 m in length and was perhaps 6·1 m high, although this height had been reduced to 3·8 m by the time of the excavation.

The finds from this, and most of Pitt-Rivers's other excavations, are in the important private Pitt-Rivers Museum at Farnham in Dorset, which regrettably is closed to the public.

S. Piggott: *Neolithic Cultures of the British Isles* (1954) 54

Museums containing archaeological material

Bridport Museum and Art Gallery, South Street, Bridport
Dorset County Museum,* Dorchester
Poole Museum, South Road, Poole
Priest's House Museum, High Street, Wimborne Minster

* Main county collection

1 AMBERSBURY BANKS · Iron Age
Epping Forest · 161 (TL:438004)

*In the northern part of the Forest, east of the A11, opposite and slightly
north of the road to Upshire.*

A single rampart and ditch with traces of a counterscarp bank surround
a shield-shaped area of 4·5 ha. Early excavation of the ditch showed it to
be V-shaped, 3·1 m deep and 6·7 m wide. The bank, which is much
damaged, varies in height between 1·2 m and 2·1 m. A stream rose
inside the fort, thus providing a water supply: an unusual feature in
most hillforts, although also present at Loughton to the south (No. 7,
page 112). The entrance was probably on the west. That at the south-
west, though inturned, is apparently medieval.

R.C.H.M. Essex **2** (1921) 64

2 BARTLOW HILLS · Roman
Ashdon · 148 (TL:586448)

*Signposted footpath on road from Bartlow to Ashdon, close to the old
Bartlow Station.*

This is undoubtedly the finest group of Roman barrows in Britain.
There were originally eight steep-sided mounds in the cemetery, but
one was destroyed in the 16th century and three more in 1832. The
four existing barrows stand in a line from north to south; the northernmost being separated from the rest by the old railway line. They were
dug into by John Gage between 1835 and 1840, but unfortunately
most of the objects found in them were destroyed in a fire in 1847.

From north to south the barrows can be described as follows:

1 Beyond the railway line and inaccessible. Standing some 6·1 m high,
this barrow was first dug into by Sir Basil Harwood in 1815,
when he failed to find a burial but uncovered a bronze bowl, an iron
lamp and a bronze strigil (a curved implement used for scraping
dirt and moisture off the skin). These objects are now in Saffron
Walden Museum. John Gage tunnelled into the barrow in April 1840
but abandoned it on discovering that it had already been dug. His
tunnel collapsed in 1930 when a skeleton surrounded by flints was
dislodged.

2 This barrow was 7·6 m high and about 24·4 m in diameter. John
Gage also examined it in April 1840 and found that it had once held
a central wooden chest containing a glass jug and pottery jar, both
filled with cremated bones. It also held a bronze flagon and basin,
an iron lamp, glass and Samian vessels and the petals of a rose or
poppy.

3 This most spectacular barrow is 12·2 m high and 43·9 m in diameter.

In driving his tunnel to the centre from the north-east side in 1835 Gage observed that it had been constructed of alternate layers of earth and chalk. In the middle was a cavity left by the decay of an oak chest that had measured 1·27 m by 1·12 m and 0·6 m high. It contained a cremation in a glass urn, three glass jugs holding liquids (perhaps wine or vinegar), two long-necked scent phials, two bronze strigils, a bronze jug with silver inlay and a handle shaped like a sphinx, and an enamelled casket, rather like a biscuit barrel, elaborately coloured in red, green and blue. A folding stool with a leather seat had also been included in the chest. Leaning on the outside of the box was a globular wine jar filled with more cremated bones.

4 Opened in April 1838, this overgrown barrow, still 11·3 m high and 30·5 m in diameter, also contained a wooden chest and a cremation in a glass urn. A bronze jug and elaborate saucepan were found wrapped in linen. These were probably supplied for the funeral feast which also included chicken bones in a Samian bowl. An unusual feature was the preservation of a wreath of box leaves wrapped round the handle of an iron lamp. Gage noticed that this barrow, also, was constructed of alternate layers of chalk and earth.

An earthwork lying between the barrows, the river Granta and Bartlow church, may have formed some kind of cemetery boundary. It is likely that all the mounds were the family tombs of Romano-British nobility living in the vicinity.

M. R. Hull: *V.C.H. Essex* **3** (1963) 39

3   BRADWELL ROMAN FORT   Roman
     Bradwell-juxta-Mare   162 (TL:031082)
3 km north-east of Bradwell-on-Sea along the Roman road.

This fort of the Saxon Shore has tentatively been identified as *Othona* listed in the Roman *Notitia Dignitatum*, and probably founded under Carausius (A.D. 286–93). It lies at the extreme eastern end of Bradwell Point on the south side of the river Blackwater, on a creek that has long been silted up. Most of the fort has been destroyed by erosion, and only about 2 ha remain. It must originally have been 158·5 m long on its west and east sides, but its width is unknown. Part of the walls survives to the south of the chapel. It is 3·7 m thick and 1·2 or 1·5 m high. There is a circular bastion at the north-west angle 4·6 m in diameter, and an interval tower 38·1 m to the south. The interior of the fort is ploughed.

The chapel, built largely of Roman material, is St. Peter-on-the-Wall. It is almost certainly the original building erected by St. Cedd about A.D. 654.

4 CAMULODUNUM (Fig. 12)   Iron Age and Roman
   Colchester   149 (TL:995253 centre)

Shortly after 10 B.C. the Iron Age kingdom of the Trinovantes of
Essex was overrun by the Catuvellauni of Hertfordshire, under their
leader Tasciovanus. Addedomaros, king of the Trinovantes had
established his capital at Camulodunum, but it was Tasciovanus who
was the first to put the name of the settlement CAMV on his coins.
However, the Catuvellaunian conquest was short-lived and coins of
Addedomaros soon appear, to be followed by Dubnovellaunus of
Kent in about A.D. 1. By A.D. 10 Cunobelin, son of Tasciovanus, had
become king of the whole of south-east England, which he ruled from
Camulodunum until his death about A.D. 42.

There was nothing very remarkable about the actual town of
Camulodunum. It consisted of a collection of round and rectangular
huts of wood daubed with clay, situated around what today is Sheepen
Farm. It was bounded on the north, east and south by the rivers
Colne and Roman River. To the west were a series of dykes which can
be assigned to two main periods. The earliest protects the area around
Gosbeck's Farm (TL:965225). This earthwork is largely destroyed,
although it is visible between Oliver's Thicks Wood and Chest Wood
where it crosses the river. The later dykes, which are rectilinear in
plan, and at least three in number, protect the Sheepen area, which
was probably Cunobelin's main settlement after A.D. 10. Some
sections of these later dykes are still visible and include the *Lexden
Dyke*, part of which in Bluebottle Grove is owned by the Department
of the Environment (TL:965245). This same dyke extends north across
the river Colne where it is known as *Moat Farm Dyke*. Parts of
Gryme's Dyke which runs from the river Colne at TL:956267 to Layer
de la Haye (TL:965200) can also be followed. Probably the latest of the
dykes is that known as the *Triple Dyke*. It seems to have been a Roman
adaptation of an earlier example. The best section is in the care of the
Department of the Environment in Lexden Straight Road (TL:965246)
from where it runs south to the river Colne.

In A.D. 43 Camulodunum fell to the Legions of Claudius, and the
Emperor himself was present when the capital was entered. In A.D.
49–50 Claudius created it a *colonia* which was named COLONIA CLAUDIA
VICTRICENSIS. This was a settlement for retired veteran soldiers, each
of whom was given a home and a small plot of land. We know little
about the layout of this early town although Tacitus records that it
contained a Senate House, theatre and temple dedicated to Claudius
himself. The huge masonry base of this temple still lies buried beneath
Colchester Castle. It measures 32 m long by 24·4 m wide and 3·4 m
high, with a further 4 m below ground. The two vaults inside this
platform can still be visited. The Norman Castle above them houses
the fine Colchester and Essex Museum.

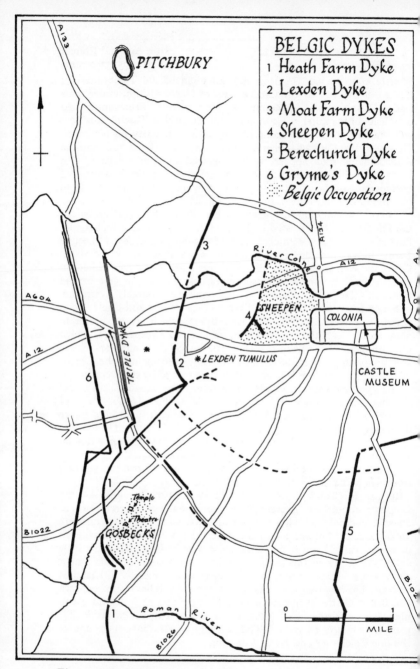

Fig. 12   The Colchester region, Essex

In A.D. 60 the town was destroyed by the Iceni, led by their Queen Boudicca. The veteran Roman soldiers, caught unawares, barricaded themselves in the temple of Claudius. After a two-day siege, the building was burnt, the soldiers killed and the town ransacked. After the rebellion, when law and order was once more established, the town began to be rebuilt, although its position on the east coast, many miles from the main arteries of Britain, was to prevent it from ever becoming the provincial capital.

Between A.D. 110 and 120 stone walls were constructed round the town enclosing 43·7 ha. They still survive today for much of their course, built of alternate layers of tiles and *septaria* (clay nodules). Six gateways entered the town: that on the western side, the *Balkerne Gate*, still has two arches surviving and a northern tower 6·1 m high. Unfortunately, half the gate lies buried beneath the 'King's Head'. Good sections of the wall survive in Balkerne Lane and on Balkerne Hill, along Park Folley and inside Castle Park. The excavated remains of a small gate can be seen at the north-east corner of Holly Tree Meadows. Part of the Roman wall containing a drain outlet is visible in an alley on the east side of St. James's churchyard. Other stretches are in Priory Street and Vineyard Street, where bastions were added, probably during the reign of Richard II.

In Holly Tree Meadows, north-east of the Castle, can be seen a subterranean room measuring 11·9 m by 5·9 m, that might have been a Mithraeum: a shrine for the practice of a popular eastern cult favoured by soldiers. There is little else to see of the Roman town, though the museum should not be missed with its remarkable collection of mosaics, tombstones and other objects from the neighbourhood.

J. and D. T.-D. Clarke: *Camulodunum* (1972)

5 COLCHESTER (LEXDEN TUMULUS) (See Fig. 12)   Iron Age
    Colchester   149 (TL:975247)
In a garden at the south end of Fitzwalter Road, near its junction with St. Clare Road.

This burial mound, excavated in 1924, produced a number of very rich grave goods, all of which had been damaged by burning. These included a number of high quality bronzes, a garment, perhaps a shirt, embroidered with gold threads, some decorative silver ears of wheat, chain mail, wine jars and a coin of Augustus struck in 17 B.C. mounted as a portrait medallion. It is reasonable to assume that this was the burial mound of Addedomarus himself or one of his relations. There is evidence to show that there were other important graves close by. All the objects found in the Lexden Tumulus are in the Colchester and Essex Museum.

P. Laver: *Archaeologia* **76** (1927) 241

6 DANBURY HILLFORT   Iron Age
   Chelmsford   162 (TL:779052)
South of the A414 around St. John's church.

This small oval fort is in a poor state of preservation. A single rampart and ditch once surrounded it. Today they are best seen on the
west in front of the Rectory, although the whole of their course can
just be made out, except on the north. Most of it is tree-covered. The
church lies in the eastern half of the camp, as does the water tank.

7 LOUGHTON CAMP   Iron Age
   Epping Forest   161 (TQ:418975)
*In Epping Forest, 0·8 km east of the A11 and 0·8 km north-west of
Loughton church.*

Oval in shape and 2·6 ha in extent, this fort is surrounded by a single
rampart and ditch. On the west and south-west the ground drops
steeply, adding to the natural strength of that side. The ditch has been
destroyed by a road on the west. On the north it is V-shaped and 2·7 m
deep and to the south 2·1 m deep. The original entrance has not been
identified. A stream rises in marshy ground in the south-east corner.
This is an unusual feature, although it is found at Ambersbury Banks
to the north. Excavations were carried out in 1882 by General Pitt-
Rivers.

R.C.H.M. Essex **2** (1916) 165

8 MERSEA MOUNT   Roman
   West Mersea, Mersea Island   149 (TM:023143)
At Barrow Hill Farm. Preserved by the Mersea Island Society.

This Romano-British burial mound, 33·5 m in diameter and 6·1 m
high, was excavated by the Morant Club in 1912. The barrow was
composed of sand and gravel. Near its centre a brick vault, constructed
of Roman tiles was found. It measured 45·7 cm square and 53·3 cm
high with a domed brick roof. Inside was a lead casket 0·3 m square
containing a pale green glass bowl which held the cremated remains of
an adult. Dated to the latter half of the 1st century A.D., they are now
in the Colchester and Essex Museum. There is a local belief that the
barrow is haunted by a centurion who walks the Strood.

R.C.H.M. Essex **3** (1922) 229

9 PITCHBURY RAMPARTS   Iron Age
   Great Horkesley   149 (TL:966290)
*Approached along the edge of the wood from minor road between Horkesley
Heath and Westwood Park.*

This once large oval earthwork has been almost completely destroyed. Only in Pitchbury Wood does a section of rampart, ditch and counterscarp, 183 m long, still survive. Here the rampart is about 3·1 m high and the ditch 15·2 m wide. A gap at the north-west may be an original entrance.

R.C.H.M. Essex **3** (1922) 128

10 RING HILL   Iron Age
Littlebury   148 (TL:515382)
Between the A11 and the railway, west of Audley End.

This oval fort of 6·67 ha is completely overgrown with trees. The ground drops away from it on all sides except the north-west, but there seems to have been no extra effort to defend that side. A ditch about 15 m wide and 4·6 m deep surrounds the fort, but the inner rampart and counterscarp bank have been much flattened. There are four gaps through the ditch, but it is uncertain which is original. That to the north-west seems the most likely.

R.C.H.M. Essex **1** (1916) 191

11 STURMER BARROW   Roman?
Sturmer   148 (TL:688444)
1·6 km south-east of Haverhill, on the south side of the A604.

Before ploughing this barrow stood 2·4 m high and 36·6 m in diameter. Today the mound is still 1·8 m high, but its soil is scattered. It stands bold and clear on the skyline and was probably Roman in origin: a late 4th-century coin hoard was found in the vicinity. In 1801 Thomas Walford wrote that it was reputed to have been dug, but he could obtain no information about it. The barrow stands near the head of the Stow valley with a Roman road passing close by.

12 WALLBURY CAMP   Iron Age
Great Hallingbury   148 (TL:493178)
Between the Stort and the B1005 west of Little Hallingbury.

Wallbury lies at the western end of a spur overlooking the valley of the river Stort. The ground to the north and south was originally marshy, so that only on the east was really strong defence necessary. In fact two banks and ditches run along the north, east and southern sides of an enclosure 12·5 ha in extent. Above the western slope this defence is single. There are a number of gaps in the defences, but which of these are original is open to doubt without excavation. The rampart and ditch are tree-covered.

R.C.H.M. Essex **2** (1921) 93

Museums containing archaeological material

Bartlow Museum, Bartlow
Chelmsford and Essex Museum, Oaklands Park, Chelmsford
Colchester and Essex Museum,* The Castle, Colchester
Saffron Walden Museum, Museum Street, Saffron Walden

* Main county collection

GLOUCESTERSHIRE

1 AVENING BURIAL CHAMBERS   Neolithic
                                              156 (ST : 879984)

*In Avening village at the foot of a steep bank below minor road off A434,
east of stream and west of Avening Old Rectory.*

The Revd. Nathaniel Thornbury excavated these three burial chambers in 1806 from a long cairn which seems to have lain to the south-
east of the 'Nag's Head' near Avening Court (ST : 895978). The chambers
were removed 'to a grove in the rectory garden' and the cairn was
destroyed. Thornbury found eight skeletons in one chamber and three
in another, together with animal bones.

As re-erected the three chambers from west to east are as follows:

1. 0·9 m wide and 1·5 m long. It has no capstone.
2. 0·9 m wide and 1·73 m long. This chamber is approached by a
   short passage and has a single capstone. It has what may be the
   lower half of a porthole entrance.
3. 2·01 m wide and 1·8 m long, built of six wallstones and roofed by a
   single large capstone. The entrance at the south-east end consists of
   a porthole cut into the adjoining edges of two upright stones, and
   forming a hole 40·6 cm wide and 60·9 cm high. The chamber is
   entered from a passage 0·84 m wide. Porthole entrances have also
   been found at Rodmarton Windmill Tump, about 4·8 km from
   Avening. They were just large enough to allow the passage of a
   corpse, and could easily be blocked with dry-stone.

E. Clifford and G. Daniel: *P.P.S.* **6** (1940) 146

2 BAGENDON EARTHWORKS   Iron Age
                                              157 (SP : 018064)

Off the A435, 0·8 km east of Bagendon village.

The far from impressive earthworks at Bagendon have been identified
with the pre-Roman *oppidum* of the Dobunni. The main earthwork in
Cutham Lane runs down the hill-slope towards a stream. The bank
on the west is some 1·4 m high, whilst to the east of it is a ditch, shown

by excavation to have been V-shaped, 3·2 m wide and 1·8 m deep. There is a much ploughed outer line of rampart in the field east of Cutham Lane. Another line of rampart and ditch climbs the hill beside Welsh Way westwards from Perrot's Brook for about 548 m. Close to the stream, behind these minor ditches, limited excavations have shown that a settlement certainly existed there between A.D. 15 and 60. Coin moulds indicate that a mint flourished there between A.D. 20 and 30, whilst imported red Italian pottery and bronze and iron brooches of continental workmanship show that the site was of some importance.

1·6 km north of Perrot's Brook is a more substantial line of earth-works facing south known as *Scrubditch* (SP:010077). Its bank still stands 3·1 m high, and it would appear once to have cut off the spur between Merchants' Downs and North Cerney. It would seem more logical to locate the *oppidum* north of this dyke, and future excavation may well do so, perhaps showing a move south after the Dobunni came under the control of the Catuvellauni about A.D. 15.

E. Clifford: *Bagendon* (1960)

---

3 BECKBURY CAMP   Iron Age
   Hailes Abbey   144 (SP:064299)
Approached by tracks through Hailes Wood from the Hailes to Farmcote minor road.

Prominently situated on the edge of the Cotswolds, overlooking the Vale of Evesham, this small rectangular promontory fort is defended on the north and west by steep scarp slopes. A rampart and silted ditch on the east and south enclose about 1·8 ha. At the northern end of the eastern rampart a short length of dry-stone walling is exposed. This may be part of the facing wall. The most likely entrance was by the hollow-way at the north-west corner, although access might have been possible around the north-east and south-west rampart ends.

---

4 BELAS KNAP CHAMBERED CAIRN   Neolithic
   Charlton Abbots   144 (SP:021254)
Signposted from minor road at SP:022261. Small lay-by, and steep climb and walk of nearly 1·6 km. Department of the Environment. Open at any time.

Hidden behind a wall until one is almost upon it, this beautifully restored chambered cairn is well worth the long walk to reach it. Measuring 51·8 m long, 18·3 m wide and 3·7 m high at the broad northern end, it is enclosed by a dry-stone revetment wall. This curves round at the north to create a deep funnel-shaped forecourt. At the inner end of this is a blind or false entrance composed of two upright

portal stones with a lintel above, and a partial blocking stone below.
Four burial chambers have been found in the cairn; two symmetrically
opposite each other about half-way along each side, a third near the
south-eastern end, and a fourth, rather doubtfully restored, in the
narrow southern end. The two northern chambers are polygonal in
plan and probably had corbelled roofs. They seem to have been entered
by narrow dry-stone passages. The south-east chamber was probably
rectangular, measuring 2·7 m by 1·1 m. It had a flat roof and was
entered by a dry-stone walled passage. There is doubt about the original
shape of the southern chamber as only one original stone is now in
place. When excavated in 1863–5 and 1928–30 the remains of about
thirty people were found in the burial chambers, and a man's skull and
the bones of five children were found in the rubble-blocking behind
the blind entrance. This false door may have been part of an elaborate
ritual entrance designed to fool evil spirits or more mundane tomb
robbers. The name Belas Knap dates at least from 14th century and
means the Beacon Mound. A few bones and flints from the cairn are
exhibited in the church porch museum at Winchcombe; the rest of the
surviving material is in Cheltenham Museum.

There is a small ploughed-down round barrow in the field to the
west of Belas Knap.

L. V. Grinsell: *Belas Knap* (1966) (D. of E. pamphlet)

5 BLACKPOOL BRIDGE ROMAN ROAD   Roman
    Forest of Dean   156 (SO:653087)
Minor road north off B4431, beyond former railway bridge.

A stretch of paved Roman road about 2·4 m wide, with a kerbstone
edging and traces of wheel tracks, has been uncovered just inside the
woods. It was part of the industrial road system that linked Ariconium
(SO:645235) near Bromsash with Caerwent and Caerleon on the south
coast of Wales. At *The Scowles*, 6·4 km south-west of Blackpool
Bridge (SO:605047) are traces of what are believed to be Roman
iron workings, though the evidence is very slight.

6 BLAISE CASTLE HILLFORT   Iron Age
    Bristol   156 (ST:559784)
On the Blaise Castle estate, south-west of the Folk Museum.

Blaise Castle (built 1768) stands in a clearing surrounded by trees.
There are steep slopes on all sides, particularly the south, and the
double banks and ditches of the hillfort lie along the north and west.
Traces of dry-stone walling can be seen in places. There is no clear
indication of an original entrance, but recent trial excavations in the
interior have produced much Middle Iron Age pottery, brooches and
storage pits, indicating that occupation had begun by the 3rd century

B.C. There was also Roman and medieval settlement. The small fort
on King's Weston Hill, 0·4 km south-west (No. 22, page 126) seems to
have preceded Blaise Castle, exhibiting Early Iron Age traditions.

P. Rahtz: *P.U.B.S.S.* **8** (1959) 147

7 BLOODY ACRE CAMP   Iron Age
   Cromhall   156 (ST:689915)
*In Tortworth Park (H.M. Prison) beside minor road 0·8 km north of
Cromhall.*

Occupying a wooded spur of about 4 ha, this triangular promontory
fort is protected by natural slopes on the north-east and south-east.
Two strong lines of bank and ditch curve across the western side of
the promontory. These are strengthened on the south-west by a third
line of bank and ditch. In all cases the ditches are very silted. A gateway
seems to lie at the northern end of the ramparts where the inner two
banks turn eastward forming an inturned entrance.

8 BRACKENBURY DITCHES   Iron Age
   North Nibley   156 (ST:747949)
*Wooded site beside the B4060 road. Approached by footpaths from North
Nibley and Wotton Hill.*

Covered by thick woodland, this small triangular promontory fort of
3·2 ha is protected by two widely spaced banks and ditches on the
east, where it faces the relatively flat main land mass. A single rampart
and ditch surrounds the rest of the hilltop. An entrance on the south is
approached by a hollow-way. A number of pits in the vicinity are
considered to have been caused by geological action.

9 BURY HILL CAMP   Iron Age and Roman
   Winterbourne Down   156 (ST:652791)
Approached from minor road at Moorend.

Two walls built of rubble but faced with dry-stone and separated by a
U-shaped ditch 6·1 wide and 1·5 m deep, form the only defence for
this pear-shaped 2 ha fort. The western side has recently been quarried
for the local pennant stone. Excavation in the interior in 1926 revealed
abundant Romano-British material, but little of earlier periods. It is
therefore uncertain which of the three entrances to the fort belong to
the initial Iron Age structure. These gates occur in the north-east,
north-west and south-east corners. A well south of the north-west
gate, and a long mound (which covers a house) near the centre on the
western side of the fort, are both Romano-British. As yet there is no
accurate date for the founding of the camp.

J. A. Davies and C. W. Phillips: *P.U.B.S.S.* **3** (1926) 8

10 CHEDWORTH ROMAN VILLA (Fig. 13, Plate 27)   Roman
                                                   144 (SP:053134)

*Off the A429 at Fossebridge along narrow lane signposted via Yanworth
to Withington road. (Not road to Chedworth village.) National Trust
property. Open 10.00 to 13.00 hours, 14.00 to 19.00 hours daily (or dusk
if earlier). Closed on Mondays except Bank Holidays, first 15 days of
October and throughout January. Car-park beside villa.*

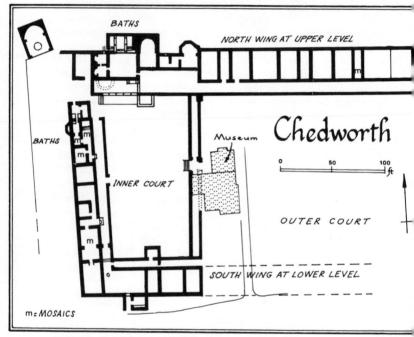

Fig. 13   Chedworth Roman villa, Gloucestershire

Tucked away amongst the woods of a narrow valley that faces east
across the river Coln, the Chedworth villa occupies one of the most
attractive sites in southern England. In the early morning it is easy to
imagine life at the villa when it was occupied during the years between
about A.D. 180 and the late 4th century. Unfortunately in summer,
long lines of cars and coaches blocking the narrow lanes rapidly dispel
the picture.

Accidentally discovered in 1864 the villa has been extensively
excavated, except on the south-east side. The site, beside a spring,
was first occupied by a small house at the head of the valley, with a

detached bath suite at the western end of what was to become the north wing, and a half-timbered building where the south wing now stands. All these buildings were destroyed by fire and later restored early in the 3rd century. At that time the north wing and the bath house were enlarged. Early in the 4th century a continuous corridor was built around the three wings, and was continued across the open eastern side to create an enclosed formal courtyard. Beyond this to the east was an outer courtyard at a lower level through which the

Plate 27   Chedworth Roman villa, Gloucestershire

main entrance probably passed. The southern wing of the existing buildings include the kitchen with adjoining furnace, the bailiff's office and a latrine. This wing could be entered at two levels, from the inner courtyard, or the lower outer courtyard. The west wing of the house included the principal rooms, in particular the dining-room (adjoining the kitchen) with an attractive mosaic floor and painted walls. Like the adjoining rooms to the north, this was heated from below by a hypocaust system. At the end of the west wing was an elaborate bath suite which included cold, warm and hot rooms of Turkish bath type. The north wing contained baths too, and these were later altered to form a Swedish sauna-type of bath in which dry heat was used to make the bathers sweat profusely. Adjoining these to the east, a large dining suite was added in the late 4th century along the north side of the villa, together with a bedroom wing, most of whose rooms were heated by a hypocaust system, although they were later used for more squalid domestic purposes. Outside the villa to the north-west is a spring covered by a shrine of the water goddess and known as the Nymphaeum. This provided the villa with its water and still supplies the present house on the site. Eventually some owners of the villa became Christian and the shrine was altered to include an octagonal basin and Chi-Rho monograms were roughly carved on the stone surround.

The original approach to the villa was probably from the White Way, a minor Roman road, through the wood to the north-west. This track passed close to a prehistoric burial mound from which came a cinerary urn now in the site museum. 0·8 km south-east of the villa, close to the river Coln, stood a square pagan temple which produced the hunting relief which is also exhibited in the museum. On the opposite side of the river valley stood a second villa, of which little is known at present.

The Villa museum was built on the east side of the Inner Court in 1866, soon after the site was discovered. It is small and cramped, but includes a number of important finds from the villa.

I. Richmond: *T.B.G.A.S.* **78** (1959) 5

---

11 CIRENCESTER (CORINIUM DOBUNNORUM)   Roman
                                                           157 (SP:020020)

There is little to see of the Roman town, but the Corinium Museum in Park Street should be visited. (Open weekdays July to September, 10.00 to 13.00 hours, 14.00 to 17.30 hours; October to June, including Saturdays, 10.00 to 13.00, 14.00 to 16.30 hours. Sundays in June to August, 14.00 to 16.30 hours.)

The settlement at Cirencester began when a small fort was established at a river crossing near the Fosse Way. The site was marshy and was soon moved north to an area now bounded by The Avenue, Chester Street, Watermoor Road and St. Michael's Fields.

As with almost all Roman forts, it was not long before a small straggling civilian settlement grew up outside the camp. Soldiers with money in their pockets provided a great attraction for local merchants and small shops and inns soon began to appear. Not long after A.D. 60 native tribesmen began to move from their Dobunnic centre, which may have been at Bagendon (page 114) to the new settlement near the fort. By A.D. 75 the fort was abandoned and pulled down.

Rapidly the civil settlement grew over the ruins, following the normal Roman pattern with a regular grid of streets. Even today roads like Lewis Lane and Watermoor Road follow the course of their Roman predecessors. A *forum* was laid out in the centre of the town, with a *basilica* on its south-east side, 97·5 m long and 21·3 m wide, with a nave, aisles and an apse at the western end. The position of the walls of the apse are marked in the cul-de-sac which opens off the south-east side of The Avenue opposite Tower Street.

During the 2nd century an *amphitheatre* was built on the west side of the town. Oval in shape it measures 48·8 m by 40·8 m and still has grass-covered banks rising 8·2 m high. Excavation has shown that it was first built with timber and earth, but later revetted with stone. It was terraced with low limestone walls which probably supported wooden seats. The two opposing entrances can still be seen, one having a passage 29·3 m long lined with stone walls. The amphitheatre is reached by a footpath in Cotswold Avenue.

In common with most towns in Britain during the second half of the 2nd century, earthen ramparts 4·6 m wide were thrown up with two external ditches and masonry towers, enclosing about 97 ha. The river Churn was diverted to run through the ditches. The Verulamium Gate, with twin carriageways and small round-fronted towers, was built at about the same time as was a bridge over the river Churn, taking the roads to Verulamium and Ratae (Leicester). Soon after A.D. 220 a stone wall 3·1 m thick was inserted into the front of the earthen rampart. A series of external stone bastions were added in the 4th century. Visitors can see parts of the earthen rampart and walls in the Beeches, Watermoor Gardens, south-east of London Road, in the Abbey Gardens and north-west of the London Road.

Excavations within the town have brought to light remains of a number of dwelling houses, though unfortunately none can be seen today. One uncovered in The Avenue in 1968 produced fragments of four patterned mosaics, some of which give clear evidence of the craft of a school of mosaic artists working in the town. This 'Corinian' school was one of the most important in the western Roman Empire in the 4th century, and examples of its mosaics have been found at the Chedworth, Woodchester and North Leigh villas, and numerous other places in the south-west Midlands.

Early in the 4th century Corinium became the provincial capital, and this probably brought about alterations to the forum and basilica, and the construction of new polygonal bastions on the city walls. Evidence of Christianity in the town is provided by the famous word square, which with the addition of the letters Alpha and Omega, forms the cryptogram *Pater noster*. It was found in 1818 scratched on the walls of a Roman house. The town continued to function into the 5th century and may even have survived at the time of the nearby battle of

Dyrham in A.D. 577 when four British kings were defeated and
Cirencester fell into Saxon hands.

P. Brown and A. McWhirr: *Ant. J.* **49** (1969) 222 and earlier reports.

12 CLEEVE HILL PROMONTORY FORT   Iron Age
    Cheltenham   144 (SO:985255)

Long walk across Cleeve Common from the A46 at SO:985269.

The only good thing about constructing a golf course over this little
0·8 ha promontory fort is that the grass of the interior is kept short,
although the two banks and ditches are overgrown. There is a wide
berm between the inner ditch and outer rampart, and no entrance is
now visible. Access was probably obtained round the ends of the
ramparts which have been eroded or quarried away. The precipitous
slope of the west makes no defence there necessary.

A linear dyke runs east to west just south of the trigonometrical
point on the hill 640 m to the north of the fort. It has a ditch on the
south side facing the fort. Since it lies on the same ridge as the much
larger Nottingham Hill to the north, it might possibly demarcate
a boundary between the two sites.

13 CLIFTON DOWN CAMP   Iron Age
    Bristol   156 (ST:566733)

*North of the Clifton suspension bridge. The Observatory stands inside the
fort, which is available at all times.*

This is a semi-circular fort enclosing 1·2 ha. There are two ramparts
and ditches with a counterscarp bank on the east, whilst the precipitous
cliffs of the Avon Gorge on the west make defence unnecessary. The
ramparts are broken by an apparent entrance gap towards their south-
east end, and there may have been another near the cliff edge on the
north-west. Vegetation and old quarry workings make the site difficult
to see clearly. The interior is grass covered, and a low bank running
east by south from a rectangular earthwork in the north-west corner can
be seen. These are believed to be more recent than the hillfort.

Clifton Down Camp is one of three forts sited on promontories
which face each other across the Avon Gorge. Stokeleigh Camp
(Somerset) is described on page 258; the other fort, Burwalls, is largely
destroyed. These camps all seem to be similar in construction and may
be contemporary, but access between them would have been rendered
difficult by the steep Gorge sides, though a ford across the Avon was
known to exist below the suspension bridge until the middle of the
last century.

A. Allcroft: *Earthwork of England* (1908) 63

14 COW COMMON BARROW CEMETERY
                                                    Neolithic and Bronze Age
Swell   144 (SP:135262)

North of minor road from Swell Hill Farm to Chalk Hill. Footpath leaves corner of wood north-eastwards to cross Cow Common.

The Cow Common long cairn is now in a disturbed state, but originally measured about 45 m long, 23 m wide and 1·5 m high. Excavation in 1867 and 1874 showed that it was surrounded by a low dry-stone wall, and that the east end was horned, although there was no indication of a blind or false portal stone. Two chambers were found in the north side which contained the skeletons of ten adults and a child, as well as neolithic pottery spoons and a Roman coin. One of the chambers was oval in shape and had a corbelled roof.

There are some ten round barrows on the Common, all suffering from the encroachment of the plough around their edges. Five form an overlapping row at the west end and were opened by William Greenwell in 1874. Each is about 13·7 m in diameter and 0·9 to 1·2 m high. The most southerly was built to cover a crouched male burial in a stone cist and two Bronze Age cremations in urns. The second barrow had a circular beehive-shaped chamber in it, entered by a passage 6·1 m long from the west. Its contents had been robbed, but it seems to belong to a group of similar corbelled chambers found in this part of Gloucestershire. The other three barrows in the row held cremation burials that seem to have been deposited in cloths secured with bone pins.

W. Greenwell: *British Barrows* (1877) 513, 445

15 CRICKLEY HILL   Neolithic and Iron Age
     Coberley   144 (SO:928161)

National Trust property west of the Air Balloon public house.

This apparently simple promontory fort of about 3·6 ha is enclosed by a main rampart some 2·7 m high at its east end, with a ditch 2·4 m deep on its eastern side. The other sides of the promontory are steep and additional defence there seems unnecessary. Excavation has shown that the defences are of three main periods of building, the earliest in the 6th or 5th century B.C. involving timber lacing, and the last the construction of solid stone bastions with a massive curving hornwork to defend an entrance passage at the north end of the rampart. The timber-laced rampart was destroyed by fire, as was the final entrance late in the Iron Age.

Some 183 m inside the rampart to the west a lesser bank and ditch stretch across the promontory. Examination in 1971 showed this to be part of a neolithic causewayed camp, with ditch sections 1·5 m deep and a bank on the inner western side. A second outer line of cause-

wayed ditches lies some 23 m to the east of this, but they are scarcely
visible on the ground. Pottery of the earliest Windmill Hill neolithic
types, and arrow-heads, were found in the excavations.

P. Dixon: *Crickley Hill Interim Reports* (1969–71)

16 DRUID STOKE BURIAL CHAMBER   Neolithic
    Bristol   156 (ST:561762)

*Near junction of Druid Hill and Druid Stoke Avenue, in garden of house
called 'Cromlech'. Public right of way to the site.*

This is the ruin of a burial chamber of uncertain type. There is now no
trace of a surrounding mound. A large slab of stone about 3 m long
which may once have been a cover stone, is supported by a small
stone on the north side. Nearby three slabs form three sides of a
burial chamber, with a large coverstone covering the fourth side. The
site was examined in 1913 with no apparent results.

F. Were: *T.B.G.A.S.* **36** (1913) 217

17 GATCOMBE LODGE CHAMBERED CAIRN   Neolithic
                                                    156 (ST:884997)

*On the south side of the road from Minchinhampton to Avening, in the
trees at the north end of Gatcombe Park.*

This long cairn, planted with beech trees, is about 58 m long and 24 m
wide and is surrounded by a low dry-stone wall. The eastern end is
horned with a false portal consisting of two upright stones. In front
of this was a paved forecourt on which lay a human skull, animal bones
and pottery, when it was excavated by Samuel Lysons in 18·70. In the
following year a workman found a burial chamber in the north-west
side of the cairn, which is still accessible, measuring 2·4 m by 1·2 m,
roofed with a single slab of stone. A single skeleton, apparently buried
'in a sitting position at the farthest end of the chamber' was found. A
large slab of stone 10·7 m from the west end of the cairn may be the
roof stone of another chamber.

The Long Stone (ST:884999) on a slight mound about 274 m north
of the long cairn may be part of a destroyed burial chamber. It is a
2·3 m high block of oolite with a number of natural holes in it. A
smaller stone block is incorporated in a wall 11 m away.

H. O'Neill and L. V. Grinsell: *Gloucestershire Barrows* (1961) 84

18 GREAT WITCOMBE VILLA   Roman
                                                    143 (SO:899142)

*Department of the Environment signpost on the A417, 400 m east of
cross-road with A46. Key at the farm, cars parked in farmyard.*

This villa lies in a beautiful position at the foot of the Cotswolds close
to springs. It was excavated by Samuel Lysons in 1818 who showed

that it was a large building surrounding three sides of a courtyard. The western wing included a bath suite with hypocausts and mosaic pavements; the latter with geometric and aquatic designs. Small pots that had contained the paints with which the walls of the rooms were painted were found during the excavations, together with fragments of a white marble cornice. Although the main part of the villa has been covered over again, the three rooms of the bath suite with mosaic pavements have been roofed over and are open to view.

19 HARESFIELD BEACON AND RING HILL   Iron Age
Haresfield   156 (SO:823090)

This is a two-period contour fort. At first a single rampart and ditch encircled Haresfield Beacon and Ring Hill, an area of about 6·5 ha. Later the defences were extended to take in the whole of Haresfield Hill to the east. There are a number of breaks in the rampart, but the only one that seems to represent an original entrance is on the south side of Ring Hill, where a track up the hillside from the west passes through an oblique entrance passage.

20 HETTY PEGLER'S TUMP LONG CAIRN   Neolithic
Uley   156 (SO:789000)

Signposted by the Department of the Environment beside the B4066. Key from house 0·8 km south beside main road. Torch or candle required.

One of the best-known chambered cairns in the Cotswolds, it was first dug in 1821 by Dr. Fry and later by John Thurnam in 1854. The mound is 36·6 m long and about 26 m wide, lying east to west on the edge of the escarpment above the vale of Berkeley and Severn. At the eastern end there is a deep forecourt with modern dry-stone walling leading to the burial chamber, whose entrance is dominated by a massive lintel stone. Within the cairn is a passage 6·7 m long, 1·4 m wide and 1·5 m high, that originally had two transepts or chambers on either side. The two on the right-hand side have been sealed off in modern times. Those on the left are both about 1·4 m square. There is a fifth chamber formed by the end of the passage. The walls are made of large slabs of stone filled in with areas of dry-stone walling, and the roof is likely to have been corbelled. Outside the entrance Thurnam found two human skeletons and the jaws and teeth of wild boars. The excavation in 1821 produced fifteen skeletons, and eight or nine others were found in 1854. A Romano-British burial with three Constantinian coins was also found high in the covering mound of the cairn. The excavators found traces of hidden lateral and transverse walls in the material of the mound near the west end, as well as a second row of concealed horn walls at the east.

The mound gets its name from Hester Pegler, whose husband owned it in the reign of Charles II.

E. Clifford: *Antiquity* **40** (1966) 129

21   HORTON CAMP HILLFORT   Iron Age
      Horton   156 (ST:765845)
Accessible from minor roads 0·4 km south of Horton.

Lying on the edge of the Cotswolds, this small rectangular fort of about 2 ha is surrounded by a bank and silted ditch. There are no clear indications of the position of the original entrance, and the whole work is somewhat depleted. The best-preserved section is under the fir-trees on the north-east. It is about 1·6 km north of the much stronger fort of Little Sodbury.

22   KING'S WESTON HILL FORT   Iron Age
      Bristol   156 (ST:557782)
Minor road or footpath from the B4057.

This tiny square-shaped fort encloses only 0·4 ha. Steep hill slopes protect it on the north and east, whilst there is a rampart and ditch on the south, and a stronger example on the west. Excavation showed that the ditch on the west is 1·6 m deep and 4·6 m wide. There are entrances at the north-west and south-west, though neither are necessarily contemporary. 274 m west of the camp is a line of rampart that is clearly an outwork of the fort. It has been damaged and its central section flattened. Roughly midway between the outwork and the fort is a circular earthwork some 18 m in diameter and defined by a low bank and shallow outer ditch. The ditch was 0·6 to 0·9 m wide and 0·6 m deep. Like the main fort ditch it contained early Iron Age pottery and both are probably contemporary. The circular earthwork may have surrounded a farming enclosure, but more excavation is needed to elucidate the problem. A scatter of 2nd century A.D. pottery suggests later occupation of the hilltop during the Roman period. The position of this fort 0·4 km south-west of the later Blaise Castle fort may be significant.

P. Rahtz: *P.U.B.S.S.* **8** (1956) 30

23   KING'S WESTON VILLA   Roman
      Bristol   156 (ST:534776)
On the north side of King's Weston Hill, close to the west end of Long Cross, Lawrence Weston. Key from caretaker at 17 Hopewell Gardens; a guide-book is available.

Only a small part of this Roman villa is accessible. Described by Sir Ian Richmond as more reminiscent of Germany than Britain, the visible part consists of east and west wings linked by a corridor and porch. The back wall of the corridor was arched and gave access to a gravelled courtyard around which further rooms (unexcavated) would have been grouped. Beside the west wing were at least five rooms forming a bath suite; unfortunately they are partly covered by a road. A weather-boarded structure houses a site museum, and is partly floored by a mosaic from a destroyed villa at Brislington (Bristol) found in 1900. Another room contains a fine geometric mosaic constructed at the end of the 3rd century. Excavation has shown that the villa was built late in the 3rd century and was altered a number of times before it was abandoned towards the end of the 4th century.

G. Boon: *T.B.G.A.S.* **69** (1950) 5

24 LAMBOROUGH BANKS CHAMBERED CAIRN   Neolithic
    Bibury   157 (SP:107094)
In Lamborough Banks covert, approached by minor road from north of Salt Way.

Lying north to south beneath the trees of the copse is the mutilated mound of a once fine long cairn. When measured by O. G. S. Crawford fifty years ago it was 85·3 m long and about 30·5 m wide. It had been contained by a double dry-stone wall, each with its face outwards, and the space between filled with rubble. At the southern end the walls curved inwards to a single block of stone 1·4 m high and 1·5 m broad, that seems to have served as a rudimentary blind or false entrance. Near the northern end in 1854 Thurnam found a long, narrow burial chamber containing a single burial.

In a copse to the south of Lamborough Banks is another long, low mound containing a dry-stone built beehive-shaped chamber (*Ablington*: SP:108092) approached by a short passage. 1·6 m in diameter with walls 1·2 m thick, it has a low bench all round the inside, and three small cupboard-like niches constructed into the thickness of the walls. The upper part of the roof, now missing, must have been corbelled. Similar chambers have been found nearby at Saltway Down, Bibury and at Cow Common (page 123). There is no evidence to show that they were used for burials or were neolithic in date, but it seems reasonable to assume both.

H. O'Neill and L. V. Grinsell: *Gloucestershire Barrows* (1961) 70, 71

25 LECKHAMPTON HILL HILLFORT AND BARROW   Iron Age
    Leckhampton   144 (SO:948184)
Approached from south by minor road off B4070 at SO:944178. Car-park at SO:951178 and 0·8 km walk, signposted 'Devil's Chimney', to the fort.

Almost every spur in this part of the Cotswolds seems to be crowned with a hillfort. Here on the south side of Cheltenham is a promontory

128   GLOUCESTERSHIRE

fort of about 3·2 ha, defended by a single rampart and rock-cut ditch
on the south and east and a precipitous modern quarry edge on the
north and west. The rampart stands 1·8 m high and recent excavations
have shown that it is dry-stone faced and badly burnt on the eastern
side. The only surviving entrance is also on the east, and was protected
by stone guard chambers. Outside the fort and to the north of the
modern entrance is an overgrown round barrow enclosed in a square
ditch. Parts of a skeleton are reputed to have been found in the mound.
The enclosure ditch may be an 18th-century tree-clump enclosure.

S. T. Champion: *T.B.G.A.S.* **90** (1971) 5

26 LEIGHTERTON LONG CAIRN   Neolithic
   Boxwell   156 (ST:819913)
*West of Leighterton village, on road to Boxwell. Tree-covered and enclosed
within modern stone wall.*

Of the many mutilated Cotswold chambered cairns, this is the largest,
measuring 82·3 m long and nearly 6 m high. Sometimes known as
'West Barrow', it was opened about 1700 by Matthew Huntley who
found three corbelled burial chambers: 'at the entrance of each was
found an earthern jar containing burnt human bones, but the skulls and
thigh bones were found unburnt.' As Huntley left the chambers exposed they have completely disintegrated. According to John Aubrey
'at the great end (in a place digged) is a stone' which was almost certainly a false portal or entrance.

O. G. S. Crawford: *Long Barrows of the Cotswolds* (1925) 136

27 LODGE PARK LONG BARROW   Neolithic
   Farmington   144 (SP:142125)
In Lodge Park, 3·2 km south-east of Northleach.

Described by O. G. S. Crawford as 'the finest long barrow I have ever
seen', this beautiful example is turf-covered and appears to be unopened. Lying north-west to south-east it measures 45·7 m long,
22·9 m wide and 2·4 m high. At the south-east end two upright stones
and a slipped coverstone protrude; whether they represent a burial
chamber or blind entrance is unknown. The tops of other large stones
can also be seen.

O. G. S. Crawford: *Long Barrows of the Cotswolds* (1925) 112

28 LOWER SWELL LONG CAIRN   Neolithic
                                                     144 (SP:170258)
North of the minor road from Lower Swell to Swell Hill Farm.

Planted with trees and surrounded by a dry-stone wall, this cairn
measures about 45·7 m by 15·2 m and is 3·1 m high. It seems to have

been trenched half across its eastern end, but this might represent a collapsed side-chamber. It stands in a ploughed field.

The Tump round barrow (SP: 166259) lies behind a wood 0·4 km west of the Lower Swell long cairn. It is also planted with trees and surrounded by a dry-stone wall. Standing about 1·5 m high and 18 m in diameter, it is typical of a number of round barrows in this part of the Cotswolds.

H. O'Neill and L. V. Grinsell: *Gloucestershire Barrows* (1961) 91, 133

29 LYDNEY HILLFORT, TEMPLE, ETC. (Fig. 14; Plate 28)
                                            Iron Age and Roman
                                            156 (SO: 616027)

Situated in Lydney Park. Permission to visit must be obtained from the agent at Lydney Park Estate Office. Access from the A48(T) at SO: 623021 and through farm.

Dr. and Mrs. R. E. M. Wheeler excavated at Lydney in 1928–9 at the invitation of the owner, Lord Bledisloe. It had long been known that a wooded hilltop within the Park was the site of Roman remains, but it was left to the Wheelers to unravel the story. The hilltop forms a steep-sided spur jutting south towards the river Severn. This was made into a promontory fort in the 1st century B.C. by the construction of two banks with external ditches across the spur on the north and east. These were breached by an entrance at their extreme eastern end, although the main entrance was probably at the south-east corner. The gap in the northern rampart is modern. The ramparts today are about 12·2 m wide and 3 m high. Excavation showed that they are built largely of rubble retained by an outer kerb of large stones, and capped by a paved rampart walk about 1·5 m wide. The inner bank on the eastern side may be a later, but still pre-Roman, addition to the fortifications. The fort seems to have been occupied until the end of the 3rd century A.D. by people living in rectangular huts and making small barrel-shaped pots known to archaeologists as 'flower pots'. They mined iron ore, exploiting veins of ferruginous marl that occur on the hill. Two of their mines have been found within the fort and one is accessible, marked by a trapdoor, about 37 m along the edge of the plateau, north of the Adam and Eve statues. The mine extends 15·2 m underground and reaches a depth of 4·6 m. There are original pick-marks on the side of the gallery. Intending visitors should wear protective clothing and carry torches. A second mine lies under the Roman bath suite on the west side of the hill, but cannot be explored.

Shortly after A.D. 364 four Roman buildings were erected on the hill and enclosed within a stone *temenos* wall, with a gate at the south-east. The most important was a temple measuring 25·9 m by 20·4 m.

Plate 28 Lydney temple wall, Gloucestershire

A flight of steps at its entrance led up through a wide ambulatory corridor, containing five alcoves or 'chapels', into the rectangular *cella* at the end of which was a triple sanctuary. Three inscriptions found in the temple show that it was dedicated to the native British god Nodens, who was responsible for healing. Numerous votive gifts including statuettes of dogs, and the famous Lydney curse begging the god to deny good health to the thief of a ring, were discovered during the excavation. The licking of sores by dogs may have been a requirement of the cult and the reason for the figurines. A narrow building running along the west side of the hill and divided into eleven rooms with a corridor in front, is thought to have been used by patients coming to the temple for cures, and perhaps forming an incubation centre for those with contagious diseases. On the other hand it might have contained lock-up shops where visitors could purchase souvenirs and votive offerings. North of this building is a very large bath house, that may well have included accommodation for ritual bathing. It was watered from a large tank in the centre of the fort. East of the baths a large guest house with central courtyard and forehall was uncovered, measuring 39·6 m by 48·8 m. Unfortunately due to deterioration it has had to be covered over again in recent years.

The collection of objects excavated from the site are housed in a private museum in Lydney Park house.

A small motte and bailey castle south-east of the hillfort and south-

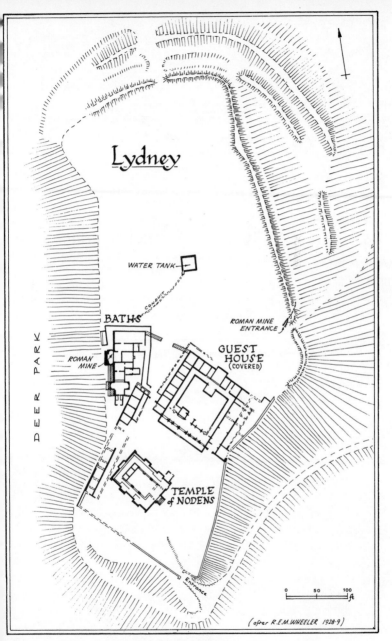

Fig. 14 Lydney hillfort and Roman buildings, Gloucestershire

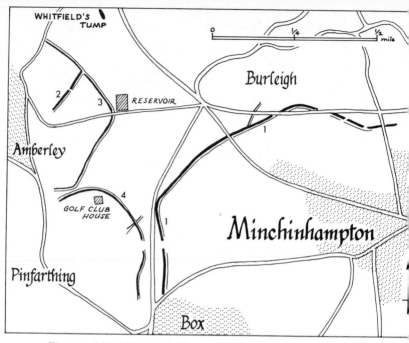

Fig. 15   *Minchinhampton Common earthworks, Gloucestershire*

Plate 29   *The Bulwarks, Minchinhampton, Gloucestershire*

west of Lydney Park house was probably built in the reign of Stephen (1135–54).

R. E. M. Wheeler: *Excavations in Lydney Park, Gloucestershire* (1932)

30 MINCHINHAMPTON COMMON EARTHWORKS (Fig. 15)

Iron Age

156

A series of earthworks on Minchinhampton Common (National Trust Property) are all easily accessible, although inspection is sometimes made difficult by over-enthusiastic golfers.

The Bulwarks (No. 1) (SO:857004 to 869012) (Plate 29). This is the major earthwork curving for at least 2·4 km across the Common from north of the Half Way House Inn to the north-west corner of Minchinhampton Park. The bank is 9·1 m wide and 1·5 m high, and excavation by Mrs. E. M. Clifford in about 1937 showed that the ditch on the south-east side, which is cut into solid rock, is 7 m wide at ground level, reducing to 1·5 m wide at the bottom and 2·4 m deep. Stone from the ditch had been used to build a retaining wall along the front of the bank. The position of the ditch on the south-east side of the Bulwarks suggests that the earthwork is defending some 243 ha to the north-west. Perhaps it should be seen as a territorial boundary, rather than a defence, its main purpose to demarcate land and to provide adequate penning for cattle and sheep. If the Bulwarks really protected land to the south around Minchinhampton then the alternative problem of an inner ditch, enclosing 81 ha has to be considered. Extensions of the earthwork run into the Park north of Minchinhampton and as far as Old Grange on the east at least (SO:876007).

The Cross-dyke (No. 2) (SO:852012 to 853014). This earthwork may be contemporary with the Bulwarks. It is 237·7 m long, and lies 183 m west of the reservoir. It stops inexplicably a third of the way across the Common beside the lesser earthwork (No. 3). When excavated in 1937 the ditch was shown to be 7 m wide at the top, 3·4 m wide at the flat bottom and 2·4 m deep. On its north-west side is a bank 9·8 m wide and 1·2 m high. Both the Cross-dyke and the Bulwarks have been dated to the Iron Age.

Amberley Camp (No. 3) (From SO:852009 to 851016). This minor earthwork runs in a curve along the west side of the Common. Its bank is 1·5 m wide and 0·6 m high, with an unexcavated ditch facing east 0·6 m deep and 1·2 m wide. In spite of its name, it is unlikely ever to have been a 'camp', nor is its neighbour on the south:

Pinfarthing Camp (No. 4) (From SO:856003 to 852008). Similar in character to the last this earthwork also forms an arc on the west side of the Common. Both earthworks are so slight that they do not appear to be of any great antiquity and are probably connected with fairly recent field boundaries. Both cut across a number of minor banks and ditches which may be part of the cattle-pen system mentioned above.

Whitfield's Tump (SO:854017). This disturbed long barrow measuring 22·9 m by 10·7 m lies on the northern end of the Common east of Littleworth. It was the preaching place of the Methodist George Whitfield on a number of occasions. There is an equally disturbed round barrow immediately to the east.

Pillow Mounds. There are about forty pillow mounds on the Common. Most of them are probably of medieval date and may have been constructed as artificial rabbit warrens. An easily-found example lies at the west end of the cattle-trough midway between the reservoir and the Golf House.

E. Clifford: *T.B.G.A.S.* **59** (1937) 287

31 NAN TOW'S TUMP   Bronze Age
    Didmarton   156 (ST:803893)

On the east side of the A46, some 11 km south of Nailsworth, and covered with trees.

Nan Tow was a local witch who, tradition says, was buried upright in this conical shaped barrow. Standing 2·7 m high and 30·5 m in diameter, it is one of the largest surviving round barrows in the Cotswolds. There is no record of its almost certain opening. It is densely covered with trees and undergrowth.

32 NOTGROVE LONG CAIRN   Neolithic
    Notgrove   144 (SP:095212)

Beside the B4068 road, just east of the railway bridge. Department of the Environment. Access at any time.

This important long cairn is of the transepted gallery type. It was first examined by G. B. Witts in 1881 and again by Elsie Clifford in 1934–5. The barrow has not been properly conserved and is in a disgracefully ruinous state. Originally about 48·8 m long and 24·4 m wide, it is trapezoidal in plan, and enclosed by dry-stone walling that was probably double all round. A funnel-shaped forecourt at the eastern end leads into an ante-chamber and gallery, together 8 m long. Two pairs of transepts or side-chambers lie on either side of the gallery and there is a further chamber at the end of the gallery. Each side-chamber is polygonal in plan and about 1·7 m across. These are all open to the sky. The chambers had been much disturbed prior to the excavations but the remains of at least six adults, three children and a new-born baby still remained. In the funnel-shaped forecourt traces of fire were found together with the bones of animals and the skeletons of two young people, seeming to indicate some elaborate ritual. Small pieces of neolithic pottery occurred in a number of places.

In the centre of the cairn, and beyond the western end of the gallery, Mrs. Clifford found the remains of a circular cairn 7 m in diameter enclosed by a well-built stone wall and containing a polygonal burial chamber in which was buried a crouched male skeleton fifty to sixty years of age. The roof was domed, and on top of it were the remains of a young woman in her late teens. This cairn was clearly earlier than the long cairn and may perhaps be compared with the round cairn on Cow Common and at Ablington (see Lamborough Banks, page 127). Material from the excavation is in the Cheltenham Museum.

H. O'Neill and L. V. Grinsell: *Gloucestershire Barrows* (1961) 86

33 NOTTINGHAM HILL HILLFORT   Iron Age
    Gotherington   144 (SO:984284)

Minor road north-west from the A46, 0·8 km north-east of Cleeve Hill. Farm road runs through the fort.

This massive promontory fort encloses 48·6 ha, but its defences are singularly unimpressive. The ground falls away steeply on all sides except the south-east. A small bank and ditch run all round the spur, and are doubled on the south-east, where they are much stronger and set close together. Here the inner bank reaches 3 m high and the outer 2 m high. Apart from this cross-dyke, there is little else to see. The interior is flat and ploughed and the south-west side has been quarried. This quarrying may have destroyed the only entrance through the earthwork. It has been suggested that another entrance may have existed at the extreme northern end of the fort overlooking Precott House. The fort is unexcavated but there are vague references to 'British coffins and coins' and 'Roman coins from the encampment' in the 19th-century literature. The fort, at 915 feet (279 m) above sea level, commands wide views across the vale of Gloucester to the forts on Bredon Hill, 11 km away.

34 NYMPSFIELD LONG CAIRN   Neolithic
    Frocester   156 (SO:794013)

On the west side of the B4066 on the edge of a wood.

Opened by Professor James Buckman in 1862, and again by Elsie Clifford in 1937 because of the 'deplorable condition of the monument'; it now lies open to the sky and is deteriorating rapidly. Roughly rectangular in plan it was 27·4 m long and 18·3 m broad, with two walls of dry-stone facing at the horned east end, and a thick wall of dry-stone at the concave west end. This western area produced the ash of fires and a post hole, whilst traces of a fire and a small pit were uncovered in the forecourt. The entrance led into an ante-chamber and then a short gallery with a single side-chamber to north and south and an end chamber, the whole interior being only 5·8 m long. The burial cham-

bers were seen to be enclosed in a hidden circular cairn, before the rest
of the barrow was built. Between twenty and thirty burials came from
the barrow during the two excavations, as well as neolithic pottery and
a leaf-shaped arrow-head.

E. Clifford: *P.P.S.* **4** (1938) 188

35 PAINSWICK BEACON HILLFORT   Iron Age
    Painswick   143 (SO:869121)
Beside minor road linking A46 and B4073 roads.

The defences of this unexcavated 2·8 ha site are as spectacular as the
wide views they command across Gloucester to the Malvern Hills and
Black Mountains. The interior, however, is an anticlimax, for it has
been intolerably quarried and ruined. Triangular in shape the fort is
surrounded by closely-set double ramparts and ditches, the outer line
having a berm and counterscarp bank. Only on the north where the
ground falls away steeply is the defence reduced to a low bank without
a ditch. The entrance is at the south-east end where the inner rampart
is sharply inturned for about 30 m. It is possible that this entrance has
been enlarged at some time, for the bank ends are also staggered and the
inturn seems excessive. There may have been another entrance at the
north-west corner where the inner rampart is again inturned at its
junction with a hollow-way. The only certain internal feature that is
not part of the quarrying is a funnel-shaped hollow, 2·7 m deep, in the
centre of the camp. It may represent the top of a ritual shaft connected
with Celtic religious observances as at Cadbury Castle in Devon
(page 58).

36 POLE'S WOOD EAST LONG CAIRN   Neolithic
    Swell   144 (SP:172265)
*Midway between Upper Swell and the Pole's Wood South long cairn, see
No. 37 below.*

Lying at the eastern end of Pole's Plantation, this cairn has a horned
forecourt at the north without a false portal. It is enclosed by dry-
stone walls, and is at least 36·6 m long, 12·2 m wide and 1·5 m high.
A trench-like burial chamber, cut into the subsoil, about 8·5 m long
and 1·8 m wide, ran across the centre of the barrow and contained
nineteen human skeletons together with pieces of a neolithic bowl,
animal bones and worked flints. The chamber can no longer be seen.

O. G. S. Crawford: *Long Barrows of the Cotswolds* (1925) 124

37 POLE'S WOOD SOUTH LONG CAIRN   Neolithic
    Swell   144 (SP:167264)
Farm track west from minor road linking Upper and Lower Swell.

This cairn was excavated by Canon William Greenwell and George Rolleston in 1878 and left in a deplorable state. It still measures about 54·9 m long, 21·3 m wide and 3·1 m high. It had a horned eastern end, but there is no clear indication of the existence of a false portal. A rectangular chamber 1·98 m long lies close to the western end of the tomb and can still be seen. A passage 1·8 m long leads to it. The chamber contained the remains of about six individuals, together with animal bones and two pieces of neolithic pottery. Two more skeletons lay in the entrance passage. Three intrusive Saxon burials had also been inserted into the mound of the cairn.

O. G. S. Crawford: *Long Barrows of the Cotswolds* (1925) 125

38 RANDWICK LONG CAIRN   Neolithic
Randwick   156 (SO:825069)

In National Trust woodland north-west of Randwick church.

Lying north-east to south-west this ruined long cairn is enclosed within a single revetment wall of dry-stone. Trapezoidal in plan, it measured 34·4 m long when excavated by G. B. Witts in 1883, although he considered that it must originally have been about 56·4 m long and 26 m wide. At the north-east end the walls curve inwards to form a slight forecourt, at the focus of which lies a burial chamber 1·5 m square. When opened this contained a mass of human bones, pottery and three flint flakes. Buried within the cairn was a longitudinal wall with three transverse walls. Their function is not clear, unless they helped to stabilize the mound material. At the south-west end of the cairn several crouched (and probably Bronze Age) skeletons were found, which the excavator considered were slaves buried with their chieftain. 'By direction of the owner, Mrs. Barrow, the walls and chambers have been covered up to protect them from damage' wrote Witts. An admirable action which might have been followed to advantage by many of his contemporary and subsequent barrow diggers.

O. G. S. Crawford: *Long Barrows of the Cotswolds* (1925) 129

39 SALMONSBURY CAMP   Iron Age
Bourton   144 (SP:175208)

Between Bourton-on-the-Water and the river Dikler.

This large square camp enclosing 22·7 ha, lies in the angle between the rivers Dikler and Windrush. It is surrounded by double banks and silted ditches. The inner bank is today 18·3 m wide and 0·8 m high. It was faced on its outer side with a dry-stone revetment wall that was thrown down in Roman times. In front was a V-shaped ditch 10·4 m wide and 3·7 m deep, and then the much denuded outer rampart and outer ditch dug 2·7 m deep and 5·8 m wide into the gravel. A wooden hut 6·7 m in diameter, composed of a ring of eighteen post holes and three central holes with a surrounding footing trench, was found in excavation in 1931. It had an entrance 2·4 m wide on the south-east side. Two hearths were found outside the entrance. In 1860 a hoard of 147 currency bars was found in a small gravel-pit on the north-west side of the fort. Together with the pottery found in 1931 it is likely that the camp was constructed and occupied in the 1st century B.C., although there was clear evidence for an undefended settlement on the site, perhaps as early as the 3rd century B.C.

G. Dunning: *Antiquity* 5 (1931) 489

40 SEA MILLS VILLA   Roman
     Bristol   156 (ST:551758)
At the side of the Portway at its junction with Roman Way, Sea Mills.

This villa was part of the Roman *Portus Abonae* (Sea Mills) which grew up at the point where the river Trym flowed into the Avon. The foundations of several small rooms of the house can be seen, together with other walls and stone gutters. A number of houses found in the vicinity must be related to wealthy traders using the port. From the harbour at Sea Mills (the visible remains are not Roman) a ferry service ran across the Bristol Channel to Caerwent, as indicated in the Antonine Itinerary.

G. C. Boon: *T.B.G.A.S.* **61** (1945) 258; **68** (1949) 184

41 SODBURY CAMP   Iron Age
     Little Sodbury   156 (ST:760826)
By farm road from A46 on east or from Portway Lane from Chipping Sodbury.

A fine rectangular fort on the edge of the Cotswold escarpment. A double rampart and ditches enclose 4·5 ha. The inner rampart on the north, east and south is apparently of glacis construction and rises about 1·5 m above the interior of the fort. On the west it runs half-way along the top of the natural hill-slope, but does not complete the southern half of the circuit. At this point its ditch and counterscarp bank are about 15·2 m down the hill-slope. The ditch around the rest of the inner rampart is 7·6 m wide and between 1·8 and 2·1 m deep. The main entrance is in the centre of the eastern side where the limestone core of the rampart is clearly fire-reddened, suggesting that the gate was burnt down at some time. There is a wide space between the inner and outer ramparts. The outer rampart appears to be unfinished. It is uneven in height, although in places it rises to 3·7 m. A berm separates it from an equally irregular broad ditch. There is a break in the rampart and ditch immediately opposite the main entrance in the inner rampart. There is another gap 45·7 m further north. Both may have been intended as entrance gaps. The northern one is out-turned and there are indications of what might be a guard-chamber on the northern side. The site is unexcavated.

42 SOLDIER'S GRAVE CAIRN   Neolithic
Nympsfield   156 (SO:794015)

On west side of B4066, in wood 210 m north of the Nympsfield long cairn.

This round cairn stands on the edge of the steep Cotswold escarpment. Measuring 17 m in diameter, it contained a rock-cut boat-shaped grave, lined with dry-stone walling, and measuring 3·4 m long, 1·37 m wide and 1·14 m deep. Excavations in 1937 uncovered a mass of human bones representing between twenty-eight and forty-four people, animal bones (mainly ox, pig and dog) and sherds of pottery of probable neolithic date. The burial vault is no longer visible.

E. Clifford: *P.P.S.* **4** (1938) 214

43 TINGLE STONE LONG CAIRN   Neolithic
Avening   156 (ST:882990)

On the east side of Gatcombe Park and west of lane from Avening Church to Hampton Fields.

Getting its name from a block of oolitic limestone 1·8 m high standing at the northern end of this long cairn, it is unusual only in that it is orientated north to south. It is 39·6 m long, 21·3 m wide and 1·8 m high. There are no signs of a burial chamber, and the mound is planted with beech trees and enclosed within a modern stone wall.

O. G. S. Crawford: *Long Barrows of the Cotswolds* (1925) 134

44 ULEYBURY HILLFORT (Plate 30)   Iron Age
Uley   156 (ST:785990)

Footpaths from the B4066 at West Hill, Uley or Crawley.

This 13 ha fort is perfectly sited on an almost flat hilltop, with the ground falling steeply away everywhere except at the northern corner. Any inner rampart has now all but vanished, but 4·6 m below the scarp edge is a ditch 13·7 m wide, and a further 18·3 m down the slope is a second ditch only 2·1 m wide with a counterscarp bank. This has been badly mutilated and quarried away at the southern corner. The main entrance was probably at the northern corner close to the road, and was defended by a mound and three ridges which cut across the neck of the promontory. There seems to have been another entrance at the eastern corner where the hollow-way from Crawley enters the fort. At the south there is a convincing gap where the rampart ends bulge on each side of a probable gateway, again at the head of a hollow-way. The fort is unexcavated, but has produced many worked flints from its ploughed interior and a gold stater of the Dobunni, now in Gloucester Museum.

H. S. Gracie: *Arch. J.* **122** (1965) 213

Plate 30   *Uleybury Hillfort, Gloucestershire*

45   WEST TUMP LONG CAIRN   Neolithic
    Brimpsfield   143 (SO:912133)

In Buckle Wood west of the B4070.

This long cairn was discovered by G. B. Witts in 1860 and dug by him
the following year. He records that it was 45·4 m long and 23·2 m wide,
with a height of 3·1 m. The whole mound is enclosed within ancient
dry-stone walls which curve inwards at the eastern end to form a
horned forecourt, with two upright stones forming a blind or false
entrance at its centre. 25 m from the southern horn Witts found a passage 0·9 m wide and 2·1 m long, that led into a chamber 'or trench'
walled with dry-stone and sloping below the original ground surface.
It measured 1·2 m wide and 4·7 m long. In this he discovered some
twenty skeletons, one at the furthest end lying on five flat stones was
the skeleton of a young woman with a baby close by. Four other
skeletons were found lying in the forecourt near the false entrance.

O. G. S. Crawford: *Long Barrows of the Cotswolds* (1925) 137

46 WINDMILL TUMP   Neolithic
    Rodmarton   157 (ST:932978)

*Covered with trees in arable land south of the Rodmarton to Cherington
minor road.*

The modern dry-stone wall enclosing this cairn makes it look decep-
tively larger than it really is. Measuring some 61 m long by 21·3 m
broad, it stands about 2·4 m high. It was surrounded by a low dry-
stone wall which was doubled at the eastern end, where it formed horns
on either side of a false portal which is still visible. Two great stones,
each more than 2·4 m high, stand on either side of this entrance, whilst
a third leaning slab forms the 'door' itself. On either side of the cairn
rectangular burial chambers were found during excavation in 1863 and
1939. In both three steps led down into a short gallery, across each of
which two upright stones were placed, each with a porthole cut into it,
just wide enough to allow the passage of a corpse. Beyond the portholes
were rectangular chambers, the north measuring 2·1 m by 1·07 m; the
southern 2·4 m by 1·2 m. The north chamber contained the burials of
ten adults and three children, the southern had been opened in 1863
and only fragments of several skeletons and sherds of neolithic pottery
remained. Neither chamber is now accessible.

E. Clifford and G. Daniel: *P.P.S.* **6** (1940) 133

47 WINDRUSH CAMP   Iron Age
    Windrush   144 (SP:182123)

South of the A40 between Northleach and Burford. Access by farm road.

This almost circular fort of 2·6 ha lies on a flat plateau, almost 1·6 km
south-west of the Windrush valley. It is defended by a single bank and
completely silted ditch, broken by a possible entrance on the west side.
Although almost twice as big as Chastleton Barrow Camp in Oxfordshire (page 232) 17·7 km away, it may well have served a similar cattle
ranching function.

48 WOODCHESTER ROMAN VILLA   Roman
                                               156 (ST:840030)

*On north side of the village and south of the old churchyard. Not per-
manently open. Mosaic floors uncovered at irregular intervals for exhibi-
tion.*

One of the most magnificent villas ever uncovered in Britain, it consists
of a mansion arranged around four sides of an inner courtyard, and
farm buildings around an outer court. Although excavated extensively
by Samuel Lysons between 1793 and 1796, much still remains to be
discovered, in particular the bathing suite. Some sixty-five rooms have
so far been recorded, of which the most important is the great dining-

room with its elaborate 4th-century mosaic 15 m square. This depicts
Orpheus and is the work of the Corinian (Cirencester) School of
mosaic artists. Four columns rose from the floor to support the ceiling,
and in its centre was a fountain. Although the villa is normally kept
covered over, it is opened for inspection at intervals.

M. D. Mann: *The Roman Villa at Woodchester* (1951)

Museums containing archaeological material

Bristol City Museum,* Queen's Road, Bristol 8
Chedworth Roman Villa and Museum (see page 118)
Cheltenham Art Gallery and Museum, Clarence Street, Cheltenham
The Corinium Museum, Park Street, Cirencester
City Museum and Art Gallery,* Brunswick Road, Gloucester
Stroud Museum, Lansdown, Stroud

* Main county collections

GREATER LONDON

1	CAESAR'S CAMP	Iron Age
	Wimbledon Common	170 (TQ:224711)

*From A219 at TQ:236712 follow 'The Causeway' and Camp Road direct
to the site on the west side of the golf course.*

Circular in plan, with a flattened northern side, this fort encloses
4·9 ha. It was formerly called Bensbury. It is surrounded by a single
bank and ditch, much flattened at the beginning of this century by
proposed housing and the golf course. When water pipes were laid
through the site in 1937 the opportunity was taken to observe the ditch
which was 9 m to 12 m wide and 3·7 m deep, with a wide inner bank
revetted at the front and back by strong timbers. The two were
separated by a berm some 3 m wide. There may be an original entrance
on the west. A storage pit produced pottery dated to the 3rd century
B.C.

There are round barrows on the common, now almost inextricably
mixed with the golf bunkers.

A. W. G. Lowther: *Arch. J.* **102** (1945) 15

2	GRIM'S DITCH	Iron Age
	Harrow and Stanmore	160

This is a linear dyke about 6 km in length, running at intervals from
Pinner Green (TQ:114904) to Brockley Hill (TQ:174937). The earthwork consists of a V-shaped ditch with a rampart on the northern
side. Excavations, largely unpublished, seem to confirm a late Iron Age

date, and the earthwork probably formed a boundary of the Catuvellauni, whose capital was at Prae Wood near St. Albans, 14·5 km to the
north. The best section to see is at Harrow Weald golf course (TQ:
135925) where the rampart stands 3 m high and the whole work is
about 30 m across.

3 HOLWOOD HILLFORT   Iron Age
   Keston, Bromley   171 (TQ: 422639)

In Holwood Park. Permission to visit required.

Also known as Caesar's Camp, this fort lies north of Holwood House,
whose gardens designed for William Pitt have destroyed the south and
east sides of what must once have been an extensive 17 ha site. The
strongest defences are on the west where a double rampart and ditch
with counterscarp bank still stand, the highest inner rampart rising
2·7 m high above its adjoining ditch which is 4·6 m deep. An entrance
sited in a small valley breaks the side at the northern end, its rampart
terminations being slightly inturned. Only a single line of rampart and
ditch survive along the north. It has been shown that the rampart has
been strengthened three times, and can be dated to the 2nd century
B.C.

Across the A233 to the north-west on *Keston Common* is a slight
promontory fort facing north (TQ: 418642). A single line of bank and
ditch cuts off the southern side of some 6 ha, whilst the north-east and
north-west are protected by marshy ground. There is a break in the
centre of the earthwork which may be an original entrance. At no
point does the rampart stand higher than 0·9 m, and we should probably consider it as an animal enclosure connected with the larger fort.

4 KESTON TOMBS (Plate 31)   Roman
   Warbank, Bromley   171 (TQ: 415634)

*West of the A233, in the care of Bromley Council. In grounds of 'Keston
Foreign Bird Farm'.*

The main feature of this site is a circular drum-shaped tomb, 8·8 m in
diameter and originally about 7·6 m high. (Today it is 0·9 m high.) Its
flint walls, 0·9 m thick, were supported by six external buttresses. It
had been completely filled with earth, and burials were probably
placed in it from above, since no sign of a door exists. The outside of
the tomb had been plastered and painted bright red. A second tomb
lay between two of the buttresses. It had been built of tiles set in a
large pit and covered with a roof of tiles and pink mortar. It contained
an adult cremation in a lead casket. (Vault is visible beneath modern
trapdoor.) North of the circular tomb was a second small rectangular
vault measuring 4·6 m by 3·4 m, with a buttress on the west side.

Inside was a stone coffin buried in a pit 2·1 m deep. The coffin was removed from the site in about 1880 and later smashed by a German bomb. Its pieces have been restored and returned to the tomb.

Immediately around the three tombs were a dozen graves dug into the ground. These contained three adult cremations, six children buried in wooden coffins and three new-born infants buried without any apparent ceremony. It is most probable that more burials exist on the adjoining private property. Pottery found in some of the graves dates them to between A.D. 180 and 250. It seems likely that they represent a private family cemetery connected with a nearby villa estate, traces of which have been found about 91 m to the west.

Near the cemetery a shaft, no longer visible, 4·9 m deep and 3·4 m in diameter, contained two cremated dog burials and fragments of pottery of uncertain type. This suggests a Celtic religious survival and may indicate that the site had served as an earlier Celtic sanctuary.

B. Philp: *Current Archaeology* **2** (1969) 73

Plate 31   Keston Roman tombs, Greater London

5 LONDINIUM   Roman
The Roman City of London   (160 TQ: 330810)

Centuries of intensive building and demolition, successive fires and the
blitz, have obliterated much of Roman *Londinium*. Even so, sufficient
survives to occupy a visitor for a full day within the City.

Already a thriving town by A.D. 60–1, it was at that time destroyed,
together with *Camulodunum* and *Verulamium*, by Boudicca. *Londinium*
was rebuilt on a grand scale during the procuratorship of Classicianus,
and soon became the meeting-place of the Provincial Council and the
chief town of Roman Britain. Soon after A.D. 100 a fort of 4·5 ha was
established at Cripplegate, measuring some 229 m long by 209 m wide.
This housed dispatch-riders and specialized military staff. About A.D.
200 the great city wall was erected, some 3 km in length, 6 m high and
2·4 m thick at the base, it enclosed about 133 ha. It was faced with
ashlar and tile and had a core of mortared flint rubble. At intervals
bastions were added, some solid and some hollow, but their date is not
certain. Of the city gates, only Newgate is known in any detail. It had
two carriageways with square towers on either side. Within the circuit
of the walls individual buildings, both private and public, have been
found from time to time, although hardly any are visible today.

Plate 32   London Wall, Tower Hill, City of London

THE ROMAN CITY WALL. *A map of the wall, superimposed on a modern street plan, can be purchased for 5p from the church of All Hallows-by-the-Tower, near Tower Hill Underground Station.*

A walk of two hours is sufficient to cover the complete circuit of the wall, but since much of it is missing, a few selected sections are likely to be more rewarding.

1 *Tower of London.* Behind the Wardrobe Tower is a section of Roman wall with a semicircular bastion. It is 3·1 m long and about 0·9 m high. The bastion, whose base is Roman, was rebuilt in the 13th century.

2 *Tower Hill* (Plate 32). North of Tower Hill in Wakefield Gardens is a fine stretch of the wall, only the lower part being Roman. It is about 15 m long and is built of ragstone with four courses of red bonding tiles. The foundations of an internal turret can be seen at the southern end. The Roman inscriptions are casts of pieces found in an adjoining bastion. They are from the tomb of the procurator Classicianus and the original is now in the British Museum. The fragments read in translation: 'To the spirits of the departed Gaius Julius Alpinus Classicianus' and 'Procurator of the Province of Britain, Julia Pacata I(ndiana) daughter of Indus, his wife, had this built.'

3 *Coopers Row.* Behind Midland House. Although this length of wall is largely medieval, the base is Roman and can be recognized by the squared ragstone blocks and bonding tiles.

4 *St. Alphage churchyard* lies to the north of London Wall street, and east of Wood Street. At this point the north wall of the churchyard is formed by the Roman wall. The lower part at the east is double. This is because the Roman city wall and the wall of the Cripplegate fort are seen together here. When the fort was built into the city wall it was thickened on the inside. The usual bonding courses of tiles were not used here, and only the mortared ragstone blocks are used.

5 *Noble Street.* The corner turret of the Cripplegate fort and the foundations of one of the rectangular internal towers can be looked down on to advantage from the modern street. The fort wall is beginning to curve east at this point.

6 *West Gate, Cripplegate Fort, Old Street.* (*Open weekdays 12.30 to 14.00 hours.*) Part of the Gate is preserved below the modern London Wall, where the foundations of the double gateway and the north turret with its guard room are visible.

Whilst in this area visitors must see the *Guildhall Museum* in Gillett House, 55 Basinghall Street, which is open from Monday to Saturday 10.00 to 17.00 hours, and houses many important finds from Londinium.

ROMAN BUILDINGS

1 *All Hallows-by-the-Tower crypt* (near Tower Hill Underground
  Station). Permission to visit the crypt obtainable from the Verger in
  advance. Here are the walls of a Roman house with two plain red
  tessellated floors. Roman pottery, coins and a good model of
  Londinium about A.D. 400 are also displayed.
2 *Temple of Mithras reconstruction.* The discovery of the Mithras
  temple in 1954 caused a tremendous surge of popular interest in its
  excavation and preservation. However, this was insufficient to
  prevent the building of Bucklersbury House on the site. The temple
  was moved 55 m west to the front of Temple Court in Queen Victoria Street. The plan is fairly accurate, although the internal
  features do not truly represent what was excavated. The building
  was 20·7 m long and 8 m wide with an apse at the west and vestibule
  at the east, separated by a nave with raised side aisles. A number of
  sculptures found in 1954 are in the Guildhall and London Museums.
3 *Bank of England mosaic.* At the foot of the staircase at the Thread-
  needle Street entrance to the Bank is a much restored and relaid
  mosaic from the city, of late 2nd-century date. It is decorated with
  a design of leaves and twisted ribbons, surrounded by a border of
  key pattern. Permission to visit is normally given during Bank
  business hours.

R. Merrifield: *The Roman City of London* (1965)

6 PARLIAMENT HILL BARROW   Bronze Age
   Hampstead Heath   160 (TQ:274865)

*Covered by bushes, half-way between Hampstead Ponds and Highgate
Ponds.*

This barrow, now obscured by bushes and enclosed by iron railings,
is about 41 m in diameter and 2·4 m high, with an encircling ditch
about 4·9 m wide. In 1894 Sir Hercules Read trenched the mound but
found nothing in it. Some doubt has been cast on its antiquity, but
a sketch made by Stukeley in May 1725 leaves little room for scepti-
cism. His drawing clearly shows a causeway across the ditch on the
north side, and another is reported on the south.

F. Celoria: *T.L.M.A.S.* **22** (1968) 23

Plate 33   Beacon Hill fort, Hampshire

HAMPSHIRE

1 BALKSBURY HILLFORT   Iron Age
Andover   168 (SU:352446)

The Andover bypass runs through the site, which can be reached from Upper Clatford.

There is now little to see of this once extensive triangular hillfort which occupied a plateau between the rivers Anton and Anna. Originally enclosing an area of 18 ha, it has been damaged by the encroachment of housing on the north and the Andover bypass through its centre. Only slight terracing on the south side is still visible from the slip road north from Upper Clatford. Emergency excavations indicated three phases of defences. Initially a slight bank and ditch protected a plateau enclosure. The ditch was later recut and the rampart heightened twice, with no use of timbering. There were some small huts associated with the final phase. Pottery indicates an early 6th-century date, and the fort would seem to be contemporary with Phase 1 at nearby Bury Hill (No. 5), for which it may have acted as a cattle enclosure.

G. Wainwright: *P. Hants F.C.* **26** (1969) 21

2 BEACON HILL (Plate 33)   Iron Age
  Kingsclere   168 (SU: 458573)

A very steep climb from the A34. Car-park and picnic place at the foot of
the hill which is one of the Hampshire County Parks.

This beautiful contour fort encloses 6·1 ha and lies at a height of 842
feet above sea level. Its single rampart, ditch and counterscarp are very
pronounced, and broken by only one entrance on the south-east.
There is a pronounced inturn to this entrance. Dr. St Joseph's aerial
photographs have recently shown the horned outworks to be a later
addition. There are about fifteen hut-hollows inside the fort, each
about 9 m in diameter, and some showing entrance gaps towards the
east or south-east. There are also a number of smaller hollows 2·1 to
2·4 m across which probably mark storage pits. Sir Leonard Woolley
excavated three of the circles which produced numerous animal bones
and 'black Bronze Age pottery'. Inside the fenced-off south-west
corner is the grave of Lord Carnarvon, former owner of the hill, and
discoverer of the tomb of Tutankhamun.

J. P. Williams-Freeman: *Field Archaeology as Illustrated by Hampshire*
(1915) 356

3 BUCKLAND RINGS   Iron Age
  Lymington   180 (SZ: 315968)

Between the A337 and the road to Buckland, north of Lymington.

An approximately rectangular fort enclosing some 2·8 ha is surrounded
by two banks and ditches, with an additional counterscarp bank. These
earthworks have been partially obliterated on the east where the main
entrance was situated. There is a modern gap on the west. Excavation
at the eastern entrance revealed a long funnel-like approach with a
stout gate at the western end. The approach road had been worn down
by traffic in Iron Age times. The ramparts of the fort were revetted
with timber at the front and back. Today the inner bank still stands
2·7 m high and 9·1 m wide, with a ditch averaging 2·4 m deep (unexcavated) and 9·1 m wide. The middle rampart has a broad flat top,
and is basically an extension of the unheightened natural ground
surface. The outer ditch is about 1·8 m deep, and the material taken
from it has been piled outwards to form the counterscarp. The fort
seems to have been deliberately pulled down, perhaps by order of the
Romans after their conquest of the area in about A.D. 45. Finds suggest
that it had been built in the early 1st century A.D.

C. F. C. Hawkes: *P. Hants F.C.* **13** (1936) 124

4 BULLSDOWN HILLFORT   Iron Age
   Bramley   169 (SU:671583)

South of minor road from Sherfield to Bramley Green, covered with trees.

This fort of 4 ha is roughly oval in shape. It is surrounded by two
banks and ditches, with a flat berm between them. The inner rampart
was thrown up and inwards from the ditch, whilst the outer rampart
was thrown out from the outer ditch. A probable entrance on the
north-east has been destroyed. The fort occupies a low hill, the bottom
of which was surrounded by marshy ground.

5 BURY HILL   Iron Age
   Upper Clatford   168 (SU:345435)

*Close to the road, beside which it is signposted. Ramparts tree-covered and
the interior ploughed.*

Two banks and ditches ring this hillfort. The inner bank stands 2·4 m
high, the outer bank 2·1 m high. Between them is a V-shaped ditch
which excavation has shown to be 6·1 m deep. The outer bank is
almost destroyed, but varied between 1·5 and 3·1 m in depth on
excavation. Both works belong to Phase 2 of the fort's construction.
The first phase is represented by a slighter oval earthwork which
underlies the outer ditch, described above, on the east and south-east,
but lies well outside it to the west and north, forming a marked tree-
covered terrace at the point where the hill slopes steeply downhill.
Excavation showed that the earliest work had a ditch about 3·7 m wide
and 3·4 m deep, with an inner bank at least 2·4 m high.

  Both earthworks had a common entrance of the east side. That on
the west seems to be modern. When examined the ramparts of both
phases were shown to be untimbered, like Balksbury in the valley
below. Phase 1 could be dated to around 350 B.C. and Phase 2 to about
100 B.C. The fort continued to be occupied until well into the Roman
period, but was finally dismantled and abandoned around A.D. 100.

C. F. C. Hawkes: *P. Hants F.C.* **14** (1939) 291

6 BUTSER HILL   Iron Age
   Petersfield   181 (SU:712201)

*Approached from A3 at SU:715175 along minor road round Oxen-
bourne Down. Car-park at Butser Hill County Park at top.*

This extensive flat-topped hill of about 32 ha is joined to the main mass
of the South Downs to the south-west by a narrow neck of land.
Across this neck are three cross-ridge dykes. The first is largely
obliterated (it lies at SU:709195). The second, about 503 m north-east,
is bivallate, whilst the third (behind a modern fence) is more massive,

and bow-shaped in plan. It stands about 1·5 m high with an irregular ditch to the west and south-west about 2·4 m deep. Professor Piggott considered this ditch part of a causewayed ditch of neolithic date in 1929, but it is now generally accepted as of unfinished Iron Age construction. Three other spurs of the hill are cut by lines of entrenchment. These lie to the south, north-east and west. They follow the edge of the clay-with-flint which caps Butser Hill and end approximately on the edge of the adjacent combes. Recently Richard Bradley has shown that the western of these dykes formed a division between arable and pasture land, perhaps suggesting that the whole hilltop was an enclosed area of pasture. There are a number of round barrows, including a bell-barrow, on the hill.

The north-east spur of the hill is known as Little Butser Hill (SU:719206). It is almost 61 m lower than the main hill-mass. As said above it is cut off by a cross-dyke. A hollow-way leads down to the spur where there is at least one hut platform, an incomplete ditch and a pillow mound.

This site is being developed by the British Association and the Council for British Archaeology, with the support of the Hampshire County Council, as an experimental prehistoric farm. It will include a Research Institute and controlled public access.

S. Piggott: *Antiquity* 4 (1938) 187

---

7 CASTLE DITCHES HILLFORT   Iron Age
   Whitsbury   179 (SU:128196)

Entrance by Castle Farm, east of road north from Whitsbury.

This fort is sited on the summit of a hill looking south-east over the Avon valley, and south-west over a tributary valley. Roughly oval in plan, the fort encloses about 6·5 ha. It is surrounded by double ramparts and ditches with a counterscarp bank, but on the west, where the entrance would have been, farm buildings have removed both the entrance and the adjoining ramparts. On the south the counterscarp bank has been destroyed. The inner bank is a massive affair, highest on the south where it stands 6·1 m above the original land surface; on the north the height is nearer 2·4 m. The outer rampart also exhibits considerable strength and the fort must have presented a considerable challenge to attackers, although the position of the site is scarcely spectacular. It was probably built in the last century B.C.

Considerable sections of the Grim's Ditch lie to the north and south-west of Castle Ditches and should probably be seen in the context of ranch boundaries related to the fort's territory.

H. Sumner: *Ancient Earthworks of Cranborne Chase* (1913) 20

8 DANEBURY LONG BARROWS   Neolithic
  Nether Wallop   168 (SU: 320383)

Approached beside trees from Down Farm.

The first long barrow lies immediately north-east of the end of the belt of fir trees. Like the others it has been ploughed continually but can still be clearly seen. It is about 30·5 m long and 24·4 m wide and still about 1·2 m high. It has ditches on the north and south sides. Midway along the south side of the belt of trees is a second long barrow about 52 m long and 18·3 m wide. It, too, is about 1·2 m high at the eastern end, with ditches on either side. A third long barrow lies 55 m west. It is 61 m long and 21·3 m wide. In spite of the ploughing it is still about 1·5 m high. Aerial photographs show that its side ditches are separated from the main barrow mound by a wide berm. None of these mounds have been excavated.

L. V. Grinsell: *P. Hants F.C.* **14** (1938–40) various

9 DANEBURY RING (Plate 34)   Iron Age
  Nether Wallop   168 (SU: 323377)

Road links A30 and A343 on north side of fort. A new road and car-park are provided at SU:330378 for the Hampshire County Park.

The hillfort of Danebury, covered with beech trees, has a long and complex history. Roughly oval in plan, it is surrounded by two rings of ramparts and ditches. The main inner set encloses 5·3 ha, whilst the weaker outer line surrounds 11 ha. Between them, on the south-east another crescentic line of earthwork forms an annexe. Of two entrances, one on the south-west was later blocked, whilst that on the east was in continual use and remodelled a number of times. The site is being carefully excavated by Professor Barry Cunliffe and an intriguing picture is beginning to emerge.

Perhaps as early as the Bronze Age the hilltop was marked by a number of ritual pits, each containing tall posts. In one pit the remains of a dog, torn to pieces, had been placed before the pole was set up. In the 5th century B.C. the first hillfort was constructed, defended by a timber-faced box rampart of Hollingbury type, 2·2 m in width, with a solid core of chalk. The entrance was simple, with a single gate. A number of circular huts may belong to this period. Around 400 B.C. the fort was reorganized with regular rows of streets and buildings rectangular in shape measuring some 3·0 m by 3·5 m. These buildings have produced no signs of floors or hearths, and may have had raised floors, and even an upper story. Although the hut posts were renewed from time to time, there was enough evidence to show that the area continued in the same use for about 300 years. The eastern gate was rebuilt as a double one about 400 B.C. with recesses behind the

Plate 34 *Danebury hillfort entrance, Hampshire*

gates perhaps used as guard chambers, and similar to those excavated at St. Catherine's Hill, 19 km away, in 1925. Sometime between 200 and 100 B.C. the defences were renewed. A deep V-shaped ditch was cut and a dumped rampart piled over the old box rampart, with a flint built wall at the top, thus creating a continuous glacis slope from ditch bottom to bank crest of 20 m.

About 100 B.C., perhaps in response to the threat of Belgic invasion, the eastern gateway was again remodelled, this time on a grand scale. The northern rampart end was drawn outwards from the gate to form what Professor Cunliffe has described as a 'command post'. Beyond it two parallel hornworks projected to form a pincer-like barbican. The command post, considerably higher than the rest of the ramparts, gave an unobstructed view of the whole entrance area, which was within 60 m radius of that spot, and within the range of a good slinger: finds of many sling-stones are therefore significant. The gate itself was a massive affair, with a wooden bridge over the top, and almost vertical gate passage walls faced with flints 3 m high. Within twenty years the gate had been burnt down and the fort abandoned.

It was not until about the time of the Roman conquest that the fort was recommissioned. The rampart was heightened and a broad shallow ditch, 11·6 m wide and 2 m deep, was dug. But nothing seems to have happened, the danger passed, and the fort was finally deserted.

The crescent-shaped annexe earthwork on the south of the fort dates from the main occupation between 400 and 100 B.C. It had an entrance at the northern end, destroyed by the eastern fort entrance extensions. The outer ring of bank and ditch all round the fort was constructed after 100 B.C. Both were used for cattle ranching and livestock and are slight affairs compared with the defences of the fort proper. Beyond these ditches traces of Celtic fields can be seen.

Large quantities of pottery have come from the excavations, as well as twenty-two currency bars, and large numbers of animal bones. There is also evidence to show that iron was smelted on the site. Human bones in large numbers have been found in pits and scattered over the interior of the fort, once more suggesting that exposure of the corpse was the normal method of disposing of the dead during the Iron Age.

B. Cunliffe: *Ant. J.* **51** (1971) 240

10 DUCK'S NEST LONG BARROW   Neolithic
Rockbourne   167 (SU: 104204)

East of minor road north from Rockbourne to Coombe Bissett, taking bridle road beside plantation towards Wick Down.

Lying north-east to south-west this overgrown long barrow is 39·6 m long and 21·3 m broad. It is remarkable for its height which is between 3·7 and 4·6 m. It has clearly defined side ditches.

In the field 0·4 km north-east is an extensive group of round barrows.

11 FLOWER DOWN DISC-BARROW   Bronze Age
  Littleton   168 (SU:459319)
At the southern end of Littleton, behind the bus shelter.
This magnificent disc-barrow has two tumps or burial mounds. A ditch 5·8 m wide and 54·9 m in diameter, with an outer bank 6·1 m wide and 0·6 m high, surrounds the central platform which is 30·5 m across. In the middle is a tump 0·6 m high, whilst to the south-west is a slightly lower mound. Both probably cover female burials.

12 FROXFIELD DYKES   Iron Age ?
  Froxfield   181 (SU:700245)
In trees beside A272 at Boredean: public footpath follows it north.
This defensive earthwork can be traced for some 3 km to the north, although the northern end has now been partly destroyed. It consists of a bank about 2·1 m high with a wide flat bottomed ditch on the western side. Its date and purpose are uncertain, but it certainly cuts off a large area of the high land east of Froxfield Green and might be connected with the Roman settlement near Ridge Farm. Traces of other dykes between High Cross and Weekgreen Farm have been noted by J. P. Williams-Freeman.

J. P. Williams-Freeman: *Field Archaeology as Illustrated by Hampshire* (1915) 374

13 GIANT'S GRAVE LONG BARROW   Neolithic
  Whitsbury   167 (SU:139200)
North-east of Castle Ditches hillfort. A downland track from Outwicks to Coombe Bissett passes at the foot of the hill to the west.
Lying east to west, this long barrow measures 54·9 m by 24·4 m, with its eastern end still about 3·1 m high. The western end has been badly damaged.

Nearby is the Mizmaze, a maze cut in the turf, and probably connected with Breamore Priory founded in 1129.

14 GRANS BARROW LONG BARROW   Neolithic
  Rockbourne   179 (SU:090198)
0·8 km west of the Rockbourne to Coombe Bissett road, beside a bridle track.
This barrow lies almost north to south. It is about 54·9 m long and 18·3 m wide, and reaches its greatest height of 2·7 m at the southern

end. Ditches, apparently passing all round it, can no longer be clearly seen. Knap barrow (No. 18) lies 183 m north-west.

15 GRIM'S DITCH   Bronze Age or Iron Age
                                           167 (SU:005204 to SU:126235)
Crosses A354 at SU:069223. Runs beside minor road at SU:112233.

Grim's Ditch runs for about 13 km between Middle Chase Farm and Yews Farm. It consists of a V-shaped ditch about 1·8 m wide and deep with a broad bank on either side. Its winding course suggests a Bronze or Iron Age date, and it may perhaps best be seen in the light of a ranch boundary related to nearby settlements and field systems.

16 HENGISTBURY HEAD   Bronze and Iron Ages
       Bournemouth   179 (SZ:164910)
Footpaths from Southbourne lead to the headland.

This extensive gravel headland on the south side of Christchurch harbour has been occupied from the Bronze Age onwards. A double rampart and ditch of Iron Age construction known as Double Dykes cuts off the western end of the peninsula. Windblown sand has obscured the earthworks to some extent, but examination of the southern end where the sea has cut a clear section indicates that the outer ditch is 2·1 m deep and 6·1 m wide, and its associated rampart is 1·5 m high. The inner ditch is 3·7 m deep and 12·2 m wide, and its rampart stands 3·7 m high. From these sections, it is clear that the rampart was rebuilt on a number of occasions. Excavations inside the headland (SZ:170909) have revealed four phases of Iron Age occupation extending into the Roman period. The corners of two superimposed rectangular or square buildings have also been found. During excavations in 1911–12 more than 3,000 coins were found within a small area. Almost half were minted locally and are known as Hengistbury Head types. They are dated to the end of the pre-Roman Iron Age. Hengistbury must have been one of the entrepôts for successive groups of Iron Age invaders and traders, the earthworks probably forming a beachhead. Pottery from the site has strong affinities with vessels found in France.

A round barrow near the inner northern end of the Iron Age rampart was excavated in 1911. 30·5 m in diameter and 2·1 m high it contained a cremation burial in an inverted collared urn, together with an incense cup, two gold cones, a halberd pendant, three amber beads and various pieces of flint work. Of two other mounds slightly to the east, one may be a long barrow.

Two barrows were examined on the Warren Hills (SU:170907); the westernmost contained pieces of pottery, but no burial; that next to it produced three cremations in urns. Two adjoining barrows were unopened, and others can be seen further along the headland to the east.

J. P. Bushe-Fox: *Hengistbury Head* (1915)

17 HOUGHTON DOWN LONG BARROW   Neolithic
    Broughton   168 (SU: 330357)
On hill crest east of minor road between Chattis Hill House and Danebury Down. Marked as two round barrows on O.S. map.

Although this long barrow is 51·8 m long and 12·2 m wide, it is scarcely 0·3 m high. It was dug into in the last century when a number of crouched skeletons were found, and a secondary Bronze Age cremation burial.

18 KNAP BARROW LONG BARROW   Neolithic
    Martin   179 (SU: 089199)
0·8 km west of Rockbourne to Coombe Bissett road, and south of bridle road across Toyd Down.

This is the second largest long barrow in Hampshire, being 97·5 m long, and 13·7 m wide. It is orientated north-west to south-east; the latter end being 1·8 m high. It was probably once much wider but considerable ploughing, particularly on the south-west side, has badly damaged it. The side ditches have been destroyed by the same process.

19 LADLE HILL (Plate 35)   Iron Age
    Sydmonton   168 (SU: 478568)
Bridle road approaches from the north, but steep climb uphill. Easiest approach from east at SU:492566, following bridleway and field paths, passing damaged and robbed bell-barrow and ploughed-down saucer-barrow.

Ladle Hill is remarkable in presenting a half-completed hillfort, from which it is possible to gain a good idea of the normal methods used in fort construction. A discontinuous ditch of irregular sections and the beginnings of an internal rampart enclose 2·8 ha. Between many of the ditch sections can be seen a small bank and ditch. It has been suggested that this is the remains of a setting-out ditch. This would seem to involve a tremendous effort when a row of stakes or even a plough furrow could have served the same purpose. It is more likely to have been a small agricultural enclosure ditch that surrounded the hill-top, which was later adapted to hillfort proportions. This early ditch is best seen on the eastern side.

Plate 35   Ladle Hill, unfinished hillfort, Hampshire

A number of gangs of workmen seem to have been employed to enlarge the early ditch. They worked at a number of points around the circumference, creating many unfinished sections from 15·2 m to 82·3 m in length. The topsoil and turf were removed from the ditch surface and dumped well inside the fort, clear of the intended line of the rampart. The base of the bank was to be constructed of the quarried chalk from the ditch, the turf and topsoil could then be brought back and dumped on top. However, the scare which created the sudden need for defence suddenly ceased, and the fort was frozen in a half-built state, the piles of sorted material left for posterity. Gaps on the east and west where the early ditch is also missing, were probably being left for entrances.

The fort seems to be later than a linear ditch on its western side, which in turn overlies a Celtic field system on Great Litchfield Down.

Due north of the fort is a large disc-barrow, 51·8 m in diameter with a single central mound, that shows a robbers' hollow. There is a much smaller disc-barrow inside the northern half of the fort.

S. Piggott: *Antiquity* **5** (1931) 474

20 LAMBOROUGH LONG BARROW   Neolithic
   Bramdean   168 (SU : 593284)
On north side of minor road between Cheriton and Bramdean.

This fine long barrow, lying east to west, measures 67 m long by
33·5 m wide. It is 2·1 m high at the eastern end. Although the barrow
has not been excavated, the side ditches were sectioned in 1932 when
they were shown to be 6·1 m wide and 2·4 to 3·7 m deep. They contained a single piece of Neolithic pottery.

21 MARTIN DOWN ENCLOSURE   Bronze Age
   Martin   167 (SU : 043201)
0·4 km south of A354, east of Bokerley Junction.

This rectangular enclosure of 0·8 ha was excavated by General Pitt-
Rivers and shown to be of Bronze Age date (*c.* 1000 B.C.). It was surrounded by a V-shaped ditch 2·1 to 3·1 m deep, with excavated material
piled into an internal bank, today only 0·6 m high. There is a broad gap
in the northern side which may have been filled by a hedge. There are
also entrance gaps in the south and east sides. This must have been a
cattle enclosure connected with local ranch boundaries. A shallow
ditch to the east has been dated to the same period, as has the nearby
Grim's Ditch. We must consider a pattern of large-scale cattle ranching
on Cranborne Chase at the beginning of the 1st millennium B.C.

A. Pitt-Rivers: *Excavations on Cranborne Chase* 5 (1898) 190

22 MERDON CASTLE HILLFORT   Iron Age
   Hursley   168 (SU : 421265)
Beside minor road at northern end of Hursley Park.

This oval hillfort enclosing 4·5 ha was converted into a Norman castle
in 1129. The outer earthwork is all that remains of the hillfort. Its
rampart stands 3·1 m high, with a wide flat ditch 1·5 m deep, and
counterscarp bank. It is difficult to tell where the Iron Age entrance
would have been. In all probability it was swept away when the massive
Norman earthworks were thrown up, obliterating most of the south
side of the fort.

J. P. Williams-Freeman: *Field Archaeology as Illustrated by Hampshire*
(1915) 384

23 MOODY'S DOWN LONG BARROWS   Neolithic
   Barton Stacey and Chilbolton   168 (SU : 426387)
*South of the B3420 between Newton Down Farm and Moody's Down
Farm.*

This rather shapeless barrow measures 38 m long by 27·4 m wide. It
lies east to west with its higher end 1·4 m high at the east. Slightly over

0·8 km south-west, at the end of a wood is a second long barrow 45·7 m long and 24·4 m wide (SU:417383). Ploughing has reduced it to about 0·9 m in height. It is best reached along the road to Middleton Farm from the A30 at SU:423376.

East of Moody's Down Farm beside a rifle range is the largest long barrow in the group, 67 m long, 22·9 m wide and 1·2 m high. It has clear, wide side ditches, and the barrow lies north-west to south-east (SU:435388).

24 OLD WINCHESTER HILL   Iron Age
     Meonstoke   180/1 (SU:641206)

Car-parking beside minor road at SU:648210. 0·8 km walk to fort which stands proud on the western skyline.

This is a fine example of a contour fort commanding wide views as far as the Isle of Wight. A single rampart and ditch enclose 5·7 ha, broken by inturned entrances at the east and west. That at the east has the ends of its banks raised, with two depressions 1·2 m deep forming outworks in front of the gate. On the southern side of the fort three mounds, possibly barrows, seem to have been incorporated into a counterscarp bank. Although unexcavated, the fort probably dates from the 2nd century B.C., and may have been the tribal centre for the region east of the Meon river. There are four bowl-barrows on the crest inside the fort, and six more outside the western end, including a low saucer-barrow. Two barrows recorded opposite the eastern entrance have been destroyed.

L. V. Grinsell: *Archaeology of Wessex* (1958) 181

26 PETERSFIELD HEATH BARROW CEMETERY   Bronze Age
     Petersfield   181 (SU:758232)

On golf course, widely scattered.

These barrows cover an extensive area between the Golf Club House and Heath Pond. Some are covered with fir trees or bracken, others have been mown and almost obliterated by the golf course. As no excavation record exists, it is not necessary to identify each in detail; suffice to say that the group includes one bell-barrow on the north, partially cut by a road, a disc-barrow 76·2 m south with two off-centre burial tumps, four saucer-barrows and fifteen bowl-barrows. This group offers splendid sport for the barrow hunter, who must at all times beware of the missiles hurled by ferocious native golfers.

L. V. Grinsell: *P. Hants F.C.* **14** (1940) 210

26 POPHAM BEACONS BARROW CEMETERY   Bronze Age
     Overton   168 (SU: 525439)

Close to junction of A30 with minor road north to Steventon.

A fine linear group of five barrows with firs on some of them. The
barrow nearest the main road is a bell-barrow measuring 39·6 m in
diameter and 2·1 m high. The berm, which is an important distinguish-
ing feature of bell-barrows, has been covered with material that has
spread from the mound.

9·1 m north is a bowl-barrow 1·8 m high and 36·6 m across. It
overlies, and therefore is later than, a saucer-barrow of considerable
dimensions. North again is what appears to be a mutilated bell-barrow
standing 2·4 m high and 39·6 m in diameter. It too overlies the saucer-
barrow.

Furthest north from the A30 is a bowl-barrow 27·4 m in diameter and
1·8 m high. There is no record of the contents of any of these barrows.

L. V. Grinsell: *P. Hants F.C.* **14** (1940) 210

27 PORTCHESTER CASTLE FORT (Plate 36)   Roman and Saxon
                                                   180 (SU: 625046)

*Signposted from the A27. Department of the Environment: open at
standard times.*

The promontory on which Portchester Castle stands juts out into
Portsmouth harbour. The whole of the eastern side and part of the
south are faced by the tidal mud flats. The outer walls of the Castle
measuring 185·9 m by 188·9 m are almost entirely Roman work. They
enclose 3·6 ha and were constructed as a Saxon Shore fort late in the
3rd century A.D. The D-shaped bastions belong to the same period
and were built at the same time. The fort was entered by gates in the
centre of the east and west walls, which have been obliterated by later
Norman building. There were also postern gates, 3·1 m wide, in the
north and south walls, which are for the most part blocked up. That
on the north can be traced by a barred opening in the wall. Between
this postern and the inner bailey of the Norman Castle can be seen
the best internal section of Roman wall with its characteristic flint
coursing.

Outside the fort on the north, south and southern ends of the west
side can be seen the Roman defensive ditch. This has been enlarged
in the area of the Norman keep, which like the church inside the
south-east corner, was constructed in the 12th century.

Excavation has shown that the initial occupation of the fort was a
short one. Exactly when in the late 3rd century it was built is not
certain, but by A.D. 300 the occupying troops were withdrawn and
the internal buildings demolished. Their place was taken by a civilian

Plate 36   Portchester Castle, Hampshire

population until around A.D. 340 when the roads were resurfaced and timber buildings were erected. Coins found in the fort suggest that it was abandoned again in about A.D. 370, probably in favour of new quarters at *Clausentum* (Southampton).

After the withdrawal Germanic mercenary troops almost immediately settled at Portchester, where they lived in sunken huts (*grubenhäuser*) through the 5th and 6th centuries, practising agriculture and small-holding. For the following two centuries there seems to have been little activity at the site, until about A.D. 900 when Portchester was revived as one of the 'Burghal Hidage' towns.

B. Cunliffe: *Ant. J.* **49** (1969) 62

28   PORT WAY ROMAN ROAD

Roman
167/8

Numerous sections under modern metalled roads.

There are many Roman roads in Britain that might be mentioned in this book, but space does not permit. Instead the reader is referred to Ivan D. Margary's book, *Roman Roads in Britain*, which describes them all in detail.

The Roman road from Silchester (*Calleva Atrebatum*) to Old Sarum (*Sorviodunum*) is visible for many kilometres as a modern road. More secluded sections can be found south-west of Grateley (SU:260415), in Smannell parish, where it meets the Devil's Ditch (SU:400489), and beside the plantation known as Caesar's Belt between Bradley Wood (SU:463523) and Freemantle Park Farm (SU:528558).

29 QUARLEY HILL   Iron Age
   Quarley   167 (SU:262423)

Approached from south along road linking Grateley and B3084.

This fort of 3·4 ha is pear-shaped in plan. It is defended by a single rampart, ditch and counterscarp bank, with entrances at the north-east and south-west. Gaps midway along the north-west and south-east sides were on excavation shown to be unfinished rampart sections and not entrances.

The 1938 excavations showed that the hill was first defended by a timber stockade early in the Iron Age. This was replaced by the earthworks visible today. The main rampart was about 8·2 m wide at its base and about 2·1 m high. It was built of chalk blocks without timber supports. In front the V-shaped ditch was 3·7 m deep and 7·6 m wide. The counterscarp bank, only 0·9 m high, probably represents material cleaned out of the ditch. The north-east entrance, which was completely excavated, seems never to have been finished, although the holes for gates and a bridge over the top had been dug. Pottery from the fort included red haematite-coated ware of 4th-century B.C. date.

A series of boundary ditches radiate from the hill and underly the hillfort. They are probably ranch boundaries of Bronze or early Iron Age date. They are quite conspicuous, and may have been used as boundaries by the fort builders. Indeed, the two entrances of the fort, and the unfinished gaps in the defences, each lead into different paddocks defined by the ditches.

C. F. C. Hawkes: *P. Hants F.C.* 14 (1939) 136

30 ROCKBOURNE VILLA   Roman
                                                                  179 (SU:120170)

South of Fordingbridge to Rockbourne road at eastern edge of West Park. Open Good Friday to October, weekdays 14.00 to 18.00 hours, Saturdays and Sundays 10.30 to 18.00 hours. New museum on the site. Good car-park.

Excavations have continued annually at this extensive, privately owned, villa site since 1956. Sited in a tributary valley of the Hampshire Avon, this is essentially a courtyard villa, in which more than sixty-eight rooms have so far been uncovered. The northern wing is 91·4 m long;

the west, with the main entrance is 85·3 m long. Fewer mosaics than might have been expected in a villa of this size have survived, but numerous hypocausts and a bath suite are well preserved, as are the flint wall footings often standing 0·6 to 0·9 m high. The domestic quarters of the villa lay on the north and west, whilst to the south were the farm buildings and offices, including a large shed with corn drying kilns and the bases of a series of large stone cornmills more than 1·5 m in diameter.

A. T. Morley Hewitt: *Roman Villa Report 1971* (privately printed)

31 ROUNDWOOD BARROW CEMETERY   Bronze Age
      Laverstoke   168 (SU: 507444)

East of minor road, north from A303 close to its junction with A30. Barrows lie behind hedge north of wood.

This linear cemetery on the spur of the hill consisted of two disc-barrows, a twin-barrow and a bell-barrow.

The disc-barrows, much ploughed down, occur on the west side of the hedge. That closest to the hedge was examined in 1920. Although the surrounding flat-bottomed ditch was uncovered, no burials were detected. The western disc remains unexcavated.

Beyond the hedge stands the twin-barrow. On excavation the western mound was found to be empty. The eastern covered a large pile of flints, but the burial from beneath them had been robbed. The whole barrow was surrounded by an oval ditch.

The bell-barrow was not recognized as such until the 1920 excavation. These showed that a body had been cremated, and its ashes placed in a pit that was dug through the burnt cremation pyre. Soil had then been scraped from the vicinity and placed over the grave, after which chalk from the surrounding ditch was piled on top to make a mound, now 2·7 m high and 21·3 m in diameter.

O. G. S. Crawford: *P. Hants F.C.* **9** (1922) 189

32 ST. CATHERINE'S HILL   Iron Age
      Winchester   168 (SU: 484276)

Reached from A33 at SU:482274 where there is a lay-by.

The rounded tree-capped hill south of Winchester known as St. Catherine's Hill, stands 320 feet (98 m) above sea level. In the early Iron Age its summit was occupied by an unfortified settlement that left traces of its existence in the form of storage pits and pottery.

In the 2nd century B.C. a single rampart and ditch with a dis-continuous counterscarp bank were thrown round the hill-top to enclose 9·3 ha. These defences made maximum use of the steep natural hill-slope on the south and west and are carefully positioned at the break of slope. The ditches are 3·7 m deep and 7·6 m wide, whilst the untimbered rampart must have been about 2·4 m high. The only entrance faces the main hill-ridge to the north-east. It is sharply inturned, and excavations between 1925 and 1928 showed a road causeway 12·2 m wide with square-cut ditch ends outside. It was possible to work out a four-phase sequence there. At first a timber-lined entrance passage was protected by a two-leaf gate and wooden guard chambers. These guard chambers were demolished in phase 2. Later the gate passage was reduced to one gate width and strengthened with flint walling. At the same time the ditch ends were deepened. Finally in the middle of the 1st century B.C. when the fort seems already to have fallen into partial decay, the entrance was burnt, perhaps indicating that the site was sacked by Belgic people who established their own settlement at Winchester to the north.

In the 12th century A.D. the small chapel of St. Catherine which gives the hill its name was established. Traces of it can still be made out under the clump of trees on the hill-top. The maze or labyrinth cut into the turf east of the trees is reputedly the work of boys from Winchester College in the early 18th century.

C. F. C. Hawkes *et al*: *St. Catherine's Hill, Winchester* (1930)

33 SETLEY PLAIN DISC-BARROWS   Bronze Age
    Sway   180 (SU:296000)

South of the road on the Plain. The second example is beside the footpath.

This is an example of a twin-barrow in which two disc-barrows overlap. The earlier lies to the north-west. It has a central mound 14·6 m in diameter and 1·2 m high, surrounded by a ditch and outer bank. The latter has been partly destroyed by the second barrow on its south-east side. This is larger than the first in overall diameter, although its mound is slightly smaller.

0·4 km south-east of the twin disc-barrow is a second, single example, with an overall diameter of 28 m, and a small central mound 9·1 m in diameter and 0·9 m high. Both this and one of the former barrows were opened by two local clergymen in 1792, who found considerable traces of cremation including the wood of the funeral pyre, but no grave goods.

L. V. Grinsell: *P. Hants F.C.* **14** (1940) 224

34 SEVEN BARROWS   Bronze Age
    Burghclere   168 (SU:463555)

On both sides of the A34, and visible from the road.

A group of eight or nine barrows form a linear cemetery from north to south. Some of the barrows have been under the plough in the past.

The southernmost barrow (west of the A34) seems to have been a bell-barrow whose mound material has slipped over its berm. It is about 45·7 m in diameter and 2·4 m high. There are four bowl-barrows north of the bell-barrow, the southernmost is about 27·4 m in diameter and 2·4 m high, then two close to the road are each about 24·4 m in diameter, one 2·1 m high and one 1·5 m high. A fourth, some distance west into the field has been ploughed down and is only visible from the air. Just north of this group is a disc-barrow about 39·6 m across with a single central tump. This, too, has suffered badly from ploughing.

Across the A34, and between it and the railway, are two more bowl-barrows, one about 24·4 m in diameter and 1·2 m high, the other 27·4 m in diameter and 1·8 m high. Yet one more bowl-barrow 36·6 m across and 2·4 m tall lies immediately beyond the railway embankment. Precise details of the contents of the barrows are not known, although cremations without urns, flint work and a bronze pin have come from them.

L. V. Grinsell: *P. Hants F.C.* **14** (1940)

35 SILCHESTER (CALLEVA ATREBATUM)   Roman
168 (SU:640625)

The Roman town lies east of Silchester Common, and minor roads lead to St. Mary's Church, within the Roman walls. The site museum, in the Rectory garden, is at the end of the Drove at SU:629624. It is open all the year round during daylight. The bulk of the Silchester finds are displayed in Reading Museum. The Roman walls are in the care of the Department of the Environment.

The Atrebates were part of a Belgic tribe from northern France who emigrated to Britain shortly after 57 B.C. They settled in southern England and their territory soon spread from the Solent to the Thames. It is probable that they established their earliest settlement at Silchester on the southern side of the later Roman town in Rampier Copse, but nothing definite has been found to prove this. Coins issued by King Eppillus bear the letters CALLEV showing that a wealthy royal settlement existed after about A.D. 5. Soon after the Roman arrival in Britain this native settlement was fortified, its defences represented by what is known as the *Inner Earthwork*. This was probably the work of King Cogidubnus and built for the defence of the most important town in the north-west of his territory. This earthwork is no longer visible, but the later Roman wall sags into the filled-in ditch of the earthwork, about 302 m north-east of the West Gate.

By the end of the 1st century A.D. the native settlement was showing distinct signs of Roman influence: a regular system of streets had been laid down and timber, brick and stone buildings extended over an area of 93 ha, to what is called the *Outer Earthwork*, an earthen defence probably built late in Cogidubnus's reign, which can be seen in Wall Lane near Rye House (SU:636628) and at its best in Rampier Copse (permission to visit required from Wellington estate). Amongst the earliest buildings were the Forum, the Baths, three temples and numerous houses. All of these were constructed before the regular street pattern was laid down. The Forum consisted of shops and offices around three sides of a courtyard, the fourth side being closed by the Basilica or town hall. The baths, about 128 m west of St. Mary's Church were heated by the usual hypocaust system. Of the three early temples, two underlie the modern churchyard, where a small column from one of them can still be seen as a sundial base. The earliest houses were made entirely of wood, and were of simple plan with one room leading directly into another. Later houses had a wooden framework set on flint foundations. It was not until the 2nd century that houses entirely of masonry began to appear. Near the end of the 2nd century the area enclosed by the outer earthwork was reduced and a rampart and ditch defence were thrown up along the line of the present wall. This *Wall*, enclosing 43 ha was constructed in the 3rd century, 2·3 m thick at the base and 6·1 to 7·6 m high, with internal steps leading to a rampart walk every 61 m. The 2nd-century ditch was filled in and a new one dug. Four main gates breached the walls at the north, south, east and west, as well as three small postern gates, two on the north-east and one on the south-east. Neither the East nor West Gateways, which had double portals and guard chambers, are visible. The *North* and *South Gates* had single archways. The Northern (SU:638627) can be seen from Wall Lane and visited with permission from Rye House. The Southern Gate (SU:638621) is the best preserved and can be visited with permission from Manor Farm (near the church). The Postern Gate giving access to the amphitheatre, and the sluice gate, can be seen from the nearby lanes.

The *Amphitheatre* (SU:644626) is unexcavated. Oval in shape, with an entrance on the south, it once contained wooden seats for most of the town's population. The outside can be seen from Pitfield Lane and the interior viewed from the corner of Wall Lane.

Nothing is known for certain about the end of Roman Silchester, but there is some evidence to suggest that life continued there into the middle of the 6th century A.D.

Although Silchester was totally excavated between 1890 and 1909 none of the hundreds of buildings uncovered are visible today. In summer the lines of buried streets can sometimes be seen as areas of parched corn in the ripening crop. The best impression of the town can be gained by visiting the extensive collection of objects excavated, which are housed in Reading Museum, Blagrave Street, Reading (*open weekdays 10.00 to 17.30 hours*).

G. Boon: *Roman Silchester* (1957) and G. Boon: *Archaeologia* **102** (1969) 1

36 SOLDIERS RING   Romano-British
        Damerham   179 (SU:082176)

Approached from Damerham to Martin road along south-east side of Knight's Copse.

Lying across two hollows of the downs this earthwork is hexagonal in plan and encloses about 11 ha. On the south, south-east and west the earthworks are straight with sharp angles. The northern side is made up of three straight lengths, each set at slight angles to the other to produce a bow-shaped side. Although the inner bank is only 0·6 m high, it is very conspicuous, with a ditch 0·9 m deep outside it. There is a second bank and ditch 4·9 m outside. It has been noted that the earthworks cut through a series of lynchets which are presumably earlier. The angularity suggests that the site is of Romano-British construction.

O. G. S. Crawford: *Air Survey and Archaeology* (1924) 30

37 SOUTHAMPTON (CLAUSENTUM)   Roman
                                                             180 (SU:420120)

On projecting spur on east bank of river Itchen, due north of Northam Bridge.

The eastern, landward side of the Roman port was defended by a flint wall and ditch with a rampart and second ditch outside. Of this only the street name 'Rampart Road' survives. The greater part of the site is occupied by modern flats and there is nothing to see except the remains of a small bath house excavated in 1951. Archaeological material excavated in *Clausentum* is displayed in the God's House Tower Museum, Town Quay, Southampton (*open weekdays 10.00 to 17.00 hours, Sundays 14.30 to 16.30 hours*) and in Winchester Museum.

M. A. Cotton and P. W. Gathercole: *Excavations at Clausentum, 1951–4.*

38 STOCKBRIDGE DOWN ROUND BARROWS   Bronze Age
        Stockbridge   168 (SU:375347)

National Trust downland on north side of A272.

There are sixteen low round barrows on this Common. They are widely scattered and difficult to find. None is more than 12·2 m in diameter and the highest is 0·9 m high. One important example, at approximately SU:378351, was 11 m in diameter and 0·6 m high. Excavation has shown it to contain a central crouched female skeleton accompanied by a bell-beaker and copper awl, and surrounded by a discontinuous ditch broken by five wide causeways. The barrow mound was built mainly of flints in which two cremations in urns had been buried. Later another cremation urn was placed deep in the mound, containing amongst the burnt bones of a child of fifteen, beads of faience, calcite, jet, lignite and shale, as well as two awls, one of copper and one of bronze.

J. F. S. Stone: *Ant. J.* **20** (1940) 39

39 WHITESHOOT PLANTATION BARROWS   Bronze Age
      Broughton   168 (SU:290329

On Broughton Down between Whiteshoot Plantation and line of trees to south.

There is a fine bell-barrow between two saucer-barrows. The bell stands 1·8 m high and 19·8 m in diameter, its top scarred by a robbers' hollow. It has a berm 4·6 m wide and a shallow ditch 5·5 m wide outside it. North-west of the bell-barrow is a saucer-barrow 7 m in diameter and 15·2 cm high, surrounded by a shallow ditch 3 m wide, and an outer bank 5·5 m wide and 0·3 m high. The second saucer-barrow, to the east of the bell, is 8·2 m in diameter with a ditch 3·7 m wide and a bank 4·6 m wide.

These saucer-barrows with outer banks slightly higher than the interior mound are good examples of their type. Unfortunately there is no record of their contents.

L. V. Grinsell: *P. Hants F.C.* **14** (1940) 210

40 WINCHESTER (VENTA BELGARUM)   Roman
                                               168 (SU:480295)

Winchester lies astride a ridgeway that runs east to west, at a point where it is breached by the river Itchen flowing north to south. It is not surprising that settlements have flourished here since the Iron Age at least. The Iron Age site has been identified on the west of the old town, on the sloping hillside between Clifton Road and Clifton Terrace, and is known as *Oram's Arbour*. Excavation has revealed a V-shaped ditch 4·9 m deep and 7·6 wide, cut by an inturned entrance beside Clifton Road. It dates from the 2nd to 1st centuries B.C. Nothing of this is visible today, and how far east it stretched towards the Itchen remains unknown. A Belgic coin mould found close to the Minster indicates that an *oppidum* or native township probably existed in the vicinity, but the Minster and Oram's Arbour are 0·8 km apart, which seems to be too great a distance for the *oppidum* to have covered.

The Roman town walls underlie the medieval ones and followed the same rectangular plan, except on the east where they followed the river. Although the medieval city walls exist in the south-east and north-west corners, the later masonry completely covers the Roman work underneath. Finds from the town are displayed in the Winchester City Museum.

M. Biddle: *Ant. J.* **48** (1968) 250; **52** (1972) 93

41 WOOLBURY RING   Iron Age
     Little Somborne   168 (SU:381353)

Beside National Trust property, reached across Stockbridge Common from A30. Parking at SU:388345 ensures following path through Celtic field system.

This hillfort is roughly circular in plan, and encloses 8·1 ha, with a single rampart and ditch and slight counterscarp bank. There is a single entrance on the south-west which shows no sign of inturning. In places the rampart reaches 3·1 m high, but on the east it has been destroyed by ploughing. The whole of the interior has been cultivated for many years.

   Three low dykes which run up to the fort on the west and south-west are the ends of field boundary ditches. One of these follows the western edge of the flights of Celtic fields which run down the valley to the south. There is a less well-defined group to the west.

J. P. Williams-Freeman: *Field Archaeology as Illustrated by Hampshire* (1915) 234

Museums containing archaeological material

The Curtis Museum, High Street, Alton
The Willis Museum, New Street, Basingstoke
Bournemouth Museum, 39 Christchurch Road, Bournemouth
Red House Museum and Art Gallery, Quay Road, Christchurch
Southsea Castle, Clarence Esplanade, Portsmouth
Calleva Museum, Rectory Grounds, Silchester Common
God's House Tower Museum, Town Quay, Southampton
Winchester City Museum, The Square, Winchester

HEREFORDSHIRE

1 ACONBURY HILL   Iron Age
     Kingsthorne   142 (SO:504331)

A track leads to the west end of the camp from Wriggle Brook at SO:501326.

An elongated oval in shape, this tree-covered contour fort occupies about 6·9 ha. It is defended by a single rampart and ditch with traces of a counterscarp bank. Of two entrances, that at the west end is inturned on its southern side, whilst that at the higher east end is strongly inturned on both sides. Limited excavation suggests that the ramparts may have internal stone revetting. Pottery indicates that the fort was occupied from the 1st century B.C. well into the Roman period.

K. Kenyon: *Arch. J.* **110** (1953) 25

2 ARTHUR'S STONE (Plate 37)   Neolithic
    Dorstone   142 (SO:318431)

2.4 km east of Bach, by minor road along hill crest from SO:314434. Department of the Environment signpost. Access at any time.

Nine upright stones support a massive capstone that measures 5·8 m by 2·7 m and forms the burial chamber. It is entered on the north-west by a short antechamber composed of two wall stones. This in turn is entered from a passage 4·6 m long which approaches from the west. Thus entry to the tomb is not direct, but requires turning some 70 degrees midway from the entrance. This is an unusual feature reminiscent of that found at *Les Pierres Plates* in Brittany. A stone to the south of the burial chamber is marked with a horizontal row of about a dozen small cup-marks. An oval mound about 21·3 m long seems once to have covered the tomb.

G. E. Daniel: *Prehistoric Chamber Tombs of England and Wales* (1950) 217

Plate 37   Arthur's Stone chambered tomb, Herefordshire

3 CAPLER CAMP   Iron Age
   Fownhope   142 (SO:593329)

The minor road from Ladyridge to Fownhope passes west of the fort.
A track leads from this road at SO:591324.

Forming an elongated oval this fort stretches along a narrow ridge
above the river Wye. There are two banks and ditches on the south and
west, whilst the north side is strongly scarped. An area of about 4 ha is
enclosed. The entrance, marked by a large mound of earth on its
south side, is at the extreme eastern end of the ridge. The northern
defences curve round the mound, which would have provided an
excellent observation post.

4 COXALL KNOLL   Iron Age
   Buckton and Bucknell   129 (SO:366734)

Approached through wood from the B4367 road at SO:368730.

Coxall Knoll consists of an oval hillfort with two additional enclosures
on its eastern side, the whole covering about 4·9 ha. The main fort
is defended by three banks and ditches on the north and two on the
east and west. These latter are reduced to scarps on the south side
which is naturally steeper. The western side is breached by an inturned
entrance, and another in the eastern side connects with the first
eastern enclosure. This latter has a single rampart and ditch enclosing
1·6 ha. At the eastern end are quarry scoops to provide additional
rampart material. There is an entrance at the south, and another on
the north which connects with the second enclosure. This is smaller
than the first and is protected by a rampart and ditch. It seems to have
been entered through the rampart on the north side.

R.C.H.M. Herefordshire **3** (1934) 27

5 CREDENHILL CAMP   Iron Age
   Credenhill   142 (SO:451445)

By track leading north from Credenhill off A480 road at SO:455440.

This is the largest hillfort in Herefordshire. A single rampart and
ditch follow the 500 feet contour to enclose about 20 ha. In places there
are traces of an internal quarry ditch. There is an inturned entrance at
the south-east corner, and another midway along the eastern side. Both
are approached by hollow-ways. Other breaks in the rampart appear to
be modern. Shortly after the trees covering the site were felled in
1962, limited excavations took place near the east gate. Since then the
fort has been reafforested. It was shown that the camp had been permanently occupied from about 390 B.C. until around A.D. 75, and that it
contained a number of four-post rectangular dwelling huts. The

excavator, S. C. Stanford, has suggested on the basis of similar buildings found at Croft Ambrey, 22·5 km to the north, that a population of
about 4,000 might have lived within Credenhill Camp. Furthermore, a
fort of such size might well be seen as the regional capital of a territory
broadly co-extensive with the present county of Hereford. The inhabitants, he considers, were probably the Decangi, described by Tacitus
and conquered by Scapula in A.D. 48.

S. C. Stanford: *Arch. J.* **127** (1970) 82

6 CROFT AMBREY   Iron Age
   Croft   129 (SO:444668)

*From Cock Gate on B4362, sharp left inside Croft Castle Park towards
castle, then right over cattle grid. Park at end of tarmac road on left and
walk 1.2 km uphill. National Trust.*

Extensive excavation of this hillfort in recent years has shown that it
was occupied from the middle of the 5th century B.C. until it was
destroyed, perhaps in A.D. 48. The fort is triangular in shape with three
lines of defences on the south and west sides and a steep undefended
scarp slope along the north. The total area of 17 ha includes 4·9 ha
covered by these defences. The inner part of the fort, known as the
plateau camp, covers 2·2 ha and was defended by a small rampart and
ditch. It was occupied by rows of rectangular wooden huts ranging in
size from 2·4 m by 1·8 m to 3·1 m by 3·7 m. These seem to have been
rebuilt over a very long period of time and must presumably have
served as houses and granaries as well as store sheds. In the middle of
the 3rd century B.C. the massive inner dumped rampart that still
stands today was thrown up from an internal quarry ditch, outside
the earlier defence, thus increasing the area defended to about 3·4 ha.
It had entrances at the east and south-west. Examination of the south-
west gate showed a sequence of fifteen successive sets of gate posts,
whose plans varied considerably, and included bridges and guard
chambers; the latter destroyed by fire about 225 B.C. Two small banks
and ditches parallel to the main defences and outside them to the south,
enclose another 4·5 ha, called the annexe. This has not been closely
dated, but probably belongs to the final phase of the hillfort's occupation between 50 B.C. and A.D. 48. About midway along this annexe and
close to the inner ramparts is a low mound which after excavation has
been interpreted as a Romano-British sanctuary, possibly used for
animal sacrifices and constructed late in the 1st century A.D. In its
final form it consisted of an oval mound with a flat top 4·6 m across and
0·9 m high, and was clearly in use long after the fort was abandoned as
a stronghold.

S. C. Stanford: *Croft Ambrey Interim Reports* (1960–6)

7 DINEDOR CAMP   Iron Age
   Dinedor   142 (SO:524364)

A metalled road at SO:522366 leads directly to the north rampart from Dinedor Cross.

A single stone-faced rampart and ditch enclose an area of 4·9 ha. They are best preserved on the east where there is a simple 'straight-through' type of entrance. Around the rest of the camp, which is wooded, the rampart has been somewhat levelled and the ditch remains only as a terrace at its foot. Limited excavation indicated that the fort was permanently and densely occupied as was Croft Ambrey.

8 HEREFORDSHIRE BEACON (Fig. 16, Plate 38)   Iron Age
   Colwall   143 (SO:760399)

A short but steep climb uphill from the A449 opposite the 'British Camp Hotel'.

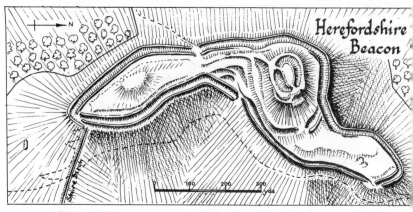

Fig. 16   The Herefordshire Beacon hillfort

Crowning a long narrow ridge of the Malvern Hills, this magnificent fort is one of the most spectacular in Britain. In its earliest form it consisted of a 3·2 ha enclosure surrounded by a bank and ditch with a counterscarp bank on the north-east, ringing the highest part of the hill at 1,100 feet (335 m) above sea-level. This was entered at the north-east and south-west.

Later in the Iron Age the fort was considerably increased in size, its new rampart, ditch and counterscarp approximately following the 1,000 feet (305 m) contour along the length of the ridge. Frequently material for the new rampart was obtained from internal quarry scoops which can be clearly seen today, especially on the eastern side. Although

Plate 38   The Herefordshire Beacon hillfort from the west

the fort is unexcavated and evidence for its occupation is lacking, the scoops may well have provided shelter for huts. Four overlapping-type entrances were incorporated, at the north-east, east, west and south. A few surface sherds of Middle Iron Age type may belong to the second phase of development.

In the 11th or 12th century A.D. the hilltop was again inhabited, this time by the builders of a ring-motte, and it is this structure that occupies the highest part of the hill. The dyke which runs eastwards downhill from the southern end of the Beacon was constructed in about 1290 by the Earl of Gloucester to mark a boundary.

R. E. M. Wheeler: *Arch. J.* **109** (1952) 145

9 IVINGTON CAMP   Iron Age
   Leominster Out   142 (SO:484547)

Off minor road from Park Gate to Gattertop, by metalled road to Camp Farm at SO:478547.

The road enters this triangular earthwork through a modern gap in its western side. The whole site covers some 19 ha. On the north, west and south the ground falls away steeply, but is still protected by a double rampart and ditch. On the east where the ground is flat the earthworks are more massive. There is an internal terrace to the rampart at the south-west where it is strongly inturned to protect an entrance that lies at the head of a steep covered way which is flanked by two banks on its south-eastern side. Between the banks is a cruciform-shaped earthwork whose purpose has not yet been satisfactorily explained, but which must be connected with an elaborate defence procedure. At the north-east is a simple overlapping entrance, with traces of ploughed-down outworks beyond.

An earlier enclosure of about 3 ha existed in the north-west corner of the fort, protected by a single bank and ditch. Its line can still be seen beneath a hedgerow, and its original entrance probably lay under the farm buildings on the south: the gap on the east looks modern. There are other banks on the west side of the hill, but they probably represent tracks of more recent times.

R.C.H.M. Herefordshire **3** (1934) 131

10 KENCHESTER (MAGNIS)   Roman
    Kenchester   142 (SO:440428)
To the north of minor road one mile south-west of Kenchester.

Lying on the Roman road from Wroxeter to Caerwent, the small town of *Magnis* was probably founded during the second half of the 1st century A.D. as an open settlement with wooden huts beside a rectangular street pattern. Perhaps in the mid 2nd century an earthen rampart and ditch were constructed reducing the size of the town on the west, and enclosing about 9 ha. A stone wall 2·1 m thick, flanked by an earth bank, may date from this time or the mid 4th century. An 18th-century plan shows four gateways, although none are visible today. Excavations have shown that the West Gate was flanked by two stone towers and had a dual-carriage road passing through it. Bastions were added to the town walls in the mid 4th century to house *ballistae*, and a new wide, shallow ditch was cut to replace the earlier one that had silted up. Early in the 5th century the gate was altered, its south carriageway being blocked up and a new road being laid through the northern one. Inside the town paved streets, drainage channels and house footings with mosaic floors and decorated wall-plaster have been uncovered. A variety of small objects, particularly pottery and coins, have been recovered, whilst inhumation and cremation burials have frequently been found inside the walls.

F. Heys and M. Thomas: *T. Woolhope Club* **36** (1958) 100; **37** (1961) 149

11 KING ARTHUR'S CAVE   Prehistoric to Roman
    Whitchurch   142 (SO:545155)
Follow Department of the Environment signpost from SO:548157 past quarry. Torch required.

In spite of its name this cave has no connection with King Arthur. It was occupied during the Upper Palaeolithic and Neolithic periods.

Two chambers lie at the ends of short passages which branch off from a wide entrance that is divided in two by a broad natural pillar of rock. First explored by W. S. Symonds in 1871 and later by the Bristol University Spelaeological Society (1924–7), the cave produced bones of late Ice Age animals in its lowest depths including mammoths and woolly rhinoceros, all covered by thick layers of stalagmite. In the cave passage and at the entrance, occupation layers dating from about 25,000 B.C. to the Roman period occurred. Here were flint implements made by Upper Palaeolithic man, as well as his mesolithic and neolithic successors. The ashes of his fires and the bones of the animals he hunted remind us of the reindeer, bison and wild horses that provided him with food and clothing. The cave mouth was only sporadically occupied, but long enough for more than 2·1 m of material to accumulate.

T. F. Hewer and H. Taylor: *P.U.B.S.S.* **2** (1925) 221; **3** (1927) 59

12 MIDSUMMER HILL   Iron Age
    Eastnor   143 (SO:761375)
National Trust property. Track north from Hollybush village.

Midsummer Hill was one of a series of border forts that were maintained in good order for four or five hundred years, prior to their destruction by the Romans, probably in A.D. 48. A bank, ditch and counterscarp bank enclose an irregular crescent-shaped area, around two hills, of about 12 ha. The bank was stone faced and is broken by entrances at the north, and in the south-west angle. This latter gate was rebuilt at least seventeen times, during which it had guard chambers both of wood and stone, and was strongly inturned. A radiocarbon date for the entrance suggests that it began about 400 to 390 B.C. Most of the buildings excavated were rectilinear in shape, measuring between 4·6 m by 3·7 m, and 3·7 m by 2·4 m. These buildings seem to have been laid out on a regular grid-iron plan suggesting a semimilitary organization. Later huts on the site were smaller, averaging 3·1 m by 2·4 m. These were finally destroyed by fire, perhaps in A.D. 48 when Ostorius Scapula attacked the Decangi. There may have been an annexe between the western side of the fort and the quarry to the south, where a line of entrenchment joins the fort. On the other hand this may be a branch of the Red Earl's Dyke, a medieval earthwork which joins the hillfort at its southern extremity.

A low mound, 48·8 m long and 12·2 m wide in the saddle between the two summits of Hollybush Hill seems to be a pillow mound of uncertain date and purpose. It has been claimed as a long barrow, but digging in 1924 failed to produce any evidence to support this. 55 m north of the pillow mound is a low, circular mound 7·6 m in diameter surrounded by a ditch 3·7 m wide, and broken by an entrance gap on the south-east. It may have been the site of a Romano-Celtic temple.

Again, digging in 1924 failed to prove this but did provide ironwork which was lying on the ground surface under the mound.

S. C. Stanford: *Midsummer Hill Interim Reports* (1967–71)

13   PYON WOOD CAMP   Iron Age
  Aymestrey   129 (SO:424664)
Along track leading west off A4110 to Ballsgate Common.

On a steep-sided hill above the river Lugg, this triangular fort encloses about 3·6 ha. It is defended by a rampart, ditch and counterscarp bank, and traces of a quarry ditch can be seen inside the rampart. A hollow-way approaches the site at an entrance on the south-east, which is clearly inturned. The whole site is covered with trees.

14   RISBURY CAMP   Iron Age
  Humber   129 (SO:542553)
East of the minor road from Stoke Prior to Risbury.

In spite of its unimpressive, low-lying position east of the Humber Brook this is one of the most strongly defended forts in southern England. Rectangular in shape, and enclosing 3·6 ha, it has two or three massive banks often 7·6 to 9·1 m high on all sides. The only probable entrance lies in the middle of the west side. Banks funnel the approach road, although the entrance itself is only slightly in-turned. Outside, and to the south of the entrance, are a number of low cross-banks and ditches. The gap which cuts through the eastern rampart seems to be modern, since there is no corresponding break in the outer earthworks. The gap has exposed a good section through the rampart which is here of dumped clay. A stone facing can be seen on the north rampart crest, and stone walling is recorded in the 19th century.

R.C.H.M. Herefordshire **3** (1934) 73

15   SUTTON WALLS   Iron Age
  Sutton   142 (SO:525464)
By cart-track leading north from Sutton St. Michael.

Almost every hill-spur in this part of the valleys of the Lugg and Wye is dominated by hillforts of the Iron Age. Long ago the area was shown to represent one of the main through routes connecting the Bristol Channel and the Welsh Marches.

   Sutton Walls crowns a narrow hill-ridge and is over 0·8 km in length. A denuded rampart and filled-in ditch enclose about 11·7 ha. These defences are broken by entrances at the east and west extremities. The gaps on the north and south are modern. Unfortunately, about a quarter of the interior has been quarried away to a depth of some 6 m, although this now allows traces of huts and storage pits to be seen in section. The hill was first occupied early in the 1st century B.C. Towards the end of the century the V-shaped ditch, 4·6 m deep, was dug and the material obtained carried up to make the rampart which may have been faced with timber or stone. Material was also scooped from shallow quarries inside the fort, in which huts were later built. About A.D. 25 the ditch was widened and the rampart enlarged. Soon afterwards a number of the camp's inhabitants were slaughtered. At the western entrance twenty-four skeletons were found in a narrow trench across the ditch, and many more probably await discovery. These are the remains of battle victims, killed either by native enemies or perhaps by the Roman attacks of A.D. 48. After the battle the fort continued to be occupied until the 3rd century A.D., although its defences had almost certainly been slighted. Material excavated from Sutton Walls, including a large pre-Roman iron anvil, is displayed in Hereford City museum.

K. Kenyon: *Arch. J.* **110** (1953) 1

16 WAPLEY CAMP   Iron Age
       Staunton-on-Avon   129 (SO:345625)

By Forestry Commission gated road at SO:353618 on Stansbatch to Byton Hand road.

Overlooking the valley of the Lugg and the Welsh border, this tri-angular fort lies at over 1,000 feet (305 m) above sea level. Although the approach and ramparts are wooded, the interior is rough but clear. On the north is an escarpment with additional scarping. On the other sides are a number of close-set steep banks and ditches, four on the south, and five on the east. An entrance in the middle of the southern side is long and oblique, and it bears to the left as it approaches the long inturned rampart ends. A gap at the south-east corner seems to be modern, although the postern gap at the north-east is more probably original. Inside the fort and west of the main southern entrance is what appears to be a well or 'ritual shaft' and at least four low pillow mounds.

R.C.H.M. Herefordshire **3** (1934) 184

Museum containing archaeological collection
Hereford City Museum, Broad Street, Hereford

Plate 39   Arbury Banks plateau fort, Hertfordshire

HERTFORDSHIRE

I   ARBURY BANKS (Plate 39)   Iron Age
    Ashwell   147 (TL:262387)

*The site, which is ploughed, can be reached along the hedgerows from either
of the roads to east or west.*

This small oval fortified farmstead consists of a rampart and ditch
enclosing 5 ha, surrounding a large off-centre circular hut: perhaps a
chieftain's house, and a number of sub-rectangular enclosures. On the
north and east the defences were levelled two centuries ago. Joseph
Beldam carried out one of the first 'rescue' digs on the site in September 1856 'the inclosure of the parish of Ashwell being immediately in
prospect'. He found that the ditch was V-shaped, 4·6 m deep and 6·1 m
wide, with a steep counterscarp bank. Within the enclosure he found
many storage pits, some pierced by gullies, which he thought were
pit dwellings. Amongst the pottery Beldam listed pipkins or cups,
cooking pots, and between thirty and forty different-shaped rims and
pierced handles, the latter suggesting the high-shouldered handled
jars characteristic of East Anglia. A specialist report on bones from the
site described *bos longifrons* (long-horned ox), deer, goat, horse, pig

and part of a human skull. Some years before Beldam's work human skulls had been found in the rampart and reburied in Ashwell church-yard. The circular hut within the site is only visible today from the air. Much of the interior has been damaged by coprolite digging.

J. K. St. Joseph: *J.R.S.* **45** (1955) 89

2 THE AUBREYS   Iron Age
  Redbourn   147/160 (TL:095113)

Approached from B487. A restaurant has been built in the southern part of the fort, from which the earthwork can be seen. North-bound carriageway of M1 overlooks the site.

This is a low-lying plateau fort in a tributary valley of the river Ver. The earthwork encloses 7·3 ha and has double ramparts and ditches on all sides except the west, where a single bank and ditch suffice. Part of the outer bank has been destroyed on the eastern side and it has been suggested that the fort may be unfinished. There is an original entrance on the western side at the point where the double rampart becomes single. As at Cholesbury (page 21) the weaker defences face the forested land to the north. It may have been used by Iron Age people mainly concerned with cattle and pig husbandry, who had perhaps moved into the area at a time when the better, unforested land was already occupied. Excavations by R. E. M. Wheeler produced two or three pieces of late hand-made Iron Age pottery.

R.C.H.M. Hertfordshire (1910) 166

3 BEECH BOTTOM DYKE (See Fig. 18)   Iron Age
  St. Albans   160 (TL:155091)

Visible at any time in Batchwood Road.

Almost certainly of Belgic construction, this linear earthwork may have bridged the open ground between the Lea and Ver valleys. It consists of a ditch on the northern side 8·8 m deep and a bank to the south: the whole feature measuring 27·4 m across. Unfortunately the dyke has suffered much in the last thirty years. Today it begins in Batchwood Road by the Townsend School playing field, crosses the A6 opposite the 'Ancient Briton' public house, and runs east under the railway line into the B651 road to Sandridge.

The Devil's Dyke at Wheathampstead (see page 188) may well be the north-eastern extension of this work which need not have been continuous, but may rather have been a link over open country between areas of forest. To the west the *Devil's Ditch* close to Mayne Farm on the Gorhambury estate (TL:123084) may be another section of the same work. It ran from the Ver into forest on the west, and may possibly have been a northern defence for the Catuvellauni living at Prae

Wood (see Verulamium, page 185). The Devil's Ditch lies beside the
drive to Gorhambury House, and permission should be sought before
visiting.

R. E. M. Wheeler: *Verulamium, a Belgic and two Roman Cities* (1936)
16

4 HARPENDEN MAUSOLEUM

Roman
147/160 (TL:119136)

*Special permission is required to visit this site preserved in the grounds of
Rothamstead Experimental Station.*

In 1937 excavations in the private grounds of the Rothamstead Experimental Station revealed the footings of a circular building 3·4 m in
diameter, surrounded by a 30·5 m-square walled enclosure, and external
V-shaped ditch, broken by an entrance on the east. The circular
building contained an altar-like plinth in front of a small alcove, which
may have housed a life-sized statue, of which pieces were found during
the excavations. Two cremation burials were found within the walls of
the square enclosure and were dated to about A.D. 130.

A. W. G. Lowther: *J.R.S.* **28** (1938) 186

5 RAVENSBURGH CASTLE
   Hexton

Iron Age
147 (TL:099295)

*The western fortifications can be seen from the Barton Hills to the west,
by taking the track from the B655 at TL:095304. The remainder of the
fort is not accessible without permission from the Hexton Estate office.*

Although covered with thick woodland, this is one of the largest and
finest of the Chiltern hillforts. It is surrounded on three sides by deep
dry valleys. A single rampart and ditch enclose 9 ha. Excavation has
shown that the ditch averages 3·7 m deep and 6·1 m wide, with an
internal rampart that has been rebuilt at least twice. At first, in about
400 B.C. the site was protected by a timber-laced rampart (two lines of
wooden fences held together with tie-beams) filled in with turf and
chalk rubble. Later in the 1st century B.C. the fort, which by then had
fallen into decay, was suddenly refortified with a glacis rampart. There
are two entrances to the fortress; the main one at the north-west is
oblique, whilst the smaller one to the south-east is of the simpler
straight-through variety. This latter gave access to the Burwell spring
below the fort, and was made when the fort was refortified. An area
inside the south-eastern gate seems to have been used for cattle pens.
The hillfort is on the northern edge of Catuvellaunian territory and
may have been the stronghold of Cassivellaunus attacked in 54 B.C.
by Julius Caesar.

6 SIX HILLS
 Stevenage

Roman
147 (TL:237237)

Beside the A602 on the south side of Stevenage New Town.

Dr. Ducarel and his friends who opened the Six Hills (or Six Boroughs) in September 1741 would have been amazed to find them as they are today, isolated by the rushing traffic to the north. The barrows average 3·1 m high and 18·3 m in diameter, and all except one appear to have been opened at some time in the past. Dr. Ducarel 'found only wood and a piece of iron'. 'An old man in the town', he recorded, 'remembers opening the fourth and finding nothing.'

J. Dyer: *Arch. J.* **116** (1961) 6

7 THERFIELD HEATH BARROW CEMETERY (Fig. 17, Plate 40)

Neolithic and Bronze Age
147/8 (TL:342402 long barrow)

 Royston

Accessible from A505, but watch out for horse riders and careless golfers.

The most extensive barrow cemetery in the Chilterns lies beside the Icknield Way on the Heath to the west of Royston. It consists of a small long barrow, ten round barrows and 0·8 km further west an

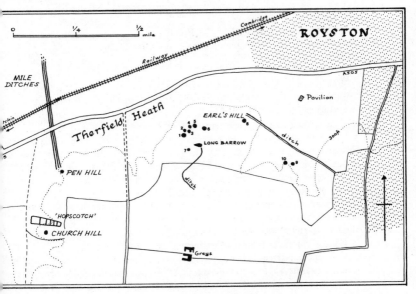

Fig. 17 Therfield Heath barrow cemetery, Hertfordshire

Plate 40   Therfield Heath barrow cemetery, Hertfordshire

Iron Age boundary dyke called the Mile ditches, with a further round barrow 'Pen Hills' at its southern end.

Many of the barrows were opened by Edmund Nunn of Royston between 1854 and 1856, and most of the objects that he found are in the Museum of Archaeology and Ethnology in Cambridge.

The long barrow, which measures 33·5 m long, 17·1 m wide, and 2·1 m high at the eastern end, was opened by Nunn in 1855 and C. W. Phillips in 1935. It contained a burial near its western end under a stack of turf.

The main group of round barrows north-west of the long barrow is known as the Five Hills. No. 1 was opened in 1854 and contained an inverted collared urn holding a cremation with a small bronze pin. There is no record of the contents of Nos. 2 and 3. No. 4, which is 3·1 m high and 18·3 m in diameter, was opened in 1856 when Nunn found 'nine human skeletons, men, women and children, covering a space 0·6 m wide by 3·7 m long, the bones lying in all directions'. No. 5 contained a rectangular flint-lined grave in which lay cremated bones and a small 17·8 cm high pottery urn.

Barrow 6 to the east of the Five Hills contained a cremation; there is no record of the contents of No. 7 or of No. 8, 'Earl's Hill'. Of the two barrows near the rifle range, 9 and 10, the eastern one produced 'a box of calcined bones' but the western was empty.

Pen Hills barrow (TL:333398) was built over two linked circular chambers that were filled with chalk, ironwork, animal bones and pieces of pottery. They were probably constructed during the Iron Age. Running north from this barrow are the three ditches of the boundary dyke called *Mile Ditches*. Today these ditches only show as darker growth in the grass and crops. Although unexcavated the dyke is in all probability part of a chain of Chiltern dykes across the Icknield Way (see Dray's Ditches, page 2).

J. Dyer: *Arch. J.* **116** (1961) 6

8 VERULAMIUM (Fig. 18, Plate 41)   Roman
    St. Albans   160 (Museum at TL: 136073)

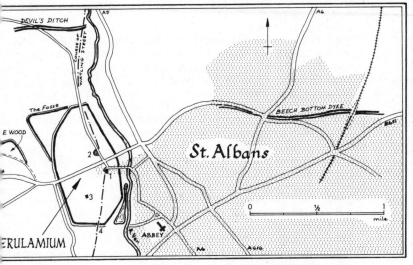

Fig. 18 Archaeological sites at St. Albans, Hertfordshire (No. 3, hypocaust)

The *municipium* (a town of self-governing status) of Verulamium was the most important Roman town in Britain. Unfortunately little is visible of it today, since most of the site, owned by the City Council, is covered by football pitches, and its potential tourist wealth is hidden from view.

In about 20 B.C. the Belgic tribe, the Catuvellauni, established their capital at Prae Wood (TL: 126070) where a somewhat primitive township grew up. Later, the Prae Wood site declined and another capital was built at Colchester. Prae Wood was not completely abandoned, though most of the inhabitants seem to have moved downhill eastwards, towards the river Ver, where they established a small defended township north of the present St. Michael's church. It was this town that was burnt to the ground by Boudicca in A.D. 60 or 61.

By A.D. 79, when Agricola was Governor, the town had been rebuilt and a splendid Basilica (town hall) erected. An earth and timber rampart was now built around the town to forestall any further native uprising. Known as The Fosse, this earthwork can best be seen at TL: 128077.

A major defence scheme about A.D. 200 resulted in the building of a flint and mortar wall around the city which by that time enclosed 81 ha. In front of the wall was a ditch 6·1 m deep and 9·1 m wide. Inside this secure boundary fine houses with mosaic floors, shops and workshops, temples and public buildings were erected. A splendid theatre was already in existence.

The end of Verulamium is obscure. Houses within the town continued to be occupied long into the 5th century, and a large Saxon cemetery outside the West (or Silchester) Gate indicates that the area continued to be occupied during early Saxon times.

The remarkable *Museum* (TL: 136073) makes the best starting point for a tour of the few visible remains. On the ground outside the museum on its western side, a line of flints outlines the corner of the Basilica. Most of that building lies under St. Michael's church. (Fig. 18, No. 1.)

Forward from the museum across the busy A414 is the *Roman theatre*, the only visible example of about six so far recognized in Britain. (TL: 134074). Staircases on the outside of the theatre led to the semicircular tiers of seats, from where the theatrical performances could be viewed. At times 'spectacles' such as bear-baiting and cock-fighting were presented in the circular 'orchestra' area in front of the stage. The bank on which visitors to the theatre walk today is the spoil from the excavation and not part of the building. (Fig. 18, No. 2.)

Beside the theatre the outlines of houses and shops have been uncovered. One house, close to the road, contained an underground shrine, of which the apsidal end is still visible.

Of the many larger houses of Verulamium practically nothing can be seen. A low, modern brick bungalow protects two rooms that were originally part of the bath wing of a magnificent town house 61 m long and 39·6 m wide (TL: 136069). The rooms are floored by mosaic pavements under which the hypocaust system of heating is clearly visible. Some of the flue tiles were removed from this floor by the Norman monks who built St. Alban's Abbey. The Museum and hypocaust are both open at the same time in summer, and the admission ticket covers both. (*Summer: weekdays 10.00 to 17.30, Sundays 14.00 to 17.30 hours. Winter: weekdays 10.00 to 16.00 hours, Sundays 14.00 to 16.00 hours.*)

A well-preserved section of the *Roman City Wall* can be seen on the southern side of the town (TL: 137066) with the excavated town ditch 6·1 m deep in front of it. The wall, which once stood about 7 m high,

Plate 41   Verulamium city walls, St. Albans, Hertfordshire

still reaches 3.1 m in places. It is constructed of flint and mortar, with layers of bonding tiles. The latter were popular with the Norman Abbey builders. At intervals along the wall are solid semicircular bastions on which war machines stood, and internal turrets both for stores and ammunition and to shelter guards on patrol. The Watling Street entered the city by the *London Gate* (TL: 138067) whose position is marked in the ground by flint foundations. The vehicular traffic entered by two large gateways, whilst pedestrians proceeded through smaller side gates. The whole was flanked by massive bastion towers. (No. 4.)

The ornamental lake (TL: 139069) lies over a Roman cemetery. It was perhaps in this area that St. Alban crossed the river Ver during the Governorship of Geta Caesar in A.D. 208 on his way up the hill to his martyrdom on the site of the present Abbey church.

Ilid Anthony: *Verulamium* (1970)

9 WHEATHAMPSTEAD DEVIL'S DYKE   Iron Age
                                          147/160 (TL:186133)
On the eastern side of Dyke Lane. National Trust Property.

The massive Devil's Dyke is about 457 m long, 12·2 m deep and 39·6 m
wide at the top. It was made by artificially deepening a natural valley
and dumping the excavated soil onto either lip to form a bank on the
east 2·7 m high and on the west 1·8 m high. A second 'dyke' to the east
called *The Slad* seems to be entirely natural, but has not been excavated
in modern times. Sir Mortimer Wheeler has suggested that together
the two earthworks (enclosing an area of about 36 ha) formed the headquarters of Cassivellaunus when his tribe was attacked by Caesar in
54 B.C. The theory is open to question, and it may be nearer the truth
to see Cassivellaunus occupying Wheathampstead after Caesar's
attack, and before establishing himself at Prae Wood.

R. E. M. Wheeler: *Antiquity* 7 (1933) 21

Museums containing archaeological material

Ashwell Village Museum, Swan Street, Ashwell
Hertford Museum, 18 Bull Plain, Hertford
Hitchin Museum, Paynes Park, Hitchin
Letchworth Museum and Art Gallery, Town Square, Letchworth
City Museum, Hatfield Road, St. Albans
Verulamium Museum, St. Michael's, St. Albans
Stevenage Museum, Lytton Way, New Town, Stevenage

   Hertfordshire material is also displayed in The Museum of
Archaeology and Ethnology, Downing Street, Cambridge

HUNTINGDONSHIRE

1 CHESTERTON ROMAN BARROW   Roman
                                          134 (TL:129946)
Approached by field track south from the A605 at Chesterton.

This probable Roman barrow crowns the northern end of a hill-ridge,
west of the Ermine Street and 2·4 km south of *Durobrivae* Roman
town. Nothing is known of its contents.

2 DUROBRIVAE (CHESTERTON) (Plate 42)   Roman
    Water Newton   134 (TL:122968)
There is a lay-by on the A1 adjoining this site to the south.

Little is visible of this Roman town of about 17·8 ha, lying between
the modern A1 road and the river Nene. The Roman road, the Ermine
Street, runs diagonally across the hexagonal area which is enclosed by

Plate 42   Chesterton Roman town, Huntingdonshire

buried walls of 2nd-century date, a rampart and ditch. These latter are
still visible and are partly marked by hedge boundaries running along
the edge of the flood plain of the river. There were at least three gates:
one where the main road enters at the south-east, a second at the north-
west, where it leaves before covering the 0·4 km to the crossing place of
the river Nene, and a third at the south-west where the rampart is
staggered. Air photographs show that irregular streets lie on either
side of the Ermine Street within the town walls in a far from typical
Roman pattern. A plan of 1828 shows no fewer than twenty-two buildings and aerial photographs of the ploughed area have confirmed this.

The importance of *Durobrivae* must be seen in its relationship with
the surrounding Castor pottery industry, one of the largest industrial
complexes so far known from Roman Britain. The town must once
have been surrounded by kilns, warehouses and potters' cottages, of
which some traces have been found in the neighbouring countryside. A
number of larger houses or *villas* in the area may represent the houses
of pottery owners or managers.

North of *Durobrivae* and west of the Billing Brook aerial photographs have shown a Roman fort measuring 155·5 m by 140·2 m and
clearly guarding the Nene crossing.

J. K. St. Joseph: *J.R.S.* **48** (1958) 98

3   GREAT STUKELEY BARROW   Roman
                                                          134 (TL:219748)

The barrow on the north side of the A14, Ermine Street Roman road,
is probably of Roman origin, but nothing is known of its contents.

4   THORNHAUGH HENGE   Neolithic
                                                          123 (TF:066008)

Via footpath 0·4 km north from Thornhaugh village, by Manor Farm.

Classically situated for a henge monument in low marshy ground
sloping down to a stream, this site, 83·8 m in diameter, consists of an
inner ditch surrounded by a low bank and outer ditch. All except the
outer ditch are broken by entrances on the north-north-west and south-
south-east. There are traces of a bank on the inside of the inner ditch.
All the ditches have carefully squared-off ends beside the entrance
causeways which is a characteristic of many henges. It has been suggested by C. W. Phillips that the site might be a 17th-century
pleasaunce or water-garden associated with the nearby Manor Farm.

R. J. C. Atkinson: *Excavations at Dorchester, Oxon. 1* (1951) 104

Museum containing archaeological material

Norris Library and Museum, The Broadway, St. Ives, Huntingdonshire

ISLE OF WIGHT

1 AFTON DOWN LONG BARROW AND BARROWS

Neolithic and Bronze Age

Freshwater   180 (SZ:352857)

North of A3055 at west end of golf course. National Trust.

Some two dozen barrows are spread along the ridge of Afton Down. At
the western end are two bell-barrows, eleven bowl-barrows and a disc-
barrow. West of these is a long barrow 36·6 m in length and 0·9 m
high, opened without result by the Revd. J. Skinner in 1817. A disc-
barrow that has been made into a golf-tee follows, with three bowl-
barrows and two more bell-barrows, one of which is uncertain. This
particular group is completed with three bowl-barrows. A number of
the round barrows were opened by Skinner who found cremations in
them. 1·6 km further east on East Afton Down is another small group
of bowl-barrows and one bell-barrow.

L. V. Grinsell and G. A. Sherwin: *P.I.W.N.H.S.* **3** (1941) various

2 BRADING ROMAN VILLA (Fig. 19)   Roman

Morton   180 (SZ:599863)

*West of the A3055 at Morton on the south-west side of the town. Open
May to October, weekdays 9.30 to 18.00 hours, Sundays 15.00 to 18.00*

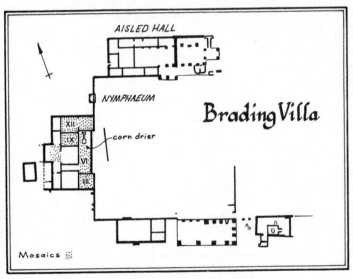

Fig. 19   The Brading Roman villa, Isle of Wight

hours. Winter months by appointment only. Telephone 235. Adults 10p, children 5p.

One of the finest accessible Roman villas in England lies at the western end of a courtyard some 55 m square, which is flanked by detached farm buildings on the north and south and is open on the east where the land slopes down towards the sea. In Roman times the sea came much closer to the front of the villa, whilst the land rose up to a ridge behind the house to the west. Here roughly square Celtic fields formed part of the farm estate. It remains unproven whether they were worked from the farm, but their steep lynchets, rising as much as 3·1 m, at least suggest that they were used over a very long period and are probably contemporary for part of the time.

The main villa building is protected by a modern roof. In front is a paved corridor, behind which are two rooms on either side of a central lobby. At each end wings containing a single room project forward. Five more rooms lie at the back, including a dining-room reached from the lobby. The central rooms were probably lit by means of clerestory windows: much window glass was found when the villa was first uncovered in 1880. The pride of the villa is its mosaics which are undoubtedly amongst the best in Britain. The most important are to be found in Rooms III, VI (the entrance corridor), IX and XII. The pavements are probably not all contemporary, and the artistic quality varies considerably, but the Brading mosaics are remarkable for the wealth of pictorial representations which at first sight seem typical of Roman mythological subjects. Orpheus and his lyre, Medusa with snakes emanating from her hair, Perseus holding the gorgon's head, all are here, together with tritons and nereids and a wealth of minor details. With deeper study the mosaics can be seen to be linked by the eclectic tastes of the villa owner, and contain such philosophical elements as the heavens, earth, air and water. A number of rooms had hypocaust heating beneath them, and finds of coal on the site suggest that it was amongst the fuels burnt.

The range of buildings to the north of the villa consisted of an aisled hall, later divided up into individual compartments and used as accommodation for a farmer or bailiff, farm-workers and animals. Most of it has been covered over, but part of its baths and a well are still visible. Between the northern range and the villa proper is a semi-circular *nymphaeum* or ornamental fountain of a quasi-religious type. A buried range on the south may have contained stables and store-houses. The villa was founded about A.D. 300 and lasted until at least the beginning of the 5th century. Towards the end of its life a corn-drying kiln was installed in the northern corner of the main entrance corridor.

A room at the southern end of the villa serves as a small site museum, and contains as well as the inevitable pottery and jewellery, a massive iron lock and key that may once have fitted the main gate of the building, and an asymmetrical ploughshare of a type belonging to a mould-board plough.

V.C.H. Hants **1** (1900) 313; A. Rivet: *The Roman Villa in Britain* (1969) various

3 CARISBROOKE CASTLE ROMAN FORT   Roman
                                                     180 (SZ:487878)

Signposted on the south-west side of the town. Department of the Environment: open at standard hours throughout the year. Museum closed on Sundays from October to Easter. Car-park, café and guide-book available.

Traces of Roman walls still survive, embedded in the earthworks of the prominent Norman Castle. Although the fort was of Saxon Shore type it is some distance from the sea, and was more likely connected with the late Roman administration of the island. Rectangular in plan, measuring some 134 m by 146 m, the fort had a wall 3·1 m thick. Little of it remains today. As one crosses the bridge over the moat to enter the Gatehouse, traces of the western wall of the Roman fort can be seen in the moat side, level with the base of the drum towers of the gateway. On the east, below the keep, a shallow Roman bastion and a deeply recessed eastern gateway have been traced, sited between the curved returns of the curtain wall. These lie on the left as one passes through the gap in the curtain wall leading to the Old Barbican.

A *Roman villa* was discovered in Carisbrooke in 1859 and excavated at that time. Most of it is now covered over, but one room, containing a mosaic pavement decorated with a vase of flowers within a geometric border, is still open and protected by a modern roof. It lies in the garden of the Vicarage and is opened only by prior arrangement.

Objects from the fort and villa are in the Isle of Wight Museum in Carisbrooke Castle.

W. Spickernell: *The Roman Villa, Carisbrooke* (1860)

4 CHILLERTON DOWN CAMP   Iron Age
      Gatcombe   180 (SZ:483842)

On the Down, 0·8 km west of Chillerton.

Known as Five Barrows Camp from the way in which the material dumped from the single line of rampart and ditch seems to make five separate mounds, there is no doubt that this earthwork is a promontory fort of the Iron Age and that it is an unfinished work. The rampart, which stands 3·1 m high with a ditch on the south-west, cuts off a steep-sided promontory which points north-eastwards. There is no apparent additional defence on these steep sides although it may have been intended. The fort thus formed encloses about 10 ha. There is an entrance at the north-western end of the rampart, which was originally approached by an Iron Age track from the main hill-mass to the south-west. This is the only Iron Age defensive work so far recognized in the Isle of Wight, and as such must be seen as the island's tribal centre.

G. C. Dunning: *P.I.W.N.H.S.* 4 (1947) 51

5 DEVIL'S PUNCHBOWL ROUND BARROW   Bronze Age
   Brading   180 (SZ:597869)
On north side of minor road across Brading Down.

This large round barrow, 18·3 m in diameter and 1·5 m high, contained a crouched burial high up in the mound, accompanied by an antler hammerhead now in the British Museum. The primary burial still awaits discovery.

L. V. Grinsell and G. A. Sherwin: *P.I.W.N.H.S.* 3 (1941) 179

6 FIVE BARROWS   Bronze Age
   Brook Down, Brightstone   180 (SZ:390852)
Beside track on highest point of Brook Down. National Trust.

Considered by L. V. Grinsell to be the best barrow group in the island, the Five Barrows do in fact consist of eight barrows: a bell-barrow 2·7 m high, a disc-barrow and six bowl-barrows. The disc-barrow lies at the eastern end of this linear cemetery. It measures 35·4 m across. The bell-barrow marks the western end. The eastern bowl-barrow has a causeway across its ditch at the north-east side, which may be indicative of some burial ceremony prior to the erection of the mound. Most of the barrows have robbers' hollows at their centres but nothing is known of their contents.

L. V. Grinsell and G. A. Sherwin: *P.I.W.N.H.S.* 3 (1941) 179

7 GALLIBURY HUMP ROUND BARROWS   Bronze Age
   Calbourne and Newport   180 (SZ:441854)
North of wood, east of footpath south-west from Rowridge.

A number of barrows are scattered over Brightstone Down including a disc-barrow. The most conspicuous is Gallibury Hump, 3·1 m high and probably the biggest round barrow in the island. It is about 30·5 m in diameter and seems to be largely composed of flints. It was described by Sir John Oglander in about 1640 as being 'where ye ffrench weare buried, being overcome theyre in a battayle'. It probably gets its name from a gallows that may have stood upon it.

L. V. Grinsell and G. A. Sherwin: *P.I.W.N.H.S.* 3 (1941) 179

8 THE LONGSTONE   Neolithic
   Mottistone   180 (SZ:408843)

In wood, south of trackway along hill-ridge.

This somewhat doubtful long barrow is 21·2 m long east to west, and
about 9 m wide. At the east it reaches its greatest height of about 1·2 m.
Excavation has shown that there is a kerb of sandstone along the north
side of the mound, but the southern side has been largely destroyed by
sand quarrying. No burials were found in the excavations. Due east of
the mound are two large blocks of sandstone, one lying on its side and
one standing 4 m upright. The fallen stone originally stood slightly
further south, but was moved to its present position after 1856. In all
probability the stones always stood free of the long barrow, as they do at
Lyneham (Oxon.) and Tinglestone (Glos.) and were never part of a
burial chamber.

J. Hawkes: *Antiquity* **31** (1957) 147

9 MICHAEL MOOREY'S HUMP ROUND BARROWS   Bronze Age
   South Arreton   180 (SZ:536874)

South of minor road along crest of Arreton Down, on edge of quarry.

Also known as Gallows Hill, this is the last of a group of four round
barrows. It is 1·8 m high and 18·3 m in diameter. Although it has not
been properly excavated Saxon secondary burials were found high in
the mound in 1815. Michael Moorey was hanged from the gallows that
once stood on the barrow in about 1730. It is claimed that one of the
oak beams in the 'Hare and Hounds' public house at Downend was the
original gallows post.

L. V. Grinsell and G. A. Sherwin: *P.I.W.N.H.S.* **3** (1941) 179

10 NEWPORT ROMAN VILLA   Roman
                                             180 (SZ:500880)

*Situated in Avondale Road, Shide (ten minutes' walk from South Street,
Newport, via Church Litten or Upper St. James's Street). Open 7 June to
10 September on Mon., Tue., Wed. and Fri.: 14.30 to 17.00 hours.
Closed 30 August. Adults 5p, children 2½p. (Isle of Wight County Council.)*

Situated on a south-east facing hill-slope leading down to the river
Medina, this small villa represents the final stage in an occupation
which began with Iron Age settlement and ended with a Romano-
British wattle-and-daub building. The villa is of the corridor type with
seven rooms beyond, and projecting wings containing a single room at
either end. Little remains of the mosaic pavements which once graced
some of the rooms. An unusual feature is an open fireplace with tiled
hearth that was installed some time after the floor of the room had been
laid down. At the west is an additional range of four bath rooms, with a

hypocaust furnace at the northern end, and a raised platform, presumably to support a water tank, outside the walls to the south. The building itself dates from the end of the 2nd century to the end of the 4th century. Finds ranging in date from the 1st to 4th centuries are displayed in a small museum on the site.

P. G. Stone: *Ant. J.* **9** (1929) 141

11 SHALCOMBE DOWN BARROW CEMETERY   Bronze Age
    Shalfleet   180 (SZ:391855)
In the plantation on the hillside south of Shalcombe.

There are five bowl-barrows and a bell-barrow amongst the fir trees in this group. Although none of the bowl-barrows are now very large, one of them, opened by J. Dennett in 1816, contained a cremation burial accompanied by a bronze knife-dagger with a bone pommel, a bronze axe, two boar's tusks and other minor items. These are now in the Carisbrooke Castle Museum. The bell-barrow is this group is very fine, measuring nearly 46 m across and 2·1 m high.

L. V. Grinsell and G. A. Sherwin: *P.I.W.N.H.S.* **3** (1941) 179

Museum containing archaeological material
Carisbrooke Castle Museum,* Newport

* Main island collection

ISLES OF SCILLY

1 BANTS CAIRN ENTRANCE GRAVE (Plate 43)   Neolithic
    St. Mary's   189 (SV:911123)
On Halangy Down near north end of golf course. Department of the Environment. Access at all times.

This round cairn is about 12 m in diameter and 1·8 m high. Composed of large blocks of stone it has inner and outer retaining walls and a well-built burial passage with an entrance on the east. Four capstones form a roof. Excavated by George Bonsor in 1899 it produced neolithic and late Bronze Age pottery.

Adjoining the cairn are the remains of a village of probable Roman date. It consists of isolated circular stone hut foundations, each about 7·6 m in diameter with a single doorway. These probably had walls standing about 1·8 m high. Traces of small gardens and pathways can be made out.

H. O. Hencken: *Ant. J.* **13** (1933) 14

Plate 43   Bants Cairn, St. Mary's, Isles of Scilly

2   CRUTHER'S HILL
    St. Martin's

Neolithic or Bronze Age
189 (SV:929152)

On the southernmost tip of the island south of Higher Town.

There are barrows on top of each of the three hills running from north to south. The northern is about 6·1 m in diameter, with a burial chamber 5·5 m long penetrating it from the south-west. There are traces of a stone peristalith that may have retained the barrow mound.

The central hill is crowned by an entrance grave 8·2 m in diameter with a burial chamber on the east 4·6 m long. Like many of the graves in the Scilly Isles it is narrow at its entrance, 0·9 m, and widens at its inner end to 1·4 m. There are two round barrows on the southern hill, one with a burial chamber, the other ruined.

G. E. Daniel: *Prehistoric Chamber Tombs of England and Wales* (1950) 245

3 GIANT'S CASTLE PROMONTORY FORT   Iron Age
      St. Mary's   189 (SV:924101)

On the cliff edge east of St. Mary's airport.

This is a strong but small example of the promontory forts more commonly found in mainland Cornwall. Three curved lines of rampart and
ditch run across the headland to isolate it from the main land mass to
the west. Early Iron Age pottery has been found inside the defended
area.

4 INNISIDGEN ENTRANCE GRAVES   Neolithic or Bronze Age
      St. Mary's   189 (SV:921127)

On the north coast of the island near road over Helvear Down.

Sometimes known as the Giant's Grave, this round cairn is 8 m in
diameter, with a well-built burial chamber, entered from the south-
east, 5·5 m long and covered with five capstones. The passage is
almost 1·5 m high. To the north is the Lower Innisidgen entrance
grave, which is overgrown and partially sand-covered, but with a
chamber on the north side. There is no record of the contents of either
barrow.

H. O. Hencken: *Ant. J.* **13** (1933) 18

5 PORTH HELLICK DOWN ENTRANCE GRAVE

                                         Neolithic or Bronze Age
      St. Mary's   189 (SV:928108)

*South-east of Tremelethen. Department of the Environment. Access at
any time.*

One of the finest entrance graves in the Scilly Isles, it has a mound
12·2 m in diameter and 1·5 m high, held in place by a dry-stone wall.
The passage, 4·3 m long and 0·9 m wide, curves left into the burial
chamber which is 3·7 m long and has four large capstones over it. A
single upright block of stone restricts the width of the passage to 0·6 m,
where it joins the burial chamber. Pottery found in the tomb is of
late Bronze Age date, suggesting that it was reused at that time. There
are four other ruined barrows close by.

H. O. Hencken: *Archaeology of Cornwall and Scilly* (1932) 21

6 SAMSON HILL   Neolithic or Bronze Age
      Bryher   189 (SV:879142)

On the southern side of Samson Hill at the south of Bryher.

This is an entrance grave 6·1 m in diameter. It has a burial chamber
entered on the north-east 5·8 m long, which widens to almost 1·5 m

midway along its length. At the northern end of the island there are lots of round barrows, especially on Shipman Head Down: one has a ruined burial chamber.

G. E. Daniel: *Prehistoric Chamber Tombs of England and Wales* (1950) 243

7 TRESCO OLD BLOCK HOUSE PROMONTORY FORT   Iron Age
    Tresco   (189 SV:897155)

On the headland east of Old Grimsby. Part owned by the Department of the Environment.

The promontory on which the Civil War defence known as the Old Block House stands is cut off by the earthworks of an Iron Age promontory fort. Three banks can be traced on the hillside running across the spur, each broken by an entrance gap. Any ditches that existed are completely silted up.

Museum containing archaeological material

Isles of Scilly Museum, Church Street, Hughtown, St. Mary's (*Summer weekdays 10.00 to 13.00 hours, 14.00 to 16.00 hours; winter Wednesdays 14.00 to 16.00 hours*)

KENT

1 ADDINGTON PARK CHAMBERED LONG BARROW   Neolithic
    Addington   171 (TQ:653591)

On either side of the road from Wrotham Heath to Addington.

Although much damaged this long barrow is clearly rectangular in shape, its edges defined by a kerb of sarsen stones 1·2 to 1·5 m high. Lying north-east to south-west, it is 61 m long and 10·7 m wide, and has been cut diagonally in half by the road. At the north-east end is a collapsed line of very large stones that represent the burial chamber; this was still in existence when examined by a local parson, L. B. Larking, in 1845, but later fell down. It is recorded that he found pieces of 'rough pottery'. The site is in a very poor state of preservation at present and urgently needs excavation and consolidation. Stone chambered barrows are unusual in southern Britain, and the small group around the Medway have cultural affinities with western Europe rather than western Britain, being particularly like the *langdysse* or long dolmens of Scandinavia. The position of The Chestnuts burial chamber, 91 m north-west on a different alignment is particularly interesting.

R. Jessup: *South-East England* (1970) 103

2 BARHAM DOWN BARROWS AND EARTHWORKS   Roman
    Kingston   173 (TR:202518)
Beside the A2 road.

These three barrows, lying in a line beside the Watling Street, are almost certainly of Roman date. They were 'turned over' by the Revd. Bryan Faussett, when he examined a group of about 250 mounds close by. The latter were of Saxon date and one produced the famous Kingston brooch.

West of the A2, along the footpath from TR:206515 is what appears to be a linear earthwork 594 m long. In places it appears as a scarping rather than true earthwork, and it is uncertain whether it is a lynchet, dyke or ancient trackway.

B. Faussett: *Inventorium Sepulchrale* (1856) Ed: C. R. Smith

3 BENENDEN ROMAN FORD   Roman
    Benenden   184 (TQ:802323)
Beside Stream Farm, approached from Benenden to Iden Green road.

The Roman road from Rochester south to Maidstone and the Weald passes through Iden Green, where it crosses a stream by means of a paved ford 3·7 m wide. It was first recognized by O. G. S. Crawford.

O. G. S. Crawford: *J.R.S.* **12** (1922) 277

4 BIGBURY HILLFORT   Iron Age
    Harbledown   173 (TR:116576)
A public footpath passes through the annexe of the fort, leaving the Upper Harbledown road at TR:120578.

Astride the Pilgrims' Way (the North Downs Trackway) this many-sided 10 ha fort closely follows the 200 feet contour line. The main earthwork consists of a rampart 2·4 m high and an outer ditch 4·9 m wide and 1·8 m deep with a counterscarp bank 0·9 m high. There is a semi-circular annexe for cattle on the north-west. It encloses 3·2 ha and has two entrance gaps. The main fort has entrances on the east and west, the former being approached by a sunken trackway and defended by two deep staggered ditches and an outer bank. Excavations show that the fort began during the earliest Iron Age and was again in use during the Belgic Iron Age. It is usually believed that Bigbury was the strongly held fort described by Caesar on his second expedition to Britain: the Britons 'occupied a well-fortified post of great natural strength, previously prepared, no doubt, for some war among themselves, since all the entrances were blocked by felled trees laid close together.' Many discoveries made during gravel digging inside the fort have produced many types of late Iron Age domestic objects ranging from a fire-dog and slave chain with barrel padlock, to saws and plough-shares, cauldron hooks and horse-bits.

R. F. Jessup: *Arch. Cantiana* **48** (1936) 151

5 CANTERBURY, WALLS AND MOSAICS   Roman
                                                  173 (TR:151578)

As is the case with all major Roman towns in Britain that lie beneath our modern cities, little is now visible to stimulate the visitor. In Canterbury it is the medieval cathedral and city walls that create the major impression; but of *Durovernum Cantiacorum*, the town of the Cantii, little survives above ground.

A stone wall was thrown around the town about A.D. 280, and it was on top of this that the medieval city walls were built. Part of a Roman gateway can be seen behind the car-park in Broad Street, just south of the square bastion. Jamb-stones of Kentish rag and a few courses of the brick turn of the arch are visible.

In Longmarket steps lead down to a Roman townhouse with two small mosaic pavements and a hypocaust visible. These consist of part of a corridor with north and south wings and a bath house foundation. The part uncovered is a 2nd-century addition to a 1st-century house, whilst the tessellated floors are even later, perhaps early 3rd-century. A number of Roman objects from Canterbury are also displayed at the site. (*It is open from April to September 10.00 to 13.00 hours, 14.00 to 18.00 hours (Sundays 14.00 to 18.00 hours); October to March 14.00 to 16.00 hours. Weekdays only.*)

S. S. Frere: *Roman Canterbury* (1965); F. Jenkins: *Arch. Cantiana* **86** (1971) 239

6 CASTLE HILL   Iron Age
   Tonbridge   171 (TQ:608438)

On the east side of the A21, mainly in woodland.

This small contour fort has been badly damaged. In the trees on the east is a double bank and ditch broken by an entrance. On the north-east this has been reduced to a single line of defence, whilst the south and west are entirely destroyed, save for a short section on the south-west. Partially excavated in 1921, the site produced no finds, but almost certainly belongs to the Iron Age.

J. H. Money: *Arch. Cantiana* **86** (1971) 233

7 CHESTNUTS CHAMBER TOMB   Neolithic
   Addington   171 (TQ:652592)

Beside house, north of road from Wrotham Heath to Addington. Permission from house. Admission 5p.

This is the most recently excavated of three important chambered tombs at the foot of the North Downs and west of the river Medway. Its restoration is incomplete. Surface deposits of sarsen stone in the area made it possible for early man to obtain stones large enough to construct tombs comparable in size with those found in south-western England. A rectangular burial chamber lying east to west, measuring 3·7 m long, 2·3 m wide and 2·1 m high was formed with two wall stones on either side, another stone at either end, and a septal stone midway between them. Two façade stones stand at the east end, on either side of the chamber's blocked entrance. The covering barrow mound of sand, almost destroyed, seems to have been D-shaped in plan, the straight side, 19·5 m long, being parallel with the façade, whilst the greatest length of the mound so far traced was only 15·2 m, though it may have been considerably longer. It had neither a ditch nor retaining stones along the edges.

The barrow had been dug into many times in the past, but sufficient finds remained to show that it had been used for a long period of time. Traces of at least nine cremations and one or two infant burials were still present, together with Windmill Hill and late Neolithic pottery. Some of the pottery found in front of the façade may indicate mourners leaving gifts at the tomb entrance.

J. Alexander: *Arch. Cantiana* **76** (1961) 1

8 COFFIN STONE   Neolithic ?
   Aylesford   171/172 (TQ:739605)

In a ploughed field close to Great Tottington Farm, approached by farm road from TQ:742603. Direction and permission from farm.

This great block of sarsen stone 4·4 m long and 2·4 m wide lies in a ploughed field near the Countless Stones. Another large stone used to stand beside it, and two smaller sarsen stones lie nearby. In 1836 two skulls were found under the stones, and for this reason it seems likely that it once formed part of a burial chamber. Close by at Tottington spring-head more scattered sarsen stones suggest an earlier use.

R. Jessup: *South-East England* (1970) 100

9 COLDRUM CHAMBER TOMB (Plate 44)   Neolithic
   Trottiscliffe   171 (TQ:654607)

Beside bridle road from Trottiscliffe at TQ:650606.

This example of a Medway chambered tomb is quite impressive,

Plate 44 Coldrum chambered tomb, Kent

largely due to partial restoration and the guardianship of the National Trust. As is common in this area the barrow is short and rectangular, measuring 21·3 m long and 16·8 m broad. It is surrounded by a peri-stalith of large fallen sarsen stones which would have held the earth in place. The stones on the east have fallen down an artificial terrace slope, partly created by chalk digging early in the last century. Some of these would have formed the façade on either side of the burial chamber. Coldrum, like the Chestnuts barrow, is orientated east to west, and the chamber is rectangular, measuring 4 m by 1·5 m, and was originally divided in the centre by a septal stone which seems to have had a semi-circular porthole opening in it. When opened by F. J. Bennett in 1910 the tomb held the remains of twenty-two skeletons, together with 'a flint saw and portions of rude pottery'. Sir Arthur Keith considered the skeletons to have been related, if not actually one family, and to range in age from infants to old men and women. He noted that many shinbones were flattened and that there were some signs of rheumatism.

There is a memorial inscription on the site to Benjamin Harrison, the Kent prehistorian, which wrongly describes Coldrum as a stone circle.

R. Jessup: *South-East England* (1970) 108

10 DOVER, LIGHTHOUSES, FORT AND HOUSE   Roman
                                    173 (lighthouse TR:326418)

It is now believed that the earthworks surrounding Dover Castle, with
the exception of the outwork north of St. John's tower, originally
formed an Iron Age hillfort. Within this the Romans placed their
lighthouse or *pharos*. Standing on Castle Hill, 116 m above the sea, it
would have been clearly seen from the French coast. It survives today
as a tower at the west end of the church of St. Mary-in-Castro. It is
still 18·9 m high, although only the bottom 13 m are Roman work. The
structure is hollow inside, 4·3 m square with vertical walls. Externally
it is octagonal, gradually diminishing in size as it goes upwards, though
when first built it rose in a series of stepped stages, to a height of about
24 m. The walls are 3·7 m thick at the base and become narrower
(2 m) at the present top. They have a core of rubble and mortar, and
a facing of sandstone and tufa, with brick courses. The windows and
door arch are constructed in stone and brick. Through the largest ones,
probably those in the upper part now destroyed, fires or torches must
have shone out to provide the necessary light. The west door and top
5·8 m of the tower are medieval.

A second lighthouse stood on the Western Heights 1·2 km south-
west, but was largely destroyed by the construction of Drop Redoubt.
Today only fallen masonry survives. Both lighthouses were probably
established soon after A.D. 43. The Emperor Gaius had built a similar
structure at Boulogne as early as A.D. 40, 'a tall lighthouse not unlike
the one at Pharos, in which fires were to be kept going all night to
guide ships'.

These great towers marked the entrance to Dover harbour which
must have increased in importance in the 2nd century A.D., as Richborough declined. At this time it became the headquarters of the *Classis
Britannica* or British fleet, whose great 1·2 ha fort lay in the centre of
modern Dover west of Cannon Street under the new by-pass road. To
the north of the fort is the 'painted house', a large Roman building of
brick and flint, heated by hypocausts and with the most substantial
wall paintings ever uncovered in Britain. It may possibly have been the
house of the fort commander. Excavated in 1971 the house is being
conserved by Dover Corporation, and together with a new adjoining
museum, will be opened to the public shortly.

11 FREE DOWN ROUND BARROWS   Bronze Age
        Ringwould   173 (TR:365471)

Beside a public footpath passing over Free Down from Wood Hill.

Of a once extensive group of round barrows, only two unditched bowl-
barrows still survive. Lying along one of the trading routes between
Wessex and the Low Countries, their contents reflect the culture of

both areas. Excavated in 1872 by the Revd. C. H. Woodruff, the western barrow, which measures 22·9 m in diameter and 1·2 m high, covered four small burial pits, in each of which was a cremation in an inverted urn. One of the urns was accompanied by a miniature vessel, its mouth stopped with clay. Another urn with four applied horseshoe-shaped handles, contained two incense cups, one of which seemed to have a substance like burnt linen inside. With it were three segmented and one round bead, all of light green faience. The second barrow is about the same size, and produced a burial pit which held only a fragment of a probable collared urn. A third barrow, now destroyed, covered a pile of flints mixed with sea shells and iron pyrites, under which may have been an inhumation burial.

R. Jessup: *South-East England* (1970) 116

12 GORSLEY WOOD BARROWS   Roman
    Bishopsbourne   173 (TR:171520)
Close to a drive in Gorsley Wood.

These three barrows in a row in the wood were excavated about 1882. The largest was found to cover a tiled Roman pavement with flints at its edge. It also contained a stone cist in which were the remains of a cremation. The other barrows also contained stone cists covering cremations, as well as three or four broken Roman urns, glass and ornaments. The tops of these cists can still be seen.

R. F. Jessup: *Antiquity* **10** (1936) 50

13 IFFIN WOOD ROUND BARROW   Bronze Age
    Thanington   173 (TR:133541)
In wood on east of minor road from Canterbury to Petham.

Rather overgrown, this bowl-barrow was originally 45·7 m in diameter, and covered five Bronze Age urns, all of which were found inverted, their mouths blocked with clay to prevent the cremated bones falling out. The urns have since been lost.

J. Y. Akerman: *Archaeologia* **30** (1844) 57

14 JULLIBERRIE'S GRAVE LONG BARROW   Neolithic/Roman
    Chilham   173 (TR:077532)
On the hillside due south of Chilham Mill. Badly overgrown.

Lying north-south on a chalk hill above the river Stour, Julliberrie's Grave is the only known Kentish long barrow that does not contain a stone burial chamber. A chalk pit has destroyed part of the northern end. What remains measures 44 m long, 14·6 m wide and 2·1 m high. Excavation has shown that an irregular ditch extended along the east and west sides and round the southern end. It was roughly U-shaped,

1·5 m deep and 4·6 to 6·1 m wide. The barrow had been constructed of turf covered with chalk. No burials were found when it was excavated in 1936–7. It seems possible that they had been destroyed when the chalk pit was dug. In the upper filling of the ditch on the south side four Romano-British burials had been deposited about A.D. 50, and covered with small cairns of flints. In the turf core of the long barrow a damaged flint axe-head of Scandinavian and North German type was found. This can be dated to about 2000 B.C. and suggests a Late Neolithic date for the barrow's construction. The axe and other material found is in Chilham Castle.

R. Jessup: *Ant. J.* **19** (1939) 260

15 KITS COTY HOUSE   Neolithic
    Aylesford   171 (TQ:745608)
On a footpath linking the A229 with side road to Aylesford.

Although one of the most famous sites in south-east England, Kits Coty House is something of a disappointment. The great stones of the burial chamber are herded together in a hideous iron fence as though to prevent their escape. Aesthetically ugly, but perhaps in this vandalistic age, not too great a price to pay for their safety.

Today, only three upright stones, 2·4 m high, in ground plan the shape of an H, and a large capstone 4 m by 2·7 m, still in position, survive. On the analogy of the other Kentish megaliths we may assume that stones also stood at either side of the monument thus forming two small enclosed chambers. Aerial photographs show that a mound, at least 55 m long and 13·4 m wide once existed lying roughly east and west. A sketch by William Stukeley made in 1722 shows a single large stone at the far end known as 'The General's Tomb'; this, together with other stones around the perimeter of the barrow found more recently, suggest that the mound was originally revetted. 'The General's Tomb' was destroyed in 1867. Stukeley also records that an arc of small stones lay on either side of the present chamber, seeming to indicate a façade. There is also recent evidence to show that ditches 3·8 m deep existed from which material for the mound must have been quarried.

R. Jessup: *South-East England* (1970) 98

16 LOWER KITS COTY HOUSE (COUNTLESS STONES) Neolithic
    Aylesford   171 (TQ:744604)
On the south of the road near Great Tottington Farm.

Lying beneath a clump of trees are a confused group of some twenty sarsen stones. They must have formed a burial chamber, and traces of a mound around them could still be seen in 1930. Stukeley published a third-hand reconstruction showing the stones forming a D-shaped structure, not unlike the Chestnuts and Coldrum tombs, but smaller. Today only excavation is likely to sort out the confusion.

17 LULLINGSTONE VILLA (Plate 45)   Roman
                                                        171 (TQ:529651)

South-west from Eynsford village. Car-park and guide-book available. Department of the Environment. Open standard hours.

The villa is situated on a low, artificial terrace cut back into the hillside above the little river Darent. In front of it gardens ran down to the river. Behind it, on a second terrace higher up the hill stood a circular temple and a temple-mausoleum.

The villa was probably built on the site of a late Iron Age farmstead, perhaps by the native farmer who considered it fashionable to rebuild his house in the new Roman style. Between A.D. 80 and A.D. 90 a rectangular house of flint and mortar was erected, measuring some 14·6 m by 21·3 m, with a corridor running the whole length of the house, living-rooms in the middle, and wings jutting out on either side of a verandah at the front. Below one of the wings was a cellar used for storage (Room 6). Towards the end of the 2nd century the house was enlarged by the addition of a bath suite on the south, where the normal range of cold, tepid and hot rooms and plunge baths can still be seen.

Plate 45   Mosaic pavement at Lullingstone villa, Kent

At this time the cellar became a shrine to the cult of a local water-goddess, and an adjoining room with a circular basin near its centre must have been used to celebrate the mysteries of the goddess. The owner of the house at this time was someone of high rank, and it is surprising that suddenly about A.D. 200 he deserted his home leaving many of his personal belongings and works of art behind him. What urgent business caused his hasty withdrawal can only be surmised, but in all probability his estate was confiscated by Severus because he had supported the revolt of Albinus (A.D. 197). The building was to remain tenantless and in ruins for almost a century. However, about A.D. 280 the villa was repaired, altered and enlarged and a granary 24·4 m long was built near the river. By about A.D. 330 the house had entered the most luxurious period of its existence, and was extended to include an apsidal dining-room and reception room, both with elaborate mosaic floors depicting the abduction of Europa by Jupiter, Bellerophon killing the Chimaera, and the four seasons. Soon after A.D. 360 Christianity reached the villa, and a shrine with wall paintings was constructed above Room 6, whilst the local pagan religion was still practised below. Early in the 5th century fire destroyed the house; its cause is uncertain: whether by accident or design we shall never know.

Behind the villa (and not visible) on a terrace, a circular pagan temple was built early in the 2nd century, and a square, domed temple-mausoleum, containing the remains of a young man and woman, was set up about A.D. 300. Both fell into ruins, the former to be dismantled shortly after the temple-mausoleum was built, the latter to pass out of use with the coming of Christianity.

G. W. Meates: *Lullingstone Roman Villa* (1955)

18 MILBAYS WOOD EARTHWORK   Iron Age?
   Nettlestead   171 (TQ:677508)

Private road east from B2016 at TQ:677508.

This bow-shaped earthwork, 457 m long, stands in rather marshy woodland. It consists of an inner and outer line of rampart and ditch. It is broken near the middle by a modern gap. Its age is unproven, but it is assumed to be part of an Iron Age hillfort.

19 OLDBURY HILL HILLFORT   Iron Age
   Ightham   171 (TQ:582561)

Access from Seven Wents on A25 road at TQ:582556. National Trust property. Access at any time.

This hillfort encloses 50 ha, of which the southern half belongs to the National Trust, and part of the northern half is covenanted. It is ranged north to south along a greensand ridge, and was initially defended about 100 B.C. with a small rampart of dumped soil and a V-shaped ditch 1·5 m deep. Extremely steep hill-slopes made stronger defences unnecessary, except along the northern neck of the spur, and there may never have been a rampart along much of the eastern side. Two simple entrances were constructed at the south and north-east. About 50 B.C. parts of the outer bank were strengthened by adding glacis or dumped material to them, and the ditch was recut with a broad flat bottom, in a manner which seems to denote Belgic workmanship. At the same time the north-east entrance was strengthened by raising the height of the walls and containing them with a stone revetment. There may also have been some kind of wooden breastwork above and beside the heavy wooden gate, whilst outside a protective earthwork or possible sling platform was constructed. Two Belgic cremation burials in pedestal urns, perhaps dedications, were found buried beside the gateway. The north-east gate was eventually destroyed by fire, and a large hoard of sling-stones nearby point to a probable final battle.

J. B. Ward Perkins: *Archaeologia* **90** (1944) 127

20 OLDBURY HILL ROCK SHELTERS   Palaeolithic
   Ightham   171 (TQ:584565)
On the east side of Oldbury Hill, west of Manor Farm, Oldbury.

Two rock shelters under the steep cliff-like slope of the hill were formed when softer Folkestone sandstone weathered away below harder, overhanging layers of greenstone. In the Middle Palaeolithic period the shelters were occupied, and perhaps enlarged, by men making stone implements of Mousterian type, which were found on the slopes nearby by Benjamin Harrison in 1890 for the British Association. Another cave was destroyed by quarrying in the last century, and others may still await discovery. Unfortunately the weather and modern schoolchildren have not been kind in helping to preserve these unique sites, which are National Trust property.

D. and A. Collins: *University of London Institute of Archaeology Bulletin* **8** (1970) 151

21 QUARRY WOOD CAMP   Iron Age
   Loose   172 (TQ:765515)
Amongst the orchards between Loose and Boughton Green.

This earthwork, which may once have enclosed about 12 ha, has been damaged by quarrying on the north, and deliberate levelling in the last century on the south. Only on the east and west do sections of the single rampart and ditch survive. On the west is a 274 m length, with a bank standing from 2·4 to 6·4 m in height. On the east it is almost 368

m long, with the bank averaging 2·4 m high. There is no sign of the
original entrance, the opening on the west being fairly modern.
Excavations between 1963 and 1967 showed that the rampart was of
dump construction, built in the second quarter of the 1st century A.D.,
perhaps as late as A.D. 40, in fear of the Roman invasion.

Linear earthworks to the north and south (the southern running for
4 km from Linton Park to Chart Sutton, with a ditch on the south side)
have led the excavator to suggest that Quarry Wood was a Belgic
oppidum, or native capital.

D. B. Kelly: *Arch. Cantiana* **86** (1971) 55

22   RECULVER ROMAN FORT   Roman
   Herne Bay   173 (TR:227693)

*From the A299 to the village of Reculver. Path along fort wall from
King Ethelbert Inn. Department of the Environment.*

The twin towers of a ruined church and a few houses, surrounded by
part of the fortress walls, are all that remain on the site of *Regulbium*,
a fort of the Saxon Shore. The fort, almost square in shape, with
rounded corners, and originally enclosing about 3 ha, measured
some 178 m by 173 m. More than half has now been destroyed by
erosion, although parts of the south and east walls, and a short length
of the west wall survive, and still reach heights of 2·7 m in places.
They measure about 2·4 m thick with 3·1 m wide bases. The facing
blocks of Kentish ragstone which once covered the walls have mostly
been removed, leaving the core of flints and ragstone. Only in the
centre of the eastern wall, outside the fort, do the facing stones still
remain. Also surrounding the outside of the fort were a pair of ditches,
both V-shaped and 2·1 m and 2·7 m deep respectively, which added to
the defence. Neither are now visible.

Originally the fort had four gateways, one in the centre of each wall,
but those to the north and west have been destroyed by the sea. In the
centre of the south wall is the *Porta Decumana*, the South Gate,
excavated in 1964 and still exposed to view. Only the lower wall blocks
of the single arch which spanned the 2·7 m wide roadway remain.
Inside the fortress wall a single guard chamber projected on the west
side of the entrance. The East Gate which is also visible, is almost
identical to the southern, but it has its single guard chamber at the
north. Both would have had massive double doors of wood and iron.

Excavations have shown that the fort was constructed about A.D. 210,
seventy years before the majority of Saxon Shore forts were built.
Within its walls a rectilinear road system was laid out, eventually with
a headquarters building, barracks, bath house and shrines. The First
Cohort of Baetasii, who were stationed in the fort seem finally to have
been withdrawn about A.D. 360, after which the fort was deserted.

It is now known that an earlier fort, enclosing roughly an acre, with a palisade and double ditches, was constructed about A.D. 43, but its occupation seems to have been very short-lived.

At the time that Reculver was first built it lay at the north-western end of a tidal channel separating the Isle of Thanet from the Kentish mainland. The Thames estuary lay 3 to 5 km to the north. At the southern end of the channel stood *Rutupiae*, Richborough. Since Roman times the Wantsum Channel has silted up, leaving the fort overlooking green fields to the east. Unfortunately, however, the sea to the north has slowly eroded its way towards Reculver, travelling 0·4 km in the last 400 years, until today it has removed half of the fortress.

The church within the fort is all that remains of the Minster built by the priest Bassa on land given to him by King Egbert of Kent in A.D. 669.

B. Philp: *The Roman Fort at Reculver* (1969)

23 RICHBOROUGH AMPHITHEATRE   Roman
     Ash   173 (TR:321598)
West of the road from Richborough to Sandwich.

On a hill to the south of the fortress at Richborough is the Roman amphitheatre, elliptical in shape, measuring 48·5 m by 58·8 m. It is enclosed by a flint wall 1·1 m thick, faced on the outside with chalk, and the inside with mortar. Placed against this was a clay ramp that may have supported seats. Entrances existed on the south and west, and a large one on the north. The amphitheatre might have been the work of the 2nd legion, built at the time of the Saxon Shore forts; coins suggest an occupation between Gallienus (253–68) and Arcadius (395–408), but its considerable size makes it more likely to have been built for the town of *Rutupiae*, rather than the fort. East of the amphitheatre two small square Romano-Celtic temples were found in 1926, and were subsequently destroyed.

C. R. Smith: *The Antiquities of Richborough, Reculver and Lymne* (1850) 162

24 RICHBOROUGH CASTLE (Plate 46)   Roman
     Ash   173 (TR:325602)
On minor road, 1·6 km north of Sandwich. Department of the Environment. Standard hours, car-park, museum and guide map.

This is one of the most rewarding Roman sites in Britain. Its history is long and complicated, and would need a whole book to detail it thoroughly. In Roman times the Isle of Thanet, to the north-east of Richborough, was separated from the mainland by the Wantsum Channel. Although this channel is now completely silted, it was once

Plate 46   Richborough Castle, Kent

possible to sail along it from Richborough to Reculver in the north. The channel was relatively shallow and a large natural harbour contained by a sandbank on its western side had formed on the southern side of what is now Richborough. This is what must have attracted the first Roman landing in A.D. 43 when the base camp for the Claudian invasion was established there. A pair of V-shaped ditches, running for 640 m across the neck of the narrow peninsula on which the fort stood, provided protection for the harbour and encampment to the east. Once the uncertainties of the invasion were passed the ditches were deliberately refilled, and timber store-buildings were built to provide accommodation for the accoutrements of an army fighting on foreign soil. Between A.D. 80–90, when the conquest of Britain seemed to be complete, the most elaborate public monument known in the country was set up to commemorate the event. It took the form of a Tetrapylon or Four-way Triumphal Arch. It stood at least 15·2 m high with a great arch 7 m wide on the line of the east–west road and a narrower arch passing through it from north to south. It was cased in Carrara marble and topped with a group of great bronze statues. Some indication of its size and strength is gained by knowing that the Arch stood on a stone base 9·1 m thick, and measuring 44·5 m long by 32·3 m wide. The cross-shaped foundation that survives today supported the flooring of the passageways that passed beneath the four piers of the central Arch.

Contemporary with the Arch was the large stone building which lies in the north-east corner of the fort. It is uncertain whether this was the house of some important harbour official, or an inn or *mansio* for visitors to the harbour. It was rebuilt at least twice (the different builds are marked in different coloured concrete) but was eventually levelled when the Saxon Shore fort was built.

With the growth of London and other south-coast ports, the prosperity of Richborough waned, and the settlement fell into disrepair. Early in the 3rd century a rectangular enclosure of three ditches with an internal rampart was set up around the Triumphal Arch, which by then had lost some of its statues and marble casing and was being used as a signal station. These ditches are clearly visible close to the foundations of the Arch and have an entrance through them on the west.

Late in the 3rd century the Saxon Shore fort was constructed. Its stone walls, still 7·6 m high in places and 3·7 m thick, are the most conspicuous features of the site. It formed part of a chain of forts from Portsmouth to the Wash, controlled by the 'Count of the Saxon Shore' to prevent attacks from Saxon pirates and raiders. It was probably built during the reign of Carausius (A.D. 286–93). The fort enclosed 2·4 ha, and its construction involved the final dismantling of the Triumphal Arch and the filling of the surrounding ditches. There seem to have been main gates on the east and west, but only the latter now survives. It had towers on either side, built in the characteristic Roman manner, with stone-faced rubble and tile bonding courses. It is clear that all the walls were built by gangs of men working on separate sections. Sometimes, as at the north-west corner, their sections did not join together correctly. There were postern entrances hidden in rectangular bastions on the north and south sides. At the corners of the fort round bastions were tied into the main fort walls with timbers high above the ground.

Outside the walls were two V-shaped ditches, the inner being the deeper and wider. A causeway carried the Watling Street to London through the outer ditch, whilst a timber bridge supported it over the inner one. The internal buildings of the Saxon Shore fort are largely unknown to us. The headquarters building probably stood on top of the former Arch foundations. A bath house was built over the house in the north-east corner. For the rest, timber buildings must have occupied the larger part of the site, and were probably too fragmentary to be recognized in the excavations by J. P. Bushe-Fox and others between 1922 and 1938. A 4th-century graveyard was uncovered near the car-park. Other burials were found from time to time during the excavations, and the site of one of them can be seen just inside the west gate of the Saxon Shore fort.

The late Saxon remains of the chapel of St. Augustine lie east of the Triumphal Arch foundations.

B. Cunliffe: *Richborough Excavations: 5th Report* (1968)

25 ROCHESTER ROMAN TOWN   Roman
                                                  171 (TQ:738695)

There was a Belgic settlement at Rochester, large enough to support its own coin mint. The Roman town of *Durobrivae* probably occupied the same site. Sections of the town wall still survive, but are so incorporated in the medieval town walls as to be discernible only to a specialist. On the east of the town the wall still stands 5·2 m high. It enclosed an area of 9·7 ha, in which an important public building, perhaps the baths or part of the forum, has recently been discovered. Material excavated within the town is displayed in the Rochester Museum.

26 SQUERRYES PARK HILLFORT   Iron Age
     Westerham   171 (TQ:443522)

A footpath through the park passes along the east side of the fort.

This pear-shaped contour fort is sited on a north pointing promontory enclosing about 7 ha. It is steeply scarped on the east and west with traces of a single V-shaped ditch 1·5 m deep, and counterscarp bank, the outer face of which is stone revetted. Across the wider, southern neck of the promontory are two banks with a ditch between them. They both stand about 1·5 m high. Internal ramparts do not survive on the east and west, instead the scarps rise steeply from the ditches. There is an entrance at the south-east corner with an outlying defensive bank. The interior was once wooded and part of the south-west side has been destroyed. Excavation has revealed Iron Age B occupation, but no sign of Belgic material.

N. Piercy Fox: *Arch. Cantiana* **86** (1971) 29

27 STOWTING BARROWS   Bronze Age
     Stowting   173 (TR:127426)

On west of footpath from Stowting village to Stowting Common.

The round barrow seems to be the one opened by John Brent in 1870, in which he found a large burnt area at the centre. Above it, in what must have been a secondary position were pieces of a roughly baked urn, reddish-brown in colour, with small perforated lugs beneath the rim. Brent recorded that other urns had been found in the barrow on a previous occasion. 0·8 km east beside the Roman road, Stone Street, stands another barrow which was probably of Roman origin. (TR: 135424).

28 STUTFALL CASTLE (PORTUS LEMANIS)   Roman
   Lympne   173 (TR: 117342)
A footpath leads south from Lympne village to the Royal Military Canal, passing through the site.

This remote and tumbled fort of the Saxon Shore lies on the hillside above the Romney Marshes. In Roman times an arm of the sea reached this stronghold in which the *Numerus Turnacensium,* an irregular infantry troop from Tournai, were garrisoned.

   The walls of *Lemanis* or Stutfall Castle still survive in places, although they have been much broken and disturbed by the unstable nature of the hill on which they are built. They enclose an irregular pentagonal area of about 4 ha, and still stand 7·6 m high and 4·3 m wide in places. Composed of a core of mortar and rubble, they are faced with limestone and bonding tiles, and strengthened by at least eight cylindrical bastions, three of which have chambers inside them. The main entrance was in the middle of the east side and seems to have had two projecting towers with a single gate passage 3·4 m wide between them. There were also a number of postern gates. When the main gateway was dug into, a mutilated altar was found, probably dedicated to Neptune, god of the sea and water, by Gaius Aufidius Pantera, an admiral of the *Classis Britannica.* This might suggest that for a brief period *Lemanis* was the headquarters of the fleet. The fort probably took on its final form during the reign of Carausius. During excavations in 1850, part of what was probably the headquarters building was uncovered near the northern side of the fort, whilst in the south-east angle a bath house was found.

R. Jessup: *South-East England* (1970) 177

29 SWANSCOMBE   Palaeolithic
   Barnfield Pit   171 (TQ: 596746)
National Nature Reserve.

The gravel pits around Swanscombe are reputed to have produced more than 60,000 hand-axes of Lower Palaeolithic man. In all probability a riverside beach stretched for many yards and was littered with waste flint from extensive working sites. Of all the Swanscombe pits, that known as Barnfield Pit is best known for the discovery of three pieces of human skull found in 1935 and 1955. The bones are not unlike modern man, and suggest that the people who made Acheulean hand-axes at Swanscombe were not dissimilar from *Homo sapiens.*

These are the earliest fossilized human remains from Britain and are now in the Natural History Museum, London.

J. Wymer: *Lower Palaeolithic Archaeology in Britain* (1969) 334

30 UPPER WHITE HORSE STONE   Neolithic ?
    Aylesford   172 (TQ:753603)
In trees, by a footpath east of Warren Cottages, a few metres from the A229.

As its name implies, this large block of sarsen stone resembles a horse. It measures 2·4 m long and 1·5 m high, and may once have formed part of a burial chamber. Around it are fragments of other sarsens which could have come from the same tomb.

Another burial chamber, similar to the Chestnuts and Coldrum, was discovered by a ploughman at the other end of the same field in 1823. It seems to have consisted of a tomb 2·1 m long, with three wall stones, and to have contained human bones and pottery. Known as Smythe's megalith, after the antiquary who best recorded it, it has since been destroyed.

R. Jessup: *South-East England* (1970) 101

31 WILDERNESSE BARROW (?)   Mesolithic/Bronze Age
    Sevenoaks   171 (TQ:538566)
In a park on the north side of Sevenoaks.

This mound, which is presumably a Bronze Age barrow, was found to contain a cremated burial associated with Mesolithic-type pygmy flints when it was examined by Lewis Abbott of Piltdown fame.

W. J. L. Abbott: *J. Anthrop. Inst.* **24** (1895) 122

Museums containing archaeological material
Powell-Cotton Museum, Quex Park, Birchington
Canterbury Royal Museum, High Street, Canterbury
Dartford Borough Museum, Market Street, Dartford
Deal Museum, Town Hall, High Street, Deal
Dover Corporation Museum, Ladywell, Dover
Maison Dieu, Ospringe, Faversham (Roman cemetery material)
Folkestone Museum, Grace Hill, Folkestone
Herne Bay Museum, High Street, Herne Bay
Museum and Art Gallery, St. Faith's Street, Maidstone
Margate Museum, Public Library, Victoria Road, Margate
Richborough Castle Museum
Rochester Public Museum, Eastgate House, Rochester
Royal Tunbridge Wells Museum, Civic Centre, Tunbridge Wells

1 ARMINGHALL HENGE MONUMENT   Neolithic
   Bixley   126 (TG:240060)

West of minor road from Trowse Newton to Caistor St. Edmund.

Marked 'Woodhenge' on the Ordnance Survey map, this timber circle
was discovered from the air in 1929 and excavated in 1935. Although
there is little to see on the ground except a slight circular depression
surrounded by a low bank close to the electricity pylon, it is included
because it is one of the classic sites of East Anglia. It is clear that
Arminghall belongs to the group of henge monuments, with single
entrance, that are generally interpreted as temple sites, though they
may have served some secular function as places of assembly or ob-
servatories. At Arminghall two concentric ditches, the inner 36·6 m in
diameter, were separated by a low bank some 15·2 m across. The outer
ditch was 3·7 m wide and 1·5 m deep, the inner 8·5 m wide and 2·4 m
deep. Inside was a horseshoe-shaped arrangement of eight massive
post holes, each about 2 m deep and 0·9 m in diameter. Charcoal from
one of the holes proved to be oak, and has been dated by corrected
radio-carbon to about 2350 B.C. The entrance to the site lay on the
south-west, looking along the gravel ridge above the river Tas.

G. Clark: *P.P.S.* 2 (1936) 1

2 BIRCHAM COMMON BARROWS   Bronze Age
   Great Bircham   125 (TF:775316)

*This line of barrows runs roughly north to south, and crosses the road from
Great Bircham to West Rudham.*

Three of these barrows lie on ploughed land south of the road. Two
appear to be bowl-barrows and one a bell-barrow, although a drawing
of 1842 shows both the two outer barrows as bells with wide berms.
Certainly the southernmost is a bell-barrow. It was opened by W. C.
Lukis in 1842. At that time it was 45·7 m in diameter and 3·1 m high
with a well-marked surrounding ditch, broken by a causeway on the
south-west. Lukis's trench cut into the heart of the barrow found a pile
of flints, at the centre of which was an inverted urn containing cremated
bones, a small copper pin or awl, and six or seven spherical and barrel-
shaped beads, bound with gold wire. Unfortunately they have since
been lost.

   North of the road and reached by a track beside a wood, is another
bell-barrow, 27·4 m in diameter and 1·8 m high. It is surrounded by
a ditch and external bank, and when dug by Lukis by means of a
central shaft, it produced only a fragment of pottery, suggesting that it
had already been robbed.

W. C. Lukis: *A Brief Account of the Barrows near Bircham Magna*
(1843)

3 BRANCASTER ROMAN FORT   Roman
                                                          125 (TF:782440)

0·8 km east of Brancaster cross-roads.

Although the road along the north coast of Norfolk is pleasant enough,
the remains of *Branodunum*, the Roman fort east of Brancaster, are
scarcely worth the effort of seeking them out. Only the deep hollows of
the external fort ditches, shown by excavation to be 13·7 m wide and
2·4 m deep, remain to show where this 2·4 ha fort of the Saxon Shore
once stood. The walls, originally 2·7 m thick and faced with sandstone,
were systematically destroyed in about 1770. They were broken by
gates in the east and west sides.

In Roman times the fort must have been close to a tidal inlet. It was
constructed during the second half of the 3rd century, and probably
remained in use until the final withdrawal of Roman troops from Britain.
By A.D. 400 it was occupied by Dalmatian cavalrymen. It is possible
that the Shore forts of East Anglia were linked together by a series of
small signal stations.

J. K. St. Joseph: *Ant. J.* **16** (1936) 444

4 BROOME HEATH LONG BARROW   Neolithic
   Ditchingham   137 (TM:344913)

*Approached from the minor road from Ditchingham village to Broome,
passing along the north side of Broome Heath.*

This Heath has been badly damaged by quarrying, making it difficult
to sort out the long and round barrows and a ditched enclosure from
quarry waste. The long barrow, a rarity in eastern England, lies east to
west, about 24 m long and 1·2 to 1·5 m high. Round barrows lie close
to the west end of the long barrow. A horseshoe-shaped enclosure with
low outer bank was excavated in 1970 and shown to be of early neolithic date. It produced many worked flints including scrapers and
arrow-heads, as well as pieces of neolithic pottery.

Archaeological Excavations, 1970 (1971) 9 (Dept. of Environment)

5 CAISTER-BY-YARMOUTH   Roman
   Caister-on-Sea   126 (TG:517123)

*Beside the A1064 on the western outskirts of Caister-on-Sea. Parking in
lay-by beside the site. Department of the Environment. Open at standard
hours.*

There is no evidence to show that the Romans founded seaside resorts
in Britain, but if they did, Caister-by-Yarmouth might have been a
likely choice. Excavation has found the foundations of a large *mansio*

just inside the south gate that might have provided suitable holiday accommodation, though it is perhaps better seen as a hostel for sailors. A town and port seem to have been founded in about A.D. 125 on the northern bank of a now-silted estuary. Such a port would have been ideally placed for trade with the Rhineland, importing glass, pottery and millstones into Britain. Rectangular in shape, it was initially defended by a wooden palisade backed by a clay bank and an external ditch. About A.D. 150 these were replaced by a flint wall 3·1 m thick with internal corner towers. The *mansio*, already mentioned, was built soon afterwards and continued in use for at least 200 years. The outer ditch was recut at the end of the 3rd century. At first Caister seems to have acted as a garrison town, and it was not until the 4th century that it adopted a completely civil role. It probably lasted until well into the 5th century.

Part of the *mansio*, the town wall and south gate have been conserved by the Department of the Environment.

J. A. Ellison: *Norfolk Archaeology* **34** (1963) 45

---

6 CAISTOR-BY-NORWICH (VENTA ICENORUM)   Roman
Caistor St. Edmund   126 (TG:230035)

Around the church, south-west of Caistor St. Edmund. Visitors are not permitted to walk over the ploughed interior, or on the walls, except near the church.

A great ditch and rampart partly overgrown with trees are all that remains above ground of this small Roman woollen-manufacturing town. The interior, except for the church of St. Edmund in the south-east corner, is ploughed and although excavations have taken place from time to time, they remain largely unpublished.

After the revolt of the East Anglian tribe, the Iceni, under their Queen Boudicca, in A.D. 60–1, a new town was deliberately started by the Romans and the tribes people were rehoused there. This was *Venta Icenorum*, a town of about 18 ha. Its gridiron pattern of streets was laid down around A.D. 70, but for many years only native huts stood beside them: the result, no doubt, of the poverty inflicted upon the Iceni by the Romans after their revolt. About A.D. 140–50 the first stone buildings were erected in the town centre; these were a Forum (market-place) and Basilica (town-hall). The Basilica, consisting of a long nave with aisle to the east, stood on the west side of the colonnaded market place. The latter consisted of an open courtyard 31·4 m by 29·5 m, with shops and market halls on three sides. Its entrance faced east. Slightly south of centre, along the western side of the town, were a set of Public Baths, draining into the adjoining river Tas, and also dating from soon after A.D. 140. In spite of these fine buildings, the private

houses of *Venta* continued to be built of wattle and daub until the end
of the century, when in about A.D. 200 defences were built, enclosing
only 14 ha of the town and cutting off existing streets on the north,
east and south. These defences consisted of an external ditch 24·4 m
wide, a stone wall with alternate rectangular and U-shaped bastions,
an inner earthwork, and four gates. The wall was 3·4 m thick and 6·1 m
high to the parapet walk. The South Gate, by which the main road
from Colchester and London entered the fort, was scarcely impressive:
a single arched passage 4 m wide and long led past two square guard
chambers. Outside, a wooden bridge carried the road over the ditch.
Similar bridges must have carried roads to the other three gates as well.
Two Romano-Celtic temples were excavated north of the Forum, but
like the rest are now covered over again.

The 3rd century A.D. saw changes at *Venta*. New houses of masonry
were built, but the Forum fell into decay, and was not rebuilt until
about A.D. 270. It is possible that there may have been some local
disturbance which led to the ruined state of the town centre. The
guard rooms at the south gate were used as rubbish dumps about this
time, and the Baths also had to be rebuilt. People continued to live in
Venta throughout the 4th century, but towards the end attacks by
Saxon pirates from the nearby coast led to the stationing of barbarian
federate troops in the town for the protection of the neighbourhood.
Few people seem to have remained within the walls by the early 5th
century, and a Saxon cemetery, lying 274 m south-east of the walls and
perhaps dating from as early as A.D. 450 may suggest a reason why. It
was perhaps considered safer to live in a less conspicuous area of
woodland.

C. F. C. Hawkes: *Arch. J.* **106** (1949) 62; S. S. Frere: *Britannia* **2**
(1971) 1

  7 DEVIL'S DITCH   Iron Age ?
     Garboldisham   136 (TL:988817)
Cut by the A1066 road.

This north–south linear dyke is covered with grass and bracken, but is
still sufficiently upstanding to make a notable feature in the countryside. The dyke consists of a bank about 1·8 m high with a ditch on the
east side, and traces of a low counterscarp bank. Cyril Fox pointed out
long ago that the dyke encloses a tongue of land between the rivers
Thet and Little Ouse. Its position in relationship to the Iron Age
settlement at nearby West Harling is also, perhaps, significant, if the
dyke originally ran as far north as the Thet. Excavations at West
Harling, on Micklemoor Hill (TL:975857) uncovered the type-site for
the Early Iron Age A culture in East Anglia; there is nothing to see at
the site.

Plate 47   Grime's Graves flint mine, Norfolk

8   GRIME'S GRAVES FLINT MINES (Plate 47)   Neolithic
   Weeting   136 (TL:817898)

*Signposted opposite a cottage south of the B1108. Numerous paths
through the woods, but beware of military activities. Department of the
Environment car-park; guide-books available. One of the shafts is open
at standard times. Visitors wishing to explore are advised to take overalls
and a torch.*

The flint mines of Grime's Graves are surrounded by modern conifer
forests in an area that was formerly wild undulating breckland. Here
thousands of white flints lie scattered amongst the tussocky grass:
many of them the products of human workmanship.

In this area some 7 ha are covered with the deep hollows of more than
360 filled-in mine shafts, whilst behind the custodian's hut to the
north, below apparently undisturbed ground, a further 7 ha of pits lie
buried.

The name Grime's Graves, meaning Devil's Hollows, reflects the
mystery that for centuries shrouded the scene of one of the oldest
extractive industries in Europe. Variously described as ancient fortifications, Danish encampments and a British village, it was not until

Canon Greenwell explored one of the shafts in 1870 that their true
identity was finally established, although their age remained a subject
of angry debate for the next sixty years.

Excavation has shown that the mines were of two types. In the
shallower area to the north, the flint was quarried 'opencast' from
exposures near the surface, or extracted from bell-shaped pits seldom
more than 3·7 m deep. Where the flint was far underground, shafts of
up to 12·2 m deep were sunk, with galleries opening out of them. It is
not yet clear which type of mines were the earliest. In all probability
only one pit was dug at a time, worked by perhaps as few as half a
dozen men. Material from the new shafts was thrown into the abandoned
ones. The best-quality flint, known as floor-stone was reached by
digging down through sand to reach the chalk in which the flint occurs
naturally. Then, using simple tools of red deer antlers for rakes, picks
and wedges, the miners continued through two inferior layers of flint
nodules—top stone and wall stone—until they reached the almost
continuous layers of floor-stone, which they followed along numerous
radiating passages, which often ran into neighbouring worked-out
shafts. The flint was hauled to the surface in baskets, the marks of the
ropes still being visible on the sides of the shafts when they are
excavated. Some pits also produced tallies of basket loads crudely
scratched on the gallery walls. The raw material seems to have been
shaped on the spot, before being peddled around the countryside.
Piles of flint chippings can still be seen around the mine heads.

The main shaft open to the public today is 9·1 m deep and is entered
by an iron ladder through a trap-door in the modern concrete roof.
(A new shaft on the east of the site is at present under excavation.)
Another pit, near the first, also with a concrete roof, but now unsafe
for visitors, apparently failed to produce flint of a suitable quality,
perhaps due to a geological fault. Before abandoning it the miners made
one final appeal to their diety, the Earth Mother. Setting up a crude
chalk statuette of the pregnant goddess on a ledge of chalk, they placed
a chalk phallus and a pile of flint nodules and antler picks before it,
doubtless in the hope of increasing the fertility of future shafts. The
chalk objects are now in the British Museum. Numerous other objects
are displayed in Norwich Castle Museum, whilst the custodian has a
small group of minor finds in his hut.

Radio-carbon dates for the mines show that they were worked
between 3000 and 2500 B.C. and possibly remained in use much later.
These dates suggest that the Norfolk mines began quite a long time
after mining had started on the South Downs in Sussex. It is interesting to notice that the craft of flint mining and working (knapping) on
a very limited scale has continued in the area, probably without a
break, into the 20th century, largely as a result of the need for building
stone, and later gun-flints—first in Africa and more recently in the

United States of America. The modern industry is centred on nearby Brandon.

A. L. Armstrong: *P.P.S.E.A.* **5** (1927) 91. Long outdated, but the best general account

9 HARPLEY COMMON BARROW CEMETERY   Bronze Age
  Harpley   125 (TF:755287 to TF:766279)

From the B1153 east of Anmer curving south-east towards Harpley.

There are no records of the contents of these barrows, which form a distinct linear cemetery, some of them 3 m high, and most of them overgrown. Although they lie beside the Roman Peddars' Way, they are almost certainly prehistoric in origin, and only a vestige of the many others that were once common in the district. A long barrow has been claimed for this group, though not seen by the writer.

10 HOLKHAM CAMP   Iron Age
  Holkham   125 (TF:875447)

Restricted parking opposite entrance to church in Holkam Park on A149. Private track leads across the marshes down to the camp.

Water offered a natural protection to the fort on this tidal island. Some 2 ha in extent and roughly oval in plan, it had a steep slope on its western side down to the water. The rest was defended by a single rampart and ditch, except on the south and south-east where an easier approach is checked by an additional rampart. The only entrance also faces south. A fort in such an isolated position was probably connected with some coastal beach-head, now eroded away.

11 LITTLE CRESSINGHAM BARROW CEMETERY   Bronze Age
                                         136 (TL:861986)

South of the Bodney to Little Cressingham road, and north of Seven Acre Plantation. Accessible from the track leading south to Bodney Lodge.

One of the disappointments of being an archaeologist today, is visiting what were the large barrow cemeteries of half a century ago, and finding only a few mutilated, ploughed-down survivors. Norfolk has suffered deplorably at the hands of official vandalism and hundreds of barrows have now disappeared. The Little Cressingham cemetery, not far from the Icknield Way, is no exception and ploughing on the edge of the heath has reduced many large mounds. Such an example can be seen close to the road, though it is still well over 30 m in diameter but only 0·9 m high. The round barrow at the north-west corner of Seven Acre Plantation has been described as the largest in Norfolk, being 4·6 m high and 61 m in diameter.

0·4 km north-east (TL:867992) the important Little Cressingham bell-barrow, excavated in 1849, was destroyed by ploughing some years ago. It contained the crouched skeleton of a man whose grave goods included a grooved bronze dagger with a wooden hilt, a flat bronze dagger, an amber bead necklace and decorative plates of sheet gold that had been sewn onto his clothing. These objects are now in Norwich Castle Museum. They date from the Wessex phase of the Early Bronze Age, about 1600 B.C.

T. Barton: *Norfolk Archaeology* **3** (1852) 1

12 PEDDARS' WAY   Roman
   Fring   124 and 125 (TF:733343)

The Peddars' Way forms the northern extension of the Roman road from London via Chelmsford and Ixworth to the Wash. Numerous villas and buildings have been found along its length in Norfolk but none are visible for visitors. There is a fine stretch of road running south from Fring at TF:727356 for 22 km to Castle Acre (TF:817154), well worth walking for all its length, though the last 5 km from Shepherd's Bush are metalled and suitable for driving. There are a number of Bronze Age barrows close to the road, which may indicate that a prehistoric track, a branch of the Icknield Way perhaps, once followed this route.

13 SALTHOUSE HEATH BARROW CEMETERY
   Cley and Salthouse   Neolithic and Bronze Age
                                            125 (TG:069421 to TG:077423)
Scattered over the Heath, and best visited in winter when the bracken is low.

This is an extensive group of barrows ranging in date from the neolithic to late Bronze Age. Amongst them is a fine disc-barrow of Wessex type, and a series of small mounds only about a metre in diameter containing bucket-shaped urns, which suggest that this cemetery was in use for at least 1,000 years.

14 SEVEN HILLS BARROW CEMETERY   Bronze Age
   Thetford   136 (TL:904814)
On the ridge south-east of Thetford, approached from the A1088 along the Great Snarehill Belt trackway.

Military use of this land during two World Wars has done irreparable damage to this group of barrows, situated on a hill-crest south of Thetford. 200 years ago about a dozen mounds were visible. Today only six have survived, miraculously, in two groups of three. Those on the west contain two bowl-barrows each about 0·9 m high, with a bell-barrow 2·1 m high at their eastern end. They are all about 30·5 m

in diameter. The eastern group are all bowl-barrows and from 1·2 to
1·8 m high. Although no records survive of the contents of the mounds,
damage to them shows that at least one has a central core of sand,
capped with chalk dug from a surrounding ditch.

West of the A1088 are two large bowl-barrows marked Elder Hill
and Tutt Hill on the Ordnance Survey maps.

L. V. Grinsell: *Ancient Burial Mounds of England* (1952) 201

15 TASBURGH HILLFORT   Iron Age ?
                                                        137 (TM:200960)

North of Tasburgh church and the B1135.

Situated on a low south-facing spur above the river Tas, this fort of
about 9·7 ha was defended by a single rampart and ditch. It has been
much mutilated by buildings within, but slight banks can still be
traced, particularly on the north side. A scatter of Roman objects
found around the village have led to the suggestion that this might be a
temporary Roman marching camp.

R. R. Clarke: *Arch. J.* **96** (1939) 1

16 THETFORD CASTLE   Iron Age
                                                        136 (TL:875828)

It is now generally accepted that the double ramparts and ditches
surrounding the large Norman motte originally formed the defences of
a hillfort. It may have been constructed by the Iceni in an attempt to
prevent Belgic penetration northwards into their territory.

17 WARHAM CAMP (Plates 48, 49)   Iron Age
        Warham St. Mary   125 (TF:944409)

*A grass bridletrack leads to the camp, off the minor road running south
from Warham All Saints to Wighton.*

Though not sited in a particularly dramatic position, the amazing
symmetry of the ramparts at Warham make a deep impression on
visitors. The site, which lies off the eastern side of the little river
Stiffkey consists of concentric double ramparts, each with outer
ditches, surrounding an area of 1·4 ha. In places the ramparts stand
2·7 m high above the interior, whilst the ditches are still 2·7 m deep.
The inner ditch, excavated in 1914, was found to be flat bottomed and
4·9 m wide, and contained about 1·8 m of silt. Until a hundred years
ago the site was planted with trees. It is recorded that in removing
these the gaps through the ramparts were made, though that on the
north side at least is likely to be original. Excavations there were far
from conclusive. On the south-west side by the river where no ramparts
stand today, the defences were once complete, but landscaping in the

Plate 48   Warham plateau fort defences, Norfolk

Plate 49   Warham plateau fort from the air, Norfolk

18th century is supposed to have resulted in their removal. An un-published excavation of 1959 suggested that the fort was constructed by the Iceni in the late 1st century B.C. or early 1st century A.D., per-haps as the result of the threat of Belgic expansion. In the field to the north-east the ditch of an unfinished rectangular fort of the same date was also explored.

The extreme regularity of the layout of the site has led to the idea that it might also have been occupied and perhaps modified by the Danes in the 10th century A.D. This assumption is not unreasonable but insufficient evidence is as yet available.

H. St. George Gray: *Ant. J.* **13** (1933) 399

18 WEASENHAM PLANTATION   Bronze Age
   Weasenham All Saints   125 (TF:853198)

1·6 km south of Weasenham All Saints, mainly to the east of the A1065, beside the minor road to Tittleshall.

Yet again, a once extensive barrow cemetery has been destroyed by agriculture in recent years. A fine bell-barrow 42·7 m in diameter and 2·1 m high stands in a ploughed field on the Lyngs, south of the road. Although overgrown it is possible to detect a slight bank on the edge of the berm inside the ditch, and L. V. Grinsell has described it as of intermediate bell-disc type. Two bowl-barrows that lay south of it have disappeared since 1939. Further east along the minor road, on Litcham Heath, is a bowl-barrow just inside a wood. In the field opposite (by a stile) two ploughed-down barrow mounds can still be seen. A large disc-barrow east again on Litcham Heath (TF:858200) has also been obliterated. West of the A1065 in Weasenham Plantation, an area of private woodland, are four more barrows, consisting of a bell-barrow, two saucer-barrows and a bowl-barrow called Black Hill.

L. V. Grinsell: *Ancient Burial Mounds of England* (1952) 202

19 WEST RUDHAM LONG BARROWS   Neolithic
   West Rudham and Harpley   125 (TF:810253)

These two long barrows lie north and south of a minor road from Harpley to Easenham All Saints. The northern barrow lies amongst young conifers.

By following the wire fence north from the road at the western end of the plantation the visitor will reach a stile shortly before the fence turns an angle opposite a fire break in the conifers. The northern barrow lies a few metres forward and to the north. Although not tree-planted it is overgrown and far from impressive. About 15·2 m wide and 58 m long, it lies north to south. A ditch runs all round it, which was shown on excavation in 1938 to be 3·7 m wide and 1·2 m deep. At the southern end was a small horseshoe-shaped enclosure containing a 'libation' pit. Both this enclosure and the main barrow mound were covered with sand. A body had been cremated at the southern end of the barrow. Cremation is normally considered to be a Bronze Age practice, and the barrow may be seen as a late survival. The higher end of the barrow, most likely to cover human remains, was only superficially examined, so it is possible that inhumation burials remain to be uncovered.

The southern long barrow, immediately south of the road, is badly ploughed. In 1938 it was 45·7 m long and 27·4 m wide, with side ditches 4·6 m across. It still stands 1·5 m high. Although it is unexcavated scraps of neolithic pottery have been found on its surface.

A. H. A. Hogg: *Norfolk Archaeology* **27** (1940) 315

Museums containing archaeological material

King's Lynn Museum and Art Gallery, Market Street, King's Lynn
Norwich Castle Museum,* The Castle, Norwich
The Ancient House Museum, White Hart Street, Thetford

* Major county collection

NORTHAMPTONSHIRE

1 ARBURY CAMP   Iron Age
    Chipping Warden   145 (SP:494486)
Beside the B4036, west of the road south-west of Chipping Warden.

This denuded plateau fort is one of a number of small forts, each about 13 km from its neighbours and separated from them by rivers like the Cherwell, and linked by the prehistoric ridge route, the Jurassic Way, which seem to control large tracts of partially forested country at the north-eastern end of the Cotswolds. Arbury Camp is roughly circular, about 183 m in diameter with a single low bank and shallow ditch around it. There appears to be an entrance on the south-east side. It has been somewhat ploughed away on the north-east, and the whole camp is covered with medieval ridge-and-furrow.

2 BOROUGH HILL   Iron Age
    Daventry   132 (SP:588626)
Footpath across golf course from junction of Daventry to Norton road at SP:584633. Not approachable from south side.

A small but very strong hillfort of 1·8 ha defends the northern tip of this hill, with a rampart, ditch and counterscarp bank. Its weakest side, the south, is protected by an additional ditch which is cut through by

an overlapping southern entrance. At some later date the fort was
extended to the south, by surrounding a further 6·5 ha with a much
slighter bank, ditch and counterscarp. Most of this is now inaccessible
due to the BBC wireless station on the hill. It is best preserved on the
west side, near the golf course.

3 HUNSBURY   Iron Age
   Hardingstone   133 (SP: 737584)

Via bridlepath west from the A43.

The Jurassic Way, the prehistoric route along the Cotswolds from the
Severn to the Welland and Wash, crosses the river Nene at Northampton below Hunsbury camp, which must surely have been established
to control the crossing.

A circular site of 1·6 ha, it was badly damaged between 1880 and
1886 when most of the interior was quarried for ironstone and lowered
by some 2·4 m. A single bank and ditch with counterscarp bank were
examined in 1952. The bank, probably constructed in the 4th century
B.C., covered a vertically-faced wall of ironstone, held in place with
posts, and with a V-shaped ditch 12·2 m wide and 7·6 m deep outside.
The wall was partly rebuilt in glacis style by refacing it with clay in the
1st century B.C., by people making fine pottery with curvilinear designs,
similar to that found at the south-western end of the Jurassic Way at
sites like Glastonbury. Of three gaps in the rampart, only that at the
south-east seems to have been original. From material found during
the 19th-century quarrying activities it seems likely that an undefended
ironworking site was founded on the hill in the early Iron Age. Finds
from more than 300 storage pits of varying sizes, destroyed within the
defences, show that the occupiers were agriculturalists who wove,
worked bronze and seem to have exploited the ironstone. Strong
influences from the north are shown by bridle and harness fittings of
Arras (Yorkshire) type, and 150 quernstones of Derby grit; from the
south by an engraved iron scabbard dated to about 50 B.C. and from
the south-west by 7 or 8 currency bars, spiral bronze finger rings and
decorated pottery.

C. Fell: *Arch. J.* **110** (1953) 212

4 IRCHESTER ROMAN TOWN   Roman
                                                          133 (SP: 917666)

*North of the A45 Cambridge–Northampton road, and 274 m west of
Chester House Farm.*

Situated on the south bank of the river Nene, Irchester is an almost
rectangular township of about 8 ha. Practically nothing is visible today
as the site has been ploughed for many years. There are traces of a

bank and ditch along the north side. The Roman town began as an open settlement at the beginning of the Conquest, following earlier Iron Age occupation. Between A.D. 150 and 200 it was surrounded by a bank 12·2 m wide. Later a mortared limestone wall, excavated in 1878–9 and 1962, was added at the front of the bank, and an internal turret at the south-west corner near the bend in the road. These defences were probably remodelled in the 4th century when a wide ditch was cut and the west gate was blocked. A north–south road ran through the town with two side streets branching off in curved lines to east and west. Numerous pieces of brick and stone scattered over the site indicate that there were many buildings, and aerial photographs show an octagonal temple and another within a square enclosure. A Roman cemetery outside the town to the north-east was damaged when the railway was constructed in 1873, and it is clear that Roman activity extended from the town site at least as far as the line of the railway.

J. K. Knight: *Arch. J.* **124** (1967) 100

5 RAINSBOROUGH CAMP (Plate 50)   Iron Age
   Newbottle   145 (SP:526348)

Approached by track west from Camp Farm on road from Charlton to Croughton.

Situated at the north-eastern end of a broad plateau, above a minor tributary of the Cherwell, Rainsborough Camp was strongly defended with two ramparts and ditches enclosing 2·5 ha. The outer defences have been obscured by ploughing, but the inner bank is still 3·1 m high with a ditch 1·5 m deep. Although there are a number of gaps in the defences the only certain original entrance is on the west side. Excavations between 1961 and 1965 showed that this consisted of an entrance passage 18·3 m long, with massive double gates and semi-circular stone-built guard chambers on either side, and perhaps a wooden bridge that may have carried a sentry walk over the top. The history of the site is long and complicated. The hilltop was extensively occupied in the 6th or 5th century B.C. In the 5th century B.C. the fort was erected with an inner rampart rising in three stone-faced tiers or steps above a ditch 2·4 to 4·3 m deep and 6·1 m wide, and an outer stone-faced rampart with an irregular ditch 1·8 to 4·3 m deep. After perhaps a century of use, when the defences were falling into disrepair, the fort was hastily refurbished and the inner ditch cleaned. Disaster struck and the fort was slighted and burnt. A defender was trapped in the guard room and the severed head of another lay amongst the debris at the gate. For nearly 200 years Rainsborough was all but deserted, and then in the 2nd century B.C. new occupants redug the ditches, piling the material on to the ruined ramparts to create simple glacis slopes,

Plate 50   The entrance of Rainsborough Camp, Northamptonshire

and a start was made to rehang the gates. The work was never finished: perhaps the war scare passed. With only brief attention from the Romano-British, the fort was never occupied again. In 1772 landscape gardening involved the heightening of the ramparts and the building of a drystone wall along the summit of the inner rampart, often now mistaken for Iron Age work.

M. Avery: *P.P.S.* **33** (1967) 207

6 TOWCESTER (LACTODORUM) ROMAN TOWN   Roman
  Towcester   146 (SP:692488)

A 229 m section of the earthworks which once surrounded this town can still be seen beside the police station at the northern end of the High Street. A bank 1·8 m high and 46 m wide forms the north-western corner of the town, whilst a stream runs along the ditch. The earthwork was strengthened by Edward the Elder in A.D. 918. Most of the Roman town now lies beneath the present town of Towcester: it stretched from the police station east to the Mill Race, and south to Sawpit Lane and St. Lawrence's church. It began life as an open settlement, and buildings of 1st- and 2nd-century date were destroyed when the town was surrounded by its rampart and ditch.

J.R.S. **45** (1955) 135

Museums containing archaeological material
Peterborough Museum, Priestgate, Peterborough
Westfield Museum, West Street, Kettering
Central Museum, Guildhall Road, Northampton

OXFORDSHIRE

1 ALCHESTER ROMAN TOWN   Roman
Wendlebury   145/146 (SP:573202)

2·4 km south-west of Bicester, on minor road branching south off A421.

This small Roman town is roughly square in shape. Very little is visible, except the slight earthworks, 0·9 to 1·2 m high, that surround its 10·5 ha. The raised causeway of a north to south road can be seen entering the town at the centre of the north side, and aerial photographs have revealed at least two other roads running east to west. Beside the northern of these roads a large building ranged round three sides of a courtyard and subsequently destroyed by fire was uncovered in 1892. Excavations in the 1920s dated the earliest occupation of the town from around the middle of the 1st century A.D. and continuing until late in the Roman period. The town wall and associated ditch were probably late, but have not been dated.

C. F. C. Hawkes: *Ant. J.* **7** (1927) 147; **9** (1929) 109

2 BOZEDOWN CAMP   Iron Age
Whitchurch   158 (SU:643783)

In the grounds of Bozedown House, north-east of Whitchurch.

Although much denuded, this camp once enclosed 12 ha. Today the rampart and ditch are best seen in 'The Wilderness' north of Bozedown House. Pottery excavated in 1953 indicates an early Iron Age date.

P. Wood: *Oxoniensia* **19** (1954) 10

3 CHASTLETON BARROW CAMP   ·   Iron Age
Chastleton   144 (SP:259283)

Off the A436, beside the road signposted to Chastleton House. Gated footpath from road north-west of camp.

Chastleton camp is approximately circular in shape and encloses some 1·4 ha. These are defended by a stone wall with a well-built dry-stone inner face and limestone core, and probably a similar stone outer face. The wall is about 6 m wide and 3·7 m high. Far from adequate excavations in 1928–9 failed to find an outer ditch from which the wall-stone was quarried, but one may well exist. There are two opposing entrances at the east and west, which are of the simplest straight-through type. Pottery found is of early Iron Age type, and its scarcity suggests only a spasmodic occupation. The camp may have been used for cattle ranching, and it is disturbing to observe that modern cattle are hastening its destruction.

E. T. Leeds: *Ant. J.* **11** (1931) 382

4 DORCHESTER-ON-THAMES ROMAN TOWN   Roman
158 (SU:578941)

On the west side of Dorchester between the High Street and Watling Lane.

A small Roman walled town of about 5·5 ha lies under the modern town and allotments to the west of Dorchester Abbey. Although much denuded, the earthen bank and wide ditch-hollow can still be seen on the south-west side, lying inside the angle of Watling Lane. Excavations in the allotment area in 1962 showed that the site was first occupied in Belgic times, but during the 1st and 2nd centuries rather crude timber-framed houses were constructed. An earthen rampart was built round the town at the end of the 2nd century, and towards the end of the 3rd century a stone wall was set up in front of this. The town was still in existence at the beginning of the 5th century when Roman troops seem to have been garrisoned there; but there is evidence to show that within about fifty years it was probably occupied by Saxons, who constructed a number of buildings amongst the Roman ruins.

S. Frere: *Arch. J.* **119** (1962) 114

5 DYKE HILLS PROMONTORY FORT   Iron Age
    Dorchester-on-Thames   158 (SU:574937)

By footpath from the south end of Dorchester, close to the northern end of the bridge over the Thame.

A rectangular area of 46 ha lies between the Thames and the Thame, south-west of Dorchester-on-Thames. Whilst the rivers form three sides of a low-lying promontory fort, the north side is artificially defended by two massive banks and ditches, the latter often waterlogged. Although there are a number of gaps through these defences, they all seem to be modern, and the position of the original entrance remains unknown, though it may have been on the eastern side where a late Roman road runs from Dorchester. On the evidence of aerial photographs the interior of the fort was intensively occupied. It probably represented a native stronghold which transferred to Dorchester after the Roman occupation.

6 GRIM'S DITCH   Iron Age
    Mongewell, Crowmarsh   158/159 (SU:608883 to SU:682868)

This linear earthwork runs from the river Thames to the crest of the Chilterns, some 8 km to the east at Hayden Farm. The dyke faces south and seems to form a barrier to progress from the lower land of the Thames valley to the Chiltern escarpment. The Icknield Way crosses the Grim's Ditch south of Blenheim Farm and the dyke must be connected with folk movements along that trackway. Its date is probably in the 1st century B.C. No clear connection seems to exist between the Mongewell Grim's Ditch and the Chiltern Grim's Ditch (page 22). A good 4·8 km stretch for walking along lies between the B479 and Nuffield village.

At Ipsden, 2·5 km south (SU:633851) is a circle of seven stones called *The Devil's Ninepins*, with a flat stone at its centre resting on four others. In spite of its name and antique appearance, it was constructed in 1827 by E. A. Reade as 'a sort of Druid's Temple'.

R. Bradley: *Oxoniensia* **33** (1968) 1 (Grim's Ditch)
H. G. d'Almaine: *P.S.A.L.* **32** (1920) 111 (Devil's Ninepins)

7 GRIM'S DITCH   Iron Age
   North Oxfordshire   145

Excavation of the Oxfordshire Grim's Ditch has shown that it consists of a rampart 6·1 m wide at the base and still 1·8 m high, with a V-shaped ditch on the northern side that is also 6·1 m wide and 1·8 m deep. It is not a continuous work, but seems to have run in a series of lengths, perhaps across open country between rivers and woods. It seems likely that it originally formed the northern boundary of some 5,698 ha (22 sq. miles) of territory between the rivers Evenlode on the west and Glyme on the east. The dykes seem to have been dug during the 1st century B.C. by Belgic Iron Age people who had moved west from Hertfordshire. Sections of the dyke to be seen today are:

1 *In Blenheim Park* (SP:427183) 0·8 km south of Ditchley Gate on the B4437 road. The Roman Akeman Street appears to utilize a gap through the dyke.
2 *Glympton Assarts Farm* (SP:423197) along the main approach track from the A34(T) and running parallel to the main road.
3 *Berrings Wood* and *Out Wood* (SP:413208). A footpath leads through Berrings Wood from the A34(T) at SP:419209 and crosses the dyke after 0·4 km. Both butt ends of this section can be clearly seen.
4 East of *Home Farm* (SP:402215); it is visible beside the minor road from Over Kiddington to Charlbury.
5 *Model Farm* (SP:383209). It runs beside the farm road west to east through the Model Farm into the wood, where the eastern butt end is clearly visible.
6 *Charlbury*. A section of ditch between the B4022 and the river, south of Charlbury (SP:360185), may also be part of the system.

Callow Hill (SP:409195). Almost equidistant within these dykes sections are two ploughed-down additional lines of ditch running north-south across a spur facing the river Glyme. A small Romano-British settlement lies north of the B4437 and west of these ditches, where traces of a rectangular platform for a building can still be seen. The site was excavated in the mid 1950s.

N. Thomas: *Oxoniensia* **22** (1957) 11

8 HOAR STONE BURIAL CHAMBER   Neolithic
   Enstone   145 (SP:378236)

Just south of the junction of the B4022 with the Enstone to Fulwell road.

In a small walled enclosure just inside Enstone Plantation are the ruined remains of a chambered long cairn. The rectangular burial chamber was formed by three stones, 0·9 m, 1·5 m and 2·7 m high, with an opening on the east. In front lie three further stones which were clearly part of the tomb, and one may have formed a capstone. It is uncertain whether the barrow mound, which still stood 0·9 m high in 1824, was circular or oval in shape. The tomb probably belonged to the group of monuments now called portal dolmens.

O. G. S. Crawford: *Long Barrows of the Cotswolds* (1925) 159

9 HOAR STONE LONG BARROW   Neolithic
   Steeple Barton   145 (SP:458241)

In a wood midway along the bridle road from Barton Abbey to the Rousham Gap to Wootton road.

This long mound, at least 15·2 m long, has a pile of broken sandstones at its eastern end. It is probably the barrow described by W. Wing in 1845 as consisting of 'two side pieces and a single lintel'. It was destroyed in 1843, but the owner, perhaps feeling pangs of conscience, had the pieces of stone collected and piled on the spot. This may have been a cairn with a terminal burial chamber, or a false entrance.

O. G. S. Crawford: *Long Barrows of the Cotswolds* (1925) 162

10 LYNEHAM CAMP HILLFORT   Iron Age
   Lyneham   145 (SP:299214)

Beside the A361 road. Gate in trees just north of minor road junction.

Situated on the south-western slope of a gentle hill, this small circular camp encloses 2·6 ha with a single rampart and ditch. Like Chastleton Barrow camp, 8 km north-west, excavations have shown that its rampart, which still stands 1·8 m high, is stone faced, both inside and out. Lyneham has a ditch, best seen in the wood to the west, which was shown to be U-shaped, 2·1 m deep and 5·5 m wide. There is a gap in the rampart facing north which seems to be the original entrance. Like Chastleton and Windrush, these small plateau forts are probably more concerned with cattle husbandry than with defence.

B. Bayne: *Oxoniensia* **22** (1957) 1

11   LYNEHAM LONG CAIRN   Neolithic
      Lyneham   145 (SP:297211)

On the west side of the A361 road, 0·4 km south of Lyneham Camp.

This long cairn is about 50 m in length. It is overgrown and in a
ruinous state, with an old field wall running across its eastern end. Its
noticeable feature is a standing stone 1·8 m high, 1·5 m wide and
45·7 cm thick at the north-eastern end of the cairn. It is possible that
this formed a false portal. The barrow was opened in 1894 and it was
noticed that a ridge of very large stones ran along the spine of the
barrow from the portal stone. Two rectangular burial chambers were
found at the time, both on the south-east side. Human and animal
bones were found scattered throughout the mound, and can still be
found lying in the stony plough soil around the cairn today. Traces of
large stones still protrude from the top of the barrow.

    There appears to be another long barrow 27·4 m long, and highest
at the northern end, about 91 m to the north of the Lyneham cairn.

O. G. S. Crawford: *Long Barrows of the Cotswolds* (1925) 163

12   MADMARSTON HILLFORT   Iron Age
      Swalcliffe   145 (SP:386389)

*Bridle road north-west of Tadmarton from Lower Lea Farm towards
Farmington Farm.*

Little remains to be seen of this important site due to extensive recent
ploughing and hedgerow removal. Rectangular in shape, two ditches
with a bank between them enclose about 2 ha. An entrance lies in the
centre of the southern side. Excavation in 1957–8 has shown that the
site was first occupied by an agricultural community using pottery of
the Middle Iron Age. They seem to have been largely concerned with
cattle raising. After a long period of desertion the fort was occupied
again in the 4th century A.D. by more agriculturalists.

P. Fowler: *Oxoniensia* **25** (1960) 3

13   NORTH LEIGH VILLA (Plate 51)   Roman
                                                     145 (SP:397154)

*Signposted off the A4095. Situated at north end of East End, not at North
Leigh. Walk of 0·4 km from car-park on minor road. Department of the
Environment. In process of conservation.*

Situated on an east-facing hill-slope above the river Evenlode, 1·2 km
south of the Akeman Street Roman road. This large courtyard villa
was first excavated in 1813–17, after which it was allowed to deteriorate.
In 1908 Professor Haverfield was instrumental in efforts to conserve
parts of the site and in 1910–11 further excavations took place. Later it
became the responsibility of the University of Oxford, and is now in

Plate 51   North Leigh Roman villa, Oxfordshire

the guardianship of the Department of the Environment, who are in the process of re-excavating and conserving it.

The main house is approximately 91 m square, and is ranged around a courtyard that measures 61 m by 48·8 m. Probably single-storied, it was entered by an imposing gate on the south-east side, with a porter's lodge beside it. From there a corridor ran all round the edge of the courtyard, broken by doorways and steps that enabled it to climb the hill-slope. The villa is of more than one period. It began as a small rectangular house (in the middle of the north-west side) with a detached bath house to the north-east. This was then extended south-west along the same north-west side, and two-colour mosaic pavements of 2nd-century type were introduced. After a time wings were added to the house in a number of stages, and eventually, in the 4th century, the whole of the original building was rebuilt on a grand scale, with fine three-colour mosaics and a new bath suite. An elaborate dining-room with vaulted ceiling and heated floors and walls was set up at the western corner of the house. Its walls were plastered and painted with olive branches enclosed in panels of red, yellow and green. The floor bore a geometric pattern of a type created by a mosaicist who also worked at Chedworth (Gloucestershire). This room was first uncovered in 1816, but most of the wall and ceiling paintings have now disappeared. Piers that supported an archway over the room have partially survived. A shed now covers this part of the site. The north-west wing is open to view, as is the south-west kitchen suite. The outlines of the north and south-east sides can be made out under the grass. There was another large bath suite, for guests perhaps, in the eastern corner, and a more cramped series at the south. Aerial photographs have shown that many more buildings, as yet unexamined, lie outside the villa enclosure to the south-west, and that a metalled roadway leads through these to contemporary stone quarries 183 m to the south, beside a public footpath in the wood.

D. R. Wilson: *North Leigh Villa Official Guide* (forthcoming)

14 ROLLRIGHT STONES (Plate 52)   Bronze Age
       Rollright   145 (SP:296308)

South of the ridge road (which follows the county boundary) from Great Rollright, west to the A436 at the Cross Hands Inn. Department of the Environment. Access at all times.

Plate 52 Rollright Stones, Oxfordshire

No site in southern England seems to be more steeped in folklore than the Rollright Stones. Lying beside one of the most ancient ridge roads in the country their secluded position has given them an air of mystery that is perhaps a little unexpected less than 32 km from industrial north Oxford. Apart from the Rollright circle known as the King's Men, two other monuments are linked in the legend: the King Stone and the Whispering Knights.

The King's Men. This is a circle of about seventy stones, with a diameter of 30·5 to 33·5 m. Few of the stones are more than 1·2 m tall, and all are gnarled and worn with no signs of ever being shaped. They have been well described as 'corroded like worm-eaten wood by the harsh jaws of time'. The stones are reputedly uncountable and this is easily understood when one sees stumps barely protruding from the ground, and realizes that it has long been the custom for local farmers to add unwanted stones from their fields to the ring. No excavations have been recorded within the circle. Larger stones on the north might indicate an entrance on that side.

The King Stone. Rearing like a tiger in a hideous iron cage, this isolated stone, 2·4 m high and 1·5 m wide, stands a few metres east of the circle on the north side of the road, in Warwickshire. It may have been part of the burial chamber of the reputed Archdruid's Barrow, the long mound on its northern side described by Stukeley in 1743, but excavations in 1926 seem to show that the mound was natural. (See The King Stone (under Warwickshire) page 308.)

The Whispering Knights (SP:299308). A track beside a hedgerow leads to this site south from the road, about 0·8 km east of the Rollright circle. Four stones varying in height between 1·5 and 2·4 m, form the upright walls of a burial chamber about 1·8 m square. A fifth stone, the capstone, lies between them. Stukeley wrote: 'It stands on a round tumulus, and has a prospect south-westward down the valley, where the head of the Evenlode runs.' There is no mound visible today.

Sir Arthur Evans has recorded the most famous of the Rollright legends. It recounts how a proud king and his army were marching across the hill when they were challenged by a witch with the cry:

> Seven long strides shalt thou take
> If Long Compton thou canst see
> King of England thou shalt be.

The king, waving his sword in the air, cried:

> Stick, stock, stone,
> As king of England I shall be known.

He took seven long strides, but instead of seeing the village of Long

Compton in the valley below, a huge mound, the Archdruid's Barrow, rose up before him, blocking his view. Then with a cackle the witch exclaimed:

> As Long Compton thou canst not see,
> King of England thou shalt not be.
> Rise up stick, and stand still stone,
> For King of England thou shalt be none.
> > Thou and thy men hoar stones shall be
> > And I myself an eldern tree.

Thereupon the king was turned into a hoar stone, the King Stone; his knights into the Whispering Knights and his army into the King's Men. 'But some day the stones will turn into flesh and blood once more, and the king will start as an armed warrior at the head of his army to overcome his enemies and rule over all the land.'

O. G. S. Crawford: *Long Barrows of the Cotswolds* (1925) 176. For Folklore see Evans (reprinted in same work) 31

15   SLATEPITS COPSE LONG CAIRN   Neolithic
     Wychwood   145 (SP:329165)
In a clearing in Wychwood Forest, 0·4 km east of the Leafield to Charlbury road. The site is a nature reserve.

The mound of this ruined long cairn is 30·5 m long and 13·7 m wide. It lies east to west and is still 1·8 m high. It has a single burial chamber at its eastern end, composed of three upright stones without a roofing slab. It is recorded that the gamekeeper who discovered the barrow found three human skulls in the burial chamber in the 1850s.

O. G. S. Crawford: *Long Barrows of the Cotswolds* (1925) 164

Museums containing archaeological collections

Ashmolean Museum, Beaumont Street, Oxford
The Pitt-Rivers Museum, Parks Road, Oxford

   Both these museums contain material of national as well as local importance

SOMERSET

1   ALDERMAN'S BARROW   Bronze Age
     Exford   164 (SS:837423)
On the south side of the road from Lucott Cross to White Cross.

On the boundaries of three parishes and marking one of the bounds of Exmoor Forest, this heather-covered round barrow is 1·2 m high

and 27·4 m across. A document of 1219 refers to it as Osmundes-
burgh.

L. V. Grinsell: *Archaeology of Exmoor* (1970) 62

2 ASHEN HILL BARROWS   Bronze Age
  Chewton Mendip   165 (ST:539520)
Beside the footpath south of the B3125, west of the 'Miners' Arms'.

This fine group of eight barrows, all between 1·5 and 2·7 m high, and
18·3 to 21·3 m across, were opened by the Revd. John Skinner in 1815.
Each barrow has produced cremated bones, sometimes in considerable
quantities, and often enclosed in urns. The second from the east produced Wessex material including five amber beads and a 'blue, opaque
glass bead', a grape cup and a bronze knife-dagger with possible
traces of its wooden sheath. In most cases the cremations had been
covered with cairns of stones before the final covering of earth had
been put over the barrow.

L. V. Grinsell: *Somerset Barrows* **2** (1971) 98

3 AVELINE'S HOLE   Palaeolithic
  Burrington   165 (ST:476587)
*Beside the road in Burrington Combe, south of 'Mendip Gate Café' and
just beyond the 'Rock of Ages'.*

After its discovery late in the 18th century this cave was subjected to
a number of excavations and is now quite empty. It consists of inner
and outer chambers and an overhanging entrance area. The inner
chamber contained no archaeological material, but the outer one was
a living site in later Upper Palaeolithic times. A harpoon of stag horn
and flint work belonging to the late Cheddarian culture (which ended
about 6000 B.C.) came from the cave as well as two ceremonial burials,
both badly crushed by a roof fall, and one of them accompanied by a
necklace of perforated sea shells, animal teeth and bone. Other burials
had also been placed in the cave before it was deliberately sealed.

4 BATH (AQUAE SULIS)   Roman
                           166 (ST:751647)

The Roman town of *Aquae Sulis* grew up at the point where the Fosse
Way crossed the river Avon. It was one of the smaller Roman towns,
being only 9·3 ha in extent. Almost from the beginning it seems to
have been developed as a spa, centred around the hot mineral springs.
Towards the end of the 1st century A.D. the Great Baths were constructed, the temple of Sul Minerva was begun and hotels and hostels
were built. For the most part, however, the less pretentious domestic
buildings were strung out along the Fosse Way to the north. At the end

of the 2nd century a rampart and ditch, and later a stone wall, were built. After that houses were built within the walls.

Today 2,090 sq. m of the Roman baths are visible, whilst another 836 remain unexcavated. It is clear that a number of changes were made involving the provision of small baths in addition to the Great Bath which measured 22 m by 8·8 m and was 1·5 m deep. (*The Bath and adjoining museum are open daily during the summer from 9.00 to 18.00 hours. In winter 9.00 to 17.00 hours, Sundays 11.00 to 17.00 hours. Admission adults 20p, children 10p.*) Nothing of the Temple is visible to visitors, although some of its sculptures, including the famous Gorgon's Head, are in the Baths museum. Also in the museum are carved corners from the temple altar. One of these was built into a buttress of Compton Dando church, 11 km from Bath (ST:645646), during the medieval period. At the beginning of this century a replica of the temple portico was built in the Sydney Gardens behind the Holburne of Menstrie Museum of Art. The only other remains of Roman Bath to be seen are mosaics in the basement of the Royal Mineral Water Hospital. These can be viewed on application at the entrance.

B. Cunliffe: *Roman Bath Discovered* (1971)

5   BEACON HILL BARROWS   Bronze Age
    Ashwick   166 (ST:635462)

On the south of the road over Beacon Hill north of Shepton Mallet.

Ranged along the ridge road are about a dozen round barrows consisting of five in a field and the others in a wood on the east where they are not accessible. None are very high, 0·9 to 1·2 m being an average, and 18·3 m is the maximum diameter. One long and very low mound might be a long barrow or three or four ploughed-down round barrows in a row. There is also a doubtful bell-barrow at the western end of the group. One of the mounds, opened by Mr. Rugg in 1841, produced more than a dozen cremations in urns. Most of the barrows in the wood were opened by John Skinner and contained cremations and urns under piles of stones. None are more than 0·9 m high.

L. V. Grinsell: *Somerset Barrows* 2 (1971) 88

6   BRENT KNOLL CAMP   Iron Age
    Brent Knoll   165 (ST:341510)

Footpath from East Brent by the church, passing Lady Well.

This isolated hill rises 137 m above the surrounding Somerset Levels. Its summit is ringed by a single rampart and ditch and encloses 1·6 ha. The north-west and south sides have been artificially scarped, whilst a slightly inturned entrance exists on the east with an elaborate entrance passage. The interior has been damaged by quarrying.

7 CADBURY CAMP   Iron Age
   Tickenham   165 (ST:454725)

*Footpath up hill north from Middletown (ST:454718) on B3130, or
from minor road to north.*

Lying astride the Failand Ridge this oval fort enclosing 2·4 ha is
surrounded by two ramparts with external ditches. The limestone dug
from the ditches was built into dry-stone rampart facings. There is an
entrance at the north where the inner rampart is inturned whilst the
outer rampart turns outwards on the east and inwards on the west. At
this point there is an extra third line of rampart and ditch which is also
inturned-out-turned. Excavations in 1922 produced Iron Age and
Romano-British material demonstrating a probable continuation of
occupation. West of the fort is a line of rampart and ditch cutting off
the easy approach to the camp from that direction.

H. St. George Gray: *P. Somerset A.S.* **68** (1923) 8

8 CADBURY CONGRESBURY HILLFORT   Iron Age
                                                  165 (ST:440651)

Approached by path west of Rhodyate Hill at ST:446651.

An overgrown hilltop is crowned by a single low rampart, which is
duplicated on the north-east where easy access was possible. Elsewhere
the steep natural slopes make added protection unnecessary. There is
an entrance on the east flanked by 'gatehouses'. Excavations have
produced neolithic and Iron Age material and show that the fort was
occupied as late as the 5th century A.D.

P. Fowler *et al*: *Cadbury Congresbury, Somerset, 1968* (1970)

9 CHARTERHOUSE-ON-MENDIP SETTLEMENT   Roman
   Charterhouse   165 (ST:500565)

The earliest Roman lead mining area in Britain was at Charterhouse,
where a small settlement grew up, linked by a Roman road to Sarum
and the port of *Clausentum* (near Southampton). An inscribed pig of
lead dated as early as A.D. 49 has been found. The mines were under
Imperial control until about A.D. 170 when private lessees probably
took over. Mendip lead was exported to many parts of the Roman
Empire and has been identified as the material used to make a cistern in
Pompeii, before that town was destroyed in A.D. 79.

  The lead workings scattered around Charterhouse were in use until
the present century and so far no one has managed to identify the
Roman workings for certain. There is a small oval amphitheatre
(ST:499565) measuring 32 m by 24·4 m with entrances at the east and
west, excavated in 1908, and probably of Roman date, and close by
three rectangular enclosures of probable military origin (perhaps not

all Roman), which may have been connected with a settlement which has also been revealed by aerial photography north-east of the amphitheatre.

10 CHEDDAR CAVES   Palaeolithic
                                                    165 (ST: 466539)

Beside the B3135 through the Cheddar Gorge.

Although it should be avoided in the holiday season when the Gorge flows with almost as much traffic as Blackpool or Southend, *Gough's Cave* is well worth a visit. Its owners have realized the archaeological potential of the site and have built a small but valuable museum at its entrance. The outer part of the cave was occupied by man in Late Palaeolithic times (sometimes called Creswellian or Cheddarian) and he has left behind more than 7,000 worked flints, mostly belonging to blade industries. The cave has also produced two of the so-called 'bâtons-de-commandement' carved from bone or antler, one of which was probably found with the deliberate burial of the 'Cheddar Man', who is now displayed in the museum and has been dated by radio-carbon to about 7130 B.C. (uncorrected). One or two bones engraved with simple patterns have also been found, but no painted art of the type found on the walls of French caves has been observed anywhere in Britain.

About 183 m east and above Gough's Cave is the *Soldiers' Hole* (ST 468539), a small cave, difficult to reach, which produced Solutrean flint implements of the early Upper Palaeolithic period.

L. V. Grinsell: *The Cheddar Caves Museum* (1969)

11 COW CASTLE HILLFORT (Plate 53)   Iron Age
   Simonsbath   163 (SS: 795374)

South-east from Simonsbath to a metalled by-road leading from Blue Gate (SS:758377) via Horsens Farm to the ford about 0·4 km south-east of the camp. (If approached from Simonsbath by riverside path, beware of marshes at SS:780387.)

Undoubtedly one of the most beautifully situated hillforts in southern England, Cow Castle occupies an isolated hilltop, amidst tightly inter-locking spurs in the lonely valley of the river Barle. Its oval fortification consists of a single rampart which is faced on the outside with overgrown dry-stone walling, and which encloses about 1·2 ha. There is no external ditch, but a counterscarp bank exists on either side of an entrance at the north-east. There is a second entrance at the south-west with a small standing stone just inside, which was almost certainly one of the door jambs noted by Hadrian Allcroft in 1908. A ditch exists in places on the *inside* of the rampart, an unusual feature, but brought

Plate 53   Cow Castle hillfort, Somerset, crowns the central hill top

about no doubt by the necessity to include every available metre of the hilltop within the defence. The ground falls away steeply on all sides outside the rampart which still stands 1·8 to 2·4 m high.

L. V. Grinsell: *Archaeology of Exmoor* (1970) 85

12   DEVIL'S BED AND BOLSTER   Neolithic
   Beckington   166 (ST: 815533)

0·8 km east of A361 on parish boundary.

From the mound of this long barrow which lies east to west and measures 26 m by 20 m, protrude a large number of sarsen stones which indicate the presence of a burial chamber, perhaps with lateral chambers. It is so overgrown and ruined that it is impossible to say anything about its type without excavation.

G. E. Daniel: *Prehistoric Chamber Tombs of England and Wales* (1950) 231

Plate 54   Dolebury hillfort, Somerset

13 DOLEBURY CAMP (Plate 54)   Iron Age
       Churchill   165 (ST:450590)

*Approached by footpath between houses on A38(T) south of Churchill
Gate at ST:446592.*

A most impressive hillfort on the northern edge of Mendip encloses
7·3 ha with a single collapsed dry-stone wall and outer ditch all round,
and an additional counterscarp bank on the east, north and west.
Inside the main rampart are a series of quarry scoops that must have
provided material for the wall. (There is recent quarrying disturbance
in the north-east corner.) The only certain entrance is at the west
where two small spurs project and carry additional outworks. At the
east a rampart gap is probably connected with the mining, as is a bank
about 91 m outside the fort to the east. Almost 0·4 km north-east along
the ridge is a section of bank and ditch, perhaps unfinished, overlook-

ing dead ground. The series of long mounds inside the hillfort may be
medieval rabbit warrens, but the possibility should not be overlooked
that they might be connected with Iron Age timber structures like
those found recently on Pilsdon Pen (Dorset).

If the footpath from the fort across the rectilinear field systems on
Dolebury Warren is followed to Burrington, it is possible to pass
Read's Cavern (ST:468584) which lies south of the footpath in a limestone amphitheatre. A tiny entrance leads into a single large chamber
which was occupied during the later part of the Iron Age. Excavation
has produced a set of shackles and four bronze bands from a tankard.
A massive cliff fall killed several people and brought the occupation of
the cave to a sudden end. At ST:474585 is an excavated barrow which
contained a burial in a stone-lined grave, with a deliberately broken
long-necked beaker; a secondary cremation burial in a collared urn and
cist, and an extensive Middle Bronze Age cremation cemetery on its
south side. All the finds are in the University of Bristol Spelaeological
Society's Museum.

D. Dobson: *Archaeology of Somerset* (1931) 196

14 DOWSBOROUGH HILLFORT   Iron Age
      Holford   164 (ST:160392)
*Footpath from sharp bend in Five Lords road at ST:162387, leads up
through bushes round the west end of this fort.*

This oval fort encloses about 2·8 ha. It has steep slopes on all sides
except the west, where it is joined to the main hill-ridge. It has a rampart and ditch with counterscarp on all sides, the former standing some
1·5 m high. There is a simple straight-through entrance at the east end.
The fort and its ramparts are very overgrown except at the west end
where they open up to reveal a magnificent view across Holford and
Bridgwater Bay. There is a possible round barrow inside the fort on the
north. 0·8 km south of the fort at ST:161381 is a line of bank 1·8 m high
with a ditch on the west cutting across a hill spur. Known as *Dead
Woman's Ditch* it might be a ranch boundary connected with the
hillfort.

15 ELWORTHY BARROWS HILLFORT   Iron Age
      Brompton Ralph   164 (ST:070338)
Lies between two minor roads: gate from northern one.

Lying on a ridge of the Brendon Hills, the banks of this small oval fort
are so irregular in appearance that it is clear that the site is unfinished.
The hillfort encloses about 2·8 ha and has an inturned entrance at the
eastern side which has been carefully constructed. On the south the
ditch and part of the inner rampart have been completed, but on the

north the site is 'frozen' in an early stage of building. A shallow quarry ditch has been dug and the soil removed and piled some metres inside, thus leaving room to deepen the ditches and obtain harder stone for the main rampart work. On the north-east and north-west no defence has been started at all. The piles of earth around the fort have clearly given rise to its name, but there are no barrows at Elworthy, although there is a cairn to the north-west, possibly opened in 1833 when ashes were found surrounded by a ring of stones.

R. W. Feachem in *The Iron Age and its Hillforts* (1971) 25

16 GLASTONBURY LAKE VILLAGE   Iron Age
                                                                  165 (ST:493409)

In angle of road junction on minor road from Glastonbury to Godney. Gate marked 'British Lake Village'.

Flat meadows, dykes and willows are all that remain at this classic site excavated at the beginning of the century. When the sun is low in the early morning or late evening a series of low mounds can be made out covering a triangular area of about 1·4 ha. A careful recent study of the Glastonbury excavation reports and finds has led Dr. E. K. Tratman to suggest that the village was of two quite distinct occupations by two different groups of people. The first built square or rectangular timber-framed houses in oak, supported on piles. They had walls of hurdle work, and the whole structure stood a few metres above the ground, or water, at the lake edge. The inhabitants were clearly excellent carpenters and constructed carefully-jointed looms and lathes, ploughs and carts. In spite of the lake there was sufficient dry ground nearby for cultivation. Possibly beginning about 150 B.C. the village was abandoned by 60 B.C. Shortly afterwards the empty houses were destroyed by newcomers who constructed crannogs, or artificial islands, made of layers of brushwood and clay. On these round huts of rather flimsy type were built, with walls of wattle and daub, and floors of clay with central hearths. Much pottery decorated with beautiful flowing linear patterns belong to this later village. The inhabitants found it necessary to defend their settlement with a palisade. After only about ten years the village was peacefully abandoned, perhaps due to flooding caused by a local rise in the water level, or even an outbreak of malaria, a disease still prevalent in the area a hundred years ago.

Objects from the village, and from its neighbour at Meare (ST: 446423) 4·8 km west, are displayed in Glastonbury Lake Village Museum in the High Street of Glastonbury (*open daily 10.00 to 13.00 hours, 14.15 to 17.15 hours, admission 5p*) and in the Somerset County Museum in Taunton Castle (*Monday to Saturday: 9.30 to 13.00 hours, 14.15 to 17.30 hours*). There is nothing to see at the Meare site which has been shown to have been occupied in the Early Iron Age, the first decades of the 1st century A.D., and the 4th century A.D.

Glastonbury: E. K. Tratman: *P.U.B.S.S.* **12** (1970) 143
Meare: M. Avery: *P. Somerset A.S.* **112** (1968) 21

17 HAM HILL CAMP   Iron Age and Roman
    Hamdon   177 (ST:484164)

The road from Stoke-sub-Hamdon to Odcombe runs through the centre of the site. Parking near the Inn (ST:478168) gives access to the best preserved area to the north.

Considered to be one of the largest hillforts in Britain, the 4·8 km of ramparts around Ham Hill enclose about 85 ha. Basically the fort is rectangular, but with a triangular extension jutting north towards Stoke. The defences consist mainly of two ramparts and ditches, but these become triple at the north-west and south-west. The ditches have been cut into the golden Ham Hill limestone, which has been used for centuries for building purposes. Because of this the western side of the fort has been drastically damaged by quarrying. There are a number of breaks in the rampart, certainly one on the east side of the northern extension seems to be an original entrance as does the gap where the Stoke to Odcombe road cuts the south-east corner.

In 1923 a shallow cremation pit was found on the hill containing a pseudo-anthropomorphic iron dagger in a bronze sheath, with traces of the belt on which it had hung, an iron arrow-head and an adze and various other scraps of metalwork. The burial, of Belgic type, dates to early in the 1st century A.D. In 1866 a number of skeletons, which may have been part of a war cemetery, like that found at Maiden Castle, were found in the north-west corner of the fort. Due to the extensive quarrying of the interior numerous finds have been made, including a delightful stylized bronze bull's head ornament and a number of chariot fittings. Small-scale excavations between 1923 and 1929 confirmed that the site had been occupied from neolithic times onwards, but particularly in the Late Iron Age and Roman periods. A large villa stood on the eastern side of the fort near Bedmore Barn, and a large depression in the north-east corner of the northern extension has been interpreted by some as an amphitheatre.

W. A. Seaby: *Arch. J.* **107** (1950) 90

18 ILCHESTER (LINDINIS) ROMAN TOWN   Roman
    Ilchester   177 (ST:520226)

At the junction of the A37 and the A303 roads.

Situated at a fording place of the river Yeo (Ivel), and the junction of the Fosse Way with roads from Dorchester and the Polden Hills; it was almost inevitable that Ilchester should grow up in about A.D. 55 and flourish until early in the 5th century. Perhaps first built to replace the native settlement on Ham Hill, Ilchester became the second cantonal capital of the Durotriges. The earliest occupation consisted of a collection of wattle-and-daub huts surrounded by a bank and ditch. Before the end of the 1st century A.D. it had been replaced with the formal layout familiar in most Roman towns. By A.D. 100 the defence had been levelled. A stone wall was built round the town late in the 4th century, 0·9 m thick and enclosing 13 ha, although a number of buildings already lay outside the protected area. The river, which was navigable, had stone quays on either bank, west of the bridge. North of it a cemetery has been found, and another along either side of the Fosse Way south-east of Ilchester. There are few visible traces of the Roman town, but its surrounding earthwork can be seen on the south-east of the lane and footpath that runs towards Pill Bridge (at ST: 517226). North-west of Ilchester is one of the densest concentrations of Roman villas yet located in England. This would indicate that Ilchester was a market centre of some importance.

L. V. Grinsell: *Archaeology of Wessex* (1958) 192

19 JOANEY HOW AND ROBIN HOW   Bronze Age
    Luccombe   164 (SS:908426)
274 m east of the road passing north-south over Dunkery Hill.

Three large stone cairns crown the north-eastern promontory of Dunkery Hill. The most northerly is known as Joaney How. It is rather mutilated, but traces of a ditch still surround the barrow, which is 24·4 m in diameter and about 1·5 m high. The central barrow is Robin How, 21·9 m in diameter and 3·1 m high. The mound to the south, known as the Beacon, is 22·9 m in diameter and 1·8 m high. It has a hollow at its centre, and a series of quarry pits around it that may have provided the material from which it was built. Both Joaney How and the Beacon have modern stone heaps on top of them. Their names seem to be fairly modern, although they may reflect an older tradition. There are other barrows on the hill to the east and north-east.

L. V. Grinsell: *Somerset Barrows* I (1969) 35

20 KEYNSHAM (SOMERDALE) ROMAN BUILDINGS   Roman
    Keynsham   156
West: ST:645693. In the cemetery north of the A4.
East: ST:656690. At the entrance to the Somerdale factory of J. S. Fry and Sons. Admission during normal working hours.

West. This large villa, which is unfortunately cut through by the A4 road, was partially uncovered in 1922–4. The house may have had as many as fifty rooms, arranged around four sides of a courtyard measuring 64 m by 55 m. Some rooms were floored with mosaics depicting such subjects as Europa seated on a bull, dolphins, dancers and pipes. One room was hexagonal in shape, whilst an adjoining one had an apse. Most of them had walls with brightly coloured plaster. Unfortunately only a very few fragments of the villa are visible to the west of the chapel in the cemetery, and consist of steps and architectural features. Fortunately the finer mosaics have been moved to the museum at the entrance lodge to Fry's factory.

East. A small rectangular house with six main rooms was found in 1922 whilst the factory was being built. It was moved to its present site opposite to the entrance lodge at that time. Only 10·7 m wide and 15·5 m long, it contains a bath suite as well as living-rooms. There was a water tank in a court on the south side. R. G. Collingwood considered that it was part of a much larger building. The objects found are in the adjoining museum.

A. Bulleid and E. Horne: *Archaeologia* **75** (1926) 109

21   LITTLE SOLSBURY HILLFORT   Iron Age
     Batheaston   156 (ST:768679)
Approached by steep metalled road from Batheaston. National Trust Property.

An isolated hilltop beside the river Avon stands out from the main hill mass to the north. It is crowned by an 8·1 ha fort that is protected on all sides by a steep scarp face and rampart, best seen on the north-east. There has been much quarrying round the edge of the fort and there are now no obvious signs of a ditch, although clean stone to build the rampart, which excavation has shown to have a dry-stone inner and outer facing wall, had to be quarried from somewhere. There are no indications of any inner quarry scoops. An entrance at the north-west corner is strongly inturned on its northern side, but the outwork which protected it has been much mutilated by quarrying. It looks towards Charmy Down and there are tracks linking the hills. Professor Grimes has suggested that some of the early fields on the Down might have been the work of the hillfort builders. Excavation in the fort showed that there was a pre-rampart occupation of the hill, before the main defences were set up, perhaps in the 2nd century B.C.

Traces of the medieval open fields can be seen inside the fort, their ends marked with the original mere-stones or marker stones.

W. A. Dowden: *P.U.B.S.S.* **8** (1956) 18

22 MAESBURY CASTLE   Iron Age
    Dinder and Croscombe   166 (ST:610472)

Beyond Castle Hill Wood just north of road between Wells and Downhead.

Roughly oval in plan this contour fort encloses 2·8 ha with double
ditches and an inner rampart. On the north there are two low banks
between the ditches, separated by a gap about 3·1 m wide. The inner
rampart varies between 2 and 4 m in height, whilst its flat-bottomed
ditch is 1·8 m deep and 4·6 m wide. There is a gap of between 9·1 and
12·2 m separating the inner and outer ditch, with no trace of a second
rampart on the south side. There are entrance gaps at the north-west
and south-east. The former has traces of outworks and is clearly
original. That at the south-east seems to have been widened at some
time and might be unfinished. There was a line of bank and ditch
running east from it, but this has almost disappeared. The ditch on the
north is water-filled, an unusual feature in hillforts.

E. K. Tratman: *P.U.B.S.S.* **8** (1959) 172

23 OLD DOWN FIELD ROUND BARROWS   Bronze Age
    Cranmore   166 (ST:658427)

Footpath from the A361 at ST:663433, 0·8 km west of the village.

Beside the old railway line are a group of six or seven fine round barrows.
Two of them are bell-barrows 45·7 m in diameter and 1·8 m high,
with banks outside their ditches. They were both probably dug by
the Revd. John Skinner, who found cremations in 1827, and one of
them was again opened in 1869 when a cremation with a grooved
bronze dagger and a knife-dagger was found. There are two further
round barrows south of the old railway line.

L. V. Grinsell: *Somerset Barrows* **2** (1971) 103

24 PONTER'S BALL DYKE   Iron Age or Dark Age
    Glastonbury   165 (ST:533377)

Cut by the A361 between Glastonbury and West Pennard.

The town of Glastonbury, on the west side of the Tor, has grown up
on the edge of an 'island' of hills, surrounded by marshes. Only on the
south-east is the island connected by a long, narrow, natural causeway
to the main hill-ridge to the east. Along this ridge runs the main
Shepton Mallet road, and at right angles across it from marsh to marsh
lies the linear earthwork known as Ponter's Ball. It is 1·6 km in
length, with a rampart 9·1 m wide and 3·7 m high, and on its eastern
side a ditch of comparable size. Iron Age pottery was found under the
rampart and deep in the ditch. From this one should probably see it
as the territorial boundary of people living in the lake village at
Glastonbury (No. 16, page 248), though the possibility of its being

connected with Dark Age occupation of Glastonbury Tor should not be ruled out.

C. A. R. Radford in G. Ashe: *Quest for Arthur's Britain* (1968) 102

25 POOL FARM STONE CIST   Bronze Age
   West Harptree   165 (ST: 537541)

Through gate north of the B3134, along footpath towards Pool Farm. The cist is in the field to the west before reaching the farm.

A round barrow 30·5 m in diameter and 1·2 m high was excavated in 1930 by Ethelbert Horne, at which time its mound was almost entirely removed for road material. At its centre was a rectangular stone-lined cist which is still visible, containing the cremated remains of an adult and child. When the south-west wall slab of the cist was examined by Leslie Grinsell in 1956, a series of engravings were observed on it, consisting of six human feet, and ten cup-mark hollows. Such carvings have occasionally been found in northern England, Denmark, Norway and Brittany. The original stone is now displayed in Bristol City Museum, but it has been replaced on the site by a concrete replica.

L. V. Grinsell: *P.P.S.* **23** (1957) 231

26 PORLOCK COMMON STONE CIRCLE   Bronze Age
   Porlock   164 (SS: 846446)

Through iron gate on west of road running from A39 at Hawcombe Head to Exford.

On the southern slope of the hill, close to the road wall, is a circle lying low in the grass. It consists of ten standing stones or stumps, and eleven fallen stones. The circle is about 24·4 m in diameter, and the tallest standing stone is about 0·6 m high. The largest fallen slab is 1·8 m long. If the stones had been equally spaced around the circumference of the circle, there would originally have been about forty-three of them. There is a doubtful round barrow close to the wall to the north-west, with one stone standing on its edge.

L. V. Grinsell: *Archaeology of Exmoor* (1970) 39

27 PRIDDY CIRCLES (Plate 55)   Bronze Age
   East Harptree   165 (ST: 540530: approximate centre)

Three circles due north of the B3135, and a fourth in field opposite Bandpitt Farm on B3134.

Four circles, each about 183 m in diameter, lie in a line from north to south. The three southern circles are each about 82 m apart, but the fourth is about 457 m to the north. They each probably consisted of banks of stones contained between two rings of upright

Plate 55   The Priddy circles, Somerset

posts that originally projected high into the air. Outside were U-shaped
ditches. The excavated example at the south was 1·2 m deep and 3·7 m
wide. The two southern circles had entrances on the north side,
the third had a gap facing south, whilst any entrance to the northern
circle has been destroyed. It is assumed that the circles belong to
the group of ceremonial henge-type monuments. They most resemble
those at Thornborough, near West Tanfield in Yorkshire.

E. K. Tratman: *P.U.B.S.S.* **11** (1967) 97

28 PRIDDY NINE BARROWS   Bronze Age
  Priddy   165 (ST:538516)

By path west of the 'Miners' Arms Restaurant', south from the B3125 road.

A group of seven large barrows form a conspicuous line, with two others to the north. Each are about 3·1 m high and 45·7 m in diameter. The Revd. John Skinner dug into the north-west mound in 1815 and found ashes and charcoal, but nothing else.

L. V. Grinsell: *Somerset Barrows* **2** (1971) 113

29 ROBIN HOOD'S BUTTS   Bronze Age
  Otterford   177 (North: ST:230143; South: ST:237128)

West of the B3170 between Honiton and Taunton, and clearly visible from the road.

Of these two groups of barrows spread along the ridge of Brown Down, those to the north lie under a group of beech trees beside a farm. Each is about 1·8 m high, with mounds, which have merged into each other, varying between 18·3 and 27·4 m in diameter. Although they have probably been opened, there is no record of their contents.

Of the barrows lying 1·6 km to the south, only about four of a once much larger group survive. There is a record of one being opened in 1818 by 'a party of gentlemen from Chard'. It contained a cremation burial and had a ring of retaining stones around its edge.

L. V. Grinsell: *Somerset Barrows* **1** (1969) 37

30 SMALL DOWN CAMP AND BARROWS
                                             Iron Age and Bronze Age
  Evercreech   166 (ST:666406)

To the west of the bridle track from Westcombe to Chesterblade.

High above the river Alham, this univallate fort of about 2 m is roughly oval in plan. On three sides a single rampart, ditch and counter-scarp bank provide the defence, but at the more level eastern end, a second rampart and ditch appear. This is broken by an original entrance 10·7 m wide at its centre, with a second original opening at the north-east corner. Burials were found inside the camp and Iron Age pottery in the ditch when it was dug at the beginning of this century.

Inside the fort is a linear cemetery of eleven or twelve rather small and damaged round barrows. All have been dug at various times, either by John Skinner or others, and seem to have contained cremations. A Bronze Age urn from one of them is in the Museum at Taunton Castle.

H. St. George Gray: *P. Somerset A.S.* **50** (1905) 32

Plate 56   South Cadbury hillfort, Somerset

31 SOUTH CADBURY CASTLE (Plate 56)   Neolithic to Saxon
                                                          166 (ST:628252)

*From the A303(T) road from Chapel Cross to South Cadbury, and then
by footpath south-west beside church to the north-west entrance of the
fort. National Trust.*

This fort is roughly triangular in shape and encloses about 7·3 ha.
Four great banks and ditches ring the hilltop, some of them on the
south side rising 12·2 m from the outside. Its ditches are cut into
oolitic limestone and traces of dry-stone walling appear in places. There
is a main entrance at the south-west, another at the north-east which
forms the normal approach today, and a possible third on the east.
Extensive excavations from 1966 to 1970 showed that the earliest
occupation on the hill dated from the neolithic prior to about 3300 B.C.,

and pottery, pits and a ditch were found from this period. The massive ramparts were built and rebuilt during the Iron Age five or six times, as was the gate at the south-west, where egg-shaped guard chambers were uncovered. Inside the fort circular and rectangular Iron Age buildings, an armourer's workshop and a temple were found. A battle followed by a massacre involving at least twenty-eight adults and children marks the arrival of the Romans who slighted the ramparts and burnt down the south-west gate.

Between A.D. 400 and 600 South Cadbury was refortified and a rectangular hall was built in which the excavators found pieces of east Mediterranean pottery. This confirms that the fort was occupied during the 'Arthurian' period, when legend associates it with King Arthur and Camelot.

In the late Saxon period the hill-top was again defended when it became a *burh* during the reign of King Ethelred, and coins were minted there between A.D. 1010 and 1020. It was probably destroyed on the orders of King Cnut.

L. Alcock: *'By South Cadbury is that Camelot'* (1972)

32 STANTON DREW STONE CIRCLES (Fig. 20)   Neolithic
166 (ST:601634)

Signposted in Stanton Drew village. Partly in the care of the Department of the Environment. The Great and North-east circles are closed on Sundays. Admission fee payable at Court Farm. The south-west circle is privately owned and approached through the farm by the Church. The Cove is easily seen from the churchyard.

After Stonehenge and Avebury, Stanton Drew is the most important group of megalithic monuments in southern England, and yet, perhaps because they are in low-lying land, dominated by trees and the adjoining village, they are scarcely spectacular. Three stone circles, two with stone avenues, a cove and a fallen standing stone, form the components of Stanton Drew.

The Great Circle is 109·7 m in diameter and still has twenty-seven of its probable thirty original stones visible, though many have fallen down. Adjoining it is the *North-east Circle*, 29·6 m in diameter and made up of eight stones, of which only four are still standing. From both of these circles avenues of stones lead eastwards to where they meet and continue towards the river Chew.

The South-west Circle (ST:599631) is 44·2 m across, and has eleven stones of a possible twelve remaining. 152·5 m west of this circle is the *Cove* (ST:598631). It consists of two great, widely spaced standing stones and one, now broken in two, lying flat.

0·4 km north-north-east of the Great Circle is *Hautville's Quoit*, originally a tall standing stone, of which only 2·1 m now remain. (It lies East of Hautville Farm, and south of the road at ST:602638.) A line drawn from the South-west Circle, through the centre of the Great Circle, is aligned on the Quoit, whilst a similar line links the Cove, and the centres of the Great and North-east Circles. Although unexcavated, the monument must relate to sites like Avebury (Wiltshire) and Knowlton (Dorset) and presumably served a religious function. They can be dated to the late Neolithic period. Most of the stone used at Stanton Drew is a local dolomitic conglomerate.

L. V. Grinsell: *Stanton Drew* (1966) (D. of E. pamphlet)

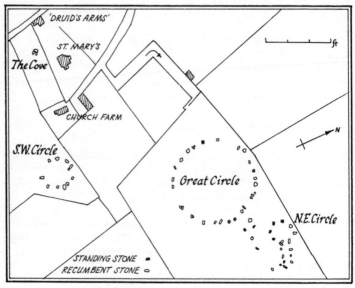

Fig. 20   Stanton Drew Circles, Somerset

33 STOKELEIGH CAMP   Iron Age
   Long Ashton   165 (ST:559733)

West of the Clifton suspension bridge, on the hill just north of Nightingale valley. National Trust property: accessible at all times.

This is one of three promontory forts facing each other across the Avon Gorge. The others are Clifton Camp (Gloucestershire, page 122) and Burwalls Camp (ST:563729) which is largely destroyed. Lying in a beech wood, Stokeleigh Camp covers 2·8 ha. It is protected by the Avon Gorge on the north-east. Elsewhere stone and earth-built ramparts form a double defence on the south-west, which is increased to three ramparts on the north-west. The inner rampart is really massive, standing 9·1 m high in places. Part of the stone core of the northern end was uncovered in 1898 and can still be seen today. The middle bank is slighter, but it also appears to have a stone outer facing. The outer bank may be unfinished. The entrance seems to have been at the north-west, close to the Avon cliffs.

34 STONEY LITTLETON LONG CAIRN (Fig. 21, Plate 57)

Neolithic

Wellow   166 (ST:735572)

From Peasedown St. John, south-east to Stoney Littleton Farm at ST:731556, from where the key can be obtained (small charge). Walk of 0·8 km from the farm to the barrow. A torch will be required. Department of the Environment.

Plate 57   Entrance to the Stoney Littleton chambered barrow, Somerset

260   SOMERSET

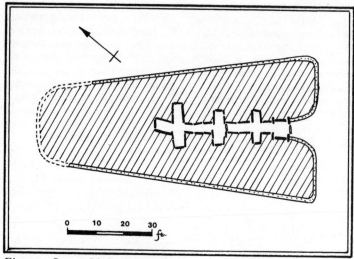

Fig. 21   Stoney Littleton chambered barrow, Somerset

After West Kennet (Wiltshire) this is the finest and most accessible
chambered long cairn in southern England, and well worth the effort
to reach it. Its grass-covered mound, retained by a dry-stone wall is
30·5 m long and 15·2 m wide at the south-eastern end. The entrance
lies between projecting horns, and beneath a massive lintel slab.
There is a conspicuous ammonite cast on the western door jamb. The
entrance passage, 1·2 m high, leads to a gallery 14·6 m long, with three
pairs of side-chambers. The barrow was opened by the Revd. John
Skinner in May 1816, by enlarging a hole made in the roof. He found
many human bones and a little pottery. Two of the skulls that he found
are in Bristol City Museum. In 1858 the site was competently restored
at a cost of sixteen shillings, and a plaque erected, declaring that it was
'the most perfect specimen of Celtic antiquity still existing in Great
Britain'.

L. V. Grinsell: *Stoney Littleton Long Barrow, Somerset* (1963) (D. of E.
pamphlet)

35 TRENDLE RING   Iron Age?
    Bicknoller   164 (ST: 118394)
Footpath west of camp between Bicknoller Hill and Quantock Moor.
This is a small circular hill-slope enclosure of about 0·8 ha, with an
outwork 0·4 km higher up the hill to the north-east. It was probably
used for stock raising during the latter part of the Iron Age.

36 WAMBARROWS   Bronze Age
  Winsford   164 (SS:876343)

On heath just north of the B3223. National Trust property.

These three closely spaced round barrows, 0·9 to 1·5 m in height, lie
in a line north of the road. There is no record of their having been
opened, but cavities at the centre of each of them clearly indicate that
this has happened. A fourth example lies a short distance south-east
of the rest.

L. V. Grinsell: *Somerset Barrows* 1 (1969) 41

37 WICK BARROW   Neolithic
  Stogursey   165 (ST:209456)

Beside road 1·6 km north-west of Wick.

This somewhat irregular looking barrow is about 24·4 m in diameter
and 3·4 m high on the southern side. It was opened by H. St. George
Gray in 1907 by trenching from east to west and then extending his
cutting in the central area.

At the centre of the barrow was a drum-shaped mound, 9·1 m in
diameter, revetted with a dry-stone wall 1·1 m high. This was covered
with a cairn of lias blocks. The primary burial at the centre of the
barrow had been robbed in Roman times. However, three secondary
crouched burials accompanied by beakers, had not been disturbed.
One of them had been buried with a fine flint dagger. Both beakers and
dagger are now in Taunton Castle Museum.

H. St. George Gray: *P. Somerset A.S.* **54** (1908) 1

38 WITHYPOOL STONE CIRCLE   Bronze Age
  Withypool   164 (SS:838343)

On the south-west side of Withypool Hill.

This is a circle of thirty-seven small stones, none more than 0·6 m
high. As they are each about 1·1 m apart, there were probably about
a hundred originally. The circle is almost 36·6 m in diameter. On the
summit of the hill to the north-east is a mutilated round barrow with
an Ordnance Survey trigonometrical point on it. It measures 18·3 m
across and 0·9 m high.

L. V. Grinsell: *Archaeology of Exmoor* (1970) 39

39 WOOKEY HOLE CAVES   Palaeolithic to Roman
    Wookey   165 (ST:532480)

Signposted at north end of Wookey Hole village. Cave privately owned.
Open summer: 09.00 hours to dusk; winter: 10.00 to 12.00, 13.30 to
17.00 hours.

Dramatically lit with electricity, the great show-cave of today must
look very different from the time when it was occupied by prehistoric
man. Lying at the head of a ravine cut by the river Axe, the cave is
formed in dolomitic conglomerate. The river issues from a lower cave
mouth, whilst visitors enter at a higher level. Early man only occupied
the first chamber, but at least six others have been discovered, the
last four requiring underwater diving apparatus to reach them. Pottery
of late Iron Age and Romano-British types suggest an intermittent
occupation close to the light of the cave mouth.

The Hyaena Den is a small cave 55 m south-east of the main cave
across a rustic bridge (ST:533478). It was explored in 1852 by the
geologist Boyd Dawkins. In it he found the bones of numerous Ice
Age animals including mammoth, woolly rhinoceros, cave bear and
many hyaenas, as well as more common animals. From time to time
the fiercer creatures had clearly used the cave as their den, and large
quantities of gnawed bones were found. Flint implements of Solutrean
type and wood ash also showed occupation by Middle and Upper
Palaeolithic man. Bones and implements from the cave are in Wells
Museum and the University Museums in Manchester and Oxford.

C. F. C. Hawkes: *Arch. J.* **107** (1950) 92

40 WORLEBURY CAMP   Iron Age
    Weston-super-Mare   165 (ST:315625)

Approached by roads from Weston-super-Mare or Worlebury.

This stone-built hillfort occupies a long narrow ridge on the north side
of Weston-super-Mare. About 4 ha are enclosed by natural cliffs on
the north and west, a single rampart and ditch on the south, and
two ramparts and five ditches on the east where the ground levels out.
The ramparts were examined in 1851 and shown to be built of rubble
faced with stone walls, and to contain at least three internal, hidden
wall-faces, presumably incorporated for stability, but perhaps representing different phases of building. There are three entrances, one at
the north-east corner, another in the west side about 46 m from the
north-west corner, and the third at the south-east, where the wall is
sharply inturned. More than ninety storage pits (originally thought to
have been pit dwellings) were found, dug as much as 1·5 m into the
limestone. They have produced pottery of Middle Iron Age B type
similar to that from the lake villages at Glastonbury and Meare, iron

spearheads, and charred wheat, barley and pulse; all suggesting permanent occupation. The concentration of these pits in the eastern half of the camp, and the sharply incurved rampart about 40 m west of the south-east corner may suggest that there was an earlier fort on the eastern knoll, later extended westwards. Remains of eighteen skeletons have been taken as evidence that the fort was assaulted, either by the Romans or rival Iron Age folk. At all events some of the stone walls were systematically slighted and the stonework thrown into the ditches. Most of the finds from the site are in Weston-super-Mare Museum.

C. W. Dymond: *Worlebury* (1902)

Museums containing archaeological material

Axbridge Caving Group and Archaeological Society, The Museum, Town Hall, Axbridge

Bath Roman Museum, Abbey Churchyard, Bath

Gough's Cave Museum, Cheddar

Glastonbury Lake Village Museum, The Tribunal, High Street, Glastonbury

Shepton Mallet Museum, Market Place, Shepton Mallet

Somerset County Museum,* Taunton Castle, Taunton

Wells Museum, Cathedral Green, Wells

Museum and Art Gallery, The Boulevard, Weston-super-Mare

Borough Museum, Hendford Manor Hall, Yeovil

Bristol City Museum, Queen's Road, Bristol 8

Spelaeological Society Museum, The University, Bristol 8

* Main county collection

SUFFOLK

I	BRIGHTWELL HEATH BARROW CEMETERY	Bronze Age
	Brightwell and Foxhall	150 (TM:236442)

Of about twenty barrows that once existed on this Heath, only a few outliers now remain. Of these, Pole Hill barrow, beside the Ipswich to Brightwell road, is a fine bowl-barrow, 0·9 m high and 24·4 m in diameter, saved from destruction, no doubt, by its crown of fir trees. The nearby saucer-barrow known as the Devil's Ring has been ploughed completely flat.

R. R. Clarke: *East Anglia* (1960) 78, for plan of former barrow cemetery

Plate 58   Burgh Castle Saxon Shore fort, Suffolk

2   BURGH CASTLE ROMAN FORT (Plate 58)   Roman
                                              126 (TG:475046)

*Signposted at west end of Burgh Castle village, to south of church. Foot-
path muddy in wet weather. Department of the Environment. Open
standard hours; guide pamphlet available.*

Late in the 3rd century A.D. a chain of fortresses were set up around
the east and south coast of England in an attempt to check the activities
of Saxon pirates, or possibly at the instigation of the usurper Carausius
against the central powers in Rome. Burgh Castle (*Gariannorum*) seems
to have been one of the first to be built. Enclosing 2 ha it lies on the
south side of the Yare estuary, Breydon Water, whilst the Roman
town of Caister-by-Yarmouth (Norfolk, page 218) lies on the northern
shore. A quadrilateral in shape, only its two long sides were parallel,
although that on the west fell into the river Waveney many centuries
ago. The existing walls stand 4·6 to 4·9 m high and this was probably

their original height, apart from a parapet along the front edge. At their base the walls are 3·4 m thick, but this reduces to 2·4 m at the top. There were six bastions jutting out from the wall, in the tops of which round holes were provided to take the turntables for *ballista* or spring guns. This can easily be seen in the fallen bastion on the south side. Each of the three surviving walls had a gateway through it, that on the east being 3·6 m wide without any protective flanking towers; but the others were narrower postern gates. The two surviving corners of the fort are rounded, a feature which bears out the early date of construction. The wide flat ditches that lie outside are completely silted up. Half-timbered buildings with stone foundations inside the fort were the barracks used by the Stablesian Cavalry (from modern Yugoslavia) stationed here about A.D. 400. The fort seems to have been built after A.D. 275 and to have been abandoned early in the 5th century.

Burgh Castle later became a 7th-century monastic site, and then a motte-and-bailey castle. The motte, which stood in the south-western corner, was removed in 1839.

A. J. Morris: *P. Suffolk Inst. Arch.* **24** (1947) 100

---

3 CLARE CAMP   Iron Age ?
                                                              149 (TL:768458)

A side road, Bridewell Street, leads off the B1063 at the northern end of Clare, on to Upper Common.

Lying on the hillside overlooking the northern end of Clare and a tributary of the river Stour, this fort of about 2·8 ha is protected by a double rampart and ditch. Houses have damaged the south and east sides. The fort may have been thrown up by the Trinovantes as a defence against the neighbouring Catuvellauni, but there is some reason for considering the whole site to be of much later Danish origin. There are possible entrances on the north and south sides. No finds have been recorded from the camp.

R. R. Clarke: *Arch. J.* **96** (1939) 1

---

4 RISBY POOR'S HEATH BARROWS   Bronze Age
        Risby   136 (TL:776678)

Beside the Cavenham to Risby road.

The area around Risby was once rich in barrows. Many have now been destroyed by agriculture. The two barrows on either side of the road both contained cremation burials in urns when examined by Canon Greenwell in 1869. In addition a crouched skeleton lay in a shallow grave in one of them, and four other burials were found higher in the same mound. A pottery vessel of Middle Iron Age date also came from the excavations. More cremations were found in two barrows

0·8 km north-east, and other burial mounds exist on the eastern side of Risby Poor's Heath at TL:793685. There is no record of their contents.

Two separate sections of dyke known as the *Black Ditches* run through Cavenham parish (TL:774684 and TL:767720). These are almost certainly of Saxon date and belong to the same series as the Cambridge dykes (page 28).

C. Fox: *Archaeology of the Cambridge Region* (1923) 327

Museums containing archaeological material

Moyse's Hall Museum, Cornhill, Bury St. Edmunds
Ipswich Museum, High Street, Ipswich
Southwold Museum, St. Bartholomew's Green, Southwold

SURREY

1   ABINGER COMMON PIT-DWELLING   Mesolithic
                                            170 (TQ:112459)
In field behind the Manor House. Key and permission at the house.

A wooden building with small museum display covers this unusual site excavated by Dr. L. S. B. Leakey in 1950. It consists of a pit 0·9 m deep, 4·3 m long and 3·1 m wide which may have been a working and sleeping place for mesolithic man, some 8,000 years ago. Dug into the natural greensand, this pit has a ledge or bench along its deeper east side, whilst at the west end burnt material and stones suggest a hearth. Above this feature and just outside the pit were two post holes that may have supported some simple shelter and bracken or saplings. Within the pit 1,056 microlithic flint implements were found, suggesting that it was in use for some considerable time, though precisely what its function was must remain obscure. It was too small for an efficient working place and lack of apparent shelter made it scarcely suitable for a sleeping place, yet it is as one of these that we must probably see it.

L. S. B. Leakey: *Surrey Arch. Soc. Report No. 3* (1951)

2   ANSTIEBURY HILLFORT   Iron Age
    Holmwood   170 (TQ:153440)
In woods immediately south of the minor road at Coldharbour Common.

This is a circular hillfort of about 4·5 ha. It is defended by three banks and two ditches on the north, east and west, but none is visible on the

steep south side. There is an entrance at the north-east which has not
been excavated. The site was probably occupied by people of the Weald
prospecting for iron ore, in the 3rd century B.C. The site is covered with
trees.

H. P. Malden: *Surrey A.C.* **12** (1895) 157

3 BANSTEAD GOLF COURSE BARROWS   Bronze Age
                                                       170 (TQ:249607)

On the golf course west of the A297 close to the highest point of the hill.

As is usual in such cases these barrows have been sadly mutilated by
the golf course. Known as the Galley Hills, the group consists of
four barrows. Two of them measure 12·2 m in diameter and 1·5 m
high, each with a robbers' pit in the centre. Another is 9·1 m across and
0·6 m high; its centre has been removed. The last bowl-barrow is
7·6 m in diameter and 0·6 m high, but has been turned into a golf
bunker making it almost unrecognizable.

L. V. Grinsell: *Surrey A.C.* **42** (1934) 43

4 CAESAR'S CAMP HILLFORT   Iron Age
    Farnham   169 (SU:825500)

On Bricksbury Hill north of A3016 from SU:832492. Military area.

A promontory fort enclosing about 11 ha faces north-east. Strongly
defended by a double rampart and ditch on the south-west, and a single
line on the south-east. The steep slopes on the north and east do not
appear to have been defended although a drawing of 1848 suggests
otherwise. There is an entrance in the centre of the south-west side.

V.C.H. Surrey **4** (1912) 385

5 CROOKSBURY COMMON TRIPLE BELL-BARROW   Bronze Age
    Elstead   169 (SU:894449)

*In woodland on the east of Crooksbury Common and south-east of footpath
at SU:892452.*

Three mounds of differing dimensions are enclosed within a single oval
ditch. The northern mound is about 9·1 m in diameter and 1·8 m high,
the central one is 14·6 m wide and 2·4 m high, whilst the southern is
18·3 m across and 2·7 m high. Berms separate the three mounds from
the ditch which encloses them all. The ditch has a slight outer bank,
and *could* be a later feature added to surround three bowl-barrows,
rather than the rare triple bell-barrow which usually tends to be more
regular in appearance.

L. V. Grinsell: *Surrey A.C.* **40** (1932) 58

6 DEERLEAP WOOD BELL-BARROW   Bronze Age
   Wotton   170 (TQ: 118480)

*North from A25, and 100 yards into wood take left fork. Barrow is off
track to right and overgrown.*

The mound of this bell-barrow is 2·1 m high and about 23 m in
diameter. A berm 6·1 m wide separates it from its ditch which is
45·7 m in diameter. Excavation in 1960 gave no conclusive evidence
for a Bronze Age date. The mound had been composed of a turf stack
overlaid by a layer of stones. No burial was found.

J. X. W. P. Corcoran: *Surrey A.C.* **60** (1963) 1

7 DRY HILL HILLFORT   Iron Age
   Lingfield   171 (TQ: 432417)

*Minor road north from B2110 at TQ:433395, then bridleway from
TQ:435404 to Beeches Farm. Footpath uphill to fort.*

A large roughly rectangular camp of about 10 ha commands extensive
views across Surrey and Kent. The defences are partially mutilated,
but on the south-west and north-east consist of double ramparts and
ditches with counterscarps. The ramparts still stand 2·7 m high in
places. The probable entrance is on the south-west where the earthworks butt obliquely to one another.

8 FARLEY HEATH ROMANO-CELTIC TEMPLE   Roman
   Albury   170 (TQ: 052449)

Beside minor road over Farley Heath.

Excavated by the Surrey poet, Martin Tupper, between 1839 and
1847, the footings of this temple are now clearly marked on the Heath.
Two squares, one inside the other, represent the inner *cella* or shrine,
with a verandah on the outside; the whole surrounded by a large
polygonal *temenos* wall. There is no evidence to suggest that an earlier
Celtic shrine stood on the spot. A decorative bronze strip which may
have formed part of the binding to a priest's sceptre was found by
Tupper. It is covered with crudely drawn figures representing the
Celtic gods Sucellus, Nantosvelta and Taranis.

R. G. Goodchild: *Ant. J.* 18 (1938) 391

9 FRENSHAM COMMON BOWL-BARROWS   Bronze Age
   Frensham   169 (SU: 854407)

*Beside footpath over Common from Rushmoor to Frensham. National
Trust property.*

A fine linear cemetery of four round barrows running north to south
along the hill-crest. The northern two round barrows are each about

1·8 m high and 22·9 m wide, the southern two slightly smaller and almost touching one another. The second barrow from the north has a prominent ditch 2·7 m wide, whilst the southernmost shows signs of having been opened at some time in the past. It also has a surrounding ditch 2·4 m wide.

L. V. Grinsell: *Surrey A.C.* **42** (1934) 59

10 FROWSBARROW ROUND BARROW   Bronze Age
   Puttenham   169 (SU:939476)
On Golf Course north of the B3000 on Puttenham Heath.

This bowl-barrow is 2·3 m high and 41 m in diameter, and is surrounded by a well-defined ditch. Unfortunately a golf-tee has been constructed on the barrow, and a commemorative stone set up, recording Queen Victoria's visit to it in 1857.

L. V. Grinsell: *Surrey A.C.* **42** (1934) 56

11 HASCOMBE HILL HILLFORT   Iron Age
   Hascombe   170 (TQ:004386)
Footpath through woods from public house at Hascombe passes through fort.

Set on a narrow, south-facing promontory, with steep slopes on all except the north-east, this fort of about 2·4 ha was strongly defended. Artificial scarping on the north-west, south-west and south-east and the digging of a ditch 1·5 m deep, some 4·6 m from the crest of the hill, made the escarpment sides almost impregnable. Across the north-east neck of the hill a ditch 2·7 m deep and 6·4 m wide was cut to provide material for a rampart 12·2 m wide and 1·5 m high. In the centre of this side was a straight-through entrance gap. The ends of the rampart at this point are strongly out-turned beyond the ends of the ditch. Slight excavation suggested a date for occupation during the 1st century B.C.

S. E. Winbolt: *Surrey A.C.* **40** (1932) 78

12 HILLBURY HILLFORT   Iron Age
   Puttenham Common   169 (SU:911469)
Various footpaths across the Common lead to the fort, which is on the hill-slope east of Hampton House.

Shaped like an irregular quadrangle this fort is protected by a single rampart and ditch on its north, east and south sides. The rampart stands about 2·7 m high. There are a number of gaps making the site of the original entrance uncertain.

13 HOLMBURY HILLFORT   Iron Age
    Shere   170 (TQ: 105430)

Footpath through woods to fort, leaving minor road at SQ:105428.

Due to sand and gravel digging this roughly square hillfort of about
3·2 ha is in a poor state of preservation. Two ramparts and ditches
defend the north and west sides. Both are now difficult to trace, but
excavation has shown that the outer ditch was originally about 2·4 m
deep and 6·1 m wide, the inner 4 m deep and 9·1 m wide. The inner
bank has been destroyed on the west where the excavation took place.
The outer bank was 2·4 m high and 10·7 m wide at its base. There
were no signs of any timbering in the rampart. On the steep south and
east sides there may have been a single rampart and ditch, but this is
not clear. Nor is it certain where the original entrance lay, although
the north-west corner seems the most likely position. Excavation
produced evidence to show that the camp was built early in the 1st
century A.D. by Belgic people.

S. E. Winbolt: *Surrey A.C.* **38** (1929–30) 156

14 HORSELL COMMON BELL-BARROWS   Bronze Age
    Horsell   170 (TQ:014598 and TQ:016598)

*North of the canal, on either side of the road from Horsell Common
roundabout to Maybury.*

These two bell-barrows have both been dug into in the past, but there is
no record of their contents. That on the west of the road has a mound
30·5 m in diameter and 1·5 m high. A berm 6·4 m wide separates it
from the ditch which has an outer diameter of 48·8 m. It has signs of
an outer bank.

   Close to the power line, east of the road, is a smaller bell-barrow
with a mound 24·4 m in diameter and 1·5 m high, a berm 4·6 m wide
and ditch 39·6 m in overall diameter. It was dug into for military
purposes during the First World War.

L. V. Grinsell: *Surrey A.C.* **40** (1932) 62

15 LEATHERHEAD DOWNS ROUND BARROW   Bronze Age
                                               170 (TQ:182547)

Barrow in wood beside minor road across Leatherhead Downs

Situated in the grounds of Cherkley Court, this round barrow, 16·2 m
in diameter and 1·1 m high, was opened in 1928 by boys of St. John's
School, Leatherhead, but nothing was found.

L. V. Grinsell: *Surrey A.C.* **42** (1934) 50

16 MILTON HEATH ROUND BARROW   Bronze Age
   Dorking   170 (TQ: 153489)

Just north of the A25 and east of the road to Milton Court.

A bowl-barrow 20·1 m in diameter and 1·5 m high, covered with
trees.

17 NEWLANDS CORNER ROUND BARROW   Bronze Age
   Guildford   170 (TQ: 045492)

In woods east of the A25 at Newlands Corner.

A bowl-barrow 18·3 m in diameter and 1·2 m high, with a large central
hollow indicating that it has been opened, although nothing is known
of its contents.

L. V. Grinsell: *Surrey A.C.* **42** (1934) 57

18 REIGATE HEATH ROUND BARROWS   Bronze Age
                                                      170 (TQ: 237504)

*On Reigate Heath and edge of woodland between A25 and windmill to
the south-west.*

There are seven round barrows in this cemetery. From north to south
they form a line varying in height between 0·3 and 2·4 m and in
diameter between 7·6 and 33 m. When the largest barrow in the group
(second from the north) was opened in 1809 it produced a cremation
burial, as did one of its neighbours. Two others that were opened failed
to satisfy the diggers.

L. V. Grinsell: *Surrey A.C.* **42** (1934) 52

19 ST. ANNE'S HILL HILLFORT   Iron Age
   Chertsey   170 (TQ: 026676)

*Footpaths through the woods lead on to St. Anne's Hill from the B388 and
minor road to the south.*

This is a steep-sided hill enclosing about 5 ha. Only on the west does
it appear to have been defended, and here a ditch and counterscarp
bank seem to be the main features. This earthwork has been cut off by
the Dingle on the south. The other sides of the hill do not seem to have
been artificially defended.

V.C.H. Surrey **4** (1912) 384

20 ST. GEORGE'S HILL HILLFORT   Iron Age
   Walton-on-Thames   170 (TQ: 085618)

Amongst woods and houses south-west of Whiteley village.

Badly damaged by the sprawl of houses it is still possible to make out
the irregular shape of this 5·7 ha fort. It is defended by a single ram-

part and ditch except at the north-west where it is doubled. At this point an entrance cuts into the fort. There is a semicircular enclosure on the north-east which seems to have been added to the existing site, perhaps as a cattle enclosure. A ditch leading off to the north-east has now been destroyed. It may have formed a ranch boundary of the type still visible in Hampshire. There are indications that the site was occupied during the 3rd century B.C. and the early 1st century A.D.

21   SOLDIERS' RING EARTHWORK   Iron Age
  Crooksbury Common, Seale   169 (SU:880462)
On north side of Crooksbury Hill not far from The Sands.

This small circular enclosure, about 46 m in diameter, is surrounded by a single bank and ditch. It lies on a low north-facing spur and was probably an animal enclosure.

More than 1·6 km to the south-east (SU:895450) are a group of at least four round barrows, two of which are surrounded by one ditch. Nothing is known of their contents.

L. V. Grinsell: *Surrey A.C.* **42** (1934) 54 (for barrows)

22   SUNNINGDALE BOWL-BARROW   Bronze Age
  Chobham   169–170 (SU:952665)
In garden of Heathside, west of Ridge Mount Road, and south-east of the A30.

This bowl-barrow is 1·5 m high and about 22·9 m in diameter. When a trench was cut through it in 1901 twenty-five cremation burials were found, twenty-three of them in bucket- and barrel-shaped urns of Deveril-Rimbury type. They were just below the surface of the barrow and were clearly not the primary burial, which was not found. They had been placed in shallow holes lined with pieces of sandstone, and covered with conglomerate slabs. The urns date the secondary use of the barrow to about 1200 B.C. and suggest that it was originally built about 1800 B.C.

L. V. Grinsell: *Surrey A.C.* **42** (1934) 36

23   THURSLEY COMMON BOWL-BARROWS   Bronze Age
  Thursley   169 (SU:909409)
North of minor road across Thursley Common.

These two bowl-barrows are best viewed when the bracken on the heath is low. The western example is 1·8 m high and 24·4 m wide; the eastern, 183 m to the east, is 2·7 m high and 22·9 m in diameter. Both have well-marked ditches surrounding them.

L. V. Grinsell: *Surrey A.C.* **42** (1934) 59

24 TITSEY PARK VILLA   Roman
    Titsey   171 (TQ:404545)
Situated in Titsey Park. Permission to visit required.

A villa of corridor type measuring some 38 m by 18·3 m was discovered
in 1847 and excavated in 1864. Two corridors, on the north and south,
communicate with a central suite of rooms, and link smaller rooms at
either end of the building. Coins suggest that the villa was occupied
from A.D. 166 to 180. Later, about A.D. 320 the rooms at the west
end were probably used for fulling and had water and heating systems
laid on. A wall running for 73 m to the south may have been part of
an enclosure wall.

V.C.H. Surrey **4** (1912) 367

25 TUMBLE BEACON ROUND BARROW   Bronze Age
    Banstead   170 (TQ:243590)
In a private garden in a side road, west off the A217.

This mound which is 4·6 m high and 33·5 m in diameter may have been
a barrow, which was later turned into a Beacon; the latter use is well
documented.

L. V. Grinsell: *Surrey A.C.* **42** (1934) 45

26 WEST END COMMON BARROWS   Bronze Age
    Chobham   169 (SU:934616)
*Beside footpath from SU:936614, 0·8 km west of Gordon Boys' School.
Military area.*

A linear cemetery of four round barrows runs east to west along a ridge,
each standing about 1·8 m high. The barrow at the west end is 25·6 m
in diameter, and has part of its ditch (2·7 m wide and 0·6 m deep)
visible to the south-west. The barrow at the east is about 27 m in
diameter and also has a slight ditch. The two smaller barrows in
between overlap one another, and measure 18·3 m and 15·2 m in
diameter respectively. A wide track running over the top of all the
mounds is badly damaging them.

L. V. Grinsell: *Surrey A.C.* **42** (1934) 39

27 WHITMOOR COMMON BARROWS   Bronze Age
    Worplesden   169 (SU:997537)
In wood close to footpath from A320 to Whitmoor House.

On the eastern corner of the Common is a low bell-barrow about
30·5 m across, with a central mound 12·2 m wide and 0·6 m high. It was
opened by Pitt-Rivers who found a small hole at the centre 'where

no doubt a burnt body had been deposited'. All trace of it had vanished.
Nearby were two bucket-type cinerary urns.

229 m west of the bridge, near Mount Pleasant, is a small round
barrow, little more than 0·3 m high and 13·7 m in diameter, with traces
of a surrounding ditch, and clear evidence of Pitt-Rivers's excavation
hole in the centre. It produced three bucket-shaped urns. The finds
from both barrows are in the Pitt-Rivers Museum in Oxford.

L. V. Grinsell: *Surrey A.C.* **42** (1934) 48

28 WISLEY COMMON BELL-BARROW   Bronze Age
   Wisley   170 (TQ:079592)

West of the A3 in woodland.

This large bell-barrow is 43·9 m in diameter and 3·1 m high, with a
berm 5·5 m wide. It appears to stand on a raised platform. When
excavated it produced a cremation from high in its mound, but no
primary burial has yet been found. It has been damaged by a parish
boundary and iron-working on its east and north-east sides. It can
probably be dated to about 1800 B.C.

L. V. Grinsell: *Surrey A.C.* **42** (1934) 59

Museums containing archaeological material

Camberley Museum, Knoll Road, Camberley
Charterhouse School Museum, Godalming
Godalming Borough Museum, Old Town Hall, Godalming
Guildford Museum,* Castle Arch, Guildford
Weybridge Museum, Church Street, Weybridge

* Main county collection

SUSSEX

I BARKHALE CAUSEWAYED CAMP   Neolithic
   Bignor Hill   181/182 (SU:976126)

*From minor road from Madehurst, walk uphill to National Trust property
on top of downs. Take bridleway south-east for 91 m to where track crosses
earthwork.*

This is one of the largest causewayed enclosures so far discovered.
Oval in shape it measures 228·6 m by 152·5 m. Unfortunately it has
been much ploughed since it was first discovered and although it is
now permanently under grass, it can only be clearly detected on the
north and north-east where traces of the ditches with internal banks

can still be made out. The south-western side, beyond the fence, is almost invisible. Minor excavation in 1930 failed to produce dating material, but more recently work by Dr. Seton Williams has confirmed the neolithic origin of the site.

Due north of the camp are two round barrows.

E. C. Curwen: *Archaeology of Sussex* (1954) 89

2 BEVIS'S THUMB LONG BARROW   Neolithic
    North Marden   181 (SU:789155)

Beside minor road between East Marden and Compton Park.

Also called Solomon's or Baverse's Thumb, this was first recognized as a long barrow by Leslie Grinsell in 1930. It is one of the largest in Sussex, measuring 64 m long, 21·3 m wide at the western end, and 1·8 m high on the east. The road has cut into its northern side destroying the ditch, and ploughing has done the same on the south, although the presence of a ditch was determined by percussion. This is one of three known long barrows in West Sussex and may be connected with the people who dug the causewayed camp at the Trundle.

L. V. Grinsell: *Sussex A.C.* **82** (1941) 122

3 BIGNOR ROMAN VILLA   Roman
                                              181/182 (SU:988147)

Clearly signposted on eastern side of Bignor village, midway between the A29 and the A285. Open daily, except Mondays, 1 March to 31 October, 10.00 to 18.30 hours. Also Bank Holidays, all Mondays in August, and Sundays in November.

Looking rather like a group of African huts under its modern thatched roofs, this famous villa, discovered in 1811, has been extensively uncovered. A number of rooms with mosaic floors have had stone huts built over them, often on the original Roman wall foundations. This means that six floors can be viewed, whilst the outlines of other rooms, particularly those of the west wing, are marked out in stones and concrete.

The villa, which faces north-west, was built 0·4 km from where Stane Street climbs the chalk escarpment of Bignor Hill on its way to Chichester. In its earliest form it consisted of a rectangular five-roomed cottage-type villa, constructed largely of timber. It was built on the west of the present site, towards the end of the 2nd century. After a fire it was rebuilt in stone, and a front corridor with slightly projecting rooms at the north and south was added. This part of the villa is represented by the west wing between Rooms 33 and 41. The mosaics in Rooms 10 and 33 belong to this period. Early in the 4th century the villa was converted into a courtyard house by building out wings, each about 67 m long, to north and south, and linking them with a corridor on the east. Towards the middle of the 4th century the more elaborate mosaics were added when the villa seems to have been at its most prosperous. At this time it was one of the larger villas in Britain. How it eventually came to an end is unknown, but it seems to have survived into the 5th century before decay set in.

The mosaics at Bignor show a variety of mythical scenes and characters including a head of Venus and an amusing frieze of cupids as gladiators, all partly restored, in Room 3, the rape of Ganymede in Room 7, two masks of Medusa (Rooms 33 and 56) and the four seasons in Room 33. One of the mosaics carries the abbreviated signature *TER*, perhaps Terentius, the mosaicist who laid it. Most of the walls were originally painted although little trace now remains. For example, when first found, Room 33 had a vertically striped wall of red, greenish-blue, white and yellow above a fringe of dark brown. This is no longer standing.

In an outer courtyard at the eastern end of the villa stood a large barn 36·6 m long, as well as smaller barns, stables and ox-stalls. It has been estimated that in using these the villa could have supported an area of 769 ha.

In Room 8 there is a small modern museum of objects found on the site. It includes photographs, drawings and models, but is spoilt by badly written labels (1972).

S. S. Frere: *J.R.S.* **53** (1963) 155

4 BLACKPATCH FLINT MINES   Neolithic
   Patching   182 (TQ:094089).

A footpath runs north from the A280, passing east of Myrtlegrove Farm. The mines lie west of the path, about half-way up the hill.

Today only low hollows indicate where more than a hundred flint-mine shafts lie buried beneath the soil. Seven of the pits were excavated between 1922 and 1930. It was clear that they had been dug to reach a seam of nodular flint about 3·4 m below the surface. From most of the shafts, galleries radiated out, only as far as daylight permitted them to be worked. In order to save labour as a new gallery was dug, the chalk extracted from it was placed in one of the worked-out galleries, thus eliminating the need to carry the debris to the surface. Some of the shafts contained cremations and inhumation burials, whilst small barrows were built over the filled-up mines. From these remains it is possible to deduce that the mines had been worked intermittently for a very long period of time, perhaps 500 years, through the Neolithic to the Middle Bronze Age. A new shaft dug every five years would certainly have supplied the needs of a small community, traces of whose village were found north-east of the mines on the other side of the footpath.

J. H. Pull: *Flint Miners of Blackpatch* (1932)

5 THE CABURN HILLFORT   Iron Age
   Glynde   183 (TQ:444089)

Reached by footpath east of Ranscombe Farm on side road to Glynde off A274.

Crowning the pudding-shaped summit of Mount Caburn, at 490 feet above sea level, is the small circular hillfort of the Caburn. A massive outer rampart and ditch with a smaller inner rampart and ditch enclose some 1·4 ha. Extensive excavations by General Pitt-Rivers, Eliot and E. Cecil Curwen and A. E. Wilson give us a good idea of the history of this site.

At first an undefended farming settlement was established on the hill, perhaps as early as 500 B.C. Much later, around 150 B.C. the hill was defended by digging a V-shaped ditch 1·5 m deep round the summit and piling the excavated material onto an internal bank. They left an entrance gap at the north-east. The construction was probably carried out with great speed as the rampart was not strengthened with timbers in the normal way. This feature still survives as the inner earthwork. There was evidence to show that the fortified hill was attacked almost immediately afterwards, perhaps by folk from west Sussex expanding towards the Weald. Inside the fort occupation seems to have been permanent. More than 140 grain storage pits, mostly rectangular in plan and 0·9 to 2·4 m deep, have been excavated, and can still be seen as hollows. Hut sites proved more elusive to the excavators but must have existed. A large pit, north of the centre, dug by Pitt-Rivers may have been intended for water storage, since there is no obvious source closer than 0·8 km to the camp. With the coming of the Romans the occupants of the Caburn attempted to strengthen their fort on its northern side. They set up a palisade of stout wooden posts 3·1 m high and 0·3 m apart along the edge of their ancient ditch, with a second line of posts parallel to them forming a kind of box, 3·1 m wide, which they filled with chalk, partly obtained by cleaning out the old ditch behind the palisade, and largely from a massive new ditch in front of it. This new ditch was 2·4 m deep and 9·1 m wide, a massive affair of what is called Fécamp type, common in northern France, and found occasionally in Britain. At the same time the gateway at the north-east was remodelled, but all in vain. When the fort was attacked the gate was reduced to ashes and occupation within came to an abrupt end.

A. E. Wilson: *Sussex A.C.* **80** (1939) 193

6 CHANCTONBURY RING   Iron Age and Roman
  Washington   182 (TQ:139120)

A footpath from Lock's Farm, Washington, leads through woods to the western side of the Ring.

This is a small oval fort of 1·4 ha, surrounded by a low rampart and traces of a ditch on the south-west. In the same sector is a simple entrance. The fort has acquired a certain celebrity from the beech trees planted within its circuit in 1760, and now forming a conspicuous landmark. Amongst the roots of the trees are the foundations of two Roman buildings, one a rectangular temple with internal *cella* measuring 7·3 m by 5·2 m. Almost 0·4 km westwards at the narrowest point on the ridge from Chanctonbury is a cross-dyke, a bank 274 m long with ditch on the western side. A similar dyke, sickle-shaped in plan, lies at a similar distance to the east where the ridge is wider, and the 'handle' of the sickle to the south-west. These must be related to the defence of the fort. Near the eastern dyke was a round barrow (TQ:128120) that contained a crouched female burial with an ogival dagger of the Wessex culture. The barrow has now been destroyed by ploughing.

7 CHICHESTER (NOVIOMAGUS REGNENTIUM)   Roman
  Chichester   181 (SU:861047)

As its Roman name *Noviomagus* implies, Chichester was a new market, built on a site that had not been previously occupied. It probably succeeded a Belgic settlement at Selsey, or more likely, close to the Chichester Dykes. Considerable excavation has failed to reveal any substantial traces of settlement prior to A.D. 44, when it is likely that a military supply base was established in the eastern part of the walled town. After A.D. 47 the Roman town seems to have developed first as a somewhat disorganized series of timber buildings, with a statue of Nero amongst them, and later in the latter half of the 1st century with planned roads and public buildings including a forum and basilica, temples, amphitheatre and baths. Chichester was the government centre for Cogidubnus, the pro-Roman client king whose probable palace lay 1·6 km west at Fishbourne, and as such it may have been something of a show-town. Towards the end of the 2nd century earthen ramparts were thrown round the town, probably with stone gateways. As time went by timber buildings were replaced by stone and brick, and a flint and mortar wall encircled the town on the line of the earlier earthworks. To this wall bastions were added after the scare of A.D. 367. With the withdrawal of Roman troops from Britain, life at Chichester probably ran down slowly, and took on a somewhat impoverished air. At all events there is no evidence for any dramatic end to the town which has almost certainly been in continual occupation to the present day.

There is little to be seen of Roman remains in Chichester. The walls, although basically Roman, are completely covered or modified by later medieval work, though the remains of 4th-century forward-projecting bastions can still be seen on the south-east. In the Cathedral is a fragment of a mosaic pavement which can be viewed on request. Perhaps the most interesting feature is the 1st-century dedication of a temple to Neptune and Minerva carved in Purbeck marble and found in 1723. It is now set into the front wall of the Assembly Rooms in North Street. The inscription was authorized by Cogidubnus and a *collegium fabrorum*, a sort of trades union which seems to have originated in the busy town. In translation the inscription reads: 'To Neptune and Minerva this temple is dedicated for the safety of the Imperial Family by the authority of Tiberius Claudius Cogidubnus, King and Imperial Legate in Britain, by the Guild of Artificers and its associated members from their own contributions, the site being given by [Cle]mens son of Pudentius.'

Many finds from Roman Chichester are on display in the City Museum at 29, Little London. (*It is open from Tuesday to Saturday, 10.00 to 18.00 hours (April to September), and 10.00 to 17.00 hours (October to March)*). There is also material in the Guildhall Museum in Priory Park (*June to September, Tuesdays to Saturdays, 13.00 to 16.30 hours*) and the Cathedral Treasury.

A. Down and M. Rule: *Chichester Excavations 1* (1971)

8 CHICHESTER DYKES   Iron Age
                                                              181

Over the gravel plain north of Chichester are some 16 km of linear earthworks. To understand them it is essential to recognize that land forms have changed considerably in the 2,000 years since they were first built. At that time the little river Lavant flowed due south into Pagham Harbour whilst the Ratham Stream to the west contained considerably more water than today. The peninsula between Chichester and Selsey was thus bounded on all sides, except the north, by water. The throwing up of the dykes across this unprotected north side, created a defended area of many hectares. Richard Bradley has recently suggested that the dykes were constructed in three separate stages. Of these, the earliest and most extensive is also the more northerly. It runs west to east from a little south of West Stoke (SU: 826083) to the edge of the Lavant valley at SU: 859081. East of the valley it begins again at SU: 865085, and runs through Goodwood Park to terminate today on Boxgrove Common (SU: 921084). It probably ran further east but ploughing has destroyed all trace. Excavation has shown this ditch to be 4 m wide and 2·7 m deep, with a bank still 1·5 m high to the south of it. Later, a southern line of dyke was introduced, running west to east from SU: 818066, by an uncertain course to the B2178 road at SU: 841067, then proceeding east to Chichester barracks from where it suddenly turned south for 0·8 km to Bishop Otter College. The final stage of construction involved a number of short sections of dyke, as well as a north–south line between Midhavant and Bishop Otter College, still visible north of The Drive (SU: 862074) and in the grounds of Graylingwell Hospital. Good sections of the dyke are visible at a number of points, especially SU: 837080, SU: 847080, and between SU: 880085 and SU: 918086.

There is little dating evidence for the dykes, but they must have been constructed at different times in the last century before the Roman invasion. Their purpose seems to have been to protect the territory around the capital of the Atrebates, which lay somewhere to their south. Perhaps this was at Selsey, in which case it has been destroyed by erosion; more probably it lies nearer to the dykes (as at Colchester) and still awaits discovery. At all events, there is as yet no evidence to suggest that it lay under the present city of Chichester.

Richard Bradley in B. W. Cunliffe: *Excavations at Fishbourne* **I** (1971) 17

9 CHURCH HILL FLINT MINES   Neolithic
    Findon   182 (TQ: 112083)

Footpath south from Church Hill on A280 (at TQ:110088) to Findon (at TQ:122083) passes beside the mines.

Like so many hills in this part of the South Downs, Church Hill has its small group of flint mine shafts. Excavations have shown these to be some 4·9 m deep, and dug into rather friable chalk which prevented the digging of galleries; instead the shafts mushroom out to take in as large a floor area as possible. In the upper filling of one of these mines a neolithic beaker with 'barbed-wire' decoration was found, containing a cremation burial and accompanied by two local flint axes. It seems likely that the mining and the beaker, which can be dated to about 1700 B.C., were contemporary. Amongst the shafts flint working floors were also uncovered indicating that once dug from the chalk, the flint was fashioned on the spot. Although few in number the mines seem to have been worked spasmodically over an immense number of years, probably into the Bronze Age. An antler pick from the site has given a corrected radio-carbon date of about 4300 B.C.

E. C. Curwen: *Archaeology of Sussex* (1954) 114

10 CISSBURY HILLFORT AND FLINT MINES

Neolithic–Iron Age

Worthing   182 (*Mines* TQ:137079; *Fort* TQ:139080)

Signposted from Findon village. Small parking space at TQ:139085.

This is a magnificent hillfort, enclosing 26 ha, with ramparts highest on
the east where it overlooks the hill-spur leading to Lychpole Hill. The
earliest features on the hill are an extensive group of more than 200
flint mines, concentrated at the western end of the fort, with others on
the crest of the spur south from the southern entrance. Although today
they are overgrown with bracken and gorse, they are clearly visible due
to their deep 'bomb-like' craters. Excavations by Pitt-Rivers and
others, almost one hundred years ago, indicated shafts, some more than
12 m deep, cutting through six seams of flint. As each seam was
reached short side-galleries followed it. At the pit bottom sometimes as
many as eight longer galleries radiated horizontally from the central
shaft, often linking with adjoining exhausted shafts. In order to prove
that the mines were older than the hillfort, Pitt-Rivers dug beneath the
fort rampart in 1875, and found six shafts through which the earthworks had been dug. Near the bottom of one of them was the skeleton
of a young woman who seems to have died when she fell into the shaft
accidentally. In the filling of another shaft 9 m deep, the crouched
skeleton of a young man was found at a depth of 4·9 m. Chalk blocks
had been placed round him to make a simple grave. Pottery from the
mines suggests that they were worked in the neolithic period, but did
not continue into the Bronze Age, as happened on some of the smaller
sites. A corrected radio-carbon date of about 3500 B.C. has been obtained for antler picks from one of the mine shafts.

About 350 B.C. the great Iron Age defences were built: a strong bank
and external ditch with a smaller counterscarp bank, and traces of
internal quarry scoops on the north and east sides. The main bank has
been excavated and shown to be about 9·1 m wide at its base, with
a row of posts on its outer edge, held firm with wooden cross-beams.
Clay and chalk rubble were piled behind this to a height of about 4·6 m.
This rampart material came from a flat-bottomed ditch 2·4 m deep and
6·1 m wide, and from the quarry scoops where they existed. The
counterscarp bank, 6·1 m wide and 1·5 m high, must also have obtained its material from the ditch. Two entrances led into the fort at the
east and south. At the beginning of the 1st century A.D. the fort was
disused and remained so through the early Roman period. Cissbury
lies in the territory of the Atrebates, friendly to Rome, who had no
need to defend themselves against Roman occupation. Indeed, at that
time its interior was ploughed, and traces of the lynchets formed can
still be seen on the south-eastern slopes within the fort. At the end of
the Roman occupation or early in the post-Roman period the camp was

hastily refortified by building a turf wall on top of the old ramparts and widening the ditch at the entrances. Some small internal enclosures and Romano-British rubbish pits, now hard to find and recognize due to the long grass, may belong to this final occupation.

E. C. Curwen: *Archaeology of Sussex* (1954) 106

11 CLIFFE HILL LONG BARROW   Neolithic
     South Malling   183 (TQ:432110)

On the northern end of Cliffe Hill above Lewes. Footpath on to golf course.

Known locally as the Camel's Humps, or Warrior's Grave, this earthen long barrow is 36·6 m long and about 15·2 m wide. It stands 1·8 m high to east and west, with signs of opening in the centre, although there are no records of this. There are traces of ditches on its long sides. Most of the round barrows on Cliffe Hill, marked on the maps, have been ploughed flat.

12 COMBE HILL CAUSEWAYED CAMP   Neolithic
     Jevington   183 (TQ:574021)

A footpath over Combe Hill runs from Jevington to Upper Willingdon, and passes through the site.

This small causewayed camp encloses about 0·6 ha of the crown of the chalk escarpment. It consists of an inner chalk rampart 0·5 m high and ditch broken at sixteen points by causeways of undug chalk, and two outer incomplete arcs of causewayed ditch, 24·4 m to the west, and 15·2 m to the south-east. The ground falls away so steeply on the north that no artificial boundary is necessary. Limited excavation on the western side of the inner ditch and bank showed that no post holes existed, either beside the ditch, in the rampart, or on the causeway separating it from the adjoining segment. The ditch itself was 3·7 m wide and 0·9 m deep and contained many pieces of local neolithic Ebbsfleet-ware pottery, a leaf-shaped arrow-head and many flint flakes.

A few metres east of the camp is a large ring-barrow consisting of an earthern bank 12·2 m in diameter with an internal ditch. Unlike a disc-barrow it has no central mound. 61 m further north-east (TQ:576023) is a ditched bowl-barrow 13·7 m in diameter and 1·2 m high. When it was opened in 1908 three flanged bronze axes were found together with the blade of a fourth. The three axes had been broken into halves as though to fulfil some votive function. The barrow also contained numerous Roman coins and pots. Another bowl-barrow with an interrupted ditch lies west of the camp. It is 1·8 m high and 22·9 m in diameter and is scarred by a robbers' pit.

R. Musson: *Sussex A.C.* **89** (1950) 105

13 DEVIL'S DYKE HILLFORT   Iron Age
  Poynings   182 (TQ:259111)

Road to Devil's Dyke from Brighton (off A2038). Bus service, car-park, restaurant and cafeteria.

This large hillfort is one of the viewpoints of the South Downs, being 711 feet (217 m) above sea level and commanding enormous views in all directions. The name Dyke now refers to the dry valley on the south-east, rather than the fort itself. Enclosing more than 16 ha the earthworks form in effect a promontory fort, isolating a massive spur which juts out to the north-east. Earthworks on the long north-west and south-east sides are relatively weak and appear little more than terraces cut into the steep hillside, the material so obtained being piled into a downhill rampart. At the north-east a bank and ditch are clearly present. On the south-east side the fortification is doubled at the head of the dry valley to the south where the only entrance winds into the fort from a terraceway. The main defence, once known as Poor Man's Wall, is a massive bank and ditch, 183 m long, cutting off the neck of the promontory on the south-west side. Here the rampart stands 3·7 m high. (It has been damaged by an earlier golf course and by wartime defences at its western end.) The road runs through a modern gap in this cross-ridge dyke to show a clear section of its construction. The only certain entrance lies in the southern corner of the fort at the top of Devil's Dyke valley. An oblique break at the north end of the south-east side seems to be modern, although it could have given access to and from the valley below. Minor excavations inside the fort between the south-western rampart and the public house revealed a round hut 8·5 m in diameter whose walls were probably made of wood set into a footing trench. Into the floor were dug three small storage pits. A larger farming settlement lay 183 m south-west of the fort on the golf course. It dates from late in the Iron Age, and is probably later than the promontory fort itself, which still remains unexcavated.

14 DEVIL'S HUMPS ROUND BARROWS (Plate 59)   Bronze Age
  Bow Hill, Stoughton Down   181 (SU:819111)

No direct path. Bridle-paths across hill from various points, e.g. from Stoughton (SU:802113), the B2141 at SU:835118, or opposite 'The White Horse' at Chilgrove: SU:829144. In all cases allow two hours.

Known as the Devil's Humps or King's Graves, these four barrows lie on the open crest of Bow Hill. At the south-west are two bell-barrows with fairly conspicuous berms separating the mounds from their surrounding ditches. The most southerly is 36·6 m in diameter with a mound 3·7 m high. Although there are clear indications that it has been dug into, there is no record of its contents. The second bell-barrow is

Plate 59   Bow Hill bell-barrows, the Devil's humps, Sussex

larger, 40·2 m in diameter and 3·7 m high. It, too, has a large robbers' trench in its centre. In 1933 Leslie Grinsell sectioned the ditch which proved to be 2·4 m wide at the top and 1·2 m deep. Between the two barrows is an embanked circular depression resembling a small pond-barrow. 118·9 m north of the bell-barrows are two large bowl-barrows. The southernmost is 30·5 m in diameter and 3·1 m high, the other 19·8 m in diameter and 3·1 m high. The latter contained a cremation with a whetstone. Between the two barrow groups traces of a Roman building have been found, perhaps a Romano-Celtic temple. Immediately south of the first bell-barrow is a cross-ridge dyke, whilst a linear earthwork runs along the western edge of the group.

1·2 km west of the Devil's Humps, just inside a wood (SU:807107) is the only known Sussex example of a twin-bell-barrow, with two mounds, each about 18·3 m in diameter and 1·8 m high, set within an oval ditch measuring 53·3 m by 30·5 m.

On the south-east spur of Bow Hill are possible neolithic flint mines (at SU:825109). An undated rectangular enclosure, sometimes called Bow Hill camp, lies across the highest point of the ridge between the Devil's Humps and Goosehill camp to the north (SU:826116).

L. V. Grinsell: *Sussex A.C.* **75** (1934) 223; **82** (1942) 115

15 DEVIL'S JUMPS BELL-BARROWS   Bronze Age
    Treyford   181 (SU:825173)

Minor road for short distance from Treyford, then steep climb by footpath
uphill from SU:824182.

This is a linear cemetery of six fine bell-barrows on the south-western
side of Treyford Hill. Five of the barrows are very well preserved,
whilst the sixth, at the south-eastern end of the row is almost destroyed. Their overall measurements average 36·6 m in diameter, but
their heights vary between 1·8 and 4·9 m. They were dug into in the
past and cremations were recorded from two of them. There is a
ruined bowl-barrow a few metres west of the cemetery still standing
0·9 m high. The Didling Hill Barrow lies 0·4 m north-east (see below).

L. V. Grinsell: *Sussex A.C.* **75** (1934) 223

16 DIDLING HILL BARROW   Iron Age?
    Treyford   181 (SU:828177)

As for the Devil's Jumps, 0·4 km north-east of that group.

This badly damaged round barrow, 5·5 m in diameter and 0·6 m high,
is unusual in being surrounded by a square ditch, which has an entrance in its eastern side. Barrows in square enclosures are more
common in northern England where they are frequently of Iron Age
date, but the Didling Hill example has not been scientifically excavated.

L. V. Grinsell: *Sussex A.C.* **75** (1934) 245

17 FIRLE BEACON BARROWS   Neolithic and Bronze Age
    West Firle
    183 (*Long barrow:* TQ:486058; *round barrows* TQ:470060–508038)

A footpath climbs the face of the Downs from the A274 via Tilton
(TQ:494066). Barrows lie to right and left on the ridge.

The long barrow, which lies east to west, measures 33·5 m in length
and 21·3 m wide, and reaches a height of about 2·4 m. There are signs
that its ditch runs round most of the barrow with the exception of the
south-east end where there seems to be a causeway. A hollow at this
end is suggestive of a collapsed wooden burial chamber. In either
direction along the ridge from the barrow are round barrows. To the
west of the long barrow is a bowl-barrow 18·3 m in diameter and more
than 0·9 m high, damaged by later use as a beacon and triangulation
point. Most of the other barrows in the immediate neighbourhood are
only 10 m in diameter and 0·6 to 0·9 m high.

L. V. Grinsell: *Sussex A.C.* **75** (1934) 220

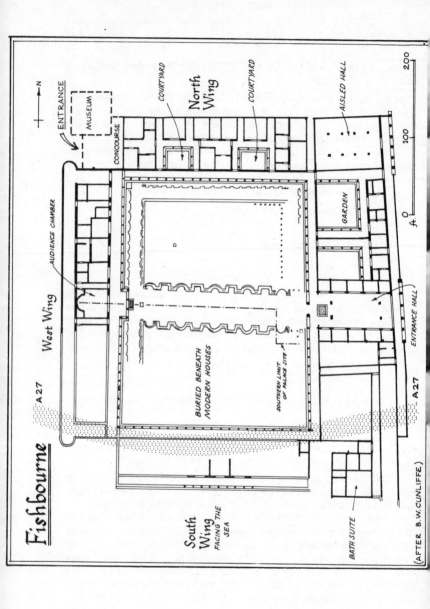

Fishbourne

N →

West Wing

A27

Audience chamber

South Wing
Facing the sea

Buried beneath modern houses

Southern limit of palace site

Entrance
Museum

Concourse

Courtyard

North Wing

Courtyard

Garden

Aisled Hall

Entrance Hall

A27

Bath Suite

(After B.W. Cunliffe)

0   100   200
ft.

SUSSEX   287

18 FISHBOURNE PALACE (Fig. 22)   Roman
    Salthill Road, Chichester   181 (SU:841047)

*Clearly signposted, 2·4 km west of Chichester by A27. Turning north into
Salthill Road. Extensive free car-park. By rail from Chichester Havant
to Fishbourne Halt (5 minutes' walk). Portsmouth to Brighton bus also
stops at Salthouse Road. Open: May to September 10.00 to 19.00 hours
(incl. Sundays); March, April, October 10.00 to 16.00 hours (incl.
Sundays); November, Saturdays and Sundays only, 10.00 to 16.00 hours.
Closed December to February. Admission adults 20p, students 15p,
children under 15, 5p.*

A group of modern buildings, reminiscent of a public swimming pool,
lead into one of the most fascinating glimpses of Rome in Britain. In
1960 workmen laying a water main dug through part of a palace
complex which at its height had covered some 4 ha. Eight years of
excavation followed by conservation have uncovered the main history
of the palace, and the north wing of the building has been laid open for
inspection. At the same time the site of the east wing has been marked
out in the grass, and half of the palace garden reconstructed. Most of
the southern half of the building lies buried beneath the A27 road and
its adjoining houses and gardens.

Excavation has shown that at first wooden buildings of a military
supply base occupied the site, constructed in about A.D. 43–4. These
were probably established at the head of Chichester harbour to support
Vespasian's attacks on south-west Britain at that time. Fishbourne lay
safely within the territory of the friendly pro-Roman client king,
Tiberius Claudius Cogidubnus. After the army had relinquished the
site a number of civilian buildings were erected including a large house
with many rooms and an elaborate bath suite, which the excavator,
Professor Barry Cunliffe, has called the 'proto-palace'. About A.D. 75
work began on the great palace that incorporated the earlier building at
the southern end of the East Wing. The new structure consisted of four
rectangular ranges of rooms enclosing a formal garden 78 m by 97·6 m,
with a second more natural garden to the south facing the sea. The
North Wing, which is open to the public, seems to have consisted of
private suites of rooms for palace guests, arranged around two small
courtyards. The West Wing was the official and administrative range,
with a large central Audience Chamber, and the Eastern Wing contained the Entrance Hall, an aisled Assembly Hall, a bath suite and two
courtyards with rooms attached. We know nothing of the South Wing
which was probably the owner's residential suite. Almost all the rooms
were decorated with wall paintings and rich mosaic floors (Plate 60),
and some were adorned with friezes of moulded stucco. Such luxury
would have required the co-operation of foreign craftsmen, for many
architectural details were unknown in Britain at the time. This sug-

Plate 60   Mosaic pavement at the Fishbourne Palace, Sussex

gests that the owner of the palace possessed considerable wealth, and may well have been King Cogidubnus himself.

After the King's death, a number of alterations were made to the palace, including the building of two new bath suites (one replacing the other) and the laying of some splendid polychrome mosaics. Somewhere between A.D. 280 and 290 the building was destroyed by a dramatic fire in the roof of the North Wing, which spread to the West Wing, leaving only the walls standing. Whether the fire was caused by accidents or sea pirates we are unlikely ever to know. At all events the palace was abandoned, and from then on became a quarry for building-stones.

The formal northern garden of the palace had a complex border of shrubs and trees, and contained fountains and statues. An attempt has been made to re-establish it, using plants that were common in Roman times.

An attractive museum has been built on the site presenting a graphical description of the Palace in all its stages, with many photographs, and models and objects found. Its labels are regrettably only in English, though brief guide-pamphlets are available in French and German.

B. W. Cunliffe: *Excavations at Fishbourne* (1971)

19 FIVE LORDS BURGH ROUND BARROW   Bronze Age
  South Heighton   183 (TQ:486036)

*At the junction of four parishes in the middle of the Downs. Footpath east
from Norton (TQ:472020) for 2 km, then north towards Firle Beacon
for 1·6 km.*

Nothing is known of the contents of this barrow which, as can be seen
from the hole at its centre, has clearly been plundered. Its interest
derives mainly from its name, Five Lords Burgh, which indicates that
it was formerly the meeting place of five parishes. It is about 14·6 m in
diameter and a little over 0·9 m high.

L. V. Grinsell: *Sussex A.C.* **75** (1934) 269

20 GOOSEHILL HILL-SLOPE FORT   Iron Age
  West Dean   181 (SU:830127)

*On east slopes of Bow Hill. Best reached by footpath from B2141 at
SU:835118. Follow path through woodland until hilltop begins to
flatten out. At first wooden sign 'Bridleway' turn right for 183 m. Earthworks to left on entering trees. Notice old field bank before first fort
earthwork.*

Overgrown with scrub, brambles and yew trees, this unusual hillslope
fort is difficult to find and explore. It consists of two concentric oval
enclosures, the inner measuring 76·2 m from north to south and 54·9 m
from east to west. This has an entrance gap on the steep downhill side.
The oval outer ring is incomplete on the south-east, but otherwise
measures 158·5 m from north to south and 137·2 m from east to west.
It has an entrance at the north. All the ditches were shown by excavation to be V-shaped and about 1·5 m deep. This site, placed on the
slope of the hill is clearly not defensive, and it can best be seen as an
example of the hill-slope cattle enclosures, normally found in south-
western Britain. It has been dated by its pottery to about 200 B.C.

J. R. Boyden: *Sussex A.C.* **94** (1956) 70

21 GRAFFHAM AND HEYSHOTT DOWNS ROUND BARROWS
                                                     Bronze Age
       181 (*Graffham* SU:915163; *Heyshott* SU:895165)

*Footpath up escarpment from Graffham at SU:919167 or 925167, from
Heyshott at SU:897172, and from the A286 at SU:875166.*

Spread out along the ridgeway between Cocking and Duncton are a
number of bowl-barrows. On Heyshott and Graffham Downs they are
sufficiently close together to constitute cemeteries in the Wessex sense.
Many of them were dug into by Thomas Honywood a hundred years
ago, but he left no records. One of the largest, the Heyshott Barrow, is

a ditched bowl-barrow, 33·5 m in diameter and 2·1 m high. They must date from the Early Bronze Age between 2000 and 1500 B.C.

L. V. Grinsell: *Sussex A.C.* **75** (1934) 246

22 HAMMER WOOD HILLFORT   Iron Age
    Iping   181 (SU:845240)
*Footpath from minor road between Chithurst and Iping at SU:849235
passes beside Hammer pond and east slope of fort.*

This wooded promontory fort is rectangular in plan and encloses about 6·9 ha. Two widely spaced ramparts and ditches cut off the promontory on the north side, and are broken by oblique entrances. On the east and west there are single ramparts with ditches, whilst on the south they are again double and fairly widely spaced. Excavation has shown that the inner rampart was stone-faced with a V-shaped ditch 2·1 to 2·4 m deep, and also produced pottery of a degenerate Early Iron Age type that the excavators considered fairly late in the local Iron Age sequence.

J. R. Boyden: *Sussex A.C.* **96** (1958) 149

23 HARDHAM POSTING STATION   Roman
    Coldwaltham   181/2 (TQ:030175)
*A footpath from the A29 at TQ:033173 leading to Hardham Mill passes
close to the east end of the site.*

The Romans built *mansio* or posting stations at intervals along all their main roads in order that messengers carrying the Imperial post could obtain fresh horses. The much damaged station at Hardham was cut through by the now disued Midhurst Branch Railway and a gravel quarry on the north-eastern side. Much of the interior is covered with trees and bushes. Lying astride the Stane Street, 19·3 km north-east of Chichester, the *mansio* was surrounded by a rectangular earthwork which measured 122 m east to west, and 134 m north to south. The Roman road cut through the centre of the longer sides and has been largely destroyed by the railway. The rampart survives 2·1 m high in places and traces of the external ditch can be seen beside it on the north and south, and partly along the east. The west side has been totally destroyed. At some time the corners of the ramparts were reinforced with stones. Inside bricks and tiles testify to simple living accommodation, cart sheds and all-important stables for the horses. It is probable that an inn also existed for travellers, but whether within the station or without only future excavation may tell. Pottery from the site shows that it was in use between A.D. 50 and 150, after which is was abandoned, perhaps in favour of Pulborough. It was later used as a Roman cemetery and a number of skeletons enclosed in wooden coffins have been found on the site.

V.C.H. Sussex **3** (1935)

24 HARROW HILL FLINT MINES AND ENCLOSURE (Fig. 23)
                                    Neolithic and Iron Age
Angmering   182 (TQ:081100)

A farm drive leaves the A280 at TQ:092073 and leads east of Michel-grove to Lee Farm, passing the foot of Harrow Hill.

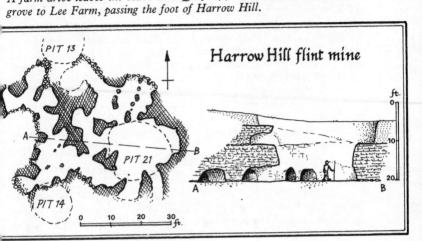

Fig. 23   Harrow Hill flint mine, Sussex

This pleasantly rounded hill, with its juniper bushes and views of the sea, is crowned by a group of at least 160 flint mines whose filled-in hollow depressions are overlaid by a later Iron Age earthwork. One large shaft and three smaller ones have been opened. There is evidence to show that some of the flint outcropped on the north side of the hill, and was worked by the open-cast method. This may have predated the digging of the deep shafts but has not been proven. Pit 21, which lies 46 m north of the Iron Age earthwork, was dug in 1924–5. It was roughly oval in plan and 6·1 m deep, and it passed through three seams of flint, all of which were of interest to the miners. The second seam, 2·4 m from the surface was followed by two 'upper' galleries on the east and west side of the shaft. Below them, on the floor of the mine were seven galleries, some penetrating so far from the shelf as to require artificial lighting. Soot from miners' lamps was found on the tunnel walls and roof in many places, and a number of scratch markings on the walls have been interpreted as miners' tallies: records of how much flint they had removed. The excavators dug out about 350 metric tons (350 tons) of chalk from the pit, and the miners would have removed an even greater quantity. Pottery and axes of neolithic type indicate that the mines were contemporary with those at Cissbury, and did not continue in use into the Bronze Age.

Early in the Iron Age a small sub-rectangular enclosure, 59·4 m by 51·8 m, with rounded corners was built over the filled-in mine shafts. Excavation of the enclosure in 1936 uncovered three of them, with a few galleries at their bottoms. The earthwork is broken by entrances on the west and north-east. The western one, when excavated, revealed two holes for stout posts on either side, connected to a wooden palisade which ran all round the enclosure, supported by a bank of earth 1·5 m high and 3·7 m wide. In front was a flat-bottomed ditch 1·5 m wide and 0·9 m deep. The tiny fort was unusual in having few traces of permanent occupation, but the limited excavation produced about seventy-five ox skulls, suggesting that here was a place where cattle were slaughtered—a prehistoric abattoir perhaps—before the carcasses were taken elsewhere for consumption.

E. Curwen: *Sussex A.C.* **67** (1926) 103; G. Holleyman: *Sussex A.C.* **78** (1937) 230

25   HARTING BEACON CAMP   Iron Age
   Harting   181 (SU:806184)

By track off road east of Turkey Island, either that signposted 'Cross-dykes', or footpath few metres east of bus stop, leading through wood to west side of hill.

This fine hill, 242 m (793 ft) high, is crowned by a large, but rather weak rectangular hillfort defended by a single rampart and ditch. Excavations at the West Gate produced two gold penannular rings, perhaps buried as a foundation deposit. There are cross-dykes on the hill ridge to the east and west. A barrow, apparently overlying the latter (SU: 797186) may indicate that they are considerably earlier than the fort. There is a small bowl-barrow inside the camp about 7·6 m in diameter and 0·6 m high.

26   HIGHDOWN HILLFORT   Iron Age
   Ferring   182 (TQ:093043)

National Trust property. Access by footpath from A27 at Clapham (TQ:093056) or from A2032 at TQ:088034.

This prominent hill north of Ferring is crowned by the damaged remains of a small rectangular hillfort of less than 0·8 ha. Excavation has shown that the fort was first defended in about 500 B.C. by a flat-bottomed ditch 3·1 m wide and 1·8 m deep, separated by a flat berm from a timber-faced rampart. An additional outer bank and ditch ran along the south side and curved round the east and west corners. On the east this outer rampart has been destroyed by a chalk pit and on the west ploughing seems to have filled it in. The original fort entrance is on the east beside the quarry. 200 years later the ditch was recut as a

V-shaped defence and a glacis face to the rampart was constructed. At that time the entrance was moved 3·1 m to the south. The entrance gap on the south-west is fairly modern and gave access to a windmill which used to stand in the south-west corner of the fort. Excavation at Highdown produced a rectangular hut in the interior of the fort, and also showed that the site was refortified by Romano-Britons at the end of the 3rd century A.D.

Traces of earlier Bronze Age settlement were found under the Iron Age rampart on the south side, and consisted of the floor and post holes of a hut containing a hearth and cooking hole. It had clearly been rebuilt more than once, suggesting a lengthy occupation.

During the Second World War most of the hillfort was again occupied by the Army who erected many buildings which did much damage to the interior. These have now been cleared away, but should provide interesting problems for future archaeologists.

A. E. Wilson: *Sussex A.C.* **89** (1950) 163

27 HIGH ROCKS HILLFORT AND ROCK SHELTERS
    Frant   Mesolithic and Iron Age
                                                171 (TQ: 561382)

Footpath between A26 at TQ:570377, and minor road south of public house at High Rocks (TQ:558382).

The sandstone cliffs which give High Rocks its name stand 6·1 to 12·2 m high around the north and west sides of this 10 ha promontory fort. On the south and east a double rampart (destroyed in parts) represents two periods of occupation. It is broken by a strong entrance at the south-east corner. The outer dump-constructed rampart and steep-sided ditch are the earliest on the site and were cut into the rock by Iron Age B people. After a period when the fort went out of use, a second line of defence was built inside the first (the nature of the site prevented building outwards). It consisted of a wide flat-bottomed ditch of Fécamp type, like that at the Caburn (Sussex) and Oldbury (Kent), with a rampart revetted with stone and some palisading. The inturned entrance had elaborate outworks added at this time. There is also a possible entrance in the north-east corner, from the top of the cliffs.

The rocks below the fort provided overhanging shelters used by mesolithic hunters, as well as by later neolithic and Iron Age communities. Numerous microlithic flints of types common in the Weald were excavated between 1954 and 1956, though radio-carbon dates of 3780 B.C. and 3700 B.C. (uncorrected) from hearth charcoal seem more likely to relate to the neolithic than the mesolithic occupation.

J. H. Money: *Sussex A.C.* **106** (1968) 158

28 HOLLINGBURY HILLFORT   Iron Age
       Brighton   182 (TQ: 322078)

Footpath from road at TQ:323083 leads south uphill to the fort, across
edge of golf course.

The visitor must take his life in his hands in crossing the golf course to
reach the comparative safety of the ramparts of this celebrated hillfort
which lies 4 km north of the sea at Brighton, and is almost surrounded
by the hideous suburban sprawl of that illustrious watering place.
Roughly square in shape, with rounded corners, and enclosing 3·6 ha,
Hollingbury is defended by a single rampart and ditch with a counterscarp bank on the southern side. There are two entrances, one with
inturned rampart ends on the west, and a single straight-through
example on the east, which was excavated in 1931. Here holes 0·9 m
deep for two oak gate posts were found. A cutting through the rampart
showed that it had been composed of chalk rubble 1·8 m high, held in
position with palisades at the front and back. Two rows of posts, 2·1 m
apart from back to front, and a similar distance apart along the line of
the rampart had supported the palisade fences, whilst horizontal tie-
beams probably linked the two together for stability. The posts were
about 15 cm in diameter. The position of these key posts has been
permanently marked on the site with metal posts that can be seen in
position today. In front of the rampart was a berm 3·1 m wide, and
then a flat-bottomed ditch with vertical sides, 2·7 m wide and 1·8 m
deep. The fort as it is seen today represents the final state of the defences in about 250 B.C.

The excavations showed that there had been an earlier enclosure on
the hill from at least 400 B.C. It followed much the same line as the later
fort, except on the east where its rampart and ditch lay between 22·9
and 30·5 m inside and roughly parallel to the present rampart, where it
can still be seen as a ridge or lynchet. It was never very strong, its
ditch being only 1·5 m wide and 0·9 m deep, with excavated material
piled on the inner side. All the material found in the excavations is now
in Brighton Museum.

There are four mounds inside the camp, one very small, which may
have been bowl-barrows. The largest once supported a beacon, and its
surface has been much disturbed. A number of bronze axes and
jewellery, now in the British Museum, were found in one of them more
than a century ago.

E. C. Curwen: *Ant. J.* **12** (1932) 1

29 HOLTYE ROMAN ROAD   Roman
                                                        171 (TQ: 461391)

Excavated section short distance south of B2110, east of Holtye, and 6·4
km east of East Grinstead. Sussex Archaeological Trust.

This is part of a secondary Roman road that ran from a point on the Watling Street south-east of London towards Lewes. Probably constructed in about A.D. 100 its purpose must have been mainly concerned with carrying iron and its ore from the area of Ashdown Forest to London and the south coast. For a considerable distance the road surface is composed almost entirely of iron slag, which has so conglomerated as to produce a surface comparable to modern road metalling. In the section uncovered and open to view, shallow wheel ruts can be clearly seen, doubtless made by heavy ore-laden Roman carts.

30 HUNTER'S BURGH LONG BARROW   Neolithic
    Wilmington   183 (TQ: 550036)

By footpaths from Wilmington or Folkington.

Lying almost north to south is this fairly well-preserved long barrow, 58 m long and 22·9 m wide at the higher southern end. There are wide ditch scoops at the southern end and along the sides, but not at the northern end. There are also indications that the south end, which is 1·8 m high, has been dug into at some time, but no records exist.

E. C. Curwen: *Sussex A.C.* **69** (1928) 93

31 ITFORD HILL   Bronze Age
    Beddingham   183 (TQ: 447053)

A track from Itford Farm curves up Itford Hill to Red Lion pond. The settlement lies amongst gorse and bramble 274 m south of the pond.

Low banks and hollows mark the site of one of the most thoroughly excavated farmstead sites in Britain. Dated to about 1000 B.C. this settlement seems to have been occupied for a relatively short time, perhaps as little as twenty-five years.

A hollow-way from the west leads to the main part of the farmstead which consisted of eleven circular wooden huts, each set in an embanked earthen enclosure. Wooden fences separated groups of huts from each other and it is possible to see separate uses for individual buildings: living huts, storage and work huts, a cooking area, barns and stables, and so on. The largest hut was 6·7 m in diameter, and had been made by erecting eight posts around a central one. It had a porch on its south-east side and may have been partitioned, although no evidence was found to show what material the walls were made of. A chalk phallus found buried beside the entrance porch was presumably a fertility charm. None of the huts contained fire-places. 76 m south-east of the main farm buildings were two more huts, lying at the end of a cross-dyke which runs westwards for a little over 0·4 km. Further south are the remains of numerous lynchets, which are probably later than the farm, and have obliterated traces of earlier fields where barley was grown and cattle and sheep pastured. 91 m north of the settlement was the cemetery, consisting of a low round barrow which covered the cremated remains of a middle-aged man. On the village side of the mound were sixteen more cremations, some in old and damaged urns. Over the surface of the cemetery hundreds of flint flakes were scattered, suggesting that this was a favourite spot above the village for flint-working. The finds from the excavations are in Lewes Museum.

G. P. Burstow and G. A. Holleyman: *P.P.S.* **23** (1957) 167; A. Selkirk: *Current Archaeology* **3** (1972) 232

32 LEWES PLATFORM-BARROW   Bronze Age
                                                                    183 (TQ:402110)
West of the A275, 1·6 km north-west of Lewes.

This is a good example of what Grinsell has called a platform-barrow, 27·4 m in diameter. It differs from a bowl-barrow in having a flat top, in this case 0·9 m high. It is surrounded by a ditch and external bank. Nearby are two normal bowl-barrows, both 0·9 m high, and one 15·2 m in diameter, the other 9·1 m across. The smaller has a robbers' hollow at its centre.

L. V. Grinsell: *Sussex A.C.* **75** (1934) 226

33 LITLINGTON LONG BARROW   Neolithic
      Litlington   183 (TQ:535006)
North of footpath across Fore Down from Clapham to Jevington via Snap Hill Barn.

This oval barrow was probably a small long barrow. It is still 24·4 m long and 13·7 m wide, and stands 1·2 m high at the south-west. There are no signs of any side ditches.

34 LONG BURGH   Neolithic
      Alfriston   183 (TQ:510034)
On the Downs immediately above Alfriston.

One of the dozen long barrows known in Sussex. It is 45·7 m long and 18·3 m wide. Its higher north-eastern end reaches 2·4 m. The material for the mound came from flanking ditches which can still just be seen.

35 LONG MAN (Plate 61)   Unknown
      Wilmington   183 (TQ:543095)
Footpath east from minor road from Wilmington to Litlington at TQ:536037.

'The Long Man of Wilmington, looks naked towards the shires' wrote

Plate 61   The Long Man of Wilmington, Sussex

Kipling. This long, thin figure, holding a staff in either hand, looks like some great skiing figure on the steep, smooth hillside. Unlike the only other ancient human chalk-cut figure, the Cerne Abbas giant in Dorset, the Long Man appears entirely in outline without internal features, though the eyes, nose and mouth are marked by turf-covered mounds, which are not visible from a distance. Standing 68·9 m high, with staffs 1·2 m higher, the figure is best viewed from the Weald where the effects of foreshortening tend to counteract the exaggerated length more apparent at close quarters. The present shape of the figure dates from 1874 when it was restored by the Revd. de Ste Croix. Its appearance before that date is subject to speculation, but earlier accounts refer to the staffs as being a rake and scythe. A detailed study by Christopher Hawkes suggests that the figure may once have held spears in his hands, and might originally have represented Woden, later demilitarized with the coming of Christianity to Sussex. There is good reason to see the figure as not later than 7th-century A.D., and quite possibly Romano-British.

C. F. C. Hawkes: *Antiquity* **39** (1965) 27

---

36 MONEY BURGH LONG BARROW   Neolithic
  Piddinghoe   183 (TQ:425037)

On the Downs behind 'Deans'.

This long barrow is about 36·6 m long, 18·3 m wide and 1·8 m high at its highest eastern end. A skeleton is recorded from the barrow, but it seems probable that this was a secondary burial. Its name may record a forgotten belief in buried treasure.

L. V. Grinsell: *Sussex A.C.* **75** (1934) 219

37 OXTEDDLE BOTTOM ROUND BARROWS   Bronze Age
   Glynde   183 (TQ:444104; TQ:447096)

Footpath from Lewes to Glyndebourne passes close to first group, whilst path from Lewes to Glynde passes second group.

Although there are more than a dozen barrows on Saxon Down, most of them are so low as to be almost unrecognizable. The barrows at the first reference above are five low bowl-barrows, from one of which two cinerary urns may have come, one containing a faience ring pendant, beads of jet and amber and a bronze spiral finger-ring. A skeleton in the same barrow seems to have been a later Saxon one. 0·8 km southeast from this group at the second grid reference are two ditched bowl-barrows, and two fine platform-barrows 24·4 m and 21·3 m in diameter respectively, both ditched and 30·5 cm high.

Most of the barrows on the hill were dug into by Dr. Gideon Mantell of Lewes about 1820. Mantell is better known for his discovery of the Iguanadon dinosaur fossils.

38 PARK BROW SETTLEMENT   Bronze Age
   Sompting   182 (TQ:153086)

Footpath passes west of Park Brow, linking bridleways from Cissbury to the south, and Findon to Steyning to the north.

This hill is covered with a Celtic-field system, and traces of settlement from the Bronze Age to Roman period. The fields are most conspicuous on the western slope of the hill, and are clearly seen from Cissbury 1·6 km south-west. Little remains of the eight circular huts, each between 6·1 and 9·1 m in diameter, dating from the Bronze Age, that stood on the slightly flattened south-west corner of the spur. The walls of the huts were of wattle and daub woven between a ring of upright posts, with a conical thatched roof above. The floor of one hut examined in 1924 had numerous small pits dug into it, some of which had been used for storage.

Early in the Iron Age two circular huts were built 183 m north-east of the earlier houses, and to the east of the drove-way which runs down the hill-spur (TQ:155088). Below their floors and in the immediate vicinity were deep pits dug into the chalk, for use in corn and food storage. One of them actually contained charred grain. Domestic rubbish usually found its way into the pits once they had ceased to function for storage. At Park Brow this included broken pottery, loom weights, spindle whorls and a weaving comb, all representative of weaving, as well as saddle querns used for grinding corn. A particularly important discovery was a silver finger ring of continental La Tène type (dated between 325 and 250 B.C.). A cremation burial in a small pottery urn was an unusual discovery, since burials of the earlier Iron Age are rare in Britain.

Later in the Iron Age, certainly by 100 B.C., the settlement had been moved again, this time back down the hill-slope (TQ:153085). Only pits remained to show where huts may once have stood. But these, too, were filled with rubbish which included typical decorated pottery of the period. When the Romans arrived in Britain, the inhabitants of the hill were sufficiently influenced to use roof tiles on their rectangular wooden houses, and to cover the wattle-and-daub walls with painted wall-plaster. Even glass windows seem to have been introduced; luxury indeed for a small farming community. This settlement came to an end in the 3rd century A.D. when it was destroyed by fire.

The fields around the settlement must represent the cumulative effect of early agriculture in the area, and cannot be assigned to any one particular period.

W. Hawley: *Archaeologia* **76** (1927) 30

39 PEVENSEY CASTLE (ANDERIDA) (Plate 62)   Roman
       Pevensey   183 (TQ:644048)

A259 road passes beside the Castle.

The outer walls of Pevensey stand on a low hill above the marshes. An irregular oval in plan, and enclosing 3·2 ha, they were built by the Romans in the second half of the 3rd century A.D. The walls are 3·7 m thick, and still reach a height of 8·5 m in some places. They are supported by ten massive U-shaped bastions. Built with stone on timber foundations, they have the usual red tile bonding-courses. The main gate is on the west, and is deeply set back into the walls, with square guard-chambers on either side of a 3·1 m wide entrance passage. Opposite, the East Gate leads to the harbour. On the north is a postern gate with its passage-way curved, thus making it impossible to see directly into the fort. Inside the walls wooden huts had been built, some with tiled hearths. They seem to have been used only for a military occupation, and there is no indication that civil buildings were ever erected in this bleak and lonely spot. Tiles bearing the stamp of Honorius (A.D. 394–423), HON AVG ANDRIA, indicate that repairs took place at the fort at about that time. On the north, nearly 61 m of the Roman wall has collapsed outwards.

Pevensey is one of the new Saxon Shore forts, constructed at the end of the 3rd century, as part of the coastal defences of south-east England; the shore most frequently attacked by Saxon raiders from that time onwards. According to the *Anglo-Saxon Chronicle* Pevensey was captured in A.D. 491 by Aelle of the South Saxons, who 'killed all who were inside, and there was not even a single Briton left alive'.

A Norman castle was built inside the eastern half of the fort, clearly

Plate 62   Pevensey Castle, Sussex

showing the trust the Normans had in the strength of the Roman
masonry, which they retained for their outer bailey wall.

R. G. Collingwood and I. Richmond: *Archaeology of Roman Britain*
(1969) 51

40   PHILPOTS CAMP   Iron Age
    West Hoathly   182 (TQ:349322)

In the grounds of Philpots, east of the B2028, and by track at TQ:346328,
then south on entering wood.

This promontory fort, like High Rocks, lies on a rocky triangular-
shaped spur. Its north-east side is cut off by a single line of rampart
that rises 2·1 m above a ditch. The other sides are protected by the
natural cliffs that rise from 4·6 to 9·1 m above the valley below. The
position of the original entrance is uncertain. A gap 61 m from the
north-east end of the rampart is known to be modern. The interior of
the fort was once ploughed, producing evidence of iron working. Now
it is forested, as are the ramparts.

E. Curwen: *Sussex A.C.* **66** (1925) 177

41   PLUMPTON PLAIN SETTLEMENT   Bronze Age
    Plumpton   183 (TQ:358122)

3 km north along the track passing Old Forge Barn and Ridge Farm,
Falmer, leaving A26 at TQ:354090. Sites are hard to find due to bushes
and bracken.

Two Bronze Age settlements have been examined on this part of
Plumpton Plain and there are traces of others to the west near Streat-
hill Farm and Horseshoe Plantation. The earliest lies astride the track
recommended above. It consists of four roughly rectangular embanked
enclosures, each surrounding a hut and linked together by roadways.
Excavation in three of the enclosures east of the modern track revealed
the post holes of circular huts, each about 6·1 m in diameter, standing
in its own yard, with what may be working hollows on the eastern sides.
None of the huts examined contained hearths. Instead cooking holes
holding charcoal and pot-boilers suggest a more temporary occupation,
and this is borne out by a lack of material finds. Pottery and flint work
indicate the continuity of native traditions in the area, and suggest that
the site was occupied around 1000 B.C.

   It may have been replaced by a second site, 0·4 km south-east of the
first on a small, gently sloping spur, at the head of the Moustone valley.
A low bank with a ditch on its north side cuts across the spur, and
below it traces of three more huts, similar to those at the first site, have
been found. Unlike the first, they do not seem to have been surrounded
by enclosure banks. Pottery of Deverel–Rimbury types was found
suggesting that the site is a little later than the first. Lynchets of Celtic
fields can be seen spreading south from the latter site for 0·8 km. They
are probably contemporary with the settlement, but it cannot be confirmed at present.

G. A. Holleyman and E. C. Curwen: *P.P.S* **1** (1935) 16

42 RANSCOMBE CAMP   Iron Age
    South Malling   183 (TQ:438092)

Reached by footpath from A274 near Ranscombe Farm.

This small promontory fort lies on the hill summit 457 m west of the
Caburn. It has been much damaged by ploughing, but the rampart and
ditch on the stronger eastern side are still upstanding where they protect the narrow neck of the promontory. The steeper slopes round the
hill required less elaborate defences, if indeed they were ever protected. It has been suggested that the fort was probably unfinished, but
it may never have consisted of more than a cross-dyke. It is broken
midway along its length by a simple entrance gap. Excavation has produced Late Iron Age and Romano-British pottery, and it was occupied
late in the 2nd century A.D., long after the Caburn had been destroyed.

There are two very low platform-barrows within the camp, each
about 10·7 m in diameter, but only a few centimetres high.

43 SAXONBURY HILLFORT   Iron Age
    Frant and Rotherfield   183 (TQ:577330)

In the woods of Eridge Park, north of minor road and west of A267.

This small hillfort is very overgrown, but it is of interest since it seems
to have originated as a fortified iron mining and smelting camp.
Excavations in 1929 revealed a narrow oval enclosure of about 0·2 ha,
surrounded by a wall of sandstone blocks 4·9 m wide at the base, with
an entrance wide enough for carts at the south. The original height of
the wall is not known, and now practically none is visible on the surface. From the amount of iron slag found within the enclosure, smelting almost certainly took place there. The excavators also noted that
some of the pottery from the site of Late Iron Age date contained
powdered iron slag. Later the site was enlarged to 0·6 ha, and lightly
protected by throwing a rampart, ditch and counterscarp around the
hill. These defences were of no great strength, the ditch being only
1·1 m deep. An entrance was cut through the earthwork at the south-
east. Pottery of Belgic and early Roman forms indicate that the site was
probably in use throughout the 1st century A.D.

The site was landscaped in the late 19th century when paths and a
tower were constructed, and rhododendrons planted.

S. E. Winbolt: *Sussex A.C.* **71** (1930) 222

44 SEAFORD HEAD HILLFORT AND BARROW   Iron Age
    Seaford   183 (TV:495978)

*On cliff edge and golf course, 1·2 km south-east of martello tower, beside
cliff-top footpath to Cuckmere Haven.*

Due to erosion Seaford Head has become a promontory fort, although in all probability it was some distance inland when first constructed. It is now triangular in shape, 4·65 ha in extent, with a rampart 1·8 m high on the east and north-west. The sea has destroyed the southern side. An external ditch, V-shaped and 2·1 m deep, has been found by excavation, but is only visible at the western end of the north-west side. There are three unexcavated gaps through the rampart of which the more northerly of those in the eastern side and that on the north-west are the more likely to be the original entrances.

Inside the camp, midway along the north-west side, is a bowl-barrow 12·2 m in diameter and about 0·6 m high. It was opened by Pitt-Rivers in 1876 who observed that it was composed of earth and flints but covered no burials. Instead broken flint axes, saws, scrapers and a barbed-and-tanged arrow-head were buried in two small pits, and probably represented some form of votive offering.

A. H. Lane-Fox (Pitt-Rivers): *J. Anthrop. Inst.* **6** (1877) 287

---

45 STANE STREET   Roman
    Bignor to Eartham   181/2 (SU:940105 to SU:970128)

4·8 km of Roman road across Bignor Hill towards Eartham belonging to the National Trust.

One of the major Roman roads of southern Britain, the Stane Street led from the East Gate of Chichester north-east through Dorking to London. In Sussex an excellent and unspoilt stretch of the road runs through woods and downland 9·7 km north-east of Chichester. On Bignor Hill the metalled road surface or *agger* can be seen as a raised, rather narrow ridge, made up of many layers of flints and chalk, pounded together by continuous use. On either side and at a distance from the agger of 7·6 m are small road ditches, which seem to be a constant feature for the whole of its 100 km length.

---

46 STOUGHTON DOWN LONG BARROWS   Neolithic
    Stoughton   181 (SU:823121)

Beside track from minor road between Stoughton and East Marden at SU:811123.

These two long barrows are rather small examples, covered with scrub, in the midst of arable land, and beside woods. The north-western is 30·5 m long and 24·4 m wide, and stands 1·8 m high. The other, on slightly higher ground to the south-east is 22·9 m long, about 12·2 m wide and 1·5 m high. Traces of side ditches have been recorded although these have now been ploughed away. Both barrows lie approximately north-west to south-east. There are indications of what may be a small round barrow between them.

L. V. Grinsell: *Sussex A.C.* **75** (1934) 219

47 THUNDERSBARROW HILL HILLFORT   Iron Age
   Old Shoreham   182 (TQ:229084)

North-west of Southwick, by footpath north-west from National Trust property on Southwick Hill, or south from Freshcombe Lodge.

A small roughly triangular hillfort of 1·2 ha and of no great strength, with a rampart rising in places about 1·8 m above the filled-in ditch. Its mutilated entrances on the north and south are both strongly inturned. Almost invisible inside the hillfort is a small rectangular enclosure, consisting of a low bank with an outer ditch 0·8 m deep. It has entrances on the east and west. There are also traces of an outer line of ditch outside and underlying the main fort on the west, which may be related to the smaller enclosure. Excavation has suggested that it is slightly earlier than the larger fort, but its pottery is of similar type, and both probably date from around 400 B.C. The hilltop was later deserted for some centuries, before being reoccupied after 100 B.C. when a small Romano-British farmstead was constructed outside the eastern rampart of the main fort. A number of hollows 4·6 to 9·1 m across indicate hut floors and storage pits, the excavation of which showed that the settlement had been in use long into Roman times, and perhaps as late as A.D. 400. A well and corn drying furnaces were also uncovered. Leading from the south gate of the hillfort is a fine ridgeway with banks on either side. Many Celtic fields have been laid out from the road, and clearly belong to the Romano-British farmstead. Close to the fort's southern gate is a modern pond which, when made in about 1870, cut into Thunders' Barrow, a bowl-barrow 13·7 m in diameter and 1·8 m high, which gave its name to the hill.

E. C. Curwen: *Ant. J.* **13** (1933) 109

48 THE TRUNDLE   Neolithic and Iron Age
   Singleton   181 (SU:877110)

Access from road to north at SU:879113, but when racing is in progress at Goodwood, better to climb up from side road, parking at SU:872110.

At 670 feet above sea level this hill commands enormous views in all directions. Unfortunately it has been much spoilt by the great radio-masts standing within the hillfort. The Trundle or 'hoop' is a work of two distinct periods. Inside the octagonal Iron Age earthwork is a complicated neolithic causewayed camp, first recognized by O. G. S. Crawford in 1925. Although much denuded this camp can in part still be clearly seen. It consists of an inner circle of ditch and bank, 122 m in diameter, an outer circle 304·8 m in diameter, of which most has been destroyed by the Iron Age defences, and between the two a spiral of ditch and bank which winds round the inner circle one and a quarter times. Like all causewayed camps the earthworks are made up of disconnected sections of ditch, varying in depth between 1·5 m in the inner ring and 2·7 m in the outer sections. The material dug out was piled into an inner bank which is more continuous than the ditches. It is noticeable that the spiral ditch has much wider gaps between the ditch sections than is normal. Pottery and bone from the ditches date the site to about 3000 B.C. At the point where the outer neolithic ditch runs under the Iron Age defence (to the north of the northern radio-mast) the flexed skeleton of a young woman was found buried in the ditch under a small cairn of chalk blocks, some time after the ditch had begun to silt up.

The Iron Age work consists of a single rampart and ditch, with small counterscarp bank, enclosing 5 ha. There are inturned entrances on the east and west. That on the east, overlooking the race course, is the only part of the Iron Age fortification that has been excavated. It has been suggested that there were three rebuilds of the entrance. At first it consisted of a dual carriageway with two gates on the outer side of the entrance passage, swinging towards a central latch post. Later this was modified by narrowing the entrance passage and adding an extra pair of gates at the inner end of the passage. In Stage 3 preparations were made for setting up enormous posts in holes 2·4 m deep, but the excavators considered that this was never completed. In the forty years since the digging took place many ideas have changed, and it is probable that some of the post holes should be interpreted as supports for a bridge or rampart walk over the gates.

At the foot of the hill to the north-west of the Trundle are two small cross-dykes.

Disturbances in the centre of the camp are the remains of the chapel of St. Roche dating from about the 15th century, and a windmill burnt down in 1773.

E. C. Curwen: *Sussex A.C.* **70** (1929) 33; **72** (1931) 200

49 WHITEHAWK CAUSEWAYED CAMP   Neolithic
    Brighton   182 (TQ:330048)

The site lies across Manor Road, at the southern end of the race-course grandstands.

Little remains to be seen of this neolithic causewayed camp partially excavated in the 1930s. Situated on a saddle between two hills, the site, which enclosed about 5 ha, is unusual in consisting of four rings of causewayed ditches, each with inner ramparts. The outer ring is partly absent on the steep east slope. Of the four concentric rings of banks and ditches, the third from the centre is perhaps easiest to see. 91 m north of Manor Road hill, it curves from the race-course, where it has been flattened out, to the south-east, and runs as a distinct ridge along the edge of the almost precipitous slope above Whitehawk Bottom. South of the road, in the rough ground, about 137 m along the track towards the TV mast more traces of the third and fourth ditches and banks can be seen.

Excavation showed that the two inner ditches were the shallowest, 1·1 and 0·8 m deep, whilst the third was the deepest at 2·4 m; and the outer ditch about 2·1 m. A number of burials from the site include some carefully buried between blocks of chalk, and the remains of others casually scattered over the ground. This suggests diverse attitudes to death; whilst some bodies required interment, others were apparently broken up and sometimes partially eaten. Perhaps class distinction was already rearing its head. Large quantities of pottery and animal bones, flint work and domestic rubbish was found in and around the central ditch and in some of the small pits also uncovered.

E. C. Curwen: *Sussex A.C.* **71** (1930) 57; **77** (1936) 60

50 WINDOVER HILL   Neolithic and Bronze Age
    Arlington   183 (TQ:542034)
Footpath from road between Wilmington and Litlington at TQ:536037.
There are a number of antiquities on Windover Hill worthy of attention. Of these two unexcavated groups of flint mines are conspicuous. They lie north-west and north-east of the large and recent quarry directly south of the 'Long Man'. On the southern edge of the quarry is a fine ditched bowl-barrow, 41·1 m in diameter and 2·1 m high. It was opened by Gideon Mantell in 1832, when he found cremation urns and a flint scraper. 274 m north-east of the bowl barrow, and south-east of the flint mines is a small platform-barrow 13·7 m across, with a flat top 0·6 m high. To the west of the quarry is a long barrow 54·9 m long and 15·2 m wide. Two terraceways climb the hill from the east and west, to meet close to the platform-barrow. There is reason to consider them to be of minor Roman construction. They should not be confused with the route of the coaching road that comes from the west and swings 91 m south of the long barrow. There are the strip-lynchets of Celtic fields on the south-west spur of the hill, but they are best seen from Fore Down, 1·6 km to the south.

E. C. Curwen: *Sussex A.C.* **69** (1928) 93

51 WOLSTONBURY HILLFORT   Iron Age
    Pyecombe   182 (TQ:284138)
Bridleway from A23 at TQ:273140 to south side of hill, where footpath climbs north; or footpath from 1·6 km west of Clayton at TQ:285143.
Looking north across to the Weald, this hill is capped by one of the more unusual hillforts of southern England. Oval in shape and measuring 182·9 m by 198 m, this fort has its ditch on the inner side of its rampart. Neither is very marked today, the bank standing only some

0·6 m above the top of the silted ditch. It seems clear that the builders used the 'downward build' method of construction, that is, they threw the earth from the ditch outwards and downhill, thus requiring less effort. Normally they would then have built an inner rampart using material from quarry scoops. If this was the intention at Wolstonbury, then it was never carried out, or else the inner rampart was later removed. The ditch, as excavated, was 1·8 m deep, 2·4 m wide at the flat bottom and 4·9 m wide at the lip. It produced a single piece of a collared urn, which might make one suspicious that here could be a very early fort with origins in the Bronze Age. The only entrance, now destroyed, was at the south, and much of the interior has been damaged by recent flint digging. Inside the fort is a very slight oval enclosure which can be dated to the early Iron Age, and may be connected with the working of Wealden iron ore.

E. C. Curwen: *Sussex A.C.* **94** (1956) 70

Museums containing archaeological material

Battle Museum, Langton House, Battle
Bexhill Museum, Egerton Park, Bexhill
Guermonprez Museum, Lyon Street, Bognor Regis
Museum and Art Gallery,* Church Street, Brighton
City Museum,* 29 Little London, Chichester
Museum and Art Gallery, John's Place, Hastings
Barbican House Museum,* High Street, Lewes
Littlehampton Museum, 12A River Road, Littlehampton
Winchelsea Museum, Court Hall, Winchelsea
Museum and Art Gallery, Chapel Road, Worthing
Bignor Villa Museum (page 275)
Fishbourne Palace Museum (page 287)

* Main county collections

WARWICKSHIRE

| 1 | BEAUSALE FORT | Iron Age |
| | *Beausale* | 131 (SP:246702) |

0·8 km south-east of Beausale beside minor road and behind farm house.

Sited on a plateau looking south-east towards Warwick, this small oval fort encloses about 2 ha with a single rampart and ditch and slight traces of a counterscarp bank. The interior has been ploughed for many years, and the rampart is sufficiently damaged to make the identification of an entrance, without excavation, impossible, though it probably lay under the farm buildings. Some kind of underground 'chamber', perhaps a grain storage pit, was recorded in the middle of the last century.

W. Gardner: *V.C.H. Warwickshire* **1** (1904) 357

2 BERRY MOUND   Iron Age
     Solihull Urban   131 (SP:095778)
0·8 km north-west of Major's Green.

Situated on a low-lying spur, surrounded on three sides by the river Cole and a smaller stream. This fort of 4·5 ha was once enclosed by three sets of ramparts and ditches, although today only a single bank and ditch survive, and are best preserved on the southern side. This part of the earthwork is tree-covered. Elsewhere a boundary bank to the field shows clearly where the fort lies. It is uncertain which of the gaps are original entrances; those on the south seem modern, but one almost certainly existed at the north-east.

3 BURROW HILL CAMP   Iron Age
     Corley   132 (SP:304850)
East of the A423 immediately south of Corley.

This camp, 183 m square, and enclosing 2·8 ha, lies on the gentle eastern slope of Burrow Hill, and is defended in part by a natural rocky outcrop and partly by a single line of rampart and ditch. A counterscarp bank existed on the uphill northern side, whilst on the south-west a slightly out-turned entrance, now damaged by ploughing, gave access to the interior. The gaps at the north-east and south-east corners are probably modern. The rampart has been shown to have been faced with a good dry-stone wall, backed by earth and rubble in which oak logs acted as a timber lacing. It belongs to the end of the Iron Age, between 50 B.C. and A.D. 50.

P. B. Chatwin: *Trans. Birmingham A.S.* **52** (1927) 282

4 CHESTERTON FORT   Roman
     Chesterton and Kingston   132 (SP:341598)
This site straddles the Fosse Way, immediately north-east of a small stream, the Chesterton brook.

Although under plough massive banks and ditches still mark the outline of this small 3·2 ha rectangular Roman fort. Dugdale (1605–86) records that 'within the Compasse' of the camp 'divers old Coynes' were 'digg'd up'.

5 THE KING STONE   Bronze Age
     Long Compton   145 (SP:297309)
North of the road which forms the county boundary. Protected by the Department of the Environment.

This standing stone is 2·4 m high and 1·5 m wide, and forms part of the Rollright Stones complex. (It is described further under Rollright Stones, Oxfordshire, page 239). It may once have been part of a burial chamber, though a long mound to the north, now much ploughed down, was shown in 1927 to be natural. Sir Arthur Evans recorded that 'on Midsummer Eve when the "eldern tree" was in blossom, it was the custom for people to come up to the King Stone and stand in a circle.' The eldern was cut, and if it bled 'the King moved his head.'

O. G. S. Crawford: *Long Barrows of the Cotswolds* (1925) 166

6 THE LUNT (Plate 63)   Roman
  Baginton   132 (SP:345752)

On the north side of the road to Baginton from the Coventry by-pass (A45) at its junction with the B4115. Coventry Museum Field Centre. Open at weekends, Easter to 1 October, 11.00 to 18.00 hours, and weekdays whilst excavations in progress. (Adults 10p, children 5p.) Car-park and picnic area adjacent.

Sited on high ground looking north, and in a loop of the river Sowe, this Roman fort has been shown by excavation to have been occupied for only about fifteen years, from A.D. 60 to A.D. 75. During that time the fort was remodelled at least three times. Throughout its existence it was bounded on the north by the steep escarpment and on the west by a line of defence which remained unchanged at all times, but in Period 1 it stretched to the south and east well beyond its present limits, and its full extent is at present unknown. At that time it contained a number of timber buildings including barrack blocks which were later realigned. Towards the end of the initial phase a circular timber arena 32·6 m in diameter was constructed. Its purpose is obscure, but it may have been a *gyrus*, a circular area for training horses. Period 2 is marked by the building of the eastern defences which are very irregular since they curve outwards round the circular arena. They also hold the eastern entrance, the *porta principalis sinistra*, which was reconstructed in 1971. This fort was some 1·2 ha in size. In the centre of the fort was the headquarters building, the *principia*, consisting of a courtyard entered from the south, with a block of five rooms along its northern side. North of the *principia* were six barrack blocks, whose foundations are now marked in concrete. These blocks each held eighty men. Between the barracks and the escarpment to the north stood three granaries. One of these is to be rebuilt and used as a site museum. The final phase of the fort, Period 3, involved the reduction in size, by cutting off the southern third along the line of the *Via Principalis* that led west from the reconstructed gateway.

Visitors will be impressed by the rebuilt rampart of turf and timber and the great wooden gateway. These have been built in the types of

Plate 63   Reconstructed fort entrance, The Lunt, Warwickshire

material that would have been used in Roman times, and are carefully based on the excavated evidence and contemporary illustrations from Trajan's Column in Rome.

B. Hobley: *Current Archaeology* **1** (1967) 86; **3** (1971) 16

7 MANCETTER ROMAN TOWN   Roman
                                                                    132 (SP:326967)
The A5 (Watling Street) runs through the site south of Witherley and around the 'Bull Inn'.

The small Roman town of *Manduessedum* (Mancetter) lies astride the Watling Street. Although there are modern buildings at its centre, the earthworks behind these, on either side of the road are fairly clear. The town, covering about 2·4 ha, is marked by a rectangular earthwork some 183 m long by 137 m wide.

There seems to have been a mid 1st-century fort on the site, after which the initial civil settlement, dated to about A.D. 60, began. This

was surrounded by a large bank and ditch which went out of use early
in the 2nd century. In the late 3rd century or early 4th, a massive stone
wall and bank were erected, separated from a wide outer ditch by a
berm. There were indications of extensive settlement outside the fort,
including potters' workshops. Another Roman fort lay 0·8 km to the
west near the present village of Mancetter.

A. Oswald: *Trans. Birmingham A.S.* **74** (1958) 30

8   MEON HILL   Iron Age
    Quinton   144 (SP : 177454)

*Via track leading west past Meon Hall off minor road from Lower
Quinton to Mickleton.*

This conspicuous hill stands out into the Vale of Evesham. Its summit
is ringed by a double rampart and ditches with a counterscarp bank
except on the wooded north-west where the slope is steepest and only
a single bank is present. The inner bank and ditch have been destroyed
by ploughing on the north, although a dry-stone wall is visible along
part of the second rampart at this point. It may be original. The
defences, which enclose about 10 ha, are best seen on the south-west.
It is not possible to identify the position of entrances without excavation. A hoard of 394 spit-shaped currency bars were found within the
fort in 1824. These long-sword-shaped bars of iron served as currency
before the introduction of coins in the Belgic Iron Age. Most of the
bars from Meon have now been lost, but examples can be seen in the
museums at Stratford-upon-Avon, Gloucester and the Ashmolean in
Oxford.

9   METCHLEY ROMAN FORTS   Roman
    Birmingham   131 (SP : 043836)

91 m west of the Birmingham University Medical School Building.

Hardly anything remains of these two forts known since the 18th
century and consisting of a small 2·5 ha structure, lying within and
aligned to a larger 6 ha fort. The larger camp was built about A.D. 48
and was surrounded by a double ditch and turf rampart. Inside
were a number of large rectangular wooden storehouses, granaries and
barracks. The fort was enlarged by adding an annexe on the north side
and continuing the ditch system around it and adding towers. After a
fire in which the internal buildings were destroyed, a new smaller fort
was built in the southern part of its predecessor. New regular buildings,
some measuring about 7·3 m by 22·9 m were set up, and in turn they
too were burned in the early part of the 2nd century A.D.

The north-west corner tower of the larger fort and its adjoining
rampart and ditch have been reconstructed and these can be visited at

any time, though they have unfortunately suffered badly from local vandals.

T. R. Rowley: *Trans. Birmingham A.S.* (forthcoming)

10 NADBURY CAMP   Iron Age
   Ratley and Upton   145 (SJ : 390482)

The main B4086 road on the north and north-east side of Edge Hill runs through the overgrown ditch of this 7 ha fort, for about half of its circumference. At the south side of the modern road on the west is the only entrance to the fort: it is approached by a hollow-way. The rampart rises high above the road, but it is much denuded around the rest of the hill where it is accompanied by a ditch and counterscarp bank. The ground falls steeply to the north and south of the ridge on which Nadbury lies, and from which it commands extensive views in most directions. A slight ditch ran southwards from the fort at its southernmost corner, perhaps connected with boundaries of some kind.

V.C.H. Warwickshire I (1904) 389 for plan

11 OLDBURY CAMP   Iron Age
   Oldbury   132 (SJ : 314947)

Immediately north of Oldbury village and surrounding Oldbury Hall.

On a ridge overlooking the river Anker, which lies to the north-west, with the Roman town of Mancetter beyond. The rectangular fort at Oldbury was once of great strength. Sir William Dugdale, in the 17th century, spoke of 'Rampires whose Height and Largenesse do still shew the Strength'. He also records a discovery of neolithic polished axes from the fort. Its banks, still 6·1 m wide and 1·8 m high in places, with an external ditch, enclose about 2·8 ha, though they are much denuded on the south-east. There are a number of gaps in the ramparts, but which one is an original entrance cannot be determined without excavation.

12 WAPPENBURY FORT   Iron Age
   Wappenbury   132 (SP : 377694)

Best seen from the B4453 to the north; the whole village lies within the earthwork.

A large rectangular earthwork encloses the village. It is marked by steep scarps on the north, west and south, and by low banks and ditches east of the church, where the rampart is almost ploughed out. The footpath west from the church leads to a hollow-way which cuts the southern scarp, forming the only entrance. A footbridge now crosses the Leam at this point. The centre of the fort is grass covered. It has been dated by excavation to the 1st century B.C. A cutting through the rampart showed it to be 12·2 m wide, and composed of gravel revetted with clay.

M. and B. Stanley: *Trans. Birmingham A.S.* **76** (1958) 1

13 WOLSTON BARROW   Bronze Age?
                                                        132 (SP: 418752)

On hill south-east of Wolston and visible from B4029 west of village.

This round barrow is conspicuous from the north and east. It stands 1·5 m high with a crater at the centre and marked by a tree that grows upon it. Its position on Lammas Hill overlooking the Fosse Way might suggest a Roman date for it.

Museums containing archaeological material

City Museum and Art Gallery, Congreve Street, Birmingham 3
Herbert Art Gallery and Museum, Jordan Well, Coventry (Whitefriars Museum of Local History)
Museum and Art Gallery, Riversley Park, Nuneaton
Warwick County Museum, Market Place, Warwick

WILTSHIRE

1 ADAM'S GRAVE CHAMBERED BARROW   Neolithic
   Alton Priors   167 (SU: 112634)

On Summit of Walker's Hill. Nature Conservancy land; numerous footpaths.

A disused quarry on the north of this chambered barrow makes it appear larger than it really is. Even so, it is 61 m long and 6·1 m high, and lies south-east to north-west. In a hollow at the southern end are traces of a sarsen stone burial chamber. There seems to have been a retaining wall of alternate sarsen stones and dry-stone around the barrow, though this cannot now be seen. On either side were ditches which are still 6·1 m wide and 0·9 m deep. It had already been opened when John Thurnam dug into it in 1860. At that time he found parts of three or four skeletons and a leaf-shaped arrow-head.

J. Thurnam: *Archaeologia* **38** (1860) 410

2 ALDBOURNE FOUR BARROWS   Bronze Age
                                                        157 (SU: 249773)

2·4 km along track which runs north and north-west from beside Aldbourne church.

This fine cemetery consists of a bowl-barrow and three bell-barrows. When the bowl-barrow at the southern end of the row was excavated by William Greenwell a century ago it produced a cremated adult burial in an hour-glass shaped pit, covered over with four sarsen stones. Above the grave were the bones of a young pig. The three bell-barrows are each about 3·1 m high and 37·8 m in diameter. At the centre of the northern one Greenwell found a cremation burial together with a small pottery vessel and some amber beads. It also held two secondary cremations and the base of a beaker. In the central barrow was a decayed skeleton with a grooved bronze dagger and a flint arrowhead. This barrow also contained a secondary burial. The southern bell-barrow provided Greenwell with another central cremation and a perforated square-headed pin.

Further north-west along the same track on top of Sugar Hill are two more bowl-barrows. In one (SU:244782) Greenwell found a cremated adult burial and traces of a funeral pyre. The other (SU:241784) also held a cremation with a riveted bronze dagger and bone pin, in a cist under a mound of sarsen stones.

South-west of the Four Barrows beside the A419 (SU:247770) is the bowl-barrow (15·2 m in diameter and 1·5 m high) which produced the small pottery vessel of unknown use which gives its name to a series of Aldbourne cups. A corpse had been cremated on a plank under this barrow. It was accompanied by a bronze dagger, two bronze awls and numerous beads and other articles of faience, amber and shale.

W. Greenwell: *Archaeologia* **52** (1890) 46

3   AMESBURY DOWN TRIPLE BELL-BARROW   Bronze Age
                                                       167 (SU:148394)
Track south-west from A345 at SU:157396. Barrow lies amongst Celtic fields 0·4 km west of spinneys.

This is the only known Wiltshire triple bell-barrow with an outer bank. The enclosing ditch is egg-shaped in plan, 4·6 m wide and 36·6 m long. The western mound is 0·5 m high and 12·2 m in diameter, the central tump 0·9 m high and 9·1 m in diameter, and the southern 0·5 m high and 6·1 m across. The whole barrow has been dug into, but nothing is known of its contents.

O. G. S. Crawford and A. Keiller: *Wessex from the Air* (1928) 205

4   AVEBURY HENGE MONUMENT (Fig. 24, Plate 64)   Neolithic
                                                       157 (SU:103699)
The eastern part of the village of Avebury lies within the site. There is a museum behind the church to the west, and a publications stall in the public car-park. National Trust and Department of the Environment (Museum).

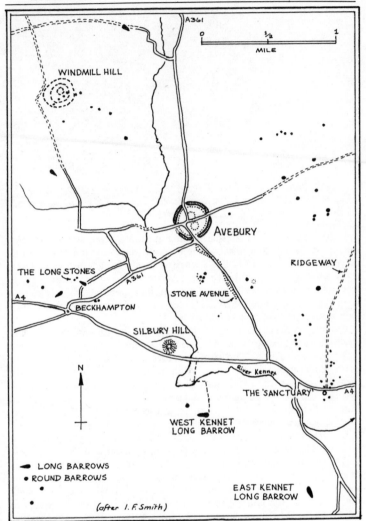

Fig. 24   The Avebury region, Wiltshire

John Aubrey, writing about 1663, claimed that Avebury 'does as much exceed in greatness the so renowned Stonehenge, as a Cathedral does a parish Church'. Today, in spite of the busy traffic rushing through this little village, there is an atmosphere of quiet seclusion about this

Plate 64   Avebury stone circle, Wiltshire

beautiful spot that is altogether lacking in the stark and over publicized setting of Stonehenge. Avebury is a secret place that needs to be explored at leisure. One is not surprised that it could disappear from the knowledge of learned men until Aubrey rediscovered it in 1648. It was not until the excavations of Alexander Keiller between 1936 and 1939 that the site was cleared of trees and undergrowth and began to look something like it does today.

Avebury consists of an approximately circular area of 11·5 ha, enclosed by a ditch 347·5 m in internal diameter and an external bank 426·7 m in diameter. The circumference of this bank is a little over 1 km. Excavations of the ditch, which is 21·3 m wide at the top, have shown that it varies considerably in depth and width at the bottom, the average dimensions being 9·1 m deep and 4 m wide. It should be noted that the flat bottom is very irregular, as though dug by gangs of workmen (a feature frequently observed in sites of this period). The bank varies between 4·3 and 5·5 m in height, and is 22·9 to 30·5 m in width at its base. The bank and ditch are separated by a berm in the south-east and north-east quadrants, but this is missing on the west, perhaps due to erosion. On the other hand this might explain why the bank on the south-west seems to have been retained by a vertical wall of chalk blocks, 0·9 m high and 1·5 m thick, although this feature is missing in other cuttings at the south-east. The four entrance causeways that run across the ditch and through the banks all seem to be original features and average 15·2 m in width.

After the initial impact of the earthworks at Avebury, one then appreciates the scale of the great sarsen stone blocks that have been set up inside it. These consist of an outer circle of at least ninety-eight stones, set at a distance of about 6·7 m inside the edge of the ditch, and two smaller inner circles of which the southern is now the most complete. A great many of the Avebury stones were destroyed during the 14th and 18th centuries. Where their holes were found during the excavations, even though the stones were missing, concrete plinths were set up to mark their places. The largest surviving stone in the outer circle is number 46 by the northern entrance. It is 4·4 m high with a further 1·2 m buried below the ground.

The southern inner circle was 51·8 m in diameter, and probably contained twenty-nine stones set at 11 m intervals. Five stones still stand on the circumference of this circle, and the holes of four others are marked. Originally a pillar stone about 6 m high known as The Obelisk stood at the centre of the circle, but this was destroyed more than 200 years ago. West of The Obelisk stood a line of a dozen small stones stretching for about 30·5 m. They seem to have been part of a rectilinear feature, and their purpose may eventually be clearer when more excavation has taken place in this circle.

The northern inner circle was about 49 m in diameter and originally contained some twenty-seven stones around an inner ring of about twelve stones. Of the outer circle only four survive, and two of those have fallen. At the centre of this circle stood three massive sarsen stones forming a three-sided enclosure known as The Cove. One of these stones fell in 1713 but the others survive, one measuring 4·9 m high by 2·4 m broad, and the other 4·3 m high and 4·9 m broad.

Former suggestions that the Avebury circles are of two or more periods of construction cannot be substantiated at present. It is clear, however, that the site retained its sanctity for something like 1,000 years, from the Neolithic into the Bronze Age, about 2600 to 1600 B.C.

Stretching for just under 2·4 km from the southern entrance at Avebury ran an avenue of a hundred pairs of sarsen stones, set two by two about 15·2 m apart transversely (Plate 65). The average height of surviv-

Plate 65   The West Kennet stone avenue, Wiltshire

ing stones is about 3 m, and it has been noticed that the stones seem to be paired alternately by shape: tall and narrow, and short and diamond. The northern third of the avenue has been restored. At its southern end the course of the avenue swings south-east at West Kennet village and climbs the hill beside the A4 road, to terminate on Overton Hill in a small stone circle called The Sanctuary.

The Sanctuary (SU: 118679) stands beside the Ridgeway on the crest of the hill above the river Kennet. Excavation in 1930 showed that it consisted of two small stone circles and six concentric circles of post holes. The post holes might represent a series of roofed wooden buildings, renewed from time to time, with a final phase in which the stone circles enclosed the last timber structure. Alternatively we may consider a series of free-standing timber circles, the posts perhaps decorated like totem poles. The outer stone circle linked the Sanctuary to the West Kennet stone avenue. Although the Sanctuary was destroyed in the 18th century, the positions of its stones and posts have been marked out with concrete plinths in the field opposite the transport café.

A second avenue leading from the west entrance of Avebury to the Longstones west of Beckhampton was described by Stukeley. Only the two *Longstones* (SU:089693) survive today, but there are reasonable arguments for believing that this avenue once existed.

I. F. Smith: *Windmill Hill and Avebury* (1965) 175

5 BARBURY CASTLE HILLFORT   Iron Age
Wroughton   157 (SU:149763)
Reached from the Ridgeway or from the road past the military hospital to Burderop Down.

Above the point where the Ridgeway drops across the valley before climbing once more to Liddington Castle, is the impressive 4·7 ha earthwork called Barbury Castle. This oval enclosure is protected by two upstanding ramparts and deep ditches, which are cut on the east and west by entrances. Direct access to the entrance on the east, where the ground levels out, is prevented by a semi-circular barbican. Colt Hoare and others dug inside from time to time and found extensive evidence of Early Iron Age occupation, including jewellery and chariot fittings: more recent air photographs have shown huts and storage pits.

There is a strong boundary dyke running from north-west to south-east on the eastern side of the fort, and it may be of comparable age. Further east on Burderop Downs are extensive Celtic fields (centred at SU:164762) of probable Iron Age or Roman date. Barbury may have been refortified in the 5th and 6th centuries, when it might have provided a rallying point in the battle of *Beranburh* in A.D. 556.

R. Colt Hoare: *Ancient Wiltshire* **2** (1819) 41

6 BATTLESBURY CAMP HILLFORT   Iron Age
    Warminster   1661/67 (ST: 898456)

Approached from Sack Hill, 2·4 km north-east of Warminster.

Woods on the south obliterate what must have been an extensive view
across the Wylye valley from this kidney-shaped contour fort of 9·7 ha.
1·6 km to the north-west the ramparts of Scratchbury can be clearly
seen. Strongly defended by double ramparts and ditches, and with an
additional line on the less-steep western side, Battlesbury was entered
by gates at the north-west and east. Both gates have outworks, that at
the east possibly having a slinging platform on the north side of the
out-turned barbican passageway. Mrs. M. E. Cunnington uncovered
eleven storage pits inside the camp in 1922. These produced Iron Age
pottery and the hub of a chariot wheel. A pit found just outside the
north-west entrance held a number of burials and included the remains
of a woman and child. This might represent a massacre by a neighbouring tribe or the work of the advancing Roman legions. A mound
just inside the camp on the south side of the hill is marked on the maps
as a barrow, but excavation by Colt Hoare failed to produce a burial. It
might be a small castle motte.

M. E. Cunnington: *W.A.M.* **42** (1924) 368; **43** (1927) 400

7 BRATTON CASTLE   Neolithic and Iron Age
                                                 166/167 (ST: 901516)

Approached by metalled road south-east from B3098 in Bratton.

This pear-shaped hillfort crowns the steep scarp-face of the Downs
above the Westbury White Horse. The defences, enclosing 10 ha,
consist of two steep banks and ditches on all sides except the north.
There are entrances on the south and north-east at the points where
the road passes through the camp. Both have outworks. Inside the
southern ramparts are traces of quarry scoops, although these might
be related to a refortification of Bratton during the post-Roman period.
Colt Hoare recorded a find of quern-stones and 'nearly a cartload of
large pebbles'; the latter may have been sling-stones.

  Perhaps forming a religious focus around which the fort was constructed is a long barrow inside the fort, which measures 70 m long,
19·8 m wide and 3·7 m high. Its uneven surface indicates the various
diggings from which it has suffered, producing secondary burials,
urns and iron objects. A hundred years ago John Thurnam found two
partially burned adult burials lying on a 'platform' at the higher
eastern end of the barrow.

  The Westbury White Horse, cut into the turf on the slope below the
western end of the hillfort is claimed to have been cut originally to

commemorate King Alfred's victory at Ethandun in A.D. 878. The present figure dates from 1778.

R. Colt Hoare: *Ancient Wiltshire* I (1812) 55

8 BURY CAMP   Iron Age
    Colerne   156 (ST:818740)

Access by road north-west from Colerne airfield passing transmitting station. All earthworks tree-covered.

Bury Camp occupies the north-western tip of a spur, whose wooded sides slope down to small brooks that eventually join the Avon. 9 ha lie within this promontory fort, and are isolated from the main hill ridge of Colerne Down by two lines of rampart and ditch. The gap by which the present track crosses this defence is modern. It is probable that originally this was a cross-dyke breeched from north-west to south-east, but later blocked when alternative entrances became available. A single bank runs round the north and east sides of the promontory; that on the north having a marked quarry ditch on its inside. At the north-west and north-east are two entrances with long inturned funnel-shaped passages. That at the north-east was of two periods, the first being brought to an end with destruction by fire, after which it was repaired and remodelled to produce a dry-stone lined passageway 12·2 m long with a bridge over the top. The north-west entrance had a longer funnel-shaped passage about 21 m long, and was approached by a terraceway from the south-west along the steep outer slope. Recent excavations have shown that the fort was first constructed about 350 B.C., but suffered a period of neglect and fires before it was repaired and resettled. Its end must have been in the 2nd century B.C. when the north-east entrance was again destroyed by fire.

At Ford Hill, 1·6 km east of the camp (ST:832744) is a fine cross-dyke with a ditch on the eastern side, and an angular bend midway along it, that is probably a territorial outwork connected with the fort.

D. Grant King: *W.A.M.* **64** (1969) 21

9 CASTERLEY CAMP HILLFORT   Iron Age
    Upavon   167 (SU:115535)

Bridle road uphill south-west from Upavon. Watch out for red flags when Army using area.

This large hillfort enclosing 27·5 ha crowns the Downs above the Avon valley. It is irregular in shape and remarkable for a curious bulge in the rampart at the northern end near the bridle road, apparently designed to cover dead ground. The defences, consisting of a single rampart and ditch, are weak and appear to be unfinished. Numerous irregularities in the rampart suggest the incomplete work of gang labour which was more advanced on the south and east where the bank is 1·5 m higher and the V-shaped ditch 1·2 to 1·5 m deep. The northern 'bulge' seems to have been added as an afterthought, and it joins uncomfortably onto the main rampart on the north-east.

Entrances exist at the south, north and west, the latter approached by a sunken road. All are probably contemporary with the fort. Excavations by the Cunningtons in 1909–12 and aerial photographs have shown that there are two enclosures in the centre, one sub-rectangular and the other roughly oval. In the latter enclosure were three pits (one with a great post, 0·9 m in diameter, rising from it) around which were four human burials and fourteen red-deer antlers. This seems to be a ritual shaft connected with Celtic religion, widely found in western Europe. This may mean that the hilltop was a local cult centre, and attracted the local population as much for worship as for defence. Belgic and Roman material suggests that the central enclosures were in use from the 1st century A.D. well into the Roman period. The interior of the fort is ploughed.

R. W. Feachem in Jesson and Hill: *The Iron Age and its Hillforts* (1970) 35

10 CASTLE DITCHES HILLFORT Iron Age
Tisbury 167 (ST:963283)
Approached by track off road between east Tisbury and Ansty at ST:954283.
This wooded hillfort crowns a steep hill above the Nadder valley. Double banks and ditches enclose 9·7 ha. On the south-east where the ground is level there is an additional line of rampart and ditch. Gaps on the east and west seem to be original entrances.

H. Sumner: *Ancient Earthworks of Cranborne Chase* (1913) 17

11 COW DOWN BARROWS Bronze Age
Collingbourne Ducis 167 (SU:229515)
Around Barrow Plantation 0·8 km south-west of A338 and A342 crossroads.
Two lines of barrows lying south-west to north-east form this cemetery. Both are composed entirely of bowl-barrows with the single exception of a disc-barrow in the northern row. Of the nine barrows in the southern row, three lie west of the wood and are badly ploughed, four are in the wood, and the other two lie to the east. The four barrows of the second row all lie north of the wood. All except the disc-barrow were opened by W. C. Lukis in 1855 or 1861.

Two of the barrows in the wood are of particular interest. The second from the west is 24·4 m in diameter and 2·4 m high. At its centre was a grave measuring almost 1·2 m long, 38·1 cm wide and 30·5 cm deep. Lukis wrote: 'The grave was cylindrical and had been lined with a plaster of powdered chalk about 1½ inches [3·8 cm] in thickness. The plaster had received the impression of the bark of a tree, and indicated that the bones of the deceased had been placed in a hollow trunk.' The body had been cremated and buried with an antler mace-head. Six further cremations, two in urns, were later added to the barrow. Next to this mound is the largest of the Cow Down barrows, 33·5 m in diameter and 3·7 m high. At the centre was the crouched skeleton of a child of three or four years, with a collared urn containing burnt bones and a food-vessel-shaped urn at its feet. Another skeleton, eighteen cremations and pieces of forty-five urns of Deverel–Rimbury type were all subsequently added to the barrow.

The disc-barrow in the northern row is about 45·7 m across with a low central mound. Colt Hoare opened it in 1805 without recording his finds, and later Lukis uncovered an empty central grave.

L. V. Grinsell: *V.C.H. Wiltshire* 1 (1957) 167

12 DEVIL'S DEN   Neolithic
    Fyfield   157 (SU: 152696)

South-west of bridleway in Clatford Bottom and 0·8 km north of A4.

The mound of this long barrow has practically disappeared, but a burial chamber at the south-east end of the barrow has been re-erected. It consists of two upright sarsen stones surmounted by a large capstone. Beneath it lie two wall stones. It probably formed a simple end chamber, but is as yet unexcavated.

A. D. Passmore: *W.A.M.* 41 (1922) 523

13 DURRINGTON WALLS   Neolithic
    Durrington   167 (SU: 150437)

The A345 from Netheravon to Amesbury runs through the site. It can be viewed from the Woodhenge lay-by, outside the site to the south-west.

Centuries of ploughing have almost obliterated this, the second largest henge monument yet recognized in Britain. It is oval in shape, and its bank and internal ditch enclose 12 ha at the head of a small dry valley. Its greatest measurements are 518 m from north to south and 500 m from east to west. The bank is best preserved on the north-east where it still rises to a height of 1·5 m, although excavation has shown it to average 27·4 m wide at its base. Inside the bank a berm from 6·1 to 42·7 m wide, extends to the edge of the ditch, which has been shown to be approximately 17·7 m wide, 5·8 m deep, and with a flat bottom 6·7 m wide. Geoffrey Wainwright, the excavator, has estimated that such a ditch would have required 900,000 man-hours to dig. Two causeways afforded access to the interior of the site: one on the north-west was 30·5 m wide and the other on the south-east 22·9 m wide, and only 61 m from the river Avon.

The bank and ditch were constructed about 2500 B.C. At that time, or soon after, a large circular timber structure 38·7 m in diameter was constructed close within the south-east entrance, and a similar, though smaller circle, approached by an avenue, was set up 118·9 m to the north of it. The large circle consisted of five concentric rings of posts, increasing in size towards the centre, which may have supported a roof. The innermost posts were about 0·6 m in diameter. The smaller circle contained only two rings of posts, 27·4 m and 18·9 m in diameter respectively, approached from the south by an avenue of irregularly placed posts. These were later replaced on a different alignment. The sites of both the large and small timber circles were destroyed in 1968 in order to build the present A345 road, under which they now lie. They were clearly related to the adjoining Woodhenge monument (page 360), and aerial photographs show that many more timber structures remain to be excavated inside Durrington Walls. There seems to be every likelihood that they formed a religious cult-centre, of which our knowledge is at present only rudimentary.

G. Wainwright: *Durrington Walls Excavations, 1966–68* (1971)

14 EAST KENNET LONG BARROW (See Fig. 24, page 315)
Neolithic
157 (SU: 116669)

In a field 0·8 km south of East Kennet village.

Like its famous neighbour across the fields at West Kennet, this barrow probably covers a stone burial chamber, but it is at present unexcavated. Since it is covered with trees, examination would be very difficult. It lies south-east to north-west, is 105·2 m long and stands 6·1 m high. Traces of sarsen stones in a hollow at the south-east end support the suggestion of a burial chamber.

L. V. Grinsell: *V.C.H. Wiltshire* I (1957) 140

15 ENFORD BOWL-BARROW
Bronze Age
167 (SU: 129516)

On the hillslope 0·4 km south-west of Compton, west of the A342 road.

One of the largest surviving bowl-barrows in southern England, it is 48·8 m in diameter and 5·2 m high. A trench has been cut into the centre from the eastern side, but nothing is known of the contents.

16 EVERLEIGH BARROWS   Bronze Age
                                                        167 (SU: 184561)

At junction of bridleways from Lower Everleigh to Pewsey Hill.

John Thurnam was responsible for digging through this small cemetery
of four barrows about 1860. He found nothing in the bowl-barrow
which today is only about 30 cm high, nor in the adjoining disc-
barrow which is 56·4 m in diameter and has a clear bank and ditch,
although its central mound is only 30 cm high. There are also two
bell-barrows in the group. That on the east is 45·7 m in diameter with
a central mound 3·4 m high which contained a cremation burial.
The western bell-barrow is slightly larger in diameter but lower in
height. There was a probable adult cremation at the centre accompanied by a flat bronze dagger. The remains of the funeral pyre lay
close by.

L. V. Grinsell: *V.C.H. Wiltshire* I (1957) 209

17 FIGSBURY RINGS HILLFORT   Iron Age
     Winterbourne   167 (SU: 188338)

National Trust Property. Approached by a track from the A30.

Sited on the flat top of a rounded spur overlooking the Bourne valley,
Figsbury Rings is at first a typical circular fort enclosing 6 ha within a
single rampart and ditch. Excavations by B. H. and M. E. Cunnington in 1924 showed that the rampart, which is 12·8 m wide and 3·4 m
high, had been enlarged twice, and was fronted by the outer V-shaped
ditch 10·7 m wide and 4·3 m deep. The inner ditch, to quote the
Cunningtons, was 'of quite different character from the outer one. It
was irregularly cut with a wide, flat bottom. Humps or promontories of
unexcavated chalk were left in the inner ditch, forming occasionally
what were tantamount to bridges across it. For a length of 60 feet
[18·3 m] the ditch had never been completely dug out.' There have
been a number of suggestions to explain this curious feature. That it
was a quarry for additional material for the outer bank is unlikely when
the distance for carting the excavated material is considered. That it
represents an unfinished defence is not improbable, though its flat
bottom and interrupted nature suggest that it may have begun life as a
neolithic causewayed camp, later remodelled as a hillfort. Certainly no
neolithic pottery was observed in 1924, but only a hundred sherds of
Bronze and early Iron Age material were found altogether, and no
evidence of permanent occupation was forthcoming. Two entrances
cut through the bank of Figsbury, on the east and west, and the Cunningtons suspected that hornworks had existed outside both.

O. G. S. Crawford and A. Keiller: *Wessex from the Air* (1928) 84

18 FYFIELD AND OVERTON DOWNS CELTIC FIELDS   Iron Age
  Fyfield, Overton and Preshute   157 (SU: 142710)

Fyfield and Overton Downs form a National Nature Reserve administered by the Nature Conservancy. They are famous for their
extensive Celtic field systems that were probably laid out at various
times from 700 or 600 B.C. onwards. During the Iron Age much of the
chalk downland was settled and farmed and at Fyfield many acres of the
associated fields have survived. Today they are divided by grass-covered
lynchets or banks standing up to 3·1 m high, formed by the gradual
building up of soil against an obstacle, such as a row of sarsen stones, a
wall or fence, or a low bank. Excavations between 1965 and 1968
revealed the grid-like markings of cross-ploughing using a simple
ard (plough). There is clear evidence that the fields continued to be
ploughed well into the Roman period, though they sometimes changed
shape and direction. Trackways for access to farms and buildings can
still be seen heading between, and sometimes across, fields.

Fyfield Down is also the probable source of the sarsen stones used
in constructing Avebury and Stonehenge. Known as the Grey Wethers
thousands lie scattered throughout the Reserve. The most accessible
groups are further south beside the A4 at Piggle Dean (SU: 143688) and
at Lockeridge Dene (SU: 145674): both National Trust properties. A
sarsen stone of particular interest was used for polishing stone axes. It
lies 91 m south-east of the north-west corner of the Reserve (approx.
SU: 128715) and its upper surface bears a characteristic smooth hollow
and five grooves. A Beaker settlement was located close to this stone.

In 1960 the British Association constructed an experimental earthwork on Overton Down (SU: 129706) in order to study the changes
which take place over a known period of time in a scientifically constructed bank and ditch, and on selected materials buried within the
structure. Sections will be cut through the earthwork at intervals of 2,
4, 8, 16, 32, 64 and perhaps 128 years.

P. A. Jewell: *The Experimental Earthwork on Overton Down, Wiltshire*
(1963)

19 GIANT'S CAVE LONG CAIRN   Neolithic
  Luckington   156 (ST: 820829)

*At the south-east corner of Badminton Park beside the road from Great
Badminton to Luckington.*

Lying on the top of a low rise above a stream, this trapezoidal cairn
measures 36·6 m long and 15·2 m wide at the higher eastern end. It
is constructed of limestone and has a blind entrance with a forecourt
between horns at the east end. In each of the long sides are two narrow
rectangular burial chambers. Of those on the north side, the western
measured 2·6 m by 1·4 m and contained the remains of at least six

individuals, three men, two women and a child. The eastern chamber, 3·4 m by 1·2 m in size, also contained the remains of at least five people including a child of twelve to fourteen years. On the south side the eastern chamber produced the bones of a woman, whilst the smaller western grave held at least seven bodies: a man, three women and three infants. The barrow has been dug into on a number of occasions, and many more remains have been destroyed. Modern excavation was carried out by A. D. Passmore in 1932, and in 1960-2 by J. X. W. P. Corcoran.

J. X. W. P. Corcoran: *W.A.M.* **65** (1970) 39

20 GIANT'S GRAVE LONG BARROW   Neolithic
   Milton Lilbourne   167 (SU: 189583)

Beside footpath from 0·4 km west of Milton Hill Farm to Pewsey Hill.

Lying above the steep escarpment of Pewsey Hill, this chalk long barrow is more than 91·4 m long, 20·1 m wide and 2·1 m high at the north-eastern end. It has clearly defined side ditches, that on the north-west being particularly well-marked. When John Thurnam excavated the barrow in about 1860 he found the remains of three or four individuals piled on the natural chalk surface below the eastern end, one with a skull cleft before burial. Nearby lay a leaf-shaped arrow-head.

J. Thurnam: *P.S.A.L.* (*2nd series*) **3** (1867) 170

21 GOPHER WOOD BARROW CEMETERY   Bronze Age
   Wilcot   167 (SU: 139639)

In front of wood on hill scarp, at end of track north from Draycot Fitz Payne.

This consists of a row of small bowl-barrows averaging 9·1 m in diameter and 0·9 m high, some of which produced cremation burials, urns and bone pins. On the steep slope at the southern end is a disc-barrow 27·4 m in diameter with a central mound 0·9 m high and a low outer bank and shallow ditch. William Cunnington found an urn in the centre with an incense cup, bone pin and bronze awl (a tattooing needle ?). There were two other cremations surrounded by flints.

L. V. Grinsell: *V.C.H. Wiltshire* **1** (1957) 219

22 GRAFTON DISC-BARROWS AND CELTIC FIELDS
                                                          Bronze and Iron Age
                                                             167 (SU: 271563)

Footpath east from road linking A346 to A338 over Fairmile Down, or 1·6 km west from Scot's Poor on Chute Causeway (SU: 286562).

These two disc-barrows are unusual since they overlap one another. Each is about 45·7 m in diameter with central mounds 0·9 m high and

9·1 to 10·7 m across. They have been excavated but no record survives. A strip lynchet of a Celtic field overlies part of each barrow, though it is clear that the main field system deliberately set out to avoid them.

23 KNAP HILL (Plate 66)   Neolithic and Iron Age
   Alton Priors   167 (SU: 121636)

East of the road from Alton Priors to Marlborough. Footpath from road at SU:116638. Note footpath inside field on east. Nature Conservancy. Access at any time.

Plate 66   Knap Hill causewayed camp, Wiltshire

Dramatically situated above the Vale of Pewsey this neolithic causewayed camp lies in an arc on the crest of the escarpment. Six, or possibly seven, ditch sections follow the 825 feet (252 m) contour along the north-west side of the hill then curve to the south-west and disappear, enclosing some 1·6 ha. Excavations have shown that the ditch sections averaged 3·7 m wide, but varied in depth between 1·2 and 2·7 m. The causeways between the ditches are about 5·5 m wide. The bank inside the ditch is today a slight affair, of dump construction. A revised radio-carbon date for the initial ditch silting of 3500 B.C. places it well within the British neolithic period, and Windmill Hill pottery, though scarce, was present. The scanty finds suggested that the site was abandoned after a fairly short period. At a later date, when the ditches were almost filled with silt, a little Beaker pottery was dropped, which can be dated by radio-carbon to 2200 B.C.

Knap Hill's skyline position may have made it an ideal place for religious and ceremonial functions. Later, in the Bronze Age, three barrows were set up at the camp, though they can scarcely be seen today. On the escarpment edge, due north of the neolithic site, and joining it, is a small Romano-British enclosure, with an entrance on the north-east side, shown by excavation to be of 1st century A.D. date. In recent times the interior of Knap Hill camp was disturbed by flint digging.

G. Connah: *W.A.M.* **60** (1965) 1

24 LAKE BARROW CEMETERY   Bronze Age
    Wilsford   167 (SU: 109402)

East of the green lane running south-west from Stonehenge, across Normanton Down to Druid's Lodge on the A360.

'A perpendicular shaft sunk into the apex, of a size proportionate to that of the barrow, rarely fails of bringing to light its contents', wrote the Revd. Edward Duke, after digging some of the Lake barrows early in the 19th century. The remainder were dug about the same time by Richard Colt Hoare, leaving little for re-examination in 1959 by W. F. Grimes.

Of approximately twenty-two barrows in the group, fifteen are bowl-barrows, four bell-barrows, two disc-barrows and one long barrow. Others flattened by ploughing certainly existed. Of the barrows outside the wood to the north-east, all have been ploughed down. Excavations have shown some of them to contain cremations, with inhumation burials under the same mound. Inside the beech wood a bowl-barrow 18·3 m in diameter and 1·8 m high known as the Prophet Barrow contained a cremation in a wooden box that had been placed in a central grave. With it was a grooved dagger and a pendant whetstone. Another bowl-barrow 3·1 m high, near the long barrow, covered a child's skeleton buried with a beaker in a deep grave. The long barrow is 42·7 m long and 2·4 m high, and it seems to be unopened. The disc-barrows are in thick undergrowth at the northern end of the wood, and although examined by Colt Hoare no record survives of their contents. Similarly the bell-barrows have been damaged and are small. One on the north-western edge of the wood produced a cremation with a bronze dagger, awl and some beads.

L. V. Grinsell: *V.C.H. Wiltshire* **1** (1957) 198

25 LAKE DOWN BARROW CEMETERY   Bronze Age
    Wilsford   167 (SU: 117393)

On south side of track from Lake to Westfield Farm, and just east of farm.

This cemetery of about sixteen barrows has, like so many others in the area, suffered destruction over the years at the hands of early excavators and the plough. This group was dug into by the Revd. Edward Duke (1790–1850) and the records he left are scanty in the extreme. An unusual feature is five pond-barrows, each about 12·2 m in diameter and 0·6 m deep, dug by Duke and either producing a cremation burial or being recorded as unproductive. A disc-barrow 54·9 m in diameter, with a low central mound, covered a primary cremation in a small urn. The bowl-barrows covered both cremations and skeletons, and contained a variety of objects datable to the Bronze Age.

L. V. Grinsell: *V.C.H. Wiltshire* **1** (1957) 199

26 LANHILL LONG CAIRN   Neolithic
    Chippenham Without   156 (ST:877747)

On the south side of the A420, 4 km north-west of Chippenham.

Few of our ancient monuments can have suffered more abominably than the Lanhill long cairn. Between the time when John Aubrey sketched it in the mid 17th century and the present day it has been subjected to one onslaught after another. Originally it seems to have been about 56·4 m long and 3·7 m high. At the eastern end there was a false entrance, removed in 1909, and a forecourt revetted with drystone walling. On the north side were two burial chambers both now destroyed. One contained a rough porthole and was roofed with a single capstone. When excavated in 1936 it held nine skeletons. At the south was another chamber, which still survives. Measuring 1·2 m by 2·4 m, it once had a corbelled roof and contained eleven or twelve burials. In 1938 Dr. A. J. E. Cave examined the bones from the northern chamber and noted marked family resemblances between the skulls of the burials, from which he deduced that Lanhill had once been a family vault.

D. Grant King: *P.P.S.* **32** (1966) 73

27 LIDDINGTON CASTLE HILLFORT   Iron Age
    Liddington   157 (SU:209797)

A steep uphill climb from the Ridgeway.

This hillfort is oval in shape. It is defended by a single rampart and ditch with a counterscarp bank, which encloses 3 ha. There are indications that this rampart may have been faced with sarsen stones. The only apparent entrance is on the south-east, facing the main hill mass where a number of outlying banks and ditches extend south for about 6 km and may mark the boundaries of once cultivated land. The present road known as the Ridgeway runs at the northern foot of the hill on which the fort is sited.

0·8 km north-east (SU:214799) are a group of pits provisionally identified as flint mines.

28 LUGBURY LONG BARROW   Neolithic
        Nettleton   156 (ST:831786)

*Beside a footpath due west from the Fosse Way at ST:834785 to Nettleton
Green.*

This barrow measures 58 m long, 27·4 m wide at the eastern end, and
1·8 m high. At the eastern end is a fine false entrance composed of three
stones; two facing each other 1·8 m and 1·5 m high, and a third leaning
against them measuring about 3·7 m by 1·8 m. In the eastern half of the
southern side were four closed burial chambers, each about 3·1 m long
and 1·2 m wide, containing at least twenty-six skeletons, ten of them
children. On 11 October 1821 Colt Hoare found what may have been
the primary burial near the eastern end, which he 'uncovered with the
greatest nicety . . . This skeleton was deposited in a cist or grave, about
0·6 m in depth, lying on its side in a direction nearly east and west, the
legs drawn up, so that the knees were on a level with the hips.'

O. G. S. Chawford: *Long Barrows of the Cotswolds* (1925) 230

29 MANTON LONG BARROW   Neolithic
        Preshute   157 (SU:152714)

Near footpath which runs north-west from Manton House.

At the south-eastern end of this damaged long barrow is a simple
burial chamber about 4·6 m long and 1·8 m wide, with a single
capstone in position. The barrow was 19·8 m long, surrounded by a
kerb of sarsens, with a forecourt in front of the empty chamber, where a
pit containing a pole-axed ox was uncovered. Neolithic pottery from
recent excavations confirms a date prior to 3000 B.C.

S. Piggott: *W.A.M.* **52** (1947) 60

30 MARDEN HENGE MONUMENT   Neolithic
                                               167 (SU:091584)

*The Marden to Woodborough road passes through the site north-east of the
river Avon.*

The valley of the Wiltshire Avon is remarkable for a series of ritual
sites apparently connected with prehistoric religion. Stonehenge,
Durrington Walls and Woodhenge are all well known, and close to the
headwaters of the river is the largest of all, Marden. This henge
monument is oval in shape and encloses 14 ha. The south and west
sides are formed by the meandering river, whilst on the north-west,
north and east is a bank, much reduced by ploughing and an inner
ditch 15·2 m wide and 1·8 m deep. The earthwork is broken by two
entrances, one at the north and one on the east; this arrangement
appears unique, two entrances normally being opposite each other.

Perhaps the possibility of two other entrances fording the river should not be ruled out.

The northern entrance was excavated in 1969, and it was soon clear that prehistoric visitors had thrown their rubbish into the ditch on either side as they entered or left. Geoffrey Wainwright, the excavator, found quantities of neolithic pottery, stone tools, animal bones and antler picks concentrated in that area. The pottery was all of the type known as grooved-ware and commonly found in henge monuments.

Close inside the northern entrance was the site of a timber circle, 9·8 m in diameter, with a possible group of three posts at its centre, presumably to support a wooden roof. The Marden earthworks have been drastically ploughed in the last century and a half, but it is still just possible to make out this great enclosure. At its centre a large barrow is reputed to have stood, 61 m in diameter and 9·1 m high. It was dug into in 1818 but there is no record of any finds. Since then it has been completely ploughed away.

G. J. Wainwright: *Ant. J.* **51** (1971) 177

31 MARTINSELL HILLFORT   Iron Age
        Pewsey   167 (SU:177639)

Approached along track beside wood from road running north-west from Wootton Rivers to Clench Common.

Strongly sited above the east-facing escarpment of Martinsell Hill this fort of 13 ha is only defended by a single rampart and ditch with a probable entrance at the north-east corner. Colt Hoare dug into it with no recorded result. A large Belgic rubbish pit was found in the copse to the north in 1907.

1·2 km south-west on the hill spur above Oare is a small promontory fort called the *Giant's Grave*, Wilcot (SU:166632). The neck of the hill is cut off by a strong rampart and ditch, broken by an entrance at its centre, and additionally protected by two outlying banks and ditches. The interior of the fort, about 1 ha in extent, is surrounded by a very slight bank and ditch. Iron Age pottery has been found within the fort indicating that it was probably of two periods.

L. V. Grinsell: *V.C.H. Wiltshire* **I** (1957) 268

32 MEMBURY HILLFORT   Iron Age
        Ramsbury   158 (SU:302753)

By minor road north from Whittonditch.

The flat interior of this fort is ploughed, and its single rampart and ditch, with counterscarp bank, are overgrown with trees. Enclosing 13·8 ha it has entrances at the north-east and south-west. The north-eastern corner of the fort is in Berkshire, the remainder in Wiltshire.

33 MILSTON DOWN LONG BARROWS   Neolithic
    Milston   167 (SU:217463)

West of the military road from Bulford Camp to Tidworth Barracks.

There are no records to indicate whether these two long barrows have
been excavated. Lying side by side and east to west, the southern is
48·8 m long, 21·3 m wide and 2·1 m high, the northern 26·8 m long,
15·2 m wide and 1·2 m high. They are both higher at the eastern end,
and have clearly defined side ditches.

L. V. Grinsell: *V.C.H. Wiltshire* I (1957) 142

34 NORMANTON BARROWS (Plate 67; see Fig. 26, p. 344)
                                              Neolithic and Bronze Age
       Wilsford   167 (centre: SU:118413)

*By green lane to Druid's Lodge, off A303 and 0·8 km south-west of
Stonehenge.*

Lying on the skyline to the north of the Normanton barrows is
Stonehenge, the religious focus for many of the barrows on this part of
Salisbury Plain. At Normanton is one of the most famous linear
cemeteries of the Bronze Age in Britain. Two dozen barrows of almost
every known type run east to west for about 1·2 km. The western end
of the line is marked by three barrows in the plantation known as
Normanton Gorse. This wood is difficult to penetrate and is scarcely
worth the effort. North of the wood is (1) what Colt Hoare described
as 'the most beautiful bowl-barrow on the plains of Stonehenge'. 53 m
in diameter and 3·4 m high, it covered the skeleton of a man, who had
been buried with a grooved bronze dagger in a wooden scabbard, a
beaker and deer antlers, all laid on a plank of wood. A cone-shaped
arrangement of poles above the corpse may have represented a funeral
hut buried within the barrow mound. (2) East of Normanton Gorse and
west of the green lane is a fine disc-barrow 61 m in diameter with a low
central mound. When opened in 1804 it contained a cremation burial in
a circular grave with beads of amber, shale and faience. (3) Almost
adjoining, but across the green lane is a second disc-barrow, 57·9 m
in diameter, opened by William Stukeley in August 1723. It contained
a cremation. (4) *Bush Barrow*, opened in September 1808 by Sir
Richard Colt Hoare, stands 2·4 m high and 14·6 m in diameter. 'On
reaching the floor of the barrow, we discovered the skeleton of a tall and
stout man, lying from south to north.' At his side were two bronze
daggers, one with a wooden hilt decorated with thousands of minute
gold pins. By his right hand was a smaller dagger, and near his leg was a
mace, its perforated head made from a rare fossil *coralline* rock, with a
wooden handle decorated with inlaid bone bands. An axe wrapped in
cloth lay by his shoulder whilst near his head was a wooden shield
decorated with bronze. No clothing had survived, but sewn onto some

Plate 67   Normanton Down barrow cemetery, Wiltshire

kind of tunic was a lozenge-shaped gold plate at his chest, and an engraved hook of hammered gold at his waist. (5) Due east lies a saucer-barrow which has been plundered. (6) Close to it is a bowl-barrow 27·4 m in diameter and 2·4 m high. It covered a skeleton accompanied by a grape-cup, amber, gold and shale beads (including one shaped like a double axe), fossil encrinites perhaps from the Frome region, and at its feet an elaborately decorated collared urn which perhaps contained food. (7) This is a bell-barrow 41·1 m in overall diameter and 3·1 m high containing a primary cremation that had been deposited with an incense cup 10·2 cm in diameter with slashed sides, a gold-plated shale cone almost 3·8 cm high, two gold-plated amber discs, a halberd pendant with an amber and gold handle, and various amber pendants. (8, 9, 10) There is no record of these three plundered bowl-barrows and none of them is now more than 0·9 m high. (11) At this point in the cemetery is a small long barrow, 19·8 m long and 2·7 m high. It was presumably the initial neolithic barrow around which the rest of the group spread. Colt Hoare examined it without result. (12) A 1·8 m high bowl barrow with an outer bank. Opened by Colt Hoare who found it unproductive. (13) This is a very fine disc-barrow, 67·1 m across, probably opened by Stukeley who found a cremation at its centre. (14) A small bowl-barrow. (15) An unusual twin bell-barrow, two mounds within a single ditch. At various times it has been dug by Stukeley, his patron Lord Pembroke, William Cunnington and Colt Hoare. The western mound covered a cremation buried with a bone belt-hook and pendant, the eastern contained a cremation with amber and shale beads and a small cup (now lost). The remainder of the group may be summarized briefly: (16) A bell-barrow opened without record. (17, 18) Bowl-barrows; 18 covered a skeleton with a bronze dagger. (19, 20) Two fine disc-barrows. (21, 22) Bowl-barrows. (23) Saucer-barrow. (24) A disc-barrow marks the end of the cemetery.

All the objects found at Normanton that have survived are in the Devizes Museum, with the exception of some of the gold which is on loan to the British Museum. Mention should also be made of two long barrows in the vicinity of the group. (25) To the south the green lane cuts the end of a long barrow 38·4 m long and 1·8 m high. Cunnington found four burials at the eastern end 'strangely huddled together'. (26) Near the A303 road is another long barrow 30·5 m in length and 1·8 m high. In it John Thurnam found three primary burials, two with cleft skulls.

L. V. Grinsell: *V.C.H. Wiltshire* I (1957) 196

35 OGBURY CAMP ENCLOSURE   Iron Age
     Durnford   167 (SU: 143383)
A minor road leads along the south side of the camp, north of Durnford.

This large heart-shaped camp is surrounded by a single rampart that encloses 25 ha, and a ditch that has been completely silted for at least 250 years. The bank has been damaged in a number of places making the positions of original entrances doubtful, though that on the east is usually considered to be ancient. Although the interior has been ploughed for many years aerial photographs show traces of internal field systems, probably later than the enclosure. William Stukeley, writing in 1724, describes 'many little banks, carried straight and meeting one another at right angles, square, oblong parallels and some oblique, as the meres and divisions between ploughed lands'. He also considered it to be a place where the inhabitants 'retired at night from the pasturage upon the river, with their cattle' rather than a defensive fort. This is a view that still holds good.

O. G. S. Crawford and A. Keiller: *Wessex from the Air* (1928) 150

36 OLD AND NEW KING BARROWS   Bronze Age
    Amesbury   167 (*New*: SU:135421; *Old*: SU:134426)
In woods north of the A303 (Amesbury by-pass) 2·4 km west of Amesbury.

Here are two groups, each of seven barrows, called by William Stukeley the Old and New King barrows. The New King group consists of five bowl- and two bell-barrows running in a line from south to north. Each averages 36·6 m in diameter and 3·1 m high. After a break in the wood through which passes the Stonehenge Avenue (not visible on the ground), the trees resume and the Old King group is reached. These are all bowl-barrows and are somewhat flatter in appearance averaging 1·2 m high. All the barrows have been dug into, but nothing is known of their contents, though the discovery is recorded 'by the Duke of Buckingham's digging, a bugle-horn tipped with silver at both ends, which his Grace kept in his closet as a great Relique'.

L. V. Grinsell: *V.C.H. Wiltshire* I (1957) 151

37 OLDBURY CASTLE HILLFORT (Plate 68)   Iron Age
    Calne   157 (SU:049693)
Footpath up the hill from the A4 opposite the Yatesbury turn at SU: 056703 (or from SU:041701).

Sited on the crest of the Cherhill Downs, 4·8 km west of Avebury and commanding wide views to north and south, this fort of 8 ha is strongly protected by a double rampart and ditches. The entrance on the eastern side is inturned, and that at the south-east may also be original. A low internal bank divides the camp into two parts. It seems to be later than the main fort. Excavation in the last century uncovered early Iron Age pottery in storage pits and on the surface. Much of the interior has suffered at the hands of 19th-century flint diggers.

Plate 68   Oldbury hillfort and White Horse, Wiltshire

The Cherhill White Horse was cut in 1780 by Dr. Christopher
Alsop, the so-called 'mad doctor' of Calne.

R. Colt Hoare: *Ancient Wiltshire* **2** (1819) 97

38 OLD SARUM   Iron Age, Roman, Medieval
       Stratford-sub-Castle   167 (SU: 137327)
*Beside the A345, 2·4 km north of Salisbury. Department of the Environ-
ment; open at standard hours. Car-park, guide-books, etc.*
Rising in tiers rather like a green wedding-cake beside the river Avon,
Old Sarum is best viewed from the west. Although today it is the
Norman Castle motte that dominates the scene, it is important to
realize that the site began life as an Iron Age hillfort. It is the outer
rampart and ditch of this structure that encircles the hill in a great oval
enclosing 11 ha. The entrance was on the east at the point where the
later Norman gate was built, and another may have existed on the
north-east (now obscured by later work). Excavations have demonstrated that the earthworks belong to the early Iron Age.

Old Sarum is generally accepted as the site of the Roman posting station of *Sorviodunum* and Roman pottery and a small Roman building were found inside the hillfort in 1909. It is more probable, however, that the main station lay to the south or west of Old Sarum.

P. A. Rhatz and J. W. Musty: *W.A.M.* **208** (1960) 353

39 OLIVER'S CASTLE HILLFORT   Iron Age
   Bromham   167 (SU:001646)

Footpath over the Downs from Roundway village or Bromham.

This promontory fort, a little over 1·2 ha in size, is protected by a single rampart and V-shaped ditch, 4·3 m deep. The defence is strongest on the east facing the open down, and is pierced on that side by an entrance, where excavations in 1907 revealed two holes for gate-posts on either side of the passageway. The same excavation produced pottery of the early Iron Age.

South-west of the camp are two round barrows, each about 9·1 m in diameter. The southern barrow is 0·5 m high and has produced a handled urn of Cornish type containing burnt bones and a riveted bronze dagger. The northern mound is 0·9 m high and covered a cist in which lay cremated bones, pieces of an incense cup and a conical bone button. On the south side of this barrow was a secondary cremation and three urns of probable late Bronze Age date.

L. V. Grinsell: *V.C.H. Wiltshire* I (1957) 162, 263

40 OVERTON HILL SEVEN BARROWS (See Fig. 24)   Bronze Age
   West Overton   157 (SU:119682)

On the east side of the Ridgeway as it crosses the A4 trunk road beside transport café.

Visitors looking for The Sanctuary at the end of the West Kennet Avenue are more likely to be impressed by the small barrow cemetery that lies beside the Ridgeway. This hill has been known locally for centuries as Seven Barrow Hill, but only six mounds survive today. One, south of the A4 and The Sanctuary, is a bowl-barrow 18·3 m in diameter and 3·7 m high. When opened by Colt Hoare it was found to contain a crouched skeleton with a flat bronze dagger and axe-head, and a crutch-headed pin of Germanic type, placed in a coffin made from a hollowed tree trunk.

The first barrow north of the A4 is a damaged bell-barrow more than 30·5 m across, opened by Colt Hoare who found a cremation and a 'very rude little cup, scratched over with the usual British pattern'. A second bell-barrow is 3·1 m high and contained a cremation. Between this mound and the next bell-barrow is a small bowl-barrow about

1·1 m high and 9·1 m in diameter. A cremation and bone pin were found in it. The third bell-barrow is 38·4 m in diameter with a mound 3·1 m high. It, too, covered a cremation, buried with a bronze dagger. A later cremation in an urn was also added to this mound. The second and third bell-barrows and intervening bowl-barrow have sometimes been described as a triple bell-barrow, their ditch seeming to surround all three mounds.

North-east of the last barrow is a bowl-barrow which covered a cremation. Further north along the Ridgeway are other barrows including a fine bell-barrow at SU:118692 and a good disc-barrow at SU:116689 close to the Avebury footpath.

L. V. Grinsell: *V.C.H. Wiltshire* 1 (1957) 195

41 PERTWOOD DOWN LONG BARROW   Neolithic
    Brixton Deverill   166 (ST:872374)

On the Down about 1·6 km east of Monkton Deverill (on B3095). Footpath passes close to west end.

Lying approximately south-east to north-east this long barrow is 76·2 m long and 1·8 m high at the south-eastern end. It is apparently unexcavated and is unusual in having a wide berm (or flat areas) between the mound and the well-preserved side ditches.

On *Cold Kitchen Hill* 2·4 km west, in the same parish, is a similar accessible long barrow (ST:847389) with side ditches. It is 70·1 m long and 3·7 m high at the south-eastern end.

L. V. Grinsell: *V.C.H. Wiltshire* 1 (1957) 139

42 RYBURY CAMP   Neolithic and Iron Age
    All Cannings   167 (SU:083640)

Footpath north uphill from All Cannings Cross Farm.

This small Iron Age fort of 1·4 ha has a single rampart and internal ditch, with traces of an unfinished rampart on the north. In 1930 E. C. Curwen suggested that the fort overlay a neolithic causewayed camp, traces of which can best be seen on the eastern side, outside the fort rampart. It was thought to consist of an inner and outer ring of causewayed ditch sections. The inner circle has been greatly mutilated by chalk digging. Recent excavations have supported this two-period theory, and the outer ditch has been shown to be neolithic, 2·1 m deep and flat-bottomed. There appears to be an outer line of causewayed ditch on Clifford's Hill 200 m to the south, but this, too, has been badly damaged by chalk digging.

D. J. Bonney: *W.A.M.* **59** (1964) 185

43 SCRATCHBURY CAMP HILLFORT   Iron Age
    Norton Bavant   166/167 (ST:912443)

Track from A36 to North Farm; steep climb at corner of wood.

Sited on the escarpment above the river Wylye with good views north-
west to Battlesbury camp. Scratchbury is irregular in shape, and its
single bank, ditch and counterscarp bank enclose about 15 ha. It has
original entrances facing along the main hill-spurs to the west, north-
east and east. The first two entrances are strong and oblique, whilst
the eastern is of the simple straight-through type. Aerial photographs
show a low bank and ditch running from the north-east entrance, to the
centre of the southern side. This may represent an earlier phase of the
fort, later enlarged to take in the land to the south-east. In the centre
is a small circular earthwork dated by excavation to about 250 B.C.

Two small barrows about 0·9 m high lie within the north-eastern
extremity of the fort, that on the east having produced a cremation
burial. In the south-west corner is a bowl-barrow 30·5 m in diameter
and 3·1 m high which was opened by Colt Hoare who found animal
bones and many burnt stones, but no burials. A fourth barrow on the
highest point of the hill at the centre of the fort is only 0·9 m high. It
produced a cremation with a small bronze dagger, a bronze pin, fifty
amber beads and a large amber ring.

The hills around the fort are terraced with strip lynchets.

O. G. S. Crawford; *Air Survey and Archaeology* (1924) 36

44 SILBURY HILL (See Fig. 24, Plate 69)   Neolithic
    Avebury   157 (SU:100685)

Beside the A4 between West Kennet and Beckhampton.

The great green 'plum-pudding' of Silbury Hill is in many ways the
most impressive and mysterious of England's prehistoric monuments.
The largest man-made prehistoric mound in Europe, it rises to a
height of 39·6 m and contains about 354,000 cubic metres of chalk. The
base of the mound covers 2·2 ha and its flat top, 30·5 m in diameter,
was once used for playing cricket.

A number of attempts have been made to explore the hill by
tunnelling from the top and sides. The latest of these was made
between 1968 and 1970 by Professor Richard Atkinson, following part
of the line of an earlier tunnel cut by Dean Merewether in 1849. This
involved driving a tunnel to the centre of the mound from the south
side. The hill has actually been built on a sloping spur of chalk, so that
the lowest 7·6 m of the mound are of solid natural chalk. Atkinson's
work has shown that Silbury was built in four phases, although its
purpose is still obscure.

Phase 1: The evidence suggests that a circular area about 19·8 m

Plate 69   Silbury Hill, Wiltshire

in diameter was surrounded by a low fence supported by widely spaced stakes. Within this a clay mound 4·9 m in diameter and 0·9 m high was constructed and covered with a heap of turf and soil that extended outwards to the fence. Over this four conical layers of gravel, chalk and subsoil were laid to complete the first mound about 34 m in diameter and 5·2 m high. The common centre of these structures was removed in 1776 when a shaft from the summit was driven into the mound. It is possible that a burial or other deposits might have been destroyed at that time.

Phase 2: Soon after the original construction the mound was enlarged by capping it with chalk quarried from an unfinished surrounding ditch about 21·3 m wide. The mound thus enlarged was 73·1 m across at the base.

Phase 3: Before the Phase 2 ditch was completed a change of plan occurred and the size of the mound was again increased. The unfinished ditch was buried under the new mound which is 158·5 m in diameter. This seems to have been built in a series of stages, producing the effect of a stepped cone. Each stage was built with a series of concentric buttressed retaining walls of chalk blocks, between which chalk rubble was piled that had been obtained from a surrounding ditch averaging 7 m deep. On its southern side this ditch measured 9·8 m deep and 26·8 m wide with a flat bottom 14 m across. The ditch sides had been protected with chalk rubble and timber shoring, presumably to counteract weathering and the slipping of the mound.

Phase 4: The last operation at Silbury seems to have been the digging of an extension of the main ditch to the west (almost to the filling station), presumably to obtain sufficient chalk to fill in the steps of the cone and to give the mound its present smooth profile. Only the topmost step seems to have been left unfilled, creating the noticeable ridge still visible today.

A revised radio-carbon reading for the building of the first mound suggests a date around 2500 B.C., and the whole construction was probably completed not long after that.

The purpose of Silbury remains a mystery. It has always been considered to be a great burial mound, but unless destroyed in the 18th century, no burial has been forthcoming. This could lie off-centre in a sarsen stone chamber, as in the great passage graves of western Britain, or it may be that its purpose was entirely different, and beyond our present comprehension. It was probably constructed at the same time as Avebury, and it could have had a religious or astronomical function. At all events, it will continue to be a subject of speculation for many years to come.

R. J. C. Atkinson: *Antiquity*: **44** (1970) 313

45 SMAY DOWN AND BOTLEY COPSE LONG BARROWS

Neolithic

Shalbourne   168 (SU:309593)

Beside lane east of Oxenwood, beyond cottage on left.

Skeletons are reputed to have been found in this long barrow which lies south-east to north-west. It is 48·8 m long and 1·8 m high at the south-east end.

In Botley Copse (SU:294599), 1·6 km north-east is a bigger long barrow 64 m in length and 3·1 m high at the southern end where there are signs of a robbers' pit. Just outside the wood and close to the long barrow is a fine disc-barrow 36·6 m in diameter. It was excavated by H. Peake and O. G. S. Crawford in 1910. Under the central mound, which had its own surrounding ditch, they found a cremation accompanied by a bronze awl and rivet. The barrow also contained a Saxon skeleton. A late ditch with bank to the north, cuts the north side of the barrow and runs on down the steep hill to the west.

L. V. Grinsell: *V.C.H. Wiltshire* **1** (1957) 218, under Grafton

46 SNAIL DOWN BARROW CEMETERY (Fig. 25, Plate 70)

Collingbourne Ducis and Kingston

Bronze Age
167 (SU:218522)

Approached by tracks leading south from A342. Edge of War Department land: observe red flags.

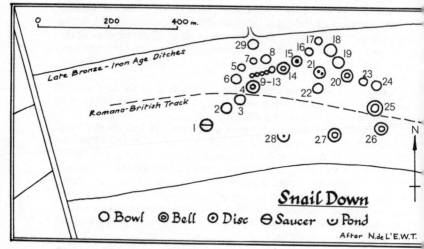

Fig. 25   Snail Down, Wiltshire

The great Bronze Age necropolis on Snail Down contained almost thirty burial mounds, a number of which have been unnecessarily destroyed by military training since 1945. Almost every barrow was dug into by Colt Hoare at the beginning of the 19th century, and most of them were again examined by Nicholas and Charles Thomas between 1953 and 1957. A careful study of the siting of the barrows and their contents has enabled Nicholas Thomas to demonstrate convincingly the growth sequence of the cemetery. Before the first burials were made a Beaker settlement existed on the downs, later to be covered by barrows 9 to 13. The first barrow to be built was probably number 23, and it can be dated to the end of the neolithic period. Shortly afterwards the row of small bowl-barrows 9 to 13, and two others were thrown up. Wessex barrows in a variety of forms: bowl, bell, disc and saucer were next added to the cemetery. One of them, a bell-barrow (4) has been dated by radio-carbon to 1540 ± 70 B.C. (uncorrected), and another double bell-barrow (25) has produced full Wessex culture material. Eventually in-filling took place (21) and additions were made to the north-west side of the group. Burials throughout the whole

Plate 70   Bell-barrows on Snail Down, Wiltshire, showing damage by tanks

cemetery were probably spread over some 200 years. Some considerable time later, at the end of the Bronze Age a Celtic field system spread around the barrows, and this in turn was cut into by V-shaped boundary ditches, seeming to indicate a change of ownership and a possible change from arable to stock rearing.

N. and C. Thomas: *W.A.M.* **56** (1959) 127

47   STONEHENGE (Figs. 26, 27; Plates 71, 72)

Neolithic and Bronze Age

Amesbury   167 (SU: 122422)

South of the A344. Department of the Environment and National Trust. Large car-park, souvenir stall, snack bar and toilets, on north side of road. Entry by sub-way. Open March to April 9.30 to 17.30 hours, May to September 9.30 to 19.00 hours, October 9.30 to 17.30 hours, November to February 9.30 to 16.00 hours. Sundays as for weekdays except October to February 14.00 hours opening time not 9.30 hours.

Henry of Huntingdon, writing in about A.D. 1130 describes Stonehenge as the second wonder of Britain 'where stones of an amazing size are set up in the manner of doorways, so that one door seems to be set upon another. Nor can anyone guess by what means so many stones were raised so high, or why they were built there.'

Though many questions still remain unanswered, excavations at intervals between 1901 and 1958 have gone a long way to explaining much of the mystery that is Stonehenge. As a structure it is unique, the fashioning of such great blocks of stone at so early a period in our

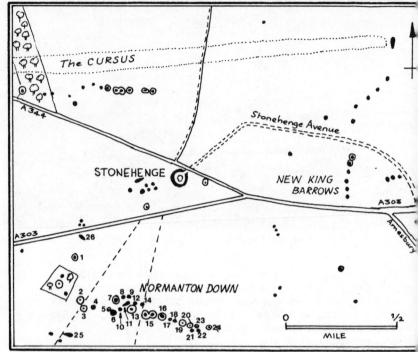

Fig. 26   The Stonehenge region, Wiltshire. Normanton Barrows, see page 332

history is a cause for constant amazement; but there is more to Stonehenge than the stones, and its history can best be divided into a number of periods.

Stonehenge 1: The outer area of the monument was marked by a low bank about 30·5 m outside the stones. It was originally about 1·8 m high and made of chalk quarried from an irregular ditch that lies immediately outside it. The bank is broken by an entrance gap on the north-east close to the isolated Heel Stone.

The Heel Stone is a block of unshaped sarsen standing 4·9 m high. It was probably the first stone erected on the site. There are traces of a circular ditch around its base. Inside the bank are a ring of fifty-six pits, marked today with white chalk, and varying in depth from 0·6 to 1·2 m. Known as the Aubrey Holes, their original purpose is obscure, though later some were used to hold cremation burials. All these features formed the first Stonehenge and can be dated to about 2600 B.C.

Stonehenge 2: About 500 years later the Beaker people made a number of changes to Stonehenge. From the entrance an avenue 12·2 m wide was marked out running for about 3·2 km to the banks of the Wiltshire Avon near West Amesbury. Its course is marked by two low banks and ditches. Today these soon disappear under arable land as they descend the hill to the north-east before turning east and then south-east. Next, about eighty blocks of spotted dolerite (blue-stone) originating in the Prescelly Mountains of Pembrokeshire were brought to Stonehenge, probably along the avenue. Each weighing about 4 metric tons (4 tons), they were dragged on sledges or rollers into the area, where they were shaped and partially set up in a double circle at the centre of the enclosure. It seems that the work was never completed for a gap was found in the stone holes of the circle on the western side.

Stonehenge 3a: Not long afterwards a major change occurred. The blue-stones were removed, and placed on one side. Great sarsen blocks averaging 26,417 kg (26 tons) each were brought from the Marlborough Downs 32 km to the north and erected in the circle and horseshoe still visible today. Each stone was carefully shaped, the uprights bulging

Plate 71   Stonehenge trilithons, Wiltshire

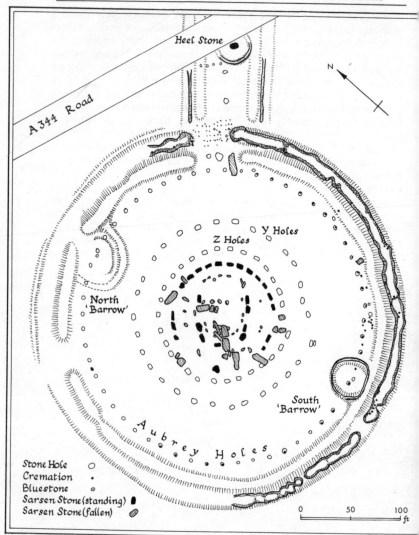

Fig. 27   Stonehenge, Wiltshire

Plate 72 Stonehenge from the air, Wiltshire

slightly in the middle to counteract the effect of perspective. The lintel stones across the top of the uprights were dovetailed into each other and morticed and tenoned to the uprights. The inner and outer faces of the lintels were also curved so that the complete ring is an almost perfect circle. The stones of the horseshoe setting are arranged in five groups of three, known as trilithons. The tallest upright stone in the group projects 6·7 m above ground level (a further 2·4 m are buried below ground) and weighs about 45,722 kg (45 tons). The refinements used in constructing this circle are truly remarkable; even more so when it is appreciated that native British craftsmen were creating a structure unique in Europe, probably 500 years before the earliest Mycenaean civilization of Greece began. It is also important to notice that the axis of the sarsen settings, like the blue-stones they replaced, points toward midsummer sunrise and midwinter sunset. On either side of the entrance at the end of the avenue large blocks of sarsen were set up to create a ceremonial gateway, perhaps through which the sun would enter the circle. One of these stones, the Slaughter Stone, though fallen, still survives.

Stonehenge 3b: It seems likely that the next move was to set up twenty of the dismantled blue-stones in an oval setting inside the sarsen horseshoe, and the rest of them in two circles outside the sarsen circle. Although the oval setting was probably completed, only the holes for the two circles were dug, (known to archaeologists as the Y and Z holes). For some reason the whole of this stage of the project was abandoned, and the oval setting was demolished.

Stonehenge 3c: By about 1800 B.C. the final modification of Stonehenge had taken place. The blue-stones were erected in the positions some of them retain today. A circle of about sixty ran between the sarsen horseshoe and circle, whilst a horseshoe of nineteen stones which increased in height towards the centre, stood inside the five trilithons. The tallest of the blue-stones, the so-called Altar Stone, was placed as an upright pillar about 3·7 m high, in front of the central sarsen trilithon. This final reconstruction must have taken place during the Middle Bronze Age.

Since that time the stones have suffered considerably from destruction by farmers, road builders and visitors, as well as the Romans who may well have made some attempt to deface what appeared to be an obnoxious shrine. It is probable that Stonehenge will for ever be connected in popular imagination with the Druids, a Celtic priesthood who flourished in Britain for about 300 years from around 250 B.C. The connection, however, is a recent one, and was founded by John Aubrey and popularized by William Stukeley in 1740. As we have seen, Stonehenge was more than 1,500 years old when the Druids first appeared in these islands, and was probably already falling in ruin. The modern so-called Druidical rites that take place at the monument are in the opinion of most archaeologists nothing more than a farce that should be discontinued before damage is done to the site

It has been observed that the central axis of Stonehenge is approximately aligned on the midsummer sunrise and midwinter sunset. This suggests that the site may have been used for a ceremony in which the ritual death and rebirth of the sun was acted out. In a more scientific vein the circle may have been used for fixing certain specific seasons of the year, although some of the complex recent theories suggesting that the site was a prehistoric computer are as wild and improbable as the modern Druids. It should be noticed that in fact the sun does *not* rise over the Heel Stone on 21 June and never has done. It has always risen some distance to the left, and will not rise exactly over the stone until about the 30th century A.D.

Some of the stones display weathered carvings of axe-heads and a dagger that can probably be dated to the early Bronze Age. The best example, a dagger, is best seen at about 5 p.m. in summer on the right-hand upright of the southern trilithon (stone number 53). Around it a number of carved axe-heads can be seen.

In 1915 Stonehenge was bought for £6,600 and presented to the nation by Mr. C. H. E. Chubb, although it has only recently been scheduled as an ancient monument.

R. J. C. Atkinson: *Stonehenge* (1960)

48 STONEHENGE CURSUS (See Fig. 26, p. 344)
                                                    Neolithic and Bronze Age
Amesbury   167 (SU:124430)

Approached along the track 0·8 km north of Stonehenge car park to Larkhill.

It was William Stukeley who discovered and named the Cursus, north of Stonehenge. This curious enclosure 2·8 km long and more than 91·4 m wide, is marked out by a low bank and a ditch which is 1·8 m wide and 0·6 to 0·9 m deep. The Cursus is clearly aligned on a long barrow which lies just beyond its eastern end, and is now badly damaged by ploughing and the trackway. When this was opened parts of the skeleton of a child were found. More than a score of these cursus monuments have been found in Britain, all clearly related to long barrows, and presumably connected with the funerary ritual. The great length of the Stonehenge example, (only the Dorset cursus is longer (page 83)) tends to increase its significance in this region. It was probably built about 2600 B.C.

Between the western end of the Cursus and the A344 are a line of barrows (SU:115428) which includes from east to west a bell-barrow, a twin bell-barrow, three more bell-barrows and a bowl-barrow. The western mound of the twin bell-barrow covered a cremation, whilst under the eastern Stukeley found the cremation of a young woman in an urn, accompanied by a flat bronze dagger, an awl, a gold-mounted amber disc, and faience, amber and shale beads. Most of the other barrows also covered cremations, some with beads of similar materials. All the existing finds are in Devizes Museum.

J. F. S. Stone: *Arch. J.* **104** (1947) 7

49 THORNY DOWN HABITATION SITE   Bronze Age
  Winterbourne   167 (SU:203339)

About 230 m north of the A30, opposite the turning to Winterslow.

Sheltered from the north by Thorny Down Wood this habitation site
stands on open downland and within sight of Figsbury Rings to the
west. At first all the visitor will observe is an uneven surface of low
banks and hollows, but with care an enclosure of less than 0·2 ha,
bounded by banks on the west and south, and a bank and ditch on the
north will be made out. Inside traces of at least nine huts have been
found which may have been circular or rectangular in plan. Storage
pits, cooking holes and holes for posts, perhaps for granaries or
corn-drying frames were excavated between 1937 and 1939. The
domestic pottery was predominantly of globular vessels of Deverel–
Rimbury type dated to about 1100 B.C.

J. F. S. Stone: *P.P.S.* 7 (1941) 114

50 TIDCOMBE LONG BARROW   Neolithic
  Tidcombe   168 (SU:292576)

Beside the road from Chute to Oxenwood.

This long barrow stands proudly on the hillside at right-angles to the
road. It is 56·4 m long and 3·1 m high at the southern end where four
sarsens in a hollow mark the remains of a burial chamber. When it was
dug in 1750 by local folk searching for treasure a skeleton was found in
the chamber. The whole barrow has been badly damaged by a longitudinal trench that was dug along it at some time in the past.

  A ditch and bank a few metres to the east may represent an Iron Age
cross-dyke.

L. V. Grinsell: *V.C.H. Wiltshire* 1 (1957) 144

51 TILSHEAD OLD DITCH LONG BARROW   Neolithic
  Tilshead   167 (SU:023468)

*War Department land (access only at special times) but clearly visible from
Tilshead to Chitterne road at SU:021475.*

Although being damaged by the Army's customary disregard for
antiquities this has been described by Leslie Grinsell as 'probably the
largest true long barrow in England'. It is 118·9 m long, 30·5 m wide
and 3·4 m high at the eastern end. It has very large side ditches. Both
William Cunnington (1802) and John Thurnam (1865) dug into the
barrow, where they found two burials at the eastern end. These represented a partially burnt man, and the flexed skeleton of a small woman
with a cleft skull. The man's remains lay on a mound of flints and
ashes, suggesting a funeral pyre, whilst a cairn of flints covered both
burials. At the other end of the barrow three further skeletons were

found beside a pit dug into the solid chalk below the mound. Whether they were a subsidiary or subsequent burial is unknown.

The *Tilshead Lodge long barrow* (SU:021475) beside the Tilshead to Chitterne road, also covered two human skeletons, one with a cleft skull, and the carcases of two slaughtered oxen. This barrow is 51·8 m long and 1·5 m high at the eastern end.

L. V. Grinsell: *V.C.H. Wiltshire* 1 (1957) 144

52 TILSHEAD WHITE BARROW   Neolithic
   Tilshead   167 (SU:033468)

National Trust property accessible along a track from the A360.

One of the many probable Bronze Age boundary ditches that wind across Salisbury Plain skirts round the White Barrow which is 77·7 m long, 45·7 m wide and 2·1 m high at the eastern end. It has well-defined side ditches from which a core of turves were first removed to make the spine of the barrow before it was covered with white chalk from deeper in the ditches which gave it its name. As long ago as 1348 it was known as *Whitebergh*. When it was dug by Colt Hoare and William Cunnington only a piece of antler was found.

L. V. Grinsell: *V.C.H. Wiltshire* 1 (1957) 144

53 UPTON GREAT BARROW   Bronze Age
   Upton Lovell   167 (ST:955423)

East of track 1·6 km north of Upton Folly on the A36 road, or 0·8 km south from Ansty Hill on the A344 road.

Sited on the crest of the Downs above the Wylye valley, this important bell-barrow, 53 m in diameter and 3·1 m high, once displayed an outer bank which is no longer clearly visible. Opened by William Cunnington and Richard Colt Hoare in 1801, it produced a primary cremation burial with a necklace of amber, shale and faience beads 'such as a British female would not in these modern days of good taste and disdain elegance to wear'.

The *Golden Barrow* which lay south of Upton Lovell (ST:944401) is now destroyed. The gold objects that were found in it are on loan to the British Museum. The rest of the material from both the Upton Lovell barrows is in Devizes Museum.

L. V. Grinsell: *V.C.H. Wiltshire* 1 (1957) 215

Plate 73   West Kennet long barrow façade, Wiltshire

54 WEST KENNET LONG BARROW (Fig. 28, Plate 73)   Neolithic
     Avebury   157 (SU: 104677)

*Clearly signposted south from the A4, 0·4 km east of Silbury Hill. Torch
required. Guide pamphlet available at Avebury. Department of the
Environment. Access at any time.*

The long climb uphill to this impressive long barrow is one of the most
rewarding in England. At the end of the pilgrimage is a grass-covered
mound of chalk, lying over a core of boulders, 100·6 m long and 2·4 m
high. Tucked into the eastern end is an accessible burial chamber,
12·2 m long, and high enough to walk into without stooping.

The barrow was badly damaged in the 17th century and it is recorded
that in 1685 a certain Dr. Troope of Marlborough came to the tomb to
dig for human bones 'and stored myself with many bushells, of which
I made a noble medicine that relieved many of my distressed neighbours'! It was partially excavated by John Thurnam in 1859, who
cleared the west chamber and 4·6 m of the passage. In the chamber he
found the burials of five male adults and a child, together with pieces
of neolithic Peterborough ware and beaker pottery.

In 1955–6 Stuart Piggott and Richard Atkinson completed the work
begun by Thurnam, and in doing so uncovered four intact burial
chambers that he had missed. Following their excavation the barrow
was restored to its present appearance.

The mound is composed of chalk from the large quarry ditches
3·1 m deep and 6·1 m wide, that lie on either side of the long barrow.
Both are now completely silted up and ploughed over. The edge of the
mound was originally marked by boulders but these have all long since
disappeared.

At the eastern end of the barrow is the façade of large upright sarsen
stones, probably dragged to the site from the Downs 1·6 km to the
south-east. In the centre of the façade, hidden behind the great central
blocking slab, is a semi-circular forecourt, out of which the burial
chamber opens. This takes the form of a roofed passage running down
the centre of the barrow, with two burial chambers opening off each
side. The gaps between the large sarsen wall stones are filled with dry-
stone walling. The roof of each side chamber is roughly corbelled and
then completed with a large capstone as much as 2·3 m above the floor,
and weighing many tons. All the side chambers contained odd bones.
In addition the north-east chamber held three more or less complete
adult burials, one man and two women, and a leaf-shaped arrow-head
close to the man's neck. The south-east chamber held a single male and
female burial as well as the remains of five infants and four babies. The
south-west and north-west chambers were smaller than the others,
with lower capstones. That on the north-west contained a mass of
disarticulated bones that seem to represent about twelve adults, whilst

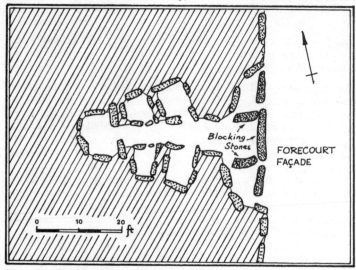

Fig. 28   The West Kennet long barrow, Wiltshire

the south-west transept had contained at least nine adults, a youth, a
child and two infants. From this it is clear that at least forty-six
individuals were buried in the tomb. How many more were removed by
Dr. Troope we shall never know. After the burial ceremonies were
finally completed the passage and chambers were filled to the roof with
chalk rubble, earth and lumps of sarsen. Throughout was a scatter of
animal bones, flints, pottery, bone tools and beads. The pottery of
Peterborough, grooved and beaker types, was in use for hundreds of
years and this suggests that the long barrow was also used for communal burial for a very long period, perhaps 1,000 years, like some
Christian cathedrals. The scatter of objects and pottery may represent
funeral gifts brought to the tomb or a nearby mortuary temple at
intervals during this time, and eventually collected together and
deposited in the burial chambers. After this the great blocking stone
3·7 m high was placed across the façade, sealing it off for ever.

On the entrance stone of the south-west chamber are two or three
areas worn smooth by the polishing of stone axes. Perhaps this was
done during the construction of the burial chambers, when timber
rollers would have been needed for moving the stones. Objects from
the 1859 and recent excavations, together with models and photographs, are well displayed in the museum at Devizes.

Stuart Piggott: *The West Kennet Long Barrow Excavations 1955–6*
(1962)

55 WHITE SHEET CASTLE HILLFORT   Iron Age
   Stourton   166 (ST:804346)

From the B3092 beside the 'Red Lion' along Long Lane. Park cars in
disused quarry at foot of hill. Walk of 1·6 km. Observe red military flags.

This roughly triangular fort is defended by a single rampart and ditch
on its south and west sides where the escarpment falls steeply on the
western edge of Salisbury Plain. On the north and east, however, where
the flat plateau top increases the need for defence three banks and
ditches are present. There are a number of gaps on this side, and not
all of them can be original entrances.

   0·4 km north is a cross-dyke facing north, whose ends run down the
hillslopes and eventually disappear.

R. Colt Hoare: *Ancient Wiltshire* I (1812) 43

56 WHITE SHEET HILL CAUSEWAYED CAMP   Neolithic
   Kilmington   166 (ST:802352)

Access via Long Lane from the B3092 near the 'Red Lion'. Sited at the
bend of the Lane on the western spur of the hill. Not to be confused with the
neighbouring hillfort (No. 55)

This small causewayed camp encloses 1·6 ha. First recognized by
L. V. Grinsell in 1950 it consists of an oval enclosure defined by a
rampart and outer ditch, the latter interrupted by twenty-one causeways of undug chalk. Trial excavations by Stuart Piggott and J. F. S.
Stone in 1951 confirmed that the site was of neolithic date and that its
ditch reached a width of 3·1 m and depths varying from 0·3 to 1·2 m.

   A large Bronze Age bowl-barrow 2·4 m high overlies the ditch of the
earthwork on the south-east side. When Colt Hoare dug into it in 1807
he found a skeleton, but observed that it had been previously opened.
A second barrow, 0·9 m high, lies to the south-west of the earthwork.
It contained a cremation.

S. Piggott: *W.A.M.* **54** (1952) 404

57 WHITE SHEET LONG BARROW AND DYKE
                                         Neolithic and Iron Age
   Ansty   167 (ST:942242)

Beside the Ridgeway over the downs from the A30.

This grass-covered long barrow, oblong in shape with clear side ditches,
measures 41·1 m long and 22·9 m wide. It is about 1·8 m high at its
eastern end, and nothing is known of its contents.

   0·4 km further east is a cross-dyke (ST:947244) 430 m long running
across the ridge from the escarpment on the north to the south. The
ditch is 7·6 m wide and 1·5 m deep, with a large flat-topped bank
9·1 m wide and 1·2 m high on the west, and a smaller example, only

0·6 m high, to the east. Yet more dykes cut off spurs to the south of Swallowcliffe Down 2 km to the east.

Dykes: P. J. Fowler: *W.A.M.* **59** (1964) 46

58 WILSFORD BARROW CEMETERY   Bronze Age
       Wilsford   167 (SU: 118398)

In a wood on the east of the green lane from Stonehenge, south to Spring-bottom Farm and Lake.

In spite of their important contents, this group of barrows has been very badly damaged in recent years. Originally it contained at least seventeen barrows, nine of bowl-type, five discs, a pond-, saucer- and bell-barrow. Half a dozen bowl-barrows survive, but there is only one overgrown disc-barrow on the south side of the group. Unfortunately there is no record of its contents. At the western end is a tall bell-barrow 3·4 m high and 45·7 m in diameter. This held the skeleton of a tall man, lying on its right side and holding a dolerite battle axe-head, a bone musical instrument, and the handle and hanging chain of a bronze cauldron dated to about 1100 B.C. Objects from this and the other barrows are displayed in Devizes Museum.

L. V. Grinsell: *V.C.H. Wiltshire* **1** (1957) 199

59 WINDMILL HILL CAUSEWAYED CAMP (See Fig. 24, page 315,
       Plate 74)   Neolithic
       Winterborne Monkton   157 (SU: 087714)

2·4 km due north of Beckhampton roundabout on A4, via minor road from Avebury Trusloe, or from the A361 at East Farm. National Trust property. Access at all times.

This rounded hill to the north of Avebury has given its name to the earliest neolithic culture recognized in England. Around its summit three approximately concentric rings of causewayed ditches form the largest neolithic camp yet found. It has an area of 8·5 ha, and its outer ditch has a diameter of 365·8 m. The mean diameter of the middle ditch is 201·1 m and the inner one measures about 85 m. The ditches do not lie precisely around the summit, but tend to droop down the steeper northern side.

Extensive excavations in the 1920s soon indicated that the ditches were all interrupted by numerous gaps or causeways varying between a few centimetres and 7·6 m, though none of them seemed to be formal entrances. The ditch sections are very irregular, and apart from flattish bottoms they have few other common features. The inner circle of ditches are the shallowest averaging 1·1 m in depth, whilst the outer ditch averaged 2·6 m in depth. The excavators considered that the work had been carried out by gangs of workmen, thus accounting for

Plate 74   Windmill Hill causewayed camp, Wiltshire

the irregularity. The ditches served as quarries for inner banks, now almost entirely ploughed away, though a section can just be seen on the eastern side of the outer circle. More than 1,300 neolithic pottery vessels were identified from the site, the bulk of them being of Windmill Hill type. Some pots had been brought to the hilltop from as far away as Devon and Cornwall, according to an analysis of their fabric. The pottery, together with wood ashes and flint and stone objects from various parts of western Britain, were found in the silting of the ditches. Broken animal bones were also found there, apparently having been carefully buried. A radio-carbon date of 2570 ± 150 B.C. indicates on correction that the site was in use about 3350 B.C.

The function of the causewayed camps found in Britain has long been questioned. That they were not 'camps' in a civil or military sense now seems certain. More probably they were centres for tribal ceremonies connected with the social and economic well-being of the local population, in which trade and barter also played a part, as in the religious fairs of medieval times. Ceremonies taking place at the camps required the throwing of objects into the ditches, and their deliberate burial by pushing some part of the inner bank over them, soon after the initial construction. This process took place a number of times until the banks had been almost completely removed.

There is a fine bell-barrow in the middle ditch enclosure on Windmill Hill called *Picket Barrow*. It is 24·4 m in diameter and 2·4 m high. Its ditch was cleared in 1939 and a number of stone axes were found in it. A burrowing rabbit also disturbed a Bronze Age cremation urn on the summit of the mound. There are a number of barrows on the hillside, although only one other occurs within the causewayed camp.

I. F. Smith: *Windmill Hill and Avebury* (1965)

60 WINKLEBURY HILL   Iron Age
    Berwick St. John   167 (ST:952218)
Above Berwick St. John. A track runs along the hilltop from north to south.

Winklebury occupies the northern 5 ha of a steep-sided promontory, whose edges are defended by a single rampart and ditch. The neck of the spur is cut off by two straight stretches of rampart and ditch, set obliquely to each other with an entrance between. Midway along the interior of the fort is a slighter, curved line of defence running from east to west, with an entrance gap towards the eastern end. Close study of the earthworks by Richard Feachem has shown that they represent three stages of construction, and each apparently unfinished. He considers that the two straight ditches across the spur that are irregular in height and appearance represent the first construction by a gang of labourers. Later a defence around the crest of the spur was begun, but again not completed. Dumps of material can still be observed lying within the rampart line. The final attempt was to construct the smaller circular enclosure at the tip of the spur. There is an entrance at the north, carrying a farm track.

Excavations by Pitt-Rivers in 1881–2 recognized two periods of construction, one with storage pits belonging to the early Iron Age, and another to the Belgic period when additional defences were commenced.

R. W. Feachem in Jesson and Hill: *The Iron Age and its Hill-Forts* (1971) 32

61 WINTERBOURNE STOKE BARROW CEMETERY (Fig. 29)
                                               Neolithic and Bronze Age
    Winterbourne Stoke and Wilsford   167 (SU:101417)
North-east of the roundabout at the junction of the A303 and A360. Barrows 2 to 10 are the property of the National Trust.

This is probably the most accessible of all the barrow cemeteries in Wiltshire. Round barrows of all types stretch north-eastwards in two

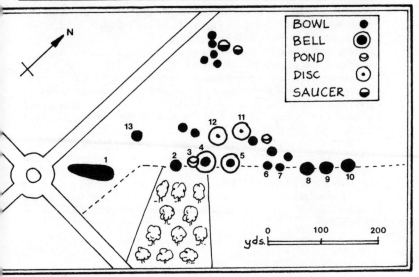

Fig. 29 Winterbourne Stoke barrow cemetery, Wiltshire

lines from the neolithic long barrow beside the roundabout. The long
barrow (1) is well-preserved, with marked side ditches. It is 73 m long
and 3·1 m high at the higher north-eastern end. After four attempts
John Thurnam found a primary male burial and an unusual flint
implement near the higher end. There were also six secondary burials,
a man, woman and four children, together with a food vessel. A number
of small post holes around the primary burial may have supported a
mortuary hut.

Along the north-western edge of the wood are (from the south-west),
(2) a low bowl-barrow, 22·9 m across, which contained a cremation.
Then a modern pond, with beyond (3) a pond-barrow measuring 11 m
across the hollow interior. It overlaps a bell-barrow and is therefore
later than it. (4) The bell-barrow is a particularly fine example, 54·8 m
in diameter with a central mound 3·7 m high. Colt Hoare, who opened
it, found traces of a wooden box with bronze fittings, that held a
cremation, two bronze daggers, a bone pin and tweezers. To the north-
east is a second bell-barrow (5), the King Barrow, about 48·8 m across,
in which Colt Hoare uncovered a skeleton in a tree-trunk coffin, with
an urn of Breton type with five handles, two bronze daggers and a
bronze awl with a bone handle. A mass of fossilized wood resembling
twigs found above the coffin, might represent a funeral wreath. Five
bowl-barrows occur next. (6) is 1·8 m high and held a cremation

beneath a mound of flints. There is no record of the contents of (7).
(8) is 24·4 m across and 1·5 m high. Built for a primary burial, it was
disturbed when a secondary cremation was added to the mound.
Amongst the objects found were a grape-cup and an incense cup, two
whetstones, a bronze pin and a beaver's tooth. Also in the barrow
mound were the bones of a dog and a deer. Bowl-barrow (9) is 27·4 m
in diameter. Colt Hoare found a boat-shaped wooden coffin containing
a skeleton, some shale and amber beads, a bronze dagger and awl and
a small pottery cup. The last of the bowl-barrows in the row (10)
covered two skeletons and a long-necked beaker.

North of the two bell-barrows (4) and (5) are two fine disc-barrows.
The northernmost (11) is 53·3 m across and has three small burial
mounds inside the enclosing ditch. Like so many other Wiltshire
barrows it was dug by Colt Hoare who found cremations in each of the
tumps. Also under the central one was a small cup and some amber
beads. The southern disc (12) is similar in size and was built to cover
a cremation.

L. V. Grinsell: *V.C.H. Wiltshire* 1 (1957) 201

62 WOODHENGE TIMBER CIRCLE   Neolithic
       Amesbury   167 (SU:150434)

On road to Larkhill, to the west of the A345, 1·6 km north of Amesbury.
Department of the Environment. Access at any time.

Lying 91 m north of the great henge monument of Durrington Walls,
which contained at least two timber circles, now under the main road,
Woodhenge should probably be seen as part of the same complex.
Discovered by aerial photography in 1925 and subsequently excavated
by the Cunningtons, it was shown to consist of six concentric ovals of
posts, enclosed by an irregular circular ditch 1·8 to 2·1 m deep and
3·7 to 4·9 m wide. At the north-east was an entrance causeway 10·7 m
wide, whilst outside the ditch was a wide, low bank of earth. The
positions of the internal wooden posts are indicated by concrete
markers. At the centre of the structure was the grave of an infant about
three years old, who had died from a blow on the skull. The position of
the grave is marked by a cairn of flints. Grooved-ware pottery from the
site indicates that it is broadly contemporary with Durrington Walls.

Timber circles, such as Woodhenge, were probably roofed buildings,
used for religious purposes, the precise nature of which remains obscure. They may have had a central court, open to the sky. If this is the
case there may have been a connection with the observation of the sun
or moon. Alternatively, Woodhenge may, as was originally suggested,
have consisted of free-standing circles of posts, some, perhaps, with
wooden lintels, looking, as its name suggests, like a timber version of

Stonehenge. Or again, the posts standing alone, carved and painted like totem poles, might be considered.

M. E. Cunnington: *Woodhenge* (1929)

63 YARNBURY CASTLE   Iron Age
   Steeple Langford   167 (SU:035404)

North of the A303, 3·2 km west of Winterbourne Stoke. Modern farm track runs into site on south side.

At the northern end of a dry valley above the river Wylye, this fine plateau fort encloses some 11 ha. It is surrounded by two banks, the inner 7·6 m high, and two ditches, as well as an outer counterscarp bank. The inside of the inner bank on the south is pitted with what appear to be quarry scoops. On the west is a strongly inturned entrance, 9·1 m wide, with an elaborate system of outworks, which direct the entrance passage south and east. A kidney-shaped enclosure is incorporated, perhaps to hold stock. All the other entrance gaps are probably modern. These earthworks have been dated to the 1st century B.C. and the Belgic Iron Age.

Inside the fort are traces of a small circular 3·6 ha enclosure, defended by a V-shaped ditch 2·7 m deep, with an entrance on its western side which excavations showed was closed by a wooden gate. This was dated to the early Iron Age and was apparently the first settlement on the site. Added to the western side of the main fort is a triangular enclosure of Roman date. This was perhaps a cattle kraal or sheepfold.

From the 18th century until 1916 an annual sheep fair was held inside Yarnbury. The sheep pens have left rectangular ridge-traces on the eastern side of the central enclosure.

C. F. C. Hawkes: *Arch. J.* **104** (1947) 29

Museums containing archaeological material

Alexander Keiller Museum, Avebury, Wiltshire
Devizes Museum,* Long Street, Devizes
Salisbury and South Wiltshire Museum,* St. Ann Street, Salisbury
Museum and Art Gallery, Bath Road, Swindon

* Main county collections. After the British Museum, Devizes Museum contains the finest British archaeological collection in England

1 BREDON HILL (Plate 75)   Iron Age
  Bredon's Norton   144 (SO:958402)
Steep climb south from Great Comberton, or 2·4 km north from Kemerton.

Plate 75   Bredon Hill hillfort, Worcestershire

This magnificent, isolated hill, almost 305 m (1,000 ft) high, and immortalized by A. E. Housman's poem, *A Shropshire Lad*, is crowned at its north-western extremity by a promontory fort enclosing 8·9 ha. At its foot, 2 km to the north-west flows the river Avon, meandering through the orchards of Evesham vale. The camp is roughly square in shape, with precipitous slopes on the north and west. On the gentle east and south slopes the hill is protected by two widely spaced lines of rampart and ditch, running from escarpment to escarpment.

Excavation in the 1930s showed the inner rampart and ditch to be the earliest part of the fort. The rampart is still 2·4 to 3·1 m high and 10·7 m wide, and is constructed of dumped clay without stone or wood revetting. The excavated ditch, dug into the solid limestone, averaged 2·4 m deep and 9·1 m wide. At the south-east corner is a diagonal passage way created by overlapping ditch ends. The position of the actual gate was not discovered. A somewhat irregular rectangular hut lay behind the rampart, together with a bronze smelting floor. Pottery from the hut and rampart is of a type made in the Malvern Hills, and may be dated as early as the 4th or 3rd century B.C.

Perhaps as late as the 1st century B.C. the hillfort was remodelled by constructing the outer bank and ditch 76·2 m outside the inner defence. The rampart still stands 1·8 to 2·4 m high and has a ditch 8·2 m wide and 1·8 m deep. The rampart is faced with an outer dry-stone wall and had a broad berm separating it from its ditch. Two entrances were provided at the east and north ends close to the escarpment (and partly destroyed by landslides). At these points the ends of the outer bank were bent backwards to form narrow passages 42·7 m long. The inner ditch was recut with a V-shaped profile, and the original entrance was remodelled as a corridor 30·5 m long and 7·6 m wide, with stone walls on either side, and probably a bridge over the top and double gates at the inner end. This is the entrance that can be seen today.

Early in the 1st century A.D. the fort was attacked, the inner gateway was burned down bringing with it a number of human skulls, probably trophies, that had been set on poles above it. Inside and outside the gate lay the hacked remains of about fifty individuals, mostly young men. Here we have clear evidence of a last stand by the inhabitants. Who the attackers were is not known. It probably happened before the arrival of the Romans and might represent a Belgic war party from the south-east, or a fierce localized skirmish. The objects found in the excavations are in a private museum at Overbury Court.

T. C. Hencken: *Arch. J.* **95** (1938) 1

2 CONDERTON CAMP (Plate 76)   Iron Age
   Conderton   144 (SO:972384)

A minor road and trackway lead to the foot of the hill from Conderton. This small 1·2 ha fort lies on a south-facing spur of Bredon Hill and may have been an outpost of the larger fort to the north-east (No. 1). A single bank and V-shaped ditch surround an oval area and have been shown by excavation to represent the earliest feature on the site. Entrances pierced the defences at the north and south. This phase, probably representing a cattle enclosure, may be dated to the 4th or 3rd century B.C. In the 1st century B.C. the area of the fort was reduced by building a dry-stone wall across the lower part of the fort and excluding 0·4 ha of the original work. The new wall was not accompanied by a ditch, but presumably obtained its material by demolishing the earlier wall to the south. A walled inturned entrance with double gates half-way along its passage was then erected in the middle of the new fort wall. The northern entrance was also redesigned with an inturned plan.

Plate 76   Reconstruction of Conderton Camp hut, Worcestershire

Circular stone huts were built inside the fort, creating a village of at
least a dozen houses, accompanied by elaborate and often stone-lined
storage pits. (A reconstruction of huts from Conderton Camp can be
seen at the Avoncroft Museum, Stoke Prior, near Bromsgrove
(Worcestershire). It is open at weekends during the summer.) At some
stage the northern entrance was completely blocked off with walling,
probably because the higher ground to the north commanded it and
afforded a tactical weakness. Occupation seems to have come to an end
prior to the Roman conquest. Field systems probably connected with
the fort can be seen in the bottom of the adjacent valley to the east.

3   GADBURY BANK   Iron Age
  Eldersfield   143 (SJ:793316)
Immediately east of the B4208 between Eldersfield and Pendock.
Although covering some 4 ha this isolated fort is protected only by a
single rampart and ditch, the latter reduced to little more than a ledge.
There is an inturned entrance at the north-east which may be original.
That side of the hilltop is wooded.

4 GARMSLEY CAMP HILLFORT   Iron Age
   Stoke Bliss   130 (SO:620618)

Beside a footpath from the B4214 at Bank Street westwards to Sallings Common.

Situated on a west-facing spur, with woods on the lower slopes, this is an oval-shaped fort of about 3·6 ha. A single rampart, ditch and counter-scarp bank surround it on all sides. The rampart is particularly strong where it faces the uphill slope to the west. There is an inturned entrance in this side, and what appears to have been another, also inturned, on the north-east.

5 WOODBURY HILL   Iron Age
   Great Witley   130 (SO:749645)

Immediately west of the B4197. Footpath from Lippetts Farm.

Completely covered by woodland, this figure-of-eight shaped fort covers 10·5 ha. It is surrounded by a strong rampart, ditch and counterscarp bank, best seen on the south and north-west. At the latter point there seems to be an original entrance. The bank ends curve inwards for a considerable distance.

6 WYCHBURY HILL CAMP   Iron Age
   Hagley   131 (SO:920818)

Track north from A456 at SO:925813.

Situated on a westward-looking spur of the Clent Hills, the steepness of which adds to the defence of this 3·2 ha fort. Triangular in shape, it is protected by two banks and a counterscarp bank on the south and a single slight bank on the steep northern side. Entrances at the east and west corners are strongly inturned. From the west entrance a bank and ditch flanks either side of a causeway that runs south for 91 m, until it is joined by another bank and ditch running north-east to join the main fort near its eastern entrance. In this way an extension is created on the south of the fort that may have acted as a cattle pound of slightly later Iron Age date.

Museums containing archaeological material

Museum and Art Gallery, St. James's Road, Dudley
Almonry Museum, Vine Street, Evesham
The Museum, Market Street, Kidderminster
Worcestershire County Museum, Hartlebury Castle, Hartlebury
City Museum and Art Gallery, Foregate Street, Worcester
Avoncroft Museum of Buildings, Stoke Prior, near Bromsgrove

   The City Museum and Art Gallery, Congreve Street, Birmingham, also contains material from Worcestershire sites

Abbreviations

Ant. J.   Antiquaries' Journal
Arch. Cantiana   Archaeologia Cantiana (Kent Archaeological Society)
Arch. J.   Archaeological Journal
Berks. A.J.   Berkshire Archaeological Journal
D. of E. pamphlet   Department of the Environment guide pamphlet.
J. Anthrop. Inst.   Journal of the Anthropological Institute
J. Brit. Archaeol. Assn.   Journal of the British Archaeological Association
J.R.S.   Journal of Roman Studies
J. R. Inst. Cornwall   Journal of Royal Institution of Cornwall
Oxoniensia   Oxford Architectural and Historical Society
P. Cambs. Ant. Soc.   Proceedings of the Cambridge Antiquarian Society
P.D.A.E.S.   Proceedings of the Devon Archaeological Exploration Society
Proc. Devon Arch. Soc.   Proceedings of the Devon Archaeological Society
Proc. Dorset N.H.A.S.   Proceedings of the Dorset Archaeological and Natural History Society
P. Hants F.C.   Proceedings of the Hampshire Field Club
P.I.W.N.H.S.   Proceedings of the Isle of Wight Natural History Society
P.P.S.   Proceedings of the Prehistoric Society
P.P.S.E.A.   Proceedings of the Prehistoric Society of East Anglia
P.S.A.L.   Proceedings of the Society of Antiquaries of London
P. Somerset A.S.   Proceedings of the Somerset Archaeological Society
P. Suffolk Arch. Inst.   Proceedings of the Suffolk Archaeological Institute
P.U.B.S.S.   Proceedings of the University of Bristol Spelaeological Society
Records of Bucks.   Records of Buckinghamshire
R.C.H.M.   Royal Commission on Historical Monuments (various counties)
Report Royal Inst. Cornwall   Report Royal Institution of Cornwall
Surrey A.C.   Surrey Archaeological Collections
Surrey Arch. Soc. Report   Surrey Archaeological Society Report
Sussex A.C.   Sussex Archaeological Collections
Trans. Birmingham A.S.   Transactions of Birmingham Archaeological Society
T.B.G.A.S.   Transactions of the Bristol and Gloucester Archaeological Society
Trans. Devon. Assn.   Transactions of the Devonshire Association
T.L.M.A.S.   Transactions of the London and Middlesex Archaeological Society

Trans. Newbury and District Field Club   *Transactions of the Newbury and District Field Club*

T. Woolhope Club   *Transactions of the Woolhope Club* (Herefordshire)

V.C.H.   *Victoria County History* (various counties)

W.A.M.   *Wiltshire Archaeological and Natural History Magazine*

Index to Sites

General Index

Alfred, King, 16–17, 57
Arthur, King, 176, 257
Atkins, Martin, 11, 14
Atkinson, R. J. C., xi, 18, 339–41, 353
Atrebates, xxiv, xxvi, 16, 166, 280, 281
Aubrey, John, 315, 344, 348
axe manufacture (stone), xvi, xvii, 33, 37, 221–3, 276, 280, 281, 284, 291, 306, 329

barrows:
  bank, 95, 96, 101
  bell-, 1, 11, 13, 30, 33, 63, 79, 80, 81, 85, 97–9, 100–1, 102, 160, 161, 164, 169, 191, 194, 196, 217, 224, 227, 252, 267, 268, 270, 274, 283, 284, 285, 313, 314, 328, 332, 335, 337, 342, 349, 351, 356, 358, 359
  chambered, xvi–xvii, xxvii, 17, 38, 41, 43, 45, 51, 54, 60, 69, 75, 86, 88, 114, 115, 123, 124, 125, 127, 128, 134, 135, 136, 137, 139, 140, 141, 171, 199, 202, 206, 216, 235, 236, 239, 240, 245, 253, 259, 313, 322, 323, 325, 329, 330, 353
  disc-, 11, 13, 80, 85, 98–9, 100–1, 155, 158, 160, 164, 165, 191, 194, 224, 227, 321, 326, 328, 332, 341, 342, 360
  earthen long, xvi, 8, 12, 17, 84, 86, 88, 97, 100, 101, 104, 105, 106, 134, 152, 154, 155, 157, 159, 183, 191, 195, 205, 218, 227, 275, 282, 295, 296, 297, 303, 306, 326, 332, 338, 341, 350, 351, 355, 359
  Roman, xxv, 9, 25, 29, 107, 112, 113, 144, 183, 188, 190, 200, 205, 313
  round, xx, xxviii, xxxi, xxxii, 1,

6, 11, 13, 14, 21, 23, 26, 29, 30, 33, 35, 40, 45, 46, 50, 53, 54, 55, 56, 57, 59, 61, 63, 65, 70, 71, 73, 75, 76, 77, 78, 79, 81, 82, 83, 85, 92, 100, 102, 104, 107, 123, 128, 129, 134, 147, 155, 156, 160, 161, 164, 165, 168, 169, 183, 191, 194, 195, 196, 204, 205, 214, 216, 217, 218, 223, 224, 227, 240, 241, 242, 250, 252, 255, 261, 263, 265, 267, 268, 269, 270, 271, 272, 273, 274, 282, 283, 285, 289, 296, 298, 303, 304, 306, 313, 314, 321, 323, 324, 326, 328, 332, 335, 337, 339, 341, 342, 349, 351, 355, 356, 358
Beaker folk, xviii, xxvi, 325
Belgae, xxiii–xxiv, xxvi, 5, 30, 154, 165, 169, 209, 214, 233, 234, 249, 270, 302, 331, 358, 361, 363
Borlase, Wm., 35, 53
Boudicca, Queen, xxv, 111, 186, 219
Bronze Age, xix, xxi, xxvi
burhs, xxvi, 57, 64, 257
burials
  Iron Age, 5, 14, 42, 81, 82, 107, 128, 298
  Roman, xxv, 9, 14, 25, 29, 102, 107, 112, 113, 144, 182, 183, 188, 190, 200, 205, 230, 290, 313

Caesar, Julius, xxiii, xxvi, 182
Cantii, xxiv
Carnarvon, Lord, 149
Catuvellauni, xxiv, xxvii, 109, 181, 182, 185, 188, 265
causewayed camps, xvii, xxvii, 3, 66, 86, 93, 123, 274, 282, 304, 305, 327, 338, 355, 356